"All of creation groans in desperate longing for God's peace. As our planet awaits ultimate redemption, we have the prophetic voices collected in *The Gospel of Peace in a Violent World* to help us imagine what peace can feel like in the current time. Marlena Graves and Shawn Graves have gathered a cross section of experts who work in a variety of settings to help guide us in the way of peace that the Lord Jesus Christ both demonstrated and proclaimed."

Dennis R. Edwards, associate professor of New Testament at North Park Theological Seminary

"This is an excellent book. The authors challenge us to consider the many ways in which the gospel of God's kingdom, the gospel of peace, confronts the violence, injustice, and threats to shalom present in our world. At a time of great division, where we do violence not only through war but also through our words, deeds, and institutions, this book does more than merely show us a better way. It gives practical advice on how to live it out."

Michael W. Austin, author of *God and Guns in America*

"We have all been through so much lately that despair can feel like the logical and natural next step. Thank God that Marlena and Shawn Graves have gathered voices who remind us that morning's joy comes through the praxis of our shared work in Christ and its impact in this world. This book is for theologians and nontheologians seeking to invigorate the work we are called to pursue."

Ange-Marie Hancock Alfaro, Dean's Professor of Gender & Sexuality Studies and chair of the Department of Political Science and International Relations at the University of Southern California

"Nonviolence is often wrongly equated with passivity and inaction. As demonstrated by this diverse and provocative collection of essays, just peacemaking and nonviolent direct action are part of a rich Christian social justice tradition that is now more important than ever."

Robert Chao Romero, associate professor in the departments of Chicana/o studies and Asian American studies at the University of California at Los Angeles, and author of *Brown Church*

"Peacemaking is not as simple as it sounds. Marlena and Shawn Graves's convicting new volume reveals how our lives are entangled in all kinds of everyday violence. Thankfully, it doesn't leave us there. This book will not only open eyes but also spark imaginations, helping us to discern how a peaceable world—one more faithful to the gospel—might come to be."

Heath W. Carter, Princeton Theological Seminary

"As a faith-rooted community activist and organizer, I have lamented how little the church has done to educate Christians in either their rich theology of biblical justice and shalom or to equip them to appropriately engage deep injustices in our world. In *The Gospel of Peace in a Violent World*, the Graveses have assembled a diverse team of relevant, scholarly contributors who speak to this missing theology and praxis of Christian discipleship. With no-stone-left-unturned vigor, this important and essential resource grounds foundational and formational theological truth with timeless and recent historical application, practically compelling Christians toward seeking a more just and peaceful world."

Michelle Ferrigno Warren, activist and author of *The Power of Proximity: Moving Beyond Awareness to Action*

"Bringing together the diverse voices of stalwart Christian writers, academics, activists, and leaders, *The Gospel of Peace in a Violent World* is a book for this moment in history—and a call to conscience to consider what Christian faith practically requires in today's world. From practices of nonviolence and peacemaking to earnest and unflinching discussions on equity, disability, immigration, environmental justice, and racial trauma, this compendium of essays pushes readers not only to contemplation but to action."

Meighan Stone, former president of the Malala Fund and board member of the Faith and Politics Institute

THE GOSPEL OF PEACE IN A VIOLENT WORLD

CHRISTIAN NONVIOLENCE FOR COMMUNAL FLOURISHING

EDITED BY SHAWN GRAVES
AND MARLENA GRAVES

An imprint of InterVarsity Press
Downers Grove, Illinois

InterVarsity Press
P.O. Box 1400 | Downers Grove, IL 60515-1426
ivpress.com | email@ivpress.com

©2022 by Shawn Graves and Marlena Graves

All rights reserved. No part of this book may be reproduced in any form without written permission from InterVarsity Press.

InterVarsity Press® is the publishing division of InterVarsity Christian Fellowship/USA®. For more information, visit intervarsity.org.

Scripture quotations, unless otherwise noted, are from the New Revised Standard Version Bible, copyright © 1989 National Council of the Churches of Christ in the United States of America. Used by permission. All rights reserved worldwide.

Cover design and image composite: David Fassett
Interior design: Jeanna Wiggins

ISBN 978-1-5140-0128-8 (print) | ISBN 978-1-5140-0129-5 (digital)

Printed in the United States of America ∞

Library of Congress Cataloging-in-Publication Data
A catalog record for this book is available from the Library of Congress.

26 25 24 23 22 | 6 5 4 3 2 1

To our dear friend Michael W. Pahl,

whose life and vision brought forth this book.

CONTENTS

Acknowledgments — xi

Introduction — 1
SHAWN GRAVES AND MARLENA GRAVES

PART ONE: BIBLICAL REFLECTIONS

1. The Old Testament as a Problem for Pacifists (and What to Do About It) — 7
   ERIC A. SEIBERT

2. Shalom for All: Toward an Old Testament Theology of Peace — 22
   T. C. HAM

3. Pride Fighter or Sacrificial Lamb? Discerning the Real Jesus in the Book of Revelation — 37
   GREGORY A. BOYD

4. "The God of Peace Will Soon Crush Satan Under Your Feet": Violence in the Gospel of Peace? — 58
   THOMAS R. YODER NEUFELD

PART TWO: LEARNING FROM OTHERS

5. A Pentagon for Peace: What America Could Learn from Its Oldest Enemy — 79
   RANDY S. WOODLEY

6. Preachers, Prophets, and Philosophers: Martin Luther King Jr.'s Moral Reasoning on Nonviolence — 105
   AARON JAMES

7	Listening for Peace: Nonviolence in William Stafford's Writing and Teaching SARAH AZARANSKY	120
8	Living Next Door to the Bronze Lady MICHAEL JIMENEZ	137
9	A Universal Love Ethic: Nonviolence and Human Rights Advocacy SHAWN GRAVES	148

PART THREE: WAR AND VIOLENCE

10	War, Terror, and Peace LISA SHARON HARPER	189
11	Christian Pacifism and the "Good War" TED GRIMSRUD	197
12	Problematic Pacifism: Pursuing Biblical Justice Toward Effective Change MAE ELISE CANNON	214
13	Lights in the Darkness: Christian Peace Practice in the Violence of Central America WILLI HUGO PEREZ LEMUS AND ADRIENNE WIEBE	238

PART FOUR: RACE, GENDER, AND DISABILITY

14	Shalom and White Supremacy DREW G. I. HART	257
15	Healing from Racial Trauma SHEILA WISE ROWE	274
16	Faith-Rooted Reconciliation: Organizing for Shalom Justice PETER GOODWIN HELTZEL	289

17 Longing Forward: Peacemaking and Violence
Toward Women and Girls   303
   ELIZABETH GERHARDT

18 Disability, Identity, and the Resurrection of the Dead:
Cultural Competency as Nonviolence   319
   CHIBUZO NIMMO PETTY

PART FIVE: IMMIGRATION AND ENVIRONMENT

19 Our Food System: The Tie to Immigration, Migrant
Workers, Exploitation, and Human Trafficking   335
   BALDEMAR VELASQUEZ

20 Immigration and the Church: Who Is My Neighbor?   346
   MARLENA GRAVES

21 Everything, Nothing, Something: Trading In
Worldviewing for Everyday Faithfulness in
Peacemaking and Sustainability   363
   JACOB ALAN COOK

22 Environmental Violence   382
   KATHY KHANG

Conclusion: Practical Steps Toward Communal Flourishing   391
   SHAWN GRAVES AND MARLENA GRAVES

List of Contributors   403

General Index   409

Scripture Index   413

ACKNOWLEDGMENTS

We would like to offer our profound thanks to each person who took the time and energy to contribute to this book. This could not have happened without you. We affirm your gifts, insights, and work and believe them to be crucial to our world and in furthering the Christlikeness of the church. We believe in this project and in what each of you have to say. For us this has been a labor of love, a long time coming. We want to thank IVP Academic for taking on this project, and David McNutt, who has been patient and kind in his feedback. In addition, we would like to thank each and every person at IVP who has been involved in bringing this book to the public.

We also want to offer our deep thanks to our dear friend, scholar, and pastor, Michael W. Pahl, who is one of the most loving and just people we know. Michael W. Pahl was a coconspirator in conceiving of this project at the very beginning.

We are deeply grateful for our readers and trust that as we learn from one another in these pages, and as we hear your feedback, we will become more just and loving people who reflect the way of Jesus in the world. We give God thanks.

INTRODUCTION

Shawn Graves and Marlena Graves

THE VOLUME YOU HOLD IN YOUR HANDS is the result of blood, sweat, and tears. Lived experience. The contributors are activists, pastors, theologians, philosophers, and more. This project was a tremendous undertaking especially because the contributors are intimately involved in the topics they cover. None of it is mere lip service. As a result, sometimes the writing and editing had to stop so they could practice the gospel they preach and thus live out their convictions. This is why it is strong. This is why it took a good while to bring it all together. This is why this book is a labor of love, a contribution to and an extension of the work of nonviolence itself.

Much has happened in the United States specifically and the world generally since this effort began and individual essays were written. And no doubt much will happen once the manuscript has left our hands and landed in yours. Frankly, it's impossible for projects like this to keep up with the frightening pace of injustice and catastrophe. Tragically, human rights violations abound, wars persist, violence multiplies, injustices radiate, and hateful ideologies take root and blossom. We are all witnesses: vulnerable and abandoned communities ravaged by a global pandemic and at the mercy of unevenly distributed health care resources and overburdened medical systems. Erupting racial terrorism, police brutality, voter suppression, and the undermining of democracy. Widening wealth inequality, climate catastrophes, gender-based violence, political scapegoating, vigilantism, humanitarian crises at the border, blatant and bald-faced lies and misinformation campaigns, truth decay, and vanishing public trust in political, economic, scientific, and religious institutions.

Our hope is that wherever you find yourself—and at whatever point in life you happen to be—you will use this book as an informative and inspiring field guide for exploring the gospel of peace. Jesus has not called us to do violence to one another nor to participate in the culture of death no matter how it manifests itself. We are to discern and use God's means to accomplish God's ends. If we use whatever means we believe will accomplish God's ends, can we truly say we are living out the gospel? No, not at all. Martin Luther King Jr. made this very point in a sermon delivered to the congregation at Ebenezer Baptist Church on Christmas Eve 1967, just a few short months before his assassination:

> So if you're seeking to develop a just society, the important thing is to get there, and the means are really unimportant; any means that will get you there—they may be violent, they may be untruthful means; they may even be unjust means to get to a just end. There have been those who have argued this throughout history. But we will never have peace in the world until men everywhere recognize that ends are not cut off from means, because the means represent the ideal in the making, and the end in process, and ultimately you can't reach good ends through evil means, because the means represent the seed and the end represents the tree.[1]

Jesus used God's means to accomplish God's ends and so must anyone who professes to follow Jesus and model their life after his. Such was the way of Jesus and his earliest followers. It is to be our way.

---

[1] See "Dr. Martin Luther King, Jr. Massey Lectures #5," PRX, https://beta.prx.org/stories/32929, May 10, 2020.

These essays open, and contribute to, conversations; they offer a way of living, a blueprint for nonviolently navigating this world riddled with injustice, indifference, indigence, inhospitality, and misinformation. But it is up to each one of us to jettison pious platitudes and put gospel truths into practice in the particular places where we find ourselves. That requires wisdom and guidance, so we encourage you to use this volume in your classes, churches, and communities, to listen and learn from one another, and together to discern how you might live out the gospel of peace with and among your local and global neighbors.

PART ONE

BIBLICAL REFLECTIONS

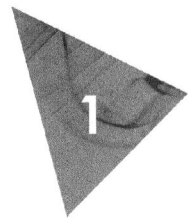

THE OLD TESTAMENT AS A PROBLEM FOR PACIFISTS (AND WHAT TO DO ABOUT IT)

Eric A. Seibert

> *If the waging of war and the military profession were in themselves wrong and displeasing to God, we should have to condemn Abraham, Moses, Joshua, David, and all the rest of the holy fathers, kings, and princes, who served God as soldiers and are highly praised in Scripture because of this service.*
>
> MARTIN LUTHER

WHILE THE SEEMINGLY ubiquitous accounts of violence, killing, and warfare in the Old Testament trouble many modern readers, they present unique—and serious—challenges for Christian pacifists.[1] What makes these accounts especially problematic for pacifists is the presence

---

[1] Portions of this chapter are adapted from Eric A. Seibert, *Disturbing Divine Behavior: Troubling Old Testament Images of God* (Minneapolis: Fortress, 2009), and *The Violence of Scripture: Overcoming the Old Testament's Troubling Legacy* (Minneapolis: Fortress, 2012). Reproduced by permission.

of Old Testament passages that sanction, and sometimes even celebrate, acts of war. God is often portrayed as a warrior, and divinely sanctioned warfare is common throughout the Hebrew Bible.[2]

For some Christians, God's involvement in warfare and killing in the pages of the Old Testament is incontrovertible evidence that the people of God can at times participate in war with God's blessing. Professor Jack Nelson-Pallmeyer reflects on an experience from his student days that illustrates this point. He writes,

> As a college student involved in protesting the U.S. wars in Indochina, I wondered why my church, including most parishioners, gave uncritical support to the U.S. war effort. Friends and I who were former leaders of our youth group were shunned when we suggested that saturation bombing, defoliation, napalm, cluster bombs, maimed civilians, destroyed villages, and elevated body counts were hard to reconcile with Jesus, who blessed peacemakers and taught love of enemies. One angry parishioner told me that if I objected to war, I shouldn't be a Christian. To bolster his case, he challenged me to read the Bible. He said . . . it was filled with stories in which a violent God approved of war.[3]

Truth be told, the Bible—specifically the Old Testament—does contain many stories that portray God approving of war. Throughout the Hebrew Bible, God ostensibly initiates, sanctions, and sometimes even participates in numerous acts of violence and war. God drowns Egyptians (Ex 14:26-30), hurls hailstones on Amorites (Josh 10:11), and commands Israelites to massacre Midianites (Num 31:1-3), kill Canaanites (Deut 7:1-2; 20:16-18), and annihilate Amalekites (1 Sam 15:1-3). Certain Old Testament passages also suggest God uses the military might of other nations, such as Assyria and Babylon, to oppress, conquer,

---

[2] "Old Testament" and "Hebrew Bible" will be used interchangeably throughout this chapter.
[3] Jack Nelson-Pallmeyer, *Is Religion Killing Us? Violence in the Bible and the Quran* (Harrisburg, PA: Trinity Press International, 2003), xii.

kill, and exile the people of Israel for sins committed (2 Kings 17:1-23; 24:1-4). Time and time again, the Old Testament portrays God as one who is intimately and actively involved in the business of war.

Many Christians believe God's frequent involvement in war in the Old Testament suggests that war in and of itself is not inherently evil. Since God (reportedly) sanctioned war to punish evildoers and save people from oppression, they believe God must not be categorically opposed to warfare and killing. Following this logic, they conclude that God's (apparent) approval of war in the past suggests that God still approves of war today, at least in certain circumstances. For many Christians, this line of reasoning is very persuasive. Herein lies the Christian pacifist's dilemma. How can Christians claim war is wrong when the Bible frequently seems to say it is right?

The primary purpose of this chapter is to help pacifists, especially Christian pacifists, mitigate the problems raised by Old Testament texts that sanction, justify, and celebrate war. This is no easy task, especially where the Old Testament is concerned. For as Terry Brensinger reminds us, "The Old Testament is clearly not a pacifistic document."[4] Before I offer some suggestions, it first may be helpful to say a few words about how Christian pacifists have traditionally addressed the problem of divinely sanctioned war in the Old Testament.

HOW PACIFISTS MAKE PEACE WITH WAR IN THE OLD TESTAMENT: A BRIEF OVERVIEW

Christian pacifists have responded to Old Testament war texts and to the image of God as warrior in a number of ways.[5] Some ignore these

---

[4]Terry L. Brensinger, "War in the Old Testament: A Journey Toward Nonparticipation," in *A Peace Reader*, ed. E. Morris Sider and Luke Keefer Jr. (Nappanee, IN: Evangel, 2002), 23.
[5]For a general survey of various options, see Dale Brown, *Biblical Pacifism,* 2nd ed. (Nappanee, IN: Evangel), 84-87. See also Willard W. Swartley, *Slavery, Sabbath, War, and Women* (Scottdale, PA: Herald, 1983), 112-18.

passages, others defend God's behavior, and some argue that God's use of violence to do justice is precisely what enables them to be nonviolent. What follows is a brief discussion and critique of these approaches, none of which I believe satisfactorily deals with the problem of divinely sanctioned warfare in the Old Testament.

Ignore problematic passages. One way some pacifists "deal with" the problem of divinely sanctioned war in the Old Testament is by choosing not to deal with it at all! Troubling texts are often ignored, and problematic passages are routinely bypassed in search of more peaceful pastures. Few churches actually use these passages, and when they do, they typically sanitize them or focus only on "positive" lessons to be learned from them (e.g., that God is a deliverer). Even individuals who have grown up in historic peace churches (Quaker, Mennonite, Brethren) are typically given little if any instruction about how to reconcile their beliefs about nonviolence with the positive portrayals of violence and war they find throughout Scripture. Surely this is a missed opportunity.

Some authors who make a case for Christian pacifism sidestep the problem as well. For example, Mennonite scholar John Roth, in his otherwise excellent book on Christian pacifism, says nothing about the problem of divinely sanctioned warfare in the Old Testament.[6] Although he devotes about a dozen pages to the Old Testament, emphasizing God's creational intention that people experience shalom (wholeness) and detailing various ways God has worked in Israel's past to invite people into that reality, nothing is said about the problems the Old Testament raises for pacifists.[7]

Other pacifists who write about the Old Testament sometimes acknowledge the presence of violent stories of warfare and killing in the Old

---

[6]John D. Roth, *Choosing Against War: A Christian View; A Love Stronger Than Our Fears* (Intercourse, PA: Good Books, 2002).
[7]Roth, *Choosing Against War*, 65-76.

Testament and may even express some discomfort with these stories—but they do not linger here. They direct the reader's attention to other parts of the Old Testament that are more promising for pacifists, such as its critique of conventional notions of warfare and its vision of peace.[8] While there is nothing wrong with focusing on these parts of the Old Testament (in fact, I think more attention should be given to these passages), neglecting the most troublesome texts fails to address the problems raised by divinely sanctioned warfare in the Hebrew Bible. If pacifists hope to counter the claim that God's involvement in warfare in the Old Testament legitimates Christian participation in war today, they will need to deal directly with the Old Testament texts used to make that claim.

Justify God's behavior. Obviously, not every Christian pacifist avoids these troubling texts. Some address them head on. In his book *Fight: A Christian Case for Nonviolence*, New Testament scholar Preston Sprinkle dedicates a number of chapters to violence and war in the Old Testament. One chapter is exclusively devoted to discussing what is arguably the most troubling account of divinely sanctioned warfare in the entire Hebrew Bible: Canaanite genocide (though Sprinkle objects to describing it as such).[9] According to Deuteronomy 7:1-2, Israel was to "utterly destroy" the Canaanites without mercy (see also Deut 20:16-18). What makes the conquest of Canaan described in Joshua 6–11 especially problematic is the way it has been used to justify subsequent acts of violence and war. As John Collins observes, "One of the most troubling aspects of this biblical story is the way it has been used, analogically, over the centuries as a legitimating paradigm of violent conquest."[10] This is deeply disturbing. What can be done to counter such a harmful way of using the Bible?

---

[8]See, for example, Brensinger, "War in the Old Testament."
[9]Preston Sprinkle, *Fight: A Christian Case for Nonviolence* (Colorado Springs: David C. Cook, 2013), 73-91.
[10]John J. Collins, *The Bible After Babel: Historical Criticism in a Postmodern Age* (Grand Rapids, MI: Eerdmans, 2005), 62-63.

Sprinkle's approach, common among evangelical scholars, is to justify God's behavior. Sprinkle works hard to minimize the problems raised by this story in an effort to convince readers that things are really not as bad as they seem. He claims the Canaanites had lots of time to repent, that God intended Israelites to kill only soldiers, and that the language used in Joshua 6–11 is hyperbolic, meaning Israel was to take control of the land, not kill every last Canaanite. Sprinkle also cautions against making contemporary applications of this command to kill. He describes the conquest of Canaan as "a one-time, non-repeatable event whereby God judged a particularly wicked people."[11]

To many people, attempts to justify God's behavior in this way seem like special pleading and are unpersuasive to those outside the Christian faith. Though space does not allow for an adequate critique of this approach, these arguments do not really address the crux of the problem.[12] Even if things are not as bad as they seem in this particular story—and that is certainly debatable—they are still very bad for Christian pacifists given the presence of so many Old Testament texts containing divinely sanctioned warfare and violence. As long as we concede that God did in fact issue commands to fight and kill in the past, there will always be those who believe God could do so again. This is precisely what prevented Richard Hays from embracing pacifism earlier in life. He writes, "I, as a young Christian during the Vietnam War era, found myself unable to justify claiming conscientious objector status because I could not claim that I would never fight; God might command me, as he had commanded Saul, to slay an enemy."[13]

---

[11]Sprinkle, *Fight*, 91.

[12]For an excellent critique of attempts to justify genocide in the Old Testament, see Thom Stark, *The Human Faces of God: What Scripture Reveals When It Gets God Wrong (and Why Inerrancy Tries to Hide It)* (Eugene, OR: Wipf & Stock, 2011), 100-150.

[13]Richard B. Hays, *The Moral Vision of the New Testament: Community, Cross, New Creation; A Contemporary Introduction to New Testament Ethics* (San Francisco: HarperSanFrancisco, 1996), 336.

Embrace God's warfare as the basis for Christian pacifism. Rather than viewing the image of God as warrior as problematic, some Christian pacifists find it beneficial to their position and regard it as the very foundation of Christian pacifism. "That God is a warrior," writes Old Testament scholar Elmer Martens, "means . . . that his people need not be warlike."[14] As Martens sees it, "The fact that Yahweh our God is a powerful warrior . . . who will deal decisively with evil, means that his followers can afford to leave the righting of wrongs in God's hand."[15] Understood this way, divine violence is neither a problem to be solved nor an obstacle to be overcome. On the contrary, since God uses warfare to stop, punish, and ultimately eradicate evil, God's warring "is not a reality about which to be embarrassed" but rather "a reality to be embraced."[16]

While I appreciate the efforts of scholars like Martens who call us to reject violence, I am troubled by the linkage between divine violence and Christian pacifism. Martens's attempt to ground pacifism in the (supposed) violence of God is problematic for a number of reasons, not least of which is the fact that it runs contrary to the teachings of Jesus. Jesus teaches us to love our enemies, not because we are confident in God's ability to judge them but because loving enemies is precisely what God does! God "is kind to the ungrateful and the wicked" (Lk 6:35), and God "makes his sun rise on the evil and on the good, and sends rain on the righteous and on the unrighteous" (Mt 5:45). When we love our enemies, we reflect God's character so clearly that we are called God's "children." Contrary to what Martens suggests, divine violence is not an appropriate basis for Christian pacifism. Instead, we are people of peace who love, forgive, and reject violence because that is what God does.

---

[14] Elmer A. Martens, "Toward Shalom: Absorbing the Violence," in *War in the Bible and Terrorism in the Twenty-First Century*, ed. Richard S. Hess and Elmer A. Martens (Winona Lake, IN: Eisenbrauns, 2008), 53.
[15] Martens, "Toward Shalom," 55. Martens cites Deut 32:35 and Rom 12:19 as support.
[16] Martens, "Toward Shalom," 53.

AN UNSTATED ASSUMPTION (AND SIGNIFICANT WEAKNESS) OF TRADITIONAL PACIFIST APPROACHES

So far, we have considered three ways Christian pacifists often respond to the problem of divinely sanctioned war in the Old Testament. But we have yet to identify an unstated assumption that governs the way many of these individuals deal with this issue. Simply stated, the assumption is as follows: God actually said and did what the Bible claims. Many Christian pacifists assume Old Testament stories of divinely sanctioned war are both historically accurate and theologically reliable. As they see it, God really did initiate, sanction, and participate in war much as the Bible describes it. This assumption has huge implications for how they address the problems that warfare in the Old Testament raises for them. It forces them to find some way to explain why God's approval of war in the past does not justify a Christian's participation in war today.

But what if this assumption is unfounded? What if God, the living God, never actually sanctioned or commanded warfare in ancient Israel? What if the Old Testament's depiction of God as warrior simply reflects common beliefs about divine involvement in war in the ancient world? If so, then the way many pacifists deal with these challenging texts is fundamentally misguided. *It makes no sense to justify God's violent behavior if, in fact, God never behaved violently in the first place.* Nor does it make sense to base one's commitment to peace on God's ability to use violence if this does not reflect how God actually behaves.

So how might we assess the validity of this assumption? A good starting point would be to place this assumption in its historical-cultural context. It is well known that people in the ancient world believed the gods were intimately involved in their experience of war. They routinely conceived of God/the gods as warriors, and they were convinced that God/the gods commissioned war, participated in it, and determined the outcome of it. People interpreted victory in battle as a sign of divine favor and defeat in battle as the consequence of divine displeasure. These assumptions about God's involvement in war are evident in many texts from the ancient world, making it unmistakably clear this was a theological given for people in antiquity.[17]

Given this historical context, it is unsurprising that Israel shared many of these same ideas about divine involvement in war. Similar to nations around them, Israel believed God sanctioned and participated in its wars, fighting for them when they were obedient and against them when they were not. Assumptions such as these dramatically influenced their view of God and, consequently, the way they portrayed God in the texts they produced. Therefore, when Israel claims that God wills, ordains, sanctions, or otherwise blesses war, it is important to recognize that claim for what it is: a culturally conditioned explanation of divine involvement in warfare that reflected widespread assumptions ancient people had about God and war.

But not every assumption from the ancient world is equally valid today. For example, the Israelites assumed the earth was flat, that people went to Sheol after they died, that it was morally right to own slaves, and that there was religious value in sacrificing animals. Yet Christians no longer share these assumptions. What then of Israel's assumption that God is a warrior? Should Christians accept this view of God? I think not.

While Christians differ over the role God plays—if any—in determining the outcome of modern wars, they realize that wars are won or lost due to a whole host of factors: troop size and strength, the number and technological sophistication of weapons used, the skill of the commanding officers, the ability to form powerful alliances, and so forth. In many significant ways, our beliefs about God's involvement in war differ considerably from those of our ancient counterparts. We therefore need

---

[17]See, e.g., Sa-Moon Kang, *Divine War in the Old Testament and in the Ancient Near East* (Berlin: de Gruyter, 1989).

to be very cautious about what we can derive about the nature of God from these texts. In many respects, it makes no more sense for us to adopt Israel's culturally conditioned view of God's involvement in warfare than it does to adopt their culturally conditioned views of cosmology, the afterlife, and animal sacrifice. Instead, Christian pacifists need to contextualize the Old Testament's warlike portrayals of God and emphasize the limitations these images have for understanding God's true character.

DEALING WITH DIVINELY SANCTIONED WARFARE: A PROPOSAL FOR CHRISTIAN PACIFISTS

At this point we are ready to return to the fundamental question driving this essay, namely, what can be done to keep the Old Testament from being used to support warfare and killing? Following are a number of suggestions offered as a response to the challenges raised by the presence of divinely sanctioned warfare in the Old Testament.

Differentiate between the textual and actual God. To begin, Christian pacifists need to learn to make distinctions between "the textual and the actual God," to borrow language from Terence Fretheim.[18] According to Fretheim, the textual God is the God located within the pages of the Bible while the actual God is the God who transcends those pages. One is a literary representation, the other a living reality. As Fretheim observes, "The God portrayed in the text does not fully correspond to the God who transcends the text, who is a living, dynamic reality that cannot be captured in words on a page."[19] Rather than simply accepting whatever the Bible says about God to be true, a more responsible way of using the Bible involves differentiating between the textual and actual God.[20]

---

[18]Terence E. Fretheim and Karlfried Froehlich, *The Bible as Word of God: In a Postmodern Age* (Minneapolis: Fortress, 1998), 116.
[19]Fretheim and Froehlich, *The Bible as Word*, 116.
[20]For some discussion about the importance of making this distinction, see Seibert, *Disturbing Divine Behavior*, 171-73.

Representations of God in the Hebrew Bible sometimes reveal and sometimes distort God's character.[21] This is because the images of God preserved in the Old Testament are best understood as human portrayals of God rather than divine self-portraits. Given the human origins of these portrayals, it is unnecessary to assume that every Old Testament image of God reflects what God is really like. While some certainly do, others most certainly do not. Hence the need to differentiate between the textual and actual God. In fact, I would argue that Christian pacifists will be unable to adequately address the problem of divinely sanctioned violence and warfare in the Old Testament without doing so.

Allow Jesus to guide our thinking about God's character. For Christian pacifists, the revelation of God in Jesus should play a key role in determining how to assess the theological reliability of violent images of God in the Old Testament. Jesus is, after all, "the image of the invisible God" (Col 1:15) and "the exact imprint of God's very being" (Heb 1:3). As Jesus himself once said, "Whoever has seen me has seen the Father" (Jn 14:9). To know what God's character is really like, we look to Jesus. When we do, we see a God who is kind to the ungrateful and the wicked, not one bent on their destruction (Lk 6:35). We see a God who seeks rather than slays sinners. In short, we see a very different picture of God than the one we find in Old Testament passages that depict God behaving violently. Therefore, when we use the Bible to think about God's character, we need to do so carefully. Not every portrayal of God is equally authoritative. We need to let Jesus guide our thinking about God. Portrayals that correspond to the God Jesus reveals may be regarded as trustworthy, while those that do not should be judged as unreliable.[22]

---

[21]This language of revealing and distorting God's character occurs repeatedly in Jack Nelson-Pallmeyer, *Jesus Against Christianity: Reclaiming the Missing Jesus* (Harrisburg, PA: Trinity Press International, 2001). See, for example, 16, 61, 65, 80, 88, 137.

[22]For a fuller treatment of these ideas, see Seibert, *Disturbing Divine Behavior*, 183-207. Although many scholars acknowledge that not all words and deeds attributed to Jesus in the Gospels reflect

As we begin to see God through the lens of Jesus, we realize that violent portrayals of God do not reveal what God is actually like.[23] As C. S. Cowles observes,

> If ours is a Christlike God, then we can categorically affirm that God is not a destroyer. . . . God does not engage in punitive, redemptive, or sacred violence. . . . God does not proactively use death as an instrument of judgment.[24]

Despite what certain Old Testament passages suggest, God does not behave violently. Since Old Testament images of a God at war do not reflect the character of God revealed in Jesus, these images should be understood as culturally conditioned depictions of God that are fundamentally incompatible with God's true nature.

State clearly and categorically that God is not a warrior. Christian pacifists should state clearly, directly, and frequently that God, the living God, is *not* a warrior. Rather than ignoring these troubling texts or trying to justify God's behavior, pacifists need to declare that God does not act this way. Doing this goes a long way toward mitigating the problem of divinely sanctioned warfare in the Old Testament since it directly challenges the rationale of those who try to use the Old Testament to justify Christian participation in war.

---

what Jesus actually said and did, there are strong and compelling reasons to believe the historical Jesus was completely and consistently nonviolent. Simon Joseph argues this point forcefully in *The Nonviolent Messiah*, and he believes it is supported by such things as "multiple attestation [evidence of Jesus' nonviolence in various layers of the tradition], the instructional content of Q [thought to be a very early collection of Jesus' sayings], Jesus' nonresistance during his arrest, and the indisputably historical tradition of early Christian pacifism" (*The Nonviolent Messiah: Jesus, Q, and the Enochic Tradition* [Minneapolis: Fortress, 2014], 39). Such evidence confirms the appropriateness of appealing to the nonviolent traditions about Jesus in the New Testament to critique violent depictions of God in the Old Testament.

[23]For some examples of this approach, see C. S. Cowles, "The Case for Radical Discontinuity," in *Show Them No Mercy: Four Views on God and Canaanite Genocide*, ed. Stanley N. Gundry (Grand Rapids, MI: Zondervan, 2003), 13-44; Gregory A. Boyd, *Crucifixion of the Warrior God: Interpreting the Old Testament's Violent Portraits of God in Light of the Cross* (Minneapolis: Fortress, 2017) and *Cross Vision: How the Crucifixion of Jesus Makes Sense of Old Testament Violence* (Minneapolis: Fortress, 2017).

[24]Cowles, "Case for Radical Discontinuity," 30.

I realize that some Christian pacifists will find it difficult to state publicly their rejection of the image of God as warrior. This is especially true for those who are part of churches and faith-based institutions in conservative contexts. These individuals may discover that being honest about their beliefs has some negative, and sometimes personally costly, repercussions. Other Christian pacifists may find it difficult to deny God's involvement in warfare because of their beliefs about the nature of Scripture. They may be unwilling to deny God is a warrior since the biblical text so plainly states God is. In order to arrive at this theological conclusion, they would first need to rethink their views about the inspiration of Scripture.

Christians who believe God actually behaved in the violent, warlike ways described in the Old Testament typically have a view of inspiration that posits a high degree of divine involvement in the formation of the Bible. While this gets nuanced in various ways, they believe God was very involved in determining the content of the Bible. This leads them to conclude that the Bible faithfully narrates God's past actions, giving them confidence that God said and did what the Bible claims.

But here's the rub. As I have argued elsewhere, these assumptions about God's very active role in determining the content of the Bible do not match the evidence at hand.[25] It appears that ancient Israelites were free to write about God in ways that made sense in their particular historical and cultural context and reflected their own perspective and worldview *even when* that resulted in portrayals of God that were inaccurate. The importance of this point cannot be overstated. It reminds us that these writers did not always get God right. This, in turn, opens the door for Christian pacifists to challenge violent images of God and to counter the efforts of those who would use God's involvement in war in the Old Testament to justify Christian participation in war today.

---

[25]See Seibert, *Disturbing Divine Behavior*, 267-70.

Demonstrate foundations for peacemaking in the Old Testament. Finally, although the image of God as warrior is prominent in the Hebrew Bible, it is by no means the only image of God found there. Numerous passages speak of God's grace and love, and these are more helpful to Christian pacifists.

Likewise, while it is true that many Old Testament passages sanction warfare and killing, some actually *critique* violence and others illustrate alternate ways of dealing with strife. Christian pacifists do well to pay special attention to Old Testament passages that promote peace and encourage the nonviolent resolution of conflict. The story of Joseph forgiving his brothers (Gen 45:1-15; 50:15-21) and the account of Abigail preventing a massacre (1 Sam 25) are two notable examples. Stories such as these remind us that the Old Testament is more than just a problem for Christian pacifists to overcome. It is a rich collection of texts containing many valuable resources for those intent on making peace.[26]

Still, as important as it is to highlight stories such as these and nonviolent images of God—and I think more should be done in this regard—I would emphasize that doing this alone is not enough to address the serious problems raised by divinely sanctioned warfare in the Old Testament. The only way to fully overcome the problems raised by God's involvement in war in the Old Testament is to confront these problematic passages directly, as noted above.

CONCLUSION

Old Testament passages that sanction war and justify slaughter have created endless problems for pacifists wishing to use the Bible to critique war and promote nonviolent peacemaking. In this chapter, I have argued

---

[26]In addition to the chapter by T. C. Ham in this volume, see also David A. Leiter, *Neglected Voices: Peace in the Old Testament* (Scottdale, PA: Herald, 2007), and John A. Wood, *Perspectives on War in the Bible* (Macon, GA: Mercer University Press, 1998), 104-20.

that properly contextualizing the Old Testament's portrayal of God as warrior and letting Jesus guide our thinking about God's character enables us to reject the notion that God sanctioned ancient Israel's wars. Doing this removes any basis for trying to use the Old Testament to legitimize war based on God's supposed approval of it.

One of the ongoing challenges for Christian pacifists who take this approach is to value and appreciate these violent Old Testament texts in spite of the difficulties they raise. It is important to find constructive ways to use these texts even while critiquing problematic dimensions of them.[27] Doing so will enable us to read the Old Testament in a manner that encourages life and peace rather than death and war. This, I submit, is a worthy goal for all Christians who take the Bible seriously and strive to read it responsibly.

---

[27]For some guidance, see Seibert, *Disturbing Divine Behavior*, 209-22.

SHALOM FOR ALL

TOWARD AN OLD TESTAMENT THEOLOGY OF PEACE

T. C. Ham

THE QUESTION USUALLY GOES SOMETHING LIKE THIS: "If a man attacks your family, will you stand by and do nothing?" Several assumptions lie behind such a question. One, peace is inactive or passive. Two, the only way to stop violence is through violence. Three, peace means the absence of conflict. Of course, seeking peace can very well include passive nonviolence. However, I sometimes answer the question with another question: "Why is this man attacking my family?" By asking this question, I am trying to humanize the hypothetical attacker. I can usually take this moment to illustrate what it means to seek biblical ideals of peace. For example, if the man is insane, it is the failure of society to help treat this person. If the man has turned to crime because he lacked other options, again the failure lies in our society.

What then is peace according to the Christian Scriptures? The Hebrew Bible uses the word "shalom" to refer to a very broad understanding of peace.[1]

---

[1] A theology of peace must be much more encompassing than the study of a single word such as "shalom," but the semantic domains of the Hebrew word serve here to organize my reflection on the topic.

While we tend to think of peace as the absence of violence or conflict, the idea of shalom in the Bible is much bigger than that. It is wholeness, healing, completeness, welfare, and, yes, peace.[2] Because of this broader sense of peace, shalom applies to many levels of brokenness. For instance, damaged relationships among nations may cause war, so bringing shalom to such brokenness would indeed diminish violence and conflict. But on a smaller scale, shalom for a broken bone brings healing, damaged relationships need the shalom of reconciliation, and the brokenness of our societies cries out for the shalom of justice.

We might envision the biblical concept of peace on four levels: individual, interpersonal, communal, and global. Peace theology, or more specifically "pacifism," typically brings to mind ideas of peace primarily in the global sense: peace between nations.[3] For example, in the case of conscientious objection to participation in war, the sought-after peace is global or international. However, the theology of peace in the Hebrew Bible includes all four levels of shalom. Therefore, healing brings wholeness, mending together the broken parts into a whole person. Reconciliation brings together broken relationships between individuals. When groups or classes of people experience shalom together in a community, the Hebrew Bible refers to this as justice. This chapter focuses on the two relatively neglected

---

[2]BDB offers the basic range of meaning for shalom as "completeness, soundness, welfare, peace." Francis Brown, S. R. Driver, and Charles A. Briggs, eds., *A Hebrew and English Lexicon of the Old Testament with an Appendix Containing the Biblical Aramaic* (Oxford: Clarendon Press, 1907), 1022. *TWOT* is correct to note, "The general meaning behind the root *sh-l-m* is of completion and fulfilment—of entering into a state of wholeness and unity, a restored relationship." *The Theological Wordbook of the Old Testament*, ed. R. Laird Harris, Gleason L. Archer Jr., and Bruce K. Waltke, vol. 2 (Chicago: Moody Press, 1980), 2401.

[3]Even when the context suggests a meaning for shalom that indicates an absence of war, for instance in the case of peace between nations during Solomon's reign, shalom "means much more than mere absence of war. Rather, the root meaning of the verb *shālēm* better expresses the true concept of shālôm. Completeness, wholeness, harmony, fulfilment, are closer to the meaning. Implicit in *shālôm* is the idea of unimpaired relationships with others and fulfilment in one's undertakings." See *TWOT*, 2401.

levels of peace found in the Bible, particularly in the Old Testament: individual and communal.

HEALING AND WELL-BEING

People of various faiths often pray when illness comes to us or to our loved ones, seeking God's help in restoring health and well-being. Really, when we are very ill, nothing else seems important. The more severe the illness, the less everything else matters. When broken, our bodies crave shalom beyond all else. The fact that so much of the ministry of Jesus involved healing the sick and lame speaks significantly of God's concern for our physical well-being. This concern is a dominant theme in the Hebrew Bible. For instance, immediately following one of the most recognizable stories in the Bible—the Red Sea miracle that saved the Israelites from the Egyptian military—the people of God experience God's faithful provision through Moses, who turns bitter water into sweet and potable water. Then, in words anticipating the Sinai covenant to come (Ex 19–20), God speaks to Israel: "If you will listen carefully to the voice of the Lord your God, and do what is right in his sight, and give heed to his commandments and keep all his statutes, I will not bring upon you any of the diseases that I brought upon the Egyptians; for I am the Lord who heals you" (Ex 15:26). What is quite startling about this verse is the self-epithet God gives.

The phrase "I am the Lord" is common in the Hebrew Bible.[4] It typically emphasizes a special relationship God has with various people. For example, it occurs for the first time in the Bible when God speaks to Abraham: "I am the Lord who brought you from Ur of the Chaldeans, to give you this land to possess" (Gen 15:7). When the phrase occurs for the second time in the Bible, God reiterates the Abrahamic covenant to Jacob: "I am the Lord, the God of Abraham your father and the God of

---

[4]In Hebrew, the construction occurs as a verbless (nominal) clause either as אנכי יהוה (11 times) or more commonly as אני יהוה (201 times).

Isaac; the land on which you lie I will give to you and to your offspring" (Gen 28:13). Those two are the only occurrences of the phrase "I am the Lord" in Genesis. Then, the phrase explodes in the book of Exodus, occurring nineteen times in clusters throughout the book.[5] What is particularly important about the occurrences of the phrase in Exodus is the connection between the Mosaic and Abrahamic covenants. Consider, for example, the first cluster of the phrase in Exodus 6. Each of these three verses contains the phrase "I am the Lord," and the self-declaration of God serves to connect God's promises to Abraham to the deliverance of Israel from Egypt:

> Say therefore to the Israelites, "I am the Lord, and I will free you from the burdens of the Egyptians and deliver you from slavery to them. I will redeem you with an outstretched arm and with mighty acts of judgment. I will take you as my people, and I will be your God. You shall know that I am the Lord your God, who has freed you from the burdens of the Egyptians. I will bring you into the land that I swore to give to Abraham, Isaac, and Jacob; I will give it to you for a possession. I am the Lord." (Ex 6:6-8)

The text has a natural progression that might be rendered this way: (1) I am Yahweh. (2) When I deliver the Israelites from Egypt, they will know that Yahweh is their God—the one who fulfills the promises made to their ancestors Abraham, Isaac, and Jacob. (3) This will be the basis for a covenant between God and the nation that is about to be formed.[6] Even before the miraculous plagues against Egypt and the giving of the law at Sinai, the basis of God's covenant with Israel mediated through Moses had been God's own character and the promises made to the

---

[5] Three times with אנכי and sixteen times with אני.
[6] The word Lord in all capital letters in most English translations, including the NRSV cited here, represents the Hebrew word יהוה (YHWH). This word, sometimes called the *Tetragrammaton* because it has four letters, is pronounced "Yahweh," and it represents a covenantal name for God.

patriarchs. In other words, the self-declaration of "I am the LORD" carries with it the power of God's own character as well as the implications of the Abrahamic and Mosaic covenants.[7]

Returning to Exodus 15:26, then, it is not at all surprising that the phrase "I am the LORD" occurs in a self-declaration from God that affirms the Mosaic covenant: "If you will listen carefully to the voice of the LORD your God, and do what is right in his sight, and give heed to his commandments and keep all his statutes. . . . " What should surprise the reader is the epithet that follows: "who heals you." Here, the ESV rendering may be preferable: "For I am the LORD, your healer."[8] Consider the context of this verse again. The Israelites face a potential physical hardship of thirst. Through Moses, God turns bitter water into sweet, potable water. Upon providing water for the Israelites, God declares, "I am the LORD"—that is, I am the one who just delivered you from Egypt and who promised to Abraham and his descendents (you!) a piece of land to which I am leading you. And as their healer, God cares for the well-being—the shalom—of the people.

The connection between shalom and healing is made explicit by the parallelism found in Isaiah 53:5:

But he was	wounded	for our transgressions,
	crushed	for our iniquities;
upon him	was the punishment	that made us whole,
and by his	bruises	we are healed.

The word translated *whole* is shalom, and the verb *heal* is the same one discussed above (*rapha*). Hebrew poetic use of parallelism—in this case

---

[7]*TWOT* correctly states that "shelôm is the result of God's activity in covenant" (2401).
[8]The Hebrew verb רפא (*rapha* heal) occurs seventy-two times in the Hebrew Bible (*BHS*), but it occurs only nine times in the participial form. It is clearly substantival in at least seven of those nine occurrences (Gen 50:2 [x2]; 2 Chron 16:12; Job 13:4; Ps 103:3; 147:3; Jer 8:22). There is one instance of the participle functioning in place of a finite verb (2 Kings 20:5). Considering the verbless construction in Ex 15:26, the participle is best understood as functioning substantivally.

synonymous—helps us understand that being healed and making shalom are comparable ideas.

A person who is already whole is experiencing shalom. A sick person needs shalom in the form of healing. A hungry person needs the shalom of food. And thirsty people—like the Israelites standing in front of bitter water—need water to experience shalom. This idea is clearly illustrated in a New Testament teaching. In demonstrating the obvious connection between faith and works, the author of James teaches us something very important about the concept of peace and physical well-being: "If a brother or sister is naked and lacks daily food, and one of you says to them, 'Go in peace; keep warm and eat your fill,' and yet you do not supply their bodily needs, what is the good of that?" (Jas 2:15-16).[9] In other words, there can be no peace without the necessities of life that make a person whole.

JUSTICE: SHALOM IN SOCIETY

An individual suffering from physical illness or pain desperately craves shalom. Likewise, people facing injustice desire justice, perhaps even above their own individual well-being. This is well attested by the civil rights movement in the United States. Oppressed people—and those who saw the evil of injustice—risked their own lives to fight for freedom and equality. But how is justice related to peace? Physical and emotional well-being can easily be conceived of as wholeness or shalom, but justice does not seem to adequately represent societal well-being. This is because contemporary Western conceptualization of justice is often legal or judicial in category. For example, a guilty verdict is often seen as serving justice. Even outside legal categories, ideas of justice for us often relate closely to fairness.

---

[9]The Greek word used here for *peace* (εἰρήνη *eirēnē*) is the one the LXX consistently uses to translate the Hebrew word *shalom*.

As was the case with the idea of peace, we need to broaden our understanding of justice in order to better appreciate the biblical teaching on the topic. Most importantly, justice and peace are very closely related ideas in the Bible. This is evident in the words of Isaiah:

> The way of peace they do not know,
> > and there is no justice in their paths.
> Their roads they have made crooked;
> > no one who walks in them knows peace.
>
> Therefore justice is far from us,
> > and righteousness does not reach us;
> we wait for light, and lo! there is darkness;
> > and for brightness, but we walk in gloom. (Is 59:8-9)

Once again, the use of parallelism in Hebrew poetry helps us here. According to the prophet, if there is no knowledge of "the way of peace," then there is no justice; if justice is far away, so is righteousness. Again, it may be somewhat foreign to contemporary readers to equate peace with righteousness and justice. However, the biblical writers conceptualized these seemingly distinct ideas into a cohesive theology of shalom. That is, peace seeks justice, and justice seeks righteousness. It is important to note that justice relates very closely—almost synonymously—to righteousness in the Bible.[10] In Isaiah 59:8-9, not only is peace in parallel position to justice, but justice is also in parallel position to righteousness. What's more, because the ideas of justice and righteousness are so closely related in the mind of the biblical writers, a single Greek word (δικαιοσύνη) in the New Testament has to be rendered in two different ways in

---

[10]In the Hebrew Bible, the two words משפט (justice) and צדקה (righteousness) occur together fifty times, often in parallel positions or as comparable ideas: Gen 18:19; Deut 33:21; 2 Sam 8:15; 1 Kings 10:9; 1 Chron 18:14; 2 Chron 9:8; Job 37:23; Ps 33:5; 36:7; 72:1; 99:4; 103:6; 106:3; Prov 8:20; 16:8; 21:3; Is 1:27; 5:7, 16; 9:6; 28:17; 32:16; 33:5; 54:17; 56:1; 58:2; 59:9, 14; Jer 4:2; 9:23; 22:3, 15; 23:5; 33:15; Ezek 18:5, 19, 21, 27; 33:14, 16, 19; 45:9; Amos 5:7, 24; 6:12; Mic 7:9.

English translations—sometimes as "justice" and other times as "righteousness." But in biblical conceptualization, doing justice is in essence acting righteously.[11]

One of the most striking features of the biblical understanding of justice is that it applies most aptly and frequently to the needs of the most vulnerable in society. Numerous passages of the Hebrew Bible illustrate this point, but a few examples will suffice here. A clear pattern emerges in the biblical use of the word "justice" *(mishpat)* in the following verses:[12]

> For the LORD your God is God of gods and Lord of lords, the great God, mighty and awesome, who is not partial and takes no bribe, who executes justice for the orphan and the widow, and who loves the strangers, providing them food and clothing. (Deut 10:17-18)

> You shall not deprive a resident alien or an orphan of justice; you shall not take a widow's garment in pledge. (Deut 24:17)

> Cursed be anyone who deprives the alien, the orphan, and the widow of justice. (Deut 27:19)

> Learn to do good;
> seek justice,
>   rescue the oppressed,
> defend the orphan,
>   plead for the widow. (Is 1:17)

> For if you truly amend your ways and your deeds, if you truly practice justice between a man and his neighbor, *if* you do not oppress the alien, the orphan, or the widow, and do not shed innocent blood in this place, nor walk after other gods to your own ruin, then I will let you dwell in

---

[11] Longman correctly notes that righteousness and justice are closely related categories that define one another. See Tremper Longman III, *Proverbs,* Baker Commentary on the Old Testament Wisdom and Psalms (Grand Rapids, MI: Baker Academic, 2006), 390.

[12] The selection represents a very small sample of similar teachings in the Hebrew Bible—from every portion of the Hebrew canon: Law, Prophets, and Writings.

this place, in the land that I gave to your fathers forever and ever. (Jer 7:5-7 NASB)

Thus says the LORD: Act with justice and righteousness, and deliver from the hand of the oppressor anyone who has been robbed. And do no wrong or violence to the alien, the orphan, and the widow, or shed innocent blood in this place. (Jer 22:3)

Thus has the LORD of hosts said, "Dispense true justice and practice kindness and compassion each to his brother; and do not oppress the widow or the orphan, the stranger or the poor; and do not devise evil in your hearts against one another." (Zech 7:9-10 NASB)

Give justice to the weak and the orphan;
    maintain the right of the lowly and the destitute. (Ps 82:3)

The LORD works vindication
    and justice for all who are oppressed. (Ps 103:6)

I know that the LORD maintains the cause of the needy,
    and executes justice for the poor. (Ps 140:12)

It is not at all surprising that justice is something that must be guarded carefully for the poor and needy. The rich and powerful can guarantee justice for themselves. Therefore, the authors of the Bible command and plead for fair treatment of the most vulnerable people in their society. But something else needs clarification. While the idea of justice certainly includes fairness and giving everyone what they rightfully deserve, the biblical picture of what everyone rightfully deserves may be different from contemporary notions of fairness.

For example, we might consider charging interest on loans to be fair. It may even be common practice in some economic systems to charge higher interest rates to poor people with bad credit ratings. In contrast to this, Mosaic law prohibits charging poor people any interest at all (Ex 22:25). Furthermore, according to the Mosaic law codes, the poor people justly deserve free access to food (Lev 19:10), means of working off debt in a reasonable period (Deut 15:12), and a living wage (Deut 15:12-15).

Often, when God speaks about the treatment of the most vulnerable people in Israelite society, the language is intense and rhetorically powerful. For instance, in Exodus 22:21-24, God tells the Israelites never to mistreat the immigrant, widow, or orphan.[13] Here, the language is provocative and powerful in several ways. First, the command never to mistreat an immigrant is grounded in the shared history of the Israelites as immigrants themselves: "for you were aliens in the land of Egypt." God reminds them not to forget their own experiences as they think about how they treat others who might be easily exploited.

Second, the command regarding the immigrant contains two verbal imperatives: "wrong or oppress." The two verbs are synonymous in Hebrew, so the addition of an extra verb does not further explain the kind of actions prohibited. Rather, the double imperative rhetorically strengthens the negative command.

Third, the word order in verse 22 is emphatic. In English, it is natural to say, "You shall not abuse any widow or orphan," but the order of words in Hebrew looks like this: any widow or orphan you shall not mistreat. By bringing the object of the verb to the beginning of the sentence, Hebrew language is able to bring emphasis.

Fourth, the word for *any* (*kol* in Hebrew) further adds emphasis. Without the word, the sentence would read just fine this way: "You shall not abuse a widow or an orphan." However, the addition of the word *any* additionally strengthens the object of the verb. In other words, while mistreatment of people might happen in any given society, these specifically identified people represent a special group under divine

---

[13]Biblical authors often identified these three classes of people together precisely because of their vulnerability in Israelite society: Deut 10:18; 14:29; 16:11, 14; 24:17, 19, 20-21; 26:12-13; 27:19; Ps 94:6; 146:9; Jer 7:6; 22:3; Ezek 22:7; Zech 7:10; Mal 3:5.

protection. It is as if God is saying, "Sure, you are going to mistreat each other, but don't even think about touching *these* people!"

Fifth, the text employs special grammatical features available in Hebrew to bring emphasis to the actions included in verse 23.[14] While English uses adverbs or short phrases to add emphasis to verbal ideas, Hebrew has a feature known as the infinitive absolute, which repeats the same verb in a different grammatical form to accomplish various emphases. The KJV renders the nuance of the infinitives absolute nicely: "If thou afflict them *in any wise*, and they cry *at all* unto me, I will *surely* hear their cry" (emphasis added).[15]

Finally, the consequence of violating this law is incredibly severe: "My wrath will burn, and I will kill you with the sword, and your wives shall become widows and your children orphans" (Ex 22:24). The punishment goes beyond the *lex talionis*. According to the law of retribution, an oppressor should in return be oppressed. But in this scenario, the oppressor is killed. Since the violator of this law would not have been responsible for the status of the widow or the orphan (as he did not kill the husband of the widow or kill the parents of the orphan), the consequences for violating this law do not meet the commensurate punishment of *lex talionis*. Rather, the punishment may be better understood as poetic justice. Those who mistreat widows and orphans will make their wives widows and their children orphans.

The above analysis shows one thing clearly. God feels strongly about the mistreatment of the vulnerable. There are good theological reasons for God's intolerance of injustice. Chief among them is God's own character:

---

[14]Three occurrences of the infinitive absolute form a triple emphatic sentence structure. Three words repeated in the infinitive absolute are *oppress* (ענה), *cry out* (צעק), and *listen* (שמע).

[15]The first two infinitive-finite pairings function emphatically by diminishing the verbal action. The final infinitive absolute functions in a more typical way of strengthening the finite verb, in this case the imperfect of שמע. Wilhelm Gesenius, E. Kautzsch, and A. E. Cowley, *Gesenius' Hebrew Grammar*, 2nd English ed. (Oxford: Clarendon Press, 1988), 342-43 §113.o.

> The Rock, his work is perfect,
>> and all his ways are just.
> A faithful God, without deceit,
>> just and upright is he. (Deut 32:4)

There is something of that attribute of God in us, created in the image of God. Something deep within us cries out when we experience injustice, even in others. If we or the people we love were to be imprisoned without guilt because of a false witness (Ex 23:1), because someone has taken a bribe (Ex 23:8), because they were poor (Ex 23:3, 6), or because they were foreigners (Ex 23:9), our outrage might begin to reflect God's wrath.

If oppressing the vulnerable in Israelite society would be met by divine wrath, what then is the positive command to seek peace for the community? In other words, how can a society experience wholeness? Here an illustration may be helpful. My mother has a placard that allows her to park in parking spaces for persons with disabilities. Once, driving in my mother's car with my sister, I suggested that we use our mother's placard even though she was not present. My sister responded by saying, "That wouldn't be fair to the person who actually needed it!" Chastised, I repented, but her use of the word *fair* has stayed with me. How is it *fair* to give preferential treatment to some drivers over others? Without intending to, my sister used the word *fair* to reflect a very biblical sense of justice.

I argued earlier that there could not be peace without the necessities of life that make a person whole. If shalom of individuals requires physical well-being, then justice in the biblical sense must also include ensuring that such needs are met. And as one might expect, the Hebrew Bible contains numerous instructions to the Israelites regarding such provisions for the most vulnerable people in society. For instance,

Leviticus 19 and Deuteronomy 24 give instructions for landowners to provide a way for the poor to find food:

> When you reap the harvest of your land, you shall not reap to the very edges of your field, or gather the gleanings of your harvest. You shall not strip your vineyard bare, or gather the fallen grapes of your vineyard; you shall leave them for the poor and the alien: I am the LORD your God. (Lev 19:9-10)

> When you reap your harvest in your field and forget a sheaf in the field, you shall not go back to get it; it shall be left for the alien, the orphan, and the widow, so that the LORD your God may bless you in all your undertakings. When you beat your olive trees, do not strip what is left; it shall be for the alien, the orphan, and the widow.
>
> When you gather the grapes of your vineyard, do not glean what is left; it shall be for the alien, the orphan, and the widow. Remember that you were a slave in the land of Egypt; therefore I am commanding you to do this. (Deut 24:19-22)

If we combine these two closely related Mosaic laws, the instructions are rather straightforward: For the benefit of the poor, immigrant, orphan, widow,

- Leave behind the gleanings (fallen grains).
- Do not harvest the corners or edges of a field.
- Do not go back for a forgotten sheaf.
- Leave behind underripened grapes and fallen (overripe) ones.
- Leave underripened olives on the branches.

Both passages provide justification for the law as being grounded in God's relationship with Israel. In Leviticus, it is God who speaks, "I am the LORD your God" (Lev 19:10). In Deuteronomy, the author spells out the relational benefit of obeying the command: "so that the LORD your God may bless you in all your undertakings" (Deut 24:19).

The reader may draw three important implications from these provisions. First, there are no obligations placed on the poor that bind them to the landowners. That is, the rich cannot use these laws to receive favors or obligations from the poor. The provision for the poor must be given freely without strings attached.[16] Second, the poor are not simply handed the grain, grapes, or olives upon completion of the harvest. Rather, the food can be gained only through hard work. Gleaning is extremely difficult labor, since there is only one way to pick up the grain that fell during sickling—one grain at a time while hunched over the ground![17] Third, precisely because the work is hard, these Mosaic laws honor the dignity of the poor person. The law does not in any way humiliate the person in need. So in a very important way, the Mosaic provision respects the image of God in the most vulnerable people in society.

CONCLUDING THOUGHTS

I am not a handy guy. If I were, I would restore a 1967 Mustang and it would be parked in the driveway of a beautifully remodeled Victorian home. Alas, I lack the knowledge and patience to accomplish such feats. When I do see a meticulously restored classic car or a beautifully remodeled home, I am amazed at how such things are actually possible. Broken things can be made whole again! When a brand new car comes off the production line, it is whole. It is shalom. Over time it will fall apart. But it can be made shalom again. This is the idea of peace in the Hebrew Bible.

---

[16]There is another system instituted by Mosaic law that does bind the poor to the rich. In it, a poor person in debt may become a servant for six years. After those six years of service, the servant must be allowed to go free, all debt forgiven, and provided generously from the wealth of the master. See Deut 15:12-18.

[17]This is the point the head servant makes to Boaz in Ruth 2:7: "She has been on her feet from early this morning until now." Even though the work itself was difficult, Ruth had been at it all day.

When the parts of a person function well together, that individual experiences shalom. When this wholeness breaks emotionally or physically, we become sick. So then healing brings peace again to brokenness. Likewise, a healthy community functions well together, creating justice. When various groups or classes of a given society can no longer experience shalom together, the necessary healing comes in the form of justice.

"If a man attacks your family, will you stand by and do nothing?" I do not honestly know how I might react in an emergency situation in which my family was threatened. I do know that seeking peace may be a little too late if such a situation has already arisen. Our theology of peace must go beyond nonviolent response to violence. Rather, our understanding of peace ought to consider the needs of shalom for both individuals and communities. Why is the hypothetical attacker acting in violence? What in our society has prompted such actions? As argued above, the two are very much related. Our Christian response to brokenness is shalom, to bring wholeness to individuals as Christ did wherever he went and to seek to build the kingdom of God in righteousness, justice, and peace.

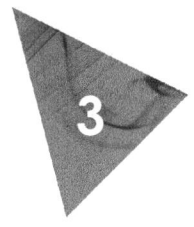

PRIDE FIGHTER OR SACRIFICIAL LAMB?

DISCERNING THE REAL JESUS IN THE BOOK OF REVELATION

Gregory A. Boyd

IN AN INTERVIEW SOME TIME AGO, Mark Driscoll claimed that in the book of Revelation, "Jesus is a pride fighter with a tattoo down His leg, a sword in His hand and the commitment to make someone bleed."[1] It is not hard to see how Driscoll came to this conclusion, for it cannot be denied that Revelation "seethes with images of blood and violence" and that a good deal of this violence is associated with "the wrath of the Lamb" (Rev 6:16).[2] This violence reaches a zenith in chapter 19, where we find Jesus going out to make war on a white horse (Rev 19:11). He is dressed in a bloodstained robe (Rev 19:13) and has a sword coming out

---

[1]Mark Driscoll, "7 Big Questions: Seven Leaders on Where the Church Is Headed," *Relevant Magazine* 24 (January/February 2007): web.archive.org/web/20071013102203/http://relevantmagazine.com/god_article.php?id=7418. Pride fighting is a form of mixed martial arts combat, closely associated with ultimate fighting or cage fighting. Some sections of this essay have been adopted with modifications from Gregory A. Boyd, *Crucifixion of the Warrior God: Interpreting the Old Testament's Violent Portraits of God in Light of the Cross*, 2 vols. (Minneapolis: Fortress, 2018), 593-628.

[2]L. L. Johns, *The Lamb Christology of the Apocalypse of John* (Eugene, OR: Wipf & Stock, 2003), 187.

of his mouth "to strike down the nations" while he "tread[s] the wine press of the fury of the wrath of God the Almighty" (Rev 19:15). Jesus and his army slay "the beast and the kings of the earth with their armies" (Rev 19:19; see also Rev 19:21), and the latter two groups end up having birds gorge on their flesh (Rev 19:21).

These violent images lead those who assume that Revelation provides a literal snapshot of end time events to conclude that Jesus will return as a pride fighter who massacres billions of people.[3] But it is not only future literalists who conclude that the Jesus of Revelation is exceedingly violent. A number of scholars also argue that the image of Jesus in this work is horrifically violent. In their view, it reflects the vindictive fantasies of a persecuted Christian community who long for their suffering to be avenged by having their enemies crushed.[4]

In this essay I will draw on the work of Richard Bauckham and an increasing number of New Testament scholars and theologians to argue that this interpretation is grossly mistaken.[5] I will begin by first offering

---

[3]This has been graphically illustrated in the wildly popular *Left Behind* series by Tim LaHaye and Jerry Jenkins and the (much less popular) *Left Behind* Hollywood movies.

[4]See, e.g., W. Carter, *The Roman Empire and the New Testament: An Essential Guide* (Nashville: Abingdon, 2006); Y. Collins, *Crisis and Catharsis: The Power of the Apocalypse* (Philadelphia: Westminster Press, 1984); D. Frankfurter, "The Legacy of Sectarian Rage: Vengeance Fantasies in the New Testament," in *Religion and Violence: The Biblical Heritage,* ed. E. Berant and J. Klawans (Sheffield, UK: Sheffield Pheonix Press, 2007); M. Grosso, *The Millennium Myth: Love and Death at the End of Time* (Wheaton, IL: Quest Books, 1995).

[5]Some of the works that have most informed my interpretation of Revelation are Richard Bauckham, *The Theology of the Book of Revelation* (Cambridge: Cambridge University Press, 1993), and *The Climax of Prophecy: Studies on the Book of Revelation* (Edinburgh: T&T Clark); M. J. Gorman, *Reading Revelation Responsibly: Uncivil Worship and Witness; Following the Lamb into the Creation* (Eugene, OR: Cascade, 2011); S. K. Tonstad, *Saving God's Reputation: The Theological Function of* Pistis Iesou *in the Cosmic Narratives of Revelation* (Edinburgh: T&T Clark, 2013); T. Grimsrud and M. Hardin, eds., *Compassionate Eschatology: The Future as Friend* (Eugene, OR: Cascade, 2011); M. Bredin, *Jesus, Revolutionary of Peace: A Nonviolent Christology in the Book of Revelation* (Waynesboro, GA: Paternoster Press, 2003); Johns, *Lamb Christology*; V. Eller, *The Most Revealing Book of the Bible: Making Sense out of Revelation* (Grand Rapids, MI: Eerdmans, 1974); T. Grimsrud, *Triumph of the Lamb: A Self-Study Guide to the Book of Revelation* (Scottdale, PA: Herald Press, 1987); D. L. Barr, "Towards an Ethical Reading of the Apocalypse: Reflections on John's Use of Power, Violence, and Misogyny," in *Society of Biblical Literature 1997 Seminar Papers,* no. 36 (Atlanta: Scholars Press, 1997); D. Weaver, *The Non-violent God* (Grand

several preliminary observations about this work that have a bearing on our interpretation of John's violent symbols. I will then discuss two dominant themes in Revelation that best indicate that John is reframing the traditional violent images he uses in a way that completely subverts their violence. And I will conclude by illustrating John's subversive technique in Revelation 19, which is commonly cited in support of the violent interpretation of Jesus in Revelation.

SEVERAL PRELIMINARY OBSERVATIONS

Several things are necessary to bear in mind as we seek to correctly interpret the violent imagery of Revelation. First, scholars generally agree that Revelation has much in common with other ancient apocalyptic works. Among other things, this work is heavily symbolic and purports to let its audience in on a divine secret by offering them a heavenly and eschatological perspective of what God is up to in the world.[6] More specifically, Revelation is written to Christians facing persecution, and it offers them a theological interpretation what they are soon going to endure if they remain faithful to Christ (Rev 1:1; 22:6). At the same time, John himself identifies his work as a prophecy (Rev 1:3), and Revelation differs from apocalyptic works in some significant respects. It is therefore important to respect the uniqueness of this work by not interpreting it through the grid of other apocalyptic works.[7] This is especially

---

Rapids, MI: Eerdmans, 2013), and *The Non-violent Atonement* (Grand Rapids, MI: Eerdmans, 2001); W. Harrington, *Revelation* (Collegeville, MN: Liturgical Press, 1993), and "Worthy Is the Lamb," *Proceedings of the Irish Biblical Association* 18 (1995); M. E. Boring, "Narrative Christology in the Apocalypse," *Catholic Biblical Quarterly* 54 (1992); H. Maier, *Apocalypse Recalled: The Book of Revelation After Christendom* (Minneapolis: Fortress, 2002); R. S. Morton, *One upon the Throne and the Lamb: A Tradition Historical/Theological Analysis of Revelation 4-5* (New York: Peter Lang, 2007); L. Morris, *Revelation* (London: Tyndale Press, 1979); W. Klassen, "Vengeance in the Apocalypse of John," *Catholic Biblical Quarterly* 28 (1966): 300-311.

[6]C. Rowland, *The Open Heaven: A Study of Apocalyptic in Judaism and Early Christianity* (London: SPCK, 1982), 20; Eller, *Most Revealing Book*, 26-28, 128.

[7]Tonstad, *Saving God's Reputation*, 18; Johns, *Lamb Christology*, 192-93; G. Linton, "Reading the Apocalypse as Apocalypse: The Limits of Genre," in *The Reality of Apocalypse: Rhetoric and*

important to remember as concerns John's use of violent imagery, for we shall see that John uses traditional violent imagery in radically unique ways.⁸

Second, while Revelation is written as though John were spontaneously reporting a series of visions as they happened, this book was actually composed "with astounding care and skill."⁹ Indeed, Bauckham goes so far as to argue that Revelation constitutes "one of the finest literary works in the N.T." and "one of the greatest theological achievements of early Christianity."¹⁰ In his view, "scarcely a word" in this book "can have been chosen without deliberate reflection on its relationship to the work as an integrated, interconnected whole."¹¹ Among other things, this means we must pay close attention to subtle details as we interpret John's violent imagery.

Third, it is important we understand that Revelation, like the Gospels, was written to be performed orally.¹² This much is reflected in the book's opening pronouncement: "Blessed is the one who reads aloud the words of the prophecy, and blessed are those who hear . . . it" (Rev 1:3). We must therefore understand Revelation along the lines of a "dramatic performance, in which the audience enters the world of the drama for its

---

Politics in the Book of Revelation, ed. D. L. Barr (Atlanta: Society of Biblical Literature, 2006), 9-42; Bauckham, *Theology*, 9-12; Bauckham, *Climax*, 175-77.

⁸Bauckham, *Climax*, 174-75; Tonstad, *Saving God's Reputation*, 5; Johns, *Lamb Christology*, 175. Caird speaks of the "rebirth of images" drawn from the OT (*Revelation: A Commentary on the Revelation of St. John the Divine*, 2nd ed. [London: A & C Black, 1984], 73). Bredin correctly observes that John often alters material in a way that "subverts and mocks" its traditional interpretation (*Jesus*, 215). J. M. Vogelgesang only slightly overstates the case when he argues that John so completely transforms traditional apocalyptic imagery that Revelation could be considered an antiapocalypse ("The Interpretation of Ezekiel in the Book of Revelation" [PhD diss., Harvard University, 1985], 300).

⁹Bauckham, *Theology*, 3.

¹⁰Bauckham, *Theology*, 3.

¹¹Bauckham, *Climax*, x. So argues Eller, *Most Revealing Book*, 213-14.

¹²D. Barr, "The Apocalypse of John as Oral Enactment," *Interpretation* 40 (1986): 243-56. For a discussion of the nature and significance of oral performance for NT studies, see P. Eddy and G. Boyd, *The Jesus Legend: A Case for the Historical Reliability of the Synoptic Jesus Tradition* (Grand Rapids, MI: Baker, 2007), 237-308.

duration and can have the perception of the world outside the drama powerfully shifted by their experience."[13] In the words of Elisabeth Schüssler Fiorenza, Revelation is a "poetic-rhetorical work" that "seeks to persuade and motivate by constructing a 'symbolic universe' that invites imaginative participation. The strength of its persuasion," she adds, "lies... in the 'evocative' power of its symbols... which engage the hearer (reader) by eliciting reactions, emotions, convictions, and identifications."[14] This means we are seriously misreading this work if we try to interpret John's symbols literally, let alone as a literal "history ahead of time."[15]

Fourth, John's ultimate goal in utilizing evocative symbols is to motivate disciples to be uncompromising in their allegiance to Christ and thus in their resistance to "Babylon," even though this resistance will likely lead to their deaths. Hence we find the theme of martyrdom permeating this book (e.g., Rev 6:9-10; 7:14; 12:11; 13:15). Moreover, he is writing to reassure these disciples that, while being put to death looks like defeat in the eyes of the world, it is actually a victory for those who belong to Christ. Hence, these disciples are to overcome Satan (the dragon) "by the blood of the Lamb and by the word of their testimony" (Rev 12:11).[16] We may thus think of Revelation as a sort of "subversive resistance manual."[17] Indeed, Bauckham goes so far as to claim that

---

[13]Barr, "Apocalypse," 248-9; Bauckham, *Theology*, 10; Johns, *Lamb Christology*, 158.

[14]E. Schüssler Fiorenza, *The Book of Revelation: Justice and Judgment* (Philadelphia: Fortress, 1985), 187. For a sampling of others who argue along these lines, see Bauckham, *Theology*, 3-5; Johns, *Lamb Christology*, 156-58, 172; L. Thompson, "Mooring the Revelation in the Mediterranean," in *Society of Biblical Literature 1992 Seminar Papers*, no. 31 (Atlanta: Scholars Press, 1992), 635-53 [635]; Bredin, *Jesus*, 181.

[15]Bauckham, *Theology*, 93. As Bauckham regularly observes, interpreting Revelation's symbols as referring to future historical events produces a multitude of contradictions and absurdities (e.g., *Theology*, 92-93, 102, 108; *Climax*, 209). Eller also offers numerous examples (e.g., *Most Revealing Book*, 56, 81,144, 181-84). On the danger of interpreting Revelation literally, see Johns, *Lamb Christology*, 185-86, 198.

[16]Bauckham notes that the "blood of the lamb" in Revelation is not primarily referring to Christ's sacrificial death but "to the deaths of the Christian martyrs, who, following Christ's example, bear witness even at the cost of their lives" (*Theology*, 75).

[17]Johns, *Lamb Christology*, 153, see also 156, 177.

Revelation constitutes "the most powerful piece of political resistance literature from the period of the early Empire."[18] We must therefore pay close attention to various ways John uses violent images that reflect the coercive power of the empire that John wants his audience to subvert.

With these preliminary words in place, I turn to discuss two important motifs in Revelation that indicate that John is drastically reframing the traditional violent images he employs.

THE TRIUMPHANT LION AND THE SLAIN LAMB

The throne room scene. The first and most important theme in Revelation that significantly affects our interpretation of its violent imagery concerns the heavenly scene of the throne room in Revelation 4–5, which most scholars agree constitutes the interpretive fulcrum of this work.[19] Here is where the audience is let in on the previously mentioned divine secret. As Bauckham argues, the throne of God and the lamb in Revelation represent heaven's perspective (and, therefore, the true perspective) on what is transpiring in history in contrast to all the inhabitants of the earth who are yet under the sway of Satan's deception (Rev 12:9; 13:14; 18:23; 20:8, 10).[20] And John captures the hidden nature of this heavenly perspective with the symbol of the mysterious sealed scroll.

The drama of this scene reaches a pinnacle when a "mighty angel" asks the question, "Who is worthy to open the scroll and break its seals?" (Rev 5:2). John initially weeps because no one is found worthy of this task (Rev 5:4), a point that arguably alludes to a prophetic tradition in

---

[18]Johns, *Lamb Christology*, 38.
[19]See, e.g., L. Hurtado, "Revelation 4–5 in the Light of Jewish Apocalyptic Analogia," *Journal for the Study of the New Testament* 25 (1985): 10; Boring, *Revelation*, 101-2; Tonstad, *Saving God's Reputation*, 37; Bauckham, *Theology*, 22-23, 40, 75; Johns, *Lamb Christology*, 158-59; D. J. Neville, "Faithful, True, and Violent? Christology and 'Divine Vengeance' in the Revelation of John," in Grimsrud and Hardin, *Compassionate Eschatology*, 56-84.
[20]Bauckham, *Theology*, 31, 74, 80-84. See also Eller, *Most Revealing Book*, 73-82; Tonstad, *Saving God's Reputation*, 141.

which weeping reflects one's sorrow "that injustice is prevailing and God's will is being thwarted."[21] The question before the heavenly throne—and the question that the unsealing of the scroll will answer—concerns why Satan and his political empire (Babylon) seem to be defeating God and his people, as evidenced by the fact that God's people are being martyred.

The lion who is a slain lamb. John does not weep for long, however, for he suddenly hears "one of the elders" declare, "The Lion of the tribe of Judah, the Root of David, has conquered" and is thus worthy "to open the scroll and its seven seals" (Rev 5:5). This depiction of Christ as the triumphant lion of the tribe of Judah reflects an ancient triumphant Jewish understanding of the Messiah (Gen 49:9). Indeed, suffering as they were under Roman oppression, most first-century Jews were hoping for this type of messiah. They anticipated a lionlike "pride fighter" who would come with an intent "to make someone bleed" in the process of liberating God's people from their oppression.[22] One might thus far assume that John was endorsing this violent conception, but immediately after hearing about the lion, John looks and sees a little lamb (*arnion*) that has already been slaughtered (Rev 5:6).[23]

The contrast between what John hears and sees is one of the previously mentioned details we need to pay close attention to, for it is one of the ways John subverts the violence of the images he employs (see Rev 7:4-9).[24] In this case John is declaring that the one who had previously been identified as a triumphant lion turns out to be a little

---

[21]Johns, *Lamb Christology*, 163n46.
[22]On the lion as a symbol that "suggests ferocity, destructiveness and irresistible strength," see Bauckham, *Climax*, 182, and *Revelation*, 67-68. On the broader background of the image of lion, see Johns, *Lamb Christology*, 164-67.
[23]Eller notes that *arnion* could be translated "lambkin" with a connotation of being a "poor little thing." The image is intended to present the strongest possible contrast with the beast (*therion*), who is depicted in chap. 13 as "a great big vicious MONSTER" (*Most Revealing Book*, 79).
[24]See Bauckham, *Theology*, 76-77; *Climax*, 179-80.

slaughtered lamb! He is proclaiming that the Messiah does indeed fight and overcome foes, but he does so not by ripping enemies apart as a lion would, but by humbly offering himself up to be sacrificed as this little lamb.[25] John has thus transformed a "symbol of power and domination" into a "symbol of vulnerability and nonviolence."[26] He has in effect turned the violent conception of the Messiah on its head and "forged a new symbol of conquest by sacrificial death."[27] Eugene Boring rightly calls this "one of the most mind-wrenching and theologically pregnant transformations of imagery in literature."[28]

It is impossible to overstate the importance of this remarkable symbolic transformation for our interpretation of Revelation. John's transformation of the lion of Judah into the sacrificial lamb constitutes the "central reversal in his apocalypse," for it anchors most of John's other symbolic reversals.[29] On this note, it is important to observe that once the lion is revealed to be the slain lamb, we find Christ depicted only this way through the remainder of Revelation.[30] Indeed, the remainder of Revelation is in essence the unveiling of Christ's lamblike victory, revealed in chapter 5, over and against the lie of the dragon that the lamb and his followers can be conquered through the military power of Babylon.[31]

The revelation of God's true character. It is precisely because the lamb has already won his battle by offering himself up that he alone is worthy to open the scroll (Rev 5:9; see also Rev 3:21).[32] No one else in

---

[25]Bauckham, *Theology*, 68. Tonstad notes that John's unexpected Messiah is consistent with the nonconformist Messiah of the rest of the New Testament (*Saving God's Reputation*, 6). For a comprehensive overview of the background the John's unique use of lamb imagery, see Johns, *Lamb Christology*, chaps 2–5.

[26]Johns, *Lamb Christology*, 170.

[27]Bauckham, *Theology*, 74; see also *Climax*, 214.

[28]Boring, "Narrative Christology," 708.

[29]Johns, *Lamb Christology*, 170. So notes Boring, *Revelation*, 110-11; Grimsrud, *Triumph of the Lamb*, 50-57; Barr, "Ethical Reading," 358-73; Eller, *Most Revealing Book*, 79.

[30]Johns, *Lamb Christology*, 191, cf. 195.

[31]Bauckham, *Theology*, 75, 88-91.

[32]So emphasizes Harrington, *Revelation*, 87-88; see also "Worthy Is the Lamb," 149, 169.

heaven is worthy, because, as Sigve Tonstad notes, "*absolutely no one else would have solved the cosmic conflict this way,*" referring to the battle between God on the one hand and the dragon and Babylon on the other.[33] Moreover, the fact that this scene takes place in the throne room, reflecting God's true perspective, along with the fact that throughout Revelation "what is said of God" is also "said of Jesus," suggests that John understands the sacrificial lamb to alone be worthy because he alone perfectly expresses God's true character.[34] As we read in 1 John, "God is love" (1 Jn 4:8)—the kind of love that is revealed when Jesus Christ "laid down his life for us" (1 Jn 3:16).

Moreover, John describes the lamb as having "seven eyes" and "seven horns" (Rev 5:6), which many scholars argue are symbols of the fullness of divine wisdom and power.[35] By identifying God's omniscience and omnipotence with the slaughtered lamb, John has transformed standard ancient (and modern) assumptions about God's wisdom and power in a radical, cruciform way. Mitchell Reddish captures the significance of this when he notes that in Revelation, "God's control over the universe is exemplified in the sacrificial, suffering work of the lamb, not in coercive domination."[36] So, too, G. B. Caird notes that John has transformed the standard conception of divine power as "the power of unlimited coercion" into "the invincible power of self-negating, self-sacrificial love."[37]

---

[33] Tonstad, *Saving God's Reputation*, 141.
[34] Neville, "Faithful, True, and Violent?" 63. As Boring notes, in Revelation "God is defined by Christ, the one who shares even his throne . . . (3.21; 12.5; 22.1, 3) so that the figures and especially the voices of God and Christ tend to fade into each other" (*Revelation*, 707). See also Bauckham, *Theology*, 54-65; Richard Bauckham, *Jesus and the God of Israel: God Crucified and Other Studies in the New Testament; Christology of Divine Identity* (Grand Rapids, MI: Eerdmans, 2008), 38-39, 45-49; Weaver, *Non-violent God*, 39, 43.
[35] See, e.g., Richard Bauckham, "The Language of Warfare in the Book of Revelation," in Grimsrud and Hardin, *Compassionate Eschatology*, 28-41 (34); Neville, "Faithful, True, and Violent?," 69.
[36] M. Reddish, *Revelation* (Macon, GA: Smyth & Helwys, 2001), 22.
[37] Caird, *Revelation*, 75. John is in this respect consistent with the apostle Paul, who also identified "the power of God" with "the cross" (1 Cor 1:18).

In short, over and against the deception of the dragon that goes back to the Garden of Eden (Gen 3:1-5), the lamb is the definitive expression of God's true character and thus of God's way of ruling the world and defeating evil.[38] While the citizens of Babylon worship the beast (Rev 13:7-8) because they are deceived into thinking coercive and violent power steers history and wins in the end, the disciples to whom John is writing are to remember that the lamb already conquered the beast by manifesting God's true self-sacrificial character on Calvary.[39] And if they will "follow the Lamb wherever he goes" (Rev 14:4, see also Rev 19:14), they will bear "the testimony [or witness] of Jesus" (Rev 12:17; 19:10; see also Rev 1:9; 2:13; 6:9; 12:11; 17:6) and thus share in his victory.[40] The secret of the scroll is thus that, while the martyrdom of those who follow the lamb looks like their defeat to citizens of Babylon (Rev 11:7; 13:4, 7-8), it is actually their victory from the true perspective of the throne room (Rev 7:9-14; 12:11; 15:2-3; see also Rev 2:10).[41]

Not only this, but according to Revelation, this is God's strategy for delivering the world from the oppressive dragon. John's central prophetic conviction is that "the sacrificial death of the Lamb and the prophetic witness of his followers are God's strategy for winning all the nations of the world from the dominion of the beast to his own kingdom."[42]

---

[38]In the words of Bauckham, "Christ's sacrificial death *belongs to the way God rules the world*" (*Revelation*, 64). See also Bauckham, *Jesus and the God of Israel*, 47-49. Similarly, Tonstad argues that the Lamb reveals "the character of the divine government" (*Saving God's Reputation*, 142), while Johns notes that the lamb is the revelation of "*how* God works in history" (*Lamb Christology*, 163, cf. 108-49). See also Bredin, *Jesus*, 33-34; Neville, "Faithful, True, and Violent?," 67, 78-79. On the importance of Genesis 3 as the background for the conception of the deceptive "ancient serpent" in Revelation (Rev 12:9; 20:2), see P. S. Minear, "Far as the Curse Is Found: The Point of Revelation 12:15-16," *Novum Testamentum* 33 (1991): 71-77.

[39]On the importance in Revelation of the question of what kind of power will turn out to be victorious, see Bauckham, *Theology*, 91.

[40]Bauckham, *Climax*, 258; see also Bauckham, *Theology*, 88-94, and "Language of Warfare," 36-38.

[41]Bauckham, *Climax*, 235, and "Language of Warfare," 37; see also Johns, *Lamb Christology*, 194. Johns notes that John radically redefines "triumph" in a self-sacrificial way, just as he does the concept of divine power (175-80). See also Bauckham, "Language of Warfare," 34.

[42]Bauckham, *Climax*, 336-37; cf. 266; Bauckham, *Theology*, 83-90.

In the words of Harry Maier, "the Apocalypse does not build heavenly Jerusalem on the foundation of glorious military might, but on the glorious defeat, both of the Lamb and of those witnesses who are faithful unto death."[43]

THE LAMBLIKE WAR OF THE SAINTS

A new kind of war. The second motif that has a direct bearing on a proper interpretation of John's violent imagery concerns his symbolic construal of holy war. The prevalence of the holy war motif in Revelation is reflected in the consistent depiction of the lamb and his people as conquerors (Rev 2:7, 11, 17, 28; 3:5, 12, 21; 5:5; 12:11; 15:2; 17:14; 21:7) and in the fact that holy war imagery permeates this book (e.g., Rev 11:7; 12:7-8, 17; 13:7; 16:14; 17:14; 19:11, 19).[44] In this light, Revelation could justifiably be described as a "war scroll," similar to the war scroll found at Qumran.

Yet just as he did with the traditional conception of the Messiah as a mighty lion, John turns this violent holy war imagery on its head by consistently associating it with the slain lamb.[45] While Qumran envisioned an eschatological battle in which God's people would violently rise up and slay God's enemies, Revelation envisions a battle that was in principle already fought and won by the lamb on Calvary when he offered up his life on behalf of enemies (Rev 3:21; 5:5).[46] The only remaining foe left to be defeated in this battle is the lie that it is the coercive and violent power of the deceptive dragon (Rev 12:9; 13:14; 20:8, 10) and of Babylon that is victorious rather than the power of the lamb's self-sacrificial love. Hence, the battle that rages throughout Revelation is not

---

[43]Maier, *Apocalypse Recalled*, 196.
[44]Bauckham, *Theology*, 69-70, 88-89. See also Bauckham, "Language of Warfare," 30.
[45]John has not rejected "eschatological war," Bauckham notes, but his holy war images must be "carefully reinterpreted in terms of faithful witness to the point of death" (*Climax*, 233).
[46]Bauckham, "Language of Warfare," 32.

physical in nature; it is rather a battle between "the power of deceit and violence, on the one hand, and the power of truth and suffering witness on the other."[47]

This is reflected in the fact that the lamb, who is always faithful and true (Rev 19:11; see also Rev 1:5; 3:14; 17:14), uses a sword that comes *out of his mouth* to vanquish "all the lies of the beast" (Rev 1:16; 2:12, 16; 19:15, 21).[48] It is reflected as well in the fact that the saints, who are without deceit (Rev 14:5), are called to overcome not by relying on physical weapons but by patiently remaining faithful to the way of the slain lamb in the face of persecution, bearing witness to the truth in their speech and by their willingness to die rather than to fight (Rev 12:11; see also Rev 13:10; 14:12; 19:11).[49] Hence, though Revelation is a sort of "war scroll," it is a war scroll of *nonviolent* warfare.

A new kind of army. John's transformation of the holy war motif is also evident in Revelation 7. John hears that 144,000 people from the twelve tribes of Israel have been sealed (Rev 7:4-8). Their military status is evident from the fact that they are listed in the form of a military census.[50] But John then looks and sees "a great multitude that no one could count, from every nation, from all tribes and peoples and languages, standing before the throne and before the Lamb" (Rev 7:9). By once again juxtaposing what he sees with what he hears, John has transformed a traditional conception of an exclusively Jewish eschatological army into an army that is transnational in character (see Rev 5:9; 7:9; 11:9; 13:7; 14:6).[51] The holy war imagery is further transformed when

---

[47]Bauckham, "Language of Warfare," 38.
[48]Bauckham, *Theology*, 68-69, 105. On the significance of Christ's verbal sword, see Bauckham, *Theology*, 105; Bredin, *Jesus*, 206-8.
[49]Johns, *Lamb Christology*, 172.
[50]Bauckham notes that the reuniting of the twelve tribes for battle fits traditional eschatological expectations and that by listing twelve thousand from twelve tribes John intends to symbolize perfection (*Climax*, 218-19).
[51]Bauckham, *Theology*, 76-77; *Climax*, 179-80, 215-34.

John notes that this transnational army is victorious because these soldiers "have washed their robes and made them white in the blood of the Lamb" (Rev 7:14). This signifies that "they are martyrs, who have triumphed by participating, through their own deaths, in the sacrificial death of the Lamb."[52]

Not only this, but the washing of the robes refers to the purification washing that Jewish soldiers were traditionally required to go through after a battle. But while traditional warriors became ceremonially clean by washing *away* the blood of their defeated foes, the lamb's warriors are cleansed by being washed *in* the shed blood of the lamb they follow. And while traditional warriors were washed *after* their battle, these warriors are washed *before* going into battle.[53] The "startling paradox" John achieves by juxtaposing these military images provides "a decisive reinterpretation of the holy war motif," for it once again indicates that the way followers of the lamb fight is exactly opposite the way Babylon's warriors fight.[54]

Waging war through sacrifice. We find a similar thing going on when John picks up the imagery of the 144,000 again in Revelation 14. In keeping with traditional Jewish eschatological expectations, the army of the lamb is depicted as standing victorious on Mount Zion (Rev 14:1) as they sing "a new song" (Rev 14:3)—namely, a song celebrating victory in a holy war (e.g., Ps 98:1-3; 144:9-10; Is 42:10-13).[55] This army is made up of virgins (Rev 14:4), symbolizing the traditional abstinence requirement of Hebrew soldiers going out to battle (Deut 23:9-14; 1 Sam 21:5; 2 Sam 11:9-13; see also 1 QM 7:3-6).[56] Yet

---

[52]Bauckham, *Theology*, 77.
[53]Baukham, *Climax*, 226-27.
[54]Baukham, *Climax*, 227.
[55]Johns, *Lamb Christology*, 168-71; Bauckham, *Climax*, 230. Bauckham elsewhere notes that whereas the victorious new song of Moses in Exodus 15 was meant to instill terror in opponents, the new song of Revelation 14 is meant to lead nations to repentance (see Rev 15:3-4) (*Theology*, 99-101). See also Gorman, *Reading Revelation*, 153-54.
[56]Bauckham, *Theology*, 77-78, and *Climax*, 231.

echoing the foundational shift from lion to lamb imagery that permeates this work, John moves from military to sacrificial imagery when he notes that these soldiers "follow the Lamb wherever he goes" and are offered "as first fruits for God and the Lamb" (Rev 14:4). He then further transforms traditional eschatological imagery by depicting this army as perfect sacrifices who fight deception with truth, specifying that "in their mouth no lie was found" (Rev 14:5; see also Zeph 3:13; Is 53:9) and that "they are blameless" (Rev 14:5; see also Ex 29:38; Lev 1:3; 3:1).[57] Bauckham summarizes the meaning of this transformed imagery when he notes that "the Lamb really does conquer, though not by force of arms, and his followers really do share his victory, though not by violence. . . . There is a holy war to be fought, but to be fought and won by sacrificial death."[58]

THE FINAL "BATTLE"

John's ingenious subversion of holy war imagery continues in Revelation 19, which is most frequently appealed to in support of the claim that this book espouses a "pride fighter" image of Jesus. I will thus close this essay by briefly considering the violent images of this chapter.

A victory without a battle. In keeping with the pervasive theme that the lamb defeated all foes on Calvary, we should first note that Revelation 19 begins not with an army preparing to fight a battle but with an army celebrating God's victory in a battle that's already been fought (Rev 19:1-4). The inhabitants of heaven proclaim that God has already defeated the prostitute (representing "the arrogance of the earthly power") and has thereby already avenged the shed blood of his servants.[59] Indeed, the smoke of Babylon's destruction already ascends to

---

[57]Bauckham, *Theology*, 78.
[58]Bauckham, *Theology*, 230.
[59]Boring, *Revelation*, 192.

the throne room of heaven "for ever and ever" as a memorial of God's victory (Rev 19:3, see also Is 34:10).[60]

The only "battle" that remains is for the truth of the lamb's victory to vanquish once and for all the demonic deception that continues to oppress the inhabitants of the earth. This is accomplished when "The Word of God" (Rev 19:13) rides to earth and brings his age-long conflict with the deceptive ancient serpent to an end.[61] The irony is that, while this chapter is frequently cited as a prime example of Jesus and his followers engaging in violence, it actually doesn't depict a single violent act! Rather, by the time "The Word of God" rides to earth, "the decisive battle is long over."[62] Yes, John utilizes traditional warfare imagery in this chapter, but if we once again pay close attention to how John uses it, it becomes apparent that he has once again ingeniously transformed it to mean the opposite of what it traditionally meant.

The apparel of Jesus and his followers. For example, John applies to Jesus Isaiah's ghoulish vision of Yahweh returning from a victorious battle with his robes soaked in the blood of enemies, whom he has trampled like grapes in a winepress during his "day of vengeance" (Is 63:4; Rev 19:13). Significantly enough, however, Jesus' robes are bloody *before* he goes into battle, indicating that the lamb goes into battle covered in his own blood and, perhaps, the blood of his martyred servants.[63] Isaiah's image of Yahweh engaging in warfare by

---

[60]On everlasting smoke as a memorial of destruction, see E. Fudge, *The Fire That Consumes: The Biblical Case For Conditional Immortality*, rev. ed. (Carlisle, UK: Paternoster, 1994), 188-89.
[61]Bauckham, *Theology*, 105.
[62]Johns, *Lamb Christology*, 184-85. Similarly, see Boring, *Revelation*, 199-200; Weaver, *Non-violent God*, 51; T. Grimsrud, "Peace Theology and the Justice of God in the Book of Revelation," in *Essays on Peace Theology and Witness,* ed. W. M. Swartley (Elkhart, IN: Institute of Mennonite Studies, 1988), 145; Eller, *Most Revealing Book*, 176-79, cf. 149; Gorman, *Reading Revelation*, 154-55. Richard Hayes also offers insights into the nonviolent dimension of this symbolic "battle" in *The Moral Vision of the New Testament: Community, Cross, New Creation; A Contemporary Introduction to New Testament Ethics* (New York: HarperCollins, 1996), 175.
[63]Bauckham, "Language of Warfare," 38; Boring, *Revelation*, 196; Johns, *Lamb Christology*, 184; Eller, *Most Revealing Book*, 176-77; Bredin, *Jesus*, 200, 214-16.

sacrificing others has been transformed into an image of warfare by self-sacrifice.

Along similar lines, the military apparel the heavenly warriors wear as they ride into battle behind their king is "white and pure," denoting their "righteous deeds" (Rev 19:14; see also Rev 19:8), as well as the fact that they've been "washed . . . in the blood of the Lamb" (Rev 7:14). And, note, this army carries no weapons. This once again expresses the truth that the lamb and his followers engage in an already won battle by testifying to the true nature of God and his lamblike way of governing the world and by bearing witness against the violent and unjust idolatry of "Babylon" and the deception of the ancient serpent that ultimately rules it.[64]

The sword and the slaughtering. Also in keeping with traditional apocalyptic symbolism, John depicts Christ wielding a "sharp sword" to "strike down the nations" (Rev 19:15). However, as was previously mentioned, this sword comes out of Christ's mouth. His weapon, in short, is nothing other than the truth he speaks and embodies, which is why he is called "Faithful and True" as he rides into battle (Rev 19:11). As Bauckham argues, "This is not the slaughtered Lamb turned slaughterer, but it is the witness turned judge."[65] For, as is true in John's Gospel as well as elsewhere in the New Testament, the same word of truth that gives eternal life to all who submit to it brings judgment on all who resist it and who thus persist in deception (see, e.g., Jn 12:48; see also Jn 3:19; 5:22-24; 9:39-41).

While the "evocative power" of the graphic "rhetorical-poetic" battle scene in Revelation 19 is clearly intended to elicit a strong, visceral reaction in the audience as it was orally performed, it is also clearly not

---

[64]Johns, *Lamb Christology*, 185. On bearing witness as warfare in Revelation, see Bauckham, "Language of Warfare," 36-38; Bredin, *Jesus*, 206.

[65]Bauckham, "Language of Warfare," 36-38, cf. 68-69. So, too, Bredin notes that "Jesus is the source of condemnation insofar as those who reject his witness condemn themselves" (*Jesus*, 203).

intended to be interpreted literally.[66] For example, while this passage depicts all kings and nations as slain and devoured by birds (Rev 19:15, 18-19, 21), we nevertheless find them still alive in subsequent chapters (Rev 20:8; 22:11). Indeed, we are even given hope that the same kings and nations that were slain in this chapter will eventually be redeemed (Rev 21:24-26; 22:2). While no one who persists in wickedness can enter the heavenly city, the gates of the city will never be shut (Rev 21:25, 27) and "the kings of the earth will bring their glory into it" (Rev 21:24). As is the case throughout Revelation (and, arguably, the entire Bible), God's judgment, while just, is nevertheless redemptive in intent (if not inevitably redemptive in effect).[67] And what is slain in Revelation is not physical kings and nations but the false identity of these kings and nations when they and "the whole world" were led astray by Satan (Rev 12:9; see also Rev 20:2-3, 7-8).

Treading in the winepress. Finally, a word should be said about John's depiction of Jesus on a white horse "tread[ing] the wine press of the fury of the wrath of God the Almighty" (Rev 19:15). John is once again employing traditional holy war imagery that is intended to poignantly express God's judgment of rebels (see Is 63:1-6; Lam 1:15; Joel 3:13). But as we should by now expect, if we pay close attention to how John uses this imagery, it becomes clear he is infusing it with a meaning that is opposite its traditional violent meaning.

It is important to first note that the "great wine press of the wrath of God" is first mentioned in Revelation 14:19-20. Interestingly enough, while sinners are crushed like grapes as punishment for their wickedness in the Old Testament, in Revelation 14 the grapes are crushed simply because they are ready to be harvested (Rev 14:15, 18). Moreover, while

---

[66]Schüssler Fiorenza, *Book of Revelation*, 187.
[67]Neville, "Faithful, True, and Violent?" 79. Eller insightfully discusses the manner in which the motifs of severe judgment and universal hope are interwoven throughout Revelation (*Most Revealing Book*, 49-51, 137-39, 195-208).

the judgment of God is expressed in the violent act of crushing grapes in the Old Testament, in Revelation the judgment is found in drinking the wine formed by the crushed grapes. That is, the crushed grapes express the wrath of God not because they are crushed, but because they form "the wine of God's wrath, poured unmixed into the cup of his anger" (Rev 14:10; see also Rev 14:8-9; 16:6; 17:6). God's wrath is thus not toward the grapes but toward the unrepentant who are made to drink from the cup that holds the wine formed by the crushed grapes.

When we add to these considerations John's pervasive theme that believers overcome by their willingness to be martyred (Rev 2:10, 13; 7:14; 12:11; 13:10; 14:12), it strongly suggests that the blood that flows from the winepress of God's fury is not the blood of God's enemies, but the blood of his servants whom these enemies murdered.[68] Similarly in Revelation 6:10-11, the time for divine judgment is reached and the cry of the martyred saints is answered when "the number would be complete both of their fellow servants and of their brothers and sisters, who were soon to be killed as they themselves had been killed"—namely, when the grapes are ready to be harvested. And the judgment of the unrepentant takes place when they are made to drink the blood of their innocent victims—meaning, they must now ingest "the murderous consequences of [their] wicked life."[69]

Reflecting the dominant way of construing divine judgment throughout the biblical narrative, the wicked in Revelation are judged when God allows the consequences of their wickedness and violence to ricochet back on them (e.g., Rev 11:18; 13:10; 16:6; 18:6; 22:18-19).[70] Indeed,

---

[68]So argues Caird, *Revelation*, 188-95; Bredin, *Jesus*, 209-16; R. Schwager, *Must There Be Scapegoats? Violence and Redemption in the Bible*, trans. M. L. Assad (New York: Gracewing, 2000), 219.
[69]Bredin, *Jesus*, 210.
[70]Bredin makes a compelling case that Rev 19:17-18 echoes Is 49:26 and Ezek 39:17-19 in which the wicked consume themselves and each other. "The violent will consume the violent," he writes, "and there will be enough even for the birds in mid-heaven" (referring to Rev 19:17, 21; *Jesus*, 213, cf. 216). For other comments on the self-destructive nature of divine judgment in

John simultaneously uses the imagery of drinking blood as a symbol of the sin that is being judged (Rev 14:8; 17:6; 18:3) and as a symbol of the judgment of this sin (Rev 14:10; 16:6). In this way, he ingeniously expresses the truth that the seeds of God's just judgment are organically present in the sin that leads to this judgment. To judge sin, therefore, God need not ever act violently. He need only turn sinners over to the self-destructive consequences of their own decisions, just as he did with his Son when he stood in our place as a sinner (see Rom 4:25; 8:32; Mt 27:46).

Understood in this light, the winepress imagery of Revelation 19:15 provides yet another stunning example of how John turns violent imagery on its head by radically reinterpreting it through the lens of the self-sacrificial lamb. It constitutes yet another illustration of the remarkable way in which John makes "lavish use of militaristic *language*" while infusing it with "a non-militaristic *sense*."[71] It once again demonstrates how "apocalyptic terror is transformed through John's Christology," for we once again see that "Christ conquers by being a lamb, not by being a lion."[72] It provides yet one more confirmation that in Revelation, followers of the lamb are called to participate in the war and the victory of the lamb by choosing to love our enemies and to suffer at their hands rather than conform to their idolatrous ways or resort to using Babylon's sword against them.[73]

Revelation, see P. G. R. de Villiers, "Unmasking and Challenging Evil: Exegetical Perspectives on Violence in Revelation 18," in *Coping with Violence in the New Testament,* ed. P. G. R. de Villiers and J. W. van Henten (Boston: Brill, 2012), 201-25; Tonstad, *Saving God's Reputation,* 142; Johns, *Lamb Christology,* 90-91; Bauckham, *Theology,* 52; Morris, *Revelation,* 102; S. Travis, *Christ and the Judgment of God: The Limits of Divine Retribution in New Testament Thought* (Colorado Springs, CO: Hendrickson, 2008), 297-98; C. Rowland, *Revelation* (London: Epworth, 1993), 87; Gorman, *Reading Revelation,* 151-53. On the self-destructive nature of sin throughout Scripture, see Travis, *Christ*; J. Krasovec, *Reward, Punishment and Forgiveness: The Thinking and Beliefs of Ancient Israel in the Light of Greek and Modern Views* (Leiden: Brill, 1999); K. Koch, "Is There a Doctrine of Retribution in the Old Testament?" in *Theodicy in the Old Testament,* ed. L. Crenshaw (Philadelphia: Fortress, 1983), 57-87.

[71]Bauckham, *Climax,* 233.
[72]Johns, *Lamb Christology,* 190.
[73]Bauckham, *Climax,* 234

CONCLUSION

I will close by noting that, if the assessment of John's subversive use of traditional violent symbols that I've offered in this essay is correct, it means those who interpret this imagery literally, as though it conveyed a "pride fighter" view of Jesus, are ascribing to this imagery a meaning that is the exact opposite of what John intended. But this forces the question: How is it that multitudes of people throughout church history and today miss John's subversive strategy and thus end up finding this violent conception of Jesus in his work?

Steven Friesen observes that John's ingenious revision of traditional warfare imagery, with its stunning reassessment of power, "is so contrary to normal human practice that most churches throughout history have not agreed with John."[74] I am convinced Friesen's observation is correct, and I suspect it goes a long way toward answering our question. John's subtlety is such that, if one wants and expects Jesus to be a "pride fighter," they will likely miss his subversion of violent images and find a violent Jesus who conforms to their wants and expectations. But if one rather wants and expects Jesus to be a self-sacrificial lamb, they will likely notice John's subversive strategy and thus find the nonviolent, self-sacrificial Jesus who John intended to convey. I submit that John could assume his audience would catch his subversive strategy because the early church knew that the Jesus they followed was a nonviolent, self-sacrificial lamb, not a violent warrior (see, e.g., Mt 5:39-45; Lk 6:27-36; Rom 12:14-21). Unfortunately, when the church was transformed into "the church triumphant" in the fourth and fifth centuries, the Jesus Christians wanted and expected was transformed, and the

---

[74]S. Friesen, *Imperial Cults and the Apocalypse of John: Reading Revelation in the Ruins* (Oxford: Oxford University Pres, 2001), 216. Similarly, Neville notes that John's reinterpretation of violent imagery is "breathtaking but all too often ignored or overlooked" ("Faithful, True, and Violent?," 67).

nonviolent, self-sacrificial lamb and his army in Revelation was thus hidden to them.

Whether John intended it or not, it seems his ingeniously subversive work functions along the lines of the all-important sealed scroll of Revelation 5 that only the slain lamb was capable of opening. For as was true of the scroll, it seems that only one who trusts in, and is committed to, the power of self-sacrificial love over the power of Babylon's sword will be able to discern Revelation's otherwise sealed-up central message: namely, that God's true character is that of a sacrificial lamb, and his lamblike way of ruling the world and defeating evil will prove victorious in the end.

"THE GOD OF PEACE WILL SOON CRUSH SATAN UNDER YOUR FEET"

VIOLENCE IN THE GOSPEL OF PEACE?

Thomas R. Yoder Neufeld

The God of peace will soon crush Satan under your feet.

ROMANS 16:20 NIV

PEACE AND VIOLENCE in one exuberant phrase? Paul's startling words highlight a vexing issue, namely, the ubiquitous presence of violence or violent vocabulary in the Bible, sometimes in close proximity to peace. This has become increasingly troubling for many Christians. Usually it has been the Old Testament that has borne the brunt of criticism. Jesus and the New Testament are more typically associated with nonviolence. To illustrate, Ephesians 2 explicitly gives Jesus the name *peace* (Eph 2:14) and says he "proclaimed peace" (Eph 2:17). In the Sermon on the Mount Jesus famously demands that those who wish to be called sons and daughters of God love their enemies and thereby imitate the perfection of their "Father in heaven" (Mt 5:38-48).

Christians of all stripes, pacifist and nonpacifist alike, agree that Jesus and peace are inseparably linked in the New Testament and in Christian tradition, even if they disagree on whether that peace is primarily social or spiritual and on what implications it has for Christian behavior.

Recently, however, the New Testament has itself come under fire for being violent.[1] Several factors have raised the level of alarm over the presence of violence. One is the pervasiveness of violence within and between nations, races, classes, genders, and religions, at both macro and micro levels. Second, what counts as violence has expanded exponentially beyond deliberate physical harm to encompass attitudes and language that exclude and thus lead to marginalization, as well as religion's absolute truth claims and the threatened consequences of not believing them. Lastly, whether or not deed or word is deemed violent has come to take into account how someone experiences them, regardless of intent.

This has had a big impact on how the Bible, specifically the New Testament, is perceived in relation to violence. The scalpel of criticism slices deep to the very bone of the biblical witness, indeed, to the very core of the gospel of peace. In the following I can do little more than identify a few aspects central to the gospel of peace—nonretaliation, love of enemies, forgiveness, subordination, and atonement—and suggest how we might wrestle with the Scriptures in a way that allows the gospel of peace to be heard clearly.[2]

---

[1] For example, see Michel Desjardins, *Peace, Violence, and the New Testament* (Sheffield, UK: Sheffield Academic, 1997); J. Harold Ellens, ed., *The Destructive Power of Religion: Violence in Judaism, Christianity, and Islam*, 4 vols. (Westport, CT: Praeger, 2004); Grace Jantzen, *Violence to Eternity*, vol. 2 of *Death and the Displacement of Beauty*, ed. Jeremy Carrette and Morny Joy (London: Routledge, 2009); Shelley Matthews and E. Leigh Gibson, eds., *Violence in the New Testament* (New York: T&T Clark, 2005).

[2] For a thorough discussion and the relevant secondary literature on these contested themes, see Thomas R. Yoder Neufeld, *Killing Enmity: Violence and the New Testament* (Grand Rapids, MI: Baker Academic, 2012), copublished in the United Kingdom as *Jesus and the Subversion of Violence: Wrestling with the New Testament Evidence* (London: SPCK, 2012).

TURNING THE CHEEK AND LOVING THE ENEMY

Those who identify the core of the gospel of peace as the practice of nonviolence predictably gravitate toward the Sermon on the Mount (Mt 5–7).[3] Most immediately relevant is Jesus' demand that his followers not resist the evildoer, that they rather turn the cheek, hand over their last article of clothing, carry the pack forced on them a second mile, and give unquestioningly to those who ask money of them (Mt 5:38-42; see also Lk 6:27-36).

Nonresistant or pacifist Christians have taken Jesus' words unambiguously to demand nonviolence in the face of abuse, a deliberate and costly vulnerability that counts on the ultimate vindication of God, even if after death in the form of resurrection. But many more Christians consider such behavior dangerously passive, opening the door to further violence.

One response has been that this is less nonresistance than a kind of "defiant vulnerability,"[4] a form of creative resistance in which victims seize the moment, surprise their tormentors, and throw them off balance, thereby subverting the predictable script of violence and counterviolence. But what prevents this from becoming a form of shaming or even goading to further violence? What keeps it from turning trust in a vindicating God into a way of stoking the fires of hell for the tormentors?[5]

The evangelists appear to have anticipated exactly this. By framing the command to turn the cheek with the command to love enemies,

---

[3]See Yoder Neufeld, *Killing Enmity*, 16-35, as well as Thomas R. Yoder Neufeld, *Recovering Jesus: The Witness of the New Testament* (Grand Rapids, MI: Brazos, 2007), 211-18.

[4]Walter Wink, "Neither Passivity nor Violence: Jesus' Third Way (Matt. 5:38-42 par.)," in *The Love of Enemy and Nonretaliation in the New Testament*, ed. Willard Swartley (Louisville, KY: Westminster John Knox, 1992), 102-25; Walter Wink, *Engaging the Powers: Discernment and Resistance in a World of Domination* (Minneapolis: Fortress, 1992), 175-93.

[5]That is how "coals on their heads" in Rom 12:19-20 has sometimes been interpreted, perhaps most strikingly by Krister Stendahl: "Why walk around with a little shotgun when the atomic blast is imminent?" ("Hate, Nonretaliation, and Love: Coals of Fire," in *Meanings: The Bible as Document and as Guide* [Philadelphia: Fortress, 1984], 139).

Luke leaves no room for passive loathing (Lk 6:27, 35). Matthew makes love of enemies into a distinct command (Mt 5:43-48), highlighting it as the apex of Jesus' commands to his followers. He makes love of enemies nothing less than the imitation of God, the essence of being sons and daughters of God. Turning the cheek may be "cheeky" ingenuity in the face of violence, certainly. More profoundly, however, it is love on the lookout to subvert violence—for the sake of the enemy! It is thus the gospel of peace in action, participating in the scandalous and merciful perfection of an enemy-loving God (Mt 5:48; Lk 6:36). Such love may sometimes look like acquiescence or falling victim to violence, as it did in the case of Jesus. It is anything but that, however, if the cross really did and does "kill enmity" (see Eph 2:16).

RAGE AND FORGIVENESS

Nothing gets closer to the core of the gospel of peace than forgiveness, both as gift and practice. Apart from the Lord's Prayer (Mt 6:9-13; Lk 11:2-4), nowhere is that more evident than in Matthew 18.[6] Similar to the Sermon on the Mount, Matthew intends this collection of Jesus' teachings to serve as a unified discourse.[7] We might characterize it as *the gospel of peace for broken relationships within the community of faith*. This discourse places forgiveness into a communal context of unequal power, abuse of the vulnerable, persistent efforts at retrieval and restoration, and, finally, the threat of judgment. There is much in this chapter that both offends and challenges contemporary sensibilities with respect to violence.

Jesus opens his "sermon on life together" by responding to his disciples' question as to who is greatest in the kingdom of God (Mt 18:1-5).

---

[6]For secondary literature and discussion of Matthew 18, see Yoder Neufeld, *Killing Enmity*, 36-56.
[7]See Yoder Neufeld, *Recovering Jesus*, 64, 199-201; Robert H. Gundry, *Matthew: A Commentary on His Literary and Theological Art* (Grand Rapids, MI: Eerdmans, 1982), 358.

His response is an attack on status and privilege and thereby on their embedded violence. Summoning a child, Jesus asserts that God's imperial reign, unlike Rome's, belongs not to the "greats" but to those of "humble" status, the "little ones" (Mt 18:6). While *kingdom* is drawn from the thesaurus of domination, Jesus turns it on its head. He caps his bracing lesson by identifying himself with the slave boy (*paidion*) he has placed before his followers, in effect incarnating himself in the most vulnerable in society. He is Lord and master, yes, but he hides himself in the weakest and most marginal, those most exposed to being abused, demanding that his followers do the same (see also Mt 25:31-46).

The depth of his identification with the vulnerable comes to shocking expression in Jesus' white-hot rage at those who abuse these "little ones" (Mt 18:6-9). To paraphrase, "Better you rip out your eye or tear off your hand and go into the kingdom maimed than go to hell in one piece!" There is no escaping the violence of this rhetoric. But is its purpose violent or antiviolent?

Matthew now follows this with Jesus' parable of the shepherd who abandons the ninety-nine of his one hundred sheep in favor of rescuing the one that has gone astray (Mt 18:10-14). Is that one of the "little ones" who has been led astray? That would seem to be consistent with what has just preceded. Or might the lost sheep also be the abuser? This possibility emerges in what immediately follows: a procedure for confronting sin and restoring the sinner (Mt 18:15-20). This is sometimes referred to as the "Rule of Christ," where if the brother or sister sins,[8] then one is to go to him or her privately. If that does not lead to change in behavior, then one is to take another individual or two along. If that does result in a change of behavior, the sinner is to be brought before

---

[8]Some important manuscripts do not contain "against you." The NA[28] Greek New Testament, for example, places it in square brackets, indicating its lack of manuscript support.

the community.[9] When that too fails, he or she is to be treated as a Gentile and a tax collector.

This text is typically employed in many communities to deal with members who have committed grievous sins. If we view this procedure in light of the preceding parable, as Matthew's arrangement urges us to do, it invests the faith community with the shepherd's responsibility of seeking and retrieving the lost "sheep." This is what love of neighbor looks like when things go wrong within the faith family (see also Lev 19:17-18; Eph 4:25-27).[10] Even the final resort of treating the wrongdoer like a "Gentile and tax collector" turns out not to be final at all. As Jesus' way of relating to tax collectors shows, the sinner is now exposed to the shepherd's relentless search for the lost sheep.

However, perhaps because of how easy it is for any procedure to morph into legalism, this text has all too frequently aided and abetted communal intolerance and ostracism, even tyranny, and thus violence. More recently these verses have come under sharp criticism in relation to sexual abuse.[11] Sexualized violence thrives on secrecy. Step one—the one-on-one confrontation—is thus viewed with great wariness as both placing the victim in further danger and in leaving the perpetrator free to engage in further abuse.

---

[9] *Ekklēsia*, usually translated as "church," is better translated for Jesus' own time as "assembly" or "community," literally, those "called out." See *BADG*, 240; *TDNT* 3:501-13.

[10] See Thomas R. Yoder Neufeld, *Ephesians*, Believers Church Bible Commentary (Scottdale, PA: Herald Press, 2002), 209-13, 221-22.

[11] See, e.g., Lauree Hersch Meyer, "The Abuse of Power and Authority: A Believer's Church Perspective," *Brethren Life and Thought* 38 (Spring 1993): 86-88, 94n45. With no little irony, given his own lengthy disciplinary process for sexual abuse, John Howard Yoder offers trenchant observations on the Rule of Christ in "Binding and Loosing," in *The Royal Priesthood: Essays Ecclesiastical and Ecumenical* (Grand Rapids, MI: Eerdmans, 1994), 323-58, reprinted as "Practicing the Rule of Christ," in *Virtues and Practices in the Christian Tradition,* ed. Nancey Murphy, Brad J. Kallenberg, and Mark Thiessen Nation (Harrisburg, PA: Trinity Press International, 1997), 132-60, and in shorter form in "Binding and Loosing," in *Body Politics: Five Practices of the Christian Community before the Watching World* (Scottdale, PA: Herald Press, 1993), 1-13. The disciplinary efforts surrounding Yoder's own failings highlight both the relevance and potential shortcomings of this text in the context of sexual abuse. See the complete issue of the *Mennonite Quarterly Review* devoted to sexual abuse in the church (89, no. 1 [2015]).

Once again we face an enigma: does the Rule of Christ open the door to violence or does it empower a community to confront it? "Binding and loosing" is, after all, both a breathtaking investment of authority in a community and, as we know from history, vulnerable to opening the door to communal tyranny. Do we resolve the dilemma by removing this text from how we respond to abuse of the vulnerable? If we do not, should we make certain that any application of the Rule of Christ not expose victims to further violence? Or might it be that a certain measure of vulnerability is inherent in any process driven by both care for victims and a desire to restore perpetrators?

Recall, importantly, that Matthew wishes us to read the discourse of chapter 18 as one whole. We are thus never to read the Rule of Christ without first hearing Jesus critique power and abuse, in effect incarnating himself in the abused, as well as the parable of the lost sheep. And we should never read or interpret it without going on to hear Jesus' exchange with Peter regarding forgiveness. In short, Matthew wishes us to see in the Rule of Christ not a means of housecleaning and exclusion, least of all keeping things under wraps for the sake of the reputation of the community, but a way to go after lost sheep with both persistent and loving confrontation and inexhaustible forgiveness ("seventy times seven"). This is surely the gospel of peace in its most radical manifestation as lived out in community.

Unsettlingly, however, in order to give further heft to forgiveness and bring the discourse to a climactic conclusion, Matthew has the "sermon" end with the parable of the unforgiving slave (Mt 18:23-35). Briefly, a slave whose master has just forgiven him an insurmountable debt refuses to forgive a comparatively minuscule amount owed him by a fellow slave. The king or master is enraged that his own mercy is not imitated and has the slave handed over to the torturers. Jesus concludes the parable brusquely with, "So my heavenly Father will also do to every one of you, if you do not forgive your brother or sister from your heart" (Mt 18:35). The discourse thus concludes with a threat of overwhelming violence.

It is hard not to be jostled by the juxtaposition in this discourse of fierce criticism of power and privilege, stern threat of judgment, and radical identification with victims on the one hand and equally intense determination to rescue, restore, and forgive perpetrators on the other. But might not the gospel of peace emerge precisely in this intersection? There is acute sensitivity to sin, particularly to violence against the vulnerable. The threat of judgment is strident testimony to the gravity of such violation. But, we note, this sensitivity is engaged for the benefit not only of victims but of victimizers. Both individual and community are given divine authority to do what it takes to restore victims and victimizers to wholeness within the community, ranging from confrontation and discipline to measureless forgiveness. If loving enemies is the imitation of God (Mt 5:43-48), so are rage at abuse and baffling forgiveness. Rage at violation without the hunger for reconciliation too easily becomes violent itself. Just so, forgiveness apart from getting to the root of the violence, holding the violent to account, and demanding a change in behavior and attitude too easily becomes impunity parading as grace.

We have an example from recent history on how this text has instilled the gospel of peace into communal reflexes in the face of extreme violence. When twice a year the Amish celebrate the Lord's Supper, Matthew 18 is read and preached. Fittingly, their most common prayer is the Lord's Prayer, which includes the phrase, "Forgive us our debts, as we also have forgiven our debtors" (Mt 6:12; see also Lk 11:4).[12] This has

---

[12]Donald B. Kraybill, Steven M. Nolt, and David L. Weaver-Zercher, *Amish Grace: How Forgiveness Trascended Tragedy* (San Francisco: Jossey-Bass, 2007), 88-98. Such startling offers of forgiveness have been offered since by Allen and Jeanne Howe, whose son James Marcus Howe was murdered in December 2013 (Sandy Banks, "True Christmas Spirit, from a Slain Man's Grieving

forged a culture such that, when in 2006 a gunman entered their little school in Nickel Mines, Pennsylvania, massacring five of their children before taking his own life, the Amish community leaders immediately went to the widow of the murderer to assure her of their forgiveness and requested she not leave the community. The world looked on in bafflement. When asked why they did this, the Amish answered, "Jesus said we are to forgive if we expect to be forgiven." No deliberation; no consultation. The father of one of the children killed said, "That is how God puts his word into the world." Stories such as this need to accompany any assessment of our text's relationship with violence, just as do those of communities that have used the Rule of Christ and the demand to forgive as a way to protect powerful abusers of the vulnerable.

SUBORDINATION AND VIOLENCE

While Christians confess Jesus to be Lord—master, boss, God—they remember him as one who came as a servant and slave, penniless, vulnerable, and obedient to the will of his Father. As we just saw in Matthew 18, Jesus is incarnate in the "little ones," demanding that his followers take on precisely such a slavelike stance. He shocks his disciples with his slavelike behavior when he washes their feet (Jn 13:1-17). So also Paul leaves no doubt that to confess Jesus as "Lord" is to become a slave as he was (Phil 2:1-11). We are at the heart of what makes the gospel of peace radical in human relationships.

The New Testament teaching on subordination owes much to Jesus' radical upending of the status cart. Ironically, its social manifestation has also spawned a great deal of violence. Several particularly notorious

---

Parents," *Los Angeles Times*, December 23, 2013, latimes.com/local/la-me-banks-reality-tv-director-killing-20131224,0,3572408.column), and most recently by the survivors and families of those murdered during Bible study at the Emmanuel AME church in Charleston, South Carolina, on June 17, 2015 (Nikita Stewart and Richard Pérez-Peña, "In Charleston, Raw Emotion at Hearing for Suspect in Church Shooting," *New York Times*, June 19, 2015, www.nytimes.com/2015/06/20/us/charleston-shooting-dylann-storm-roof.html).

texts draw on this tradition of "voluntary slavery": Romans 13:1-7, which addresses subordination to authorities generally, and the household code, present in Ephesians 5:21–6:9, Colossians 3:18–4:1, and 1 Peter 2:13–3:7, which combines both the household and public spheres.[13]

Romans 13:1-7 is relevant particularly to Christian participation in or acquiescence to the violence of the state in demanding that everyone be subordinate to the authorities. The Greek *hypotassō*, "to order under," in the passive "to be subordinate," is typically translated as "to be obedient" or "to be subject." The "authorities" are usually identified as the state, even though the text does not quite make that explicit. They are "ordered" (placed in order) by God, which again is most frequently translated as "appointed" or "instituted." The text has thus historically served to assert that whatever authorities exist, they have been put there by God. Obedience to civil authorities is obedience to God. In much of Christian history this has been the basis by which rulers have laid claim to their "divine right" to demand unquestioning obedience of their Christian subjects, including, when ordered, to commit violence.

Understandably, most especially in light of the Holocaust and the killing of millions of Jews by millions of Christians in two world wars in the past century alone, Romans 13 has come under critical scrutiny. Is Paul an apologist for Rome, and thus for every ruler since, offering up the church as little more than a willing slave? Or, could Paul possibly have been the author of these seven verses, given the evident tension with what he says both before and after this passage about non-conformity and peaceableness (Rom 12:1-21; 13:8-14)? Alternatively, if these are Paul's words, did he pen them with a wink and a nudge, so to speak, understood by readers of his day even if not by countless others

---

[13] Yoder Neufeld, *Killing Enmity*, 97-121.

in the centuries that followed? After all, who in Paul's Roman audience would have had any illusions about authorities who within living memory put Jesus their Lord to death by imperial execution? Might Paul be mostly concerned with the paying of taxes (Rom 13:7; see also Mk 12:13-17) so as to keep believers out of trouble and focused on the church's primary mission, namely, to preach and live the gospel of peace? Or, perhaps the "authorities" are not the state at all but the synagogue rulers with whom believers in Jesus are in conflict. The interpretive community clearly and rightly squirms under the impact of the legacy of these seven verses.[14]

Nevertheless, historically the majority of Christians, and not only those in positions of authority, have taken these verses to demand obedience to the state,[15] allowing this text to trump any political dimensions of Jesus' call to love the enemy and Paul's own explicit summons in the immediately preceding verses to overcome evil with good (Rom 12:17-21) and in the immediately following verses to owe nothing other than love (Rom 13:8-14). Instead of taking up the cross, Christians have obediently put others on it. Thus, whatever good the text has done in setting a standard for responsible and accountable government, which too is surely part of its legacy and one from which the church and its mission have benefited, no text has had a greater role in justifying Christian participation in state-sanctioned violence.

---

[14]For discussion of the secondary literature, see Yoder Neufeld, *Killing Enmity*, 108-21; in addition to many excellent commentaries, see John E. Toews, *Romans,* Believers Church Bible Commentary (Scottdale, PA: Herald Press, 2004), 313-18, 321-26; Lee C. Camp, "What About Romans 13: 'Let Every Soul Be Subject'?," in *A Faith Not Worth Fighting For: Commonly Asked Questions About Christian Nonviolence*, ed. Tripp York and Justin Bronson Barringer (Eugene, OR: Cascade, 2012), 140-53.

[15]Most recently Oxford University moral theologian Nigel Biggar, *In Defence of War* (Oxford: Oxford University Press, 2014). On the five hundredth anniversary of the Reformation it is sobering to see how important Romans 13 was to the Reformers in their insistence on obedience to temporal authority. See, e.g., Martin Luther's 1523 treatise *Temporal Authority: To What Extent It Should Be Obeyed* and his fierce criticisms of the Peasants' Revolt of 1524-25, e.g., *Against the Robbing and Murdering Hordes of Peasants*.

In my view, while I am tempted to think otherwise, Paul did write these verses. However, the nuggetlike nature of our passage and the absence of any reference to Christ suggests that Paul was employing a Jewish wisdom tradition to bolster his main point, which is that believers in Rome *not* engage in violence (Rom 12:17-21). We dare not remove these seven verses from their frame or bracket. On one side Paul calls for nonconformity and a transformed mind (Rom 12:1-2), vigorous pursuit of strangers and enemies with love and blessing (Rom 12:13-14),[16] and not resorting to violence (Rom 12:17-21). On the other one side, Paul insists on the centrality of love (Rom 13:8), as well as on militant identification with Jesus (e.g., putting on "armor of light" paralleled with "put[ting] on the Lord Jesus Christ," Rom 13:12, 14). It seems clear that Paul never intended Romans 13:1-7 to be more than a supporting argument for leaving "wrath" in the hands of a just God to whom all rulers are in the end accountable (Rom 12:19-20).[17] Given Paul's deep commitment to follow Jesus' command to be a servant, thus to be "subordinate," this nugget of Jewish tradition allowed Paul to express the stance of voluntary servanthood in relation to the authorities. Subordination cannot then mean blind and unquestioning obedience. In Jesus' case subordination to the authorities put him on the cross; it did not implicate him in crucifixion. Nor should it for his followers. That said, Romans 13:1-7 will remain a stone of stumbling. Two millennia of Christians taking these seven verses out of their frame and doing what the state tells them to do are too deeply ingrained to be changed easily.

For many Christians the call to subordination is troubling much closer to home, quite literally. For centuries the so-called household

---

[16]The term usually translated as "hospitality" is literally translated as "love of strangers" (*philoxenia*); the term the NRSV translates as "extend" is the same verb translated in Rom 12:14 as "persecute" (*diōkō*).

[17]Compare Wisdom of Solomon 6:1-11.

code found in Ephesians, Colossians, and 1 Peter has been used to support slavery, the subjugation of women, and patriarchy.[18] While no one any longer has the gall to defend slavery, at least publicly, the subordination of women to men is still widely prevalent. For many the household code is thus a complete betrayal of Jesus' egalitarian vision and thus of the "gospel of peace."[19]

Without being able to argue the points in detail here,[20] let me propose at the outset that we see in this tradition a precariously risky and vulnerable effort to inject Jesus' vision of mutual servanthood into the "normal" contexts of culturally embedded structures of familial, economic, and political life. Ephesians makes that explicit by attaching the code grammatically to the imperative to be filled with the Spirit and the call to mutual subordination (Eph 5:21).[21] The template husbands are given for how they are to love their wives is a Jesus who cares and finally dies for the liberation of his beloved (Eph 5:25-33). Who would opt for patriarchy if the template for ruling over others is the Jesus of Ephesians 5:25-33, Philippians 2:6-11, John 13:1-20, or Matthew 18:1-5?

While acknowledging its implication in a history of violence, might we not better see the code as a summons, given to us in our moment in time and our particular cultural and sociological context, to render the domestic and economic context one in which the drama of liberation through mutual servanthood is lived out for all to see? If so, then to employ the

---

[18]Willard M. Swartley explores the use of the Bible to support slavery and patriarchy in *Slavery, Sabbath, War, and Women: Case Studies in Biblical Interpretation* (Scottdale, PA: Herald Press, 1983).

[19]One of the most influential treatments is Elizabeth Schüssler Fiorenza, *In Memory of Her: A Feminist Theological Reconstruction of Christian Origins* (New York: Crossroads, 1985), 251-84. Her critique has set the tone for much scholarship since.

[20]For fuller discussion of text and secondary literature, see Yoder Neufeld, *Killing Enmity*, 97-108, and *Ephesians*, 253-89, 347-50.

[21]This is critical, in my view, for the reading of the code in Ephesians. See Yoder Neufeld, *Ephesians*, 255.

code as a permanent foundation for the subjugation of women, children, and slaves is indeed the most profound betrayal of the gospel of peace.

ATONEMENT

It is surely the greatest of ironies that the very center of the gospel of peace—atonement—has become the focus of the most intense debate with respect to violence.[22] Is the cross an instance of measureless love—the death of hostility, as Ephesians 2 puts it—or is it the most egregious instance of "redemptive violence,"[23] even "divine child abuse"?[24]

Every one of the three main theories of atonement—Anselm's substitutionary atonement, Abelard's moral influence or subjective atonement, and the classic "Christus victor" theory—has been criticized for making violence a constitutive element of reconciliation with God.[25] The cross comes to stand for Jesus' sacrifice on our behalf in order to satisfy God's justice, or wrath. Or, as in the case of Abelard, it displays for all to see the depth of God's love for humanity, thereby linking love and violence. Or, finally, God liberates us from captivity to Satan, offering up Jesus as ransom and then tricking the devil by raising Jesus to life. In all of these "theories," death—and thus violence—plays a decisive role.

The debate has grown fierce, the discourse sometimes brutal. Where some wish to distance God from any implication in violence, to the point where Jesus' death is solely human response to how he lived and not a constituent element in what saves sinful humanity,[26] others see in

---

[22] For literature see Yoder Neufeld, *Killing Enmity*, 73-96.
[23] This criticism is associated in the contemporary context in particular with René Girard and Walter Wink. See the collected essays in Brad Jersak and Michael Hardin, eds., *Stricken by God? Nonviolent Identification and the Victory of Christ* (Grand Rapids, MI: Eerdmans, 2007).
[24] For example, Joanne Carlson Brown and Rebecca Parker, "For God So Loved the World?" in *Christianity, Patriarchy and Abuse: A Feminist Critique*, ed. Joanne Carlson Brown and Carol R. Bohn (New York: Pilgrim, 1989), 1-30.
[25] For example, J. Denny Weaver, *Nonviolent Atonement* (Grand Rapids, MI: Eerdmans, 2001); for a concise summary of his argument, see J. Denny Weaver, "The Nonviolent Atonement: Human Violence, Discipleship and God," in *Stricken by God*, 316-55.
[26] Most insistently Weaver, *Nonviolent Atonement*, 19-69, 210-23.

such a critique nothing less than an attack on the central conviction of the Christian faith—namely, that Christ gave his life for us who deserved the punishment of death.[27] The very meaning of gospel of peace is at stake in this debate.

Much of the turbulence surrounding atonement centers on assessing this or that theory with respect to violence. It is, in my view, critical not to read the New Testament through the lens of a particular theory of atonement, as much as each of the theories finds a foothold in the biblical text and sheds some light on that central event. No theory is by itself capable of capturing the mystery of God's enemy love. For one, the whole life and teaching of Jesus, as well as the resurrection and the birth of a community of reclaimed enemies (Eph 2:11-22), easily gets marginalized in theories of atonement in ways no biblical writer would have recognized. Jesus did not come to die, as much as his death constitutes the apex of God's peacemaking ingenuity. He came to live and preach peace, to bring peace in its fullness. That makes both the Sermon on the Mount on one side of the cross and Easter on the other essential to God's work of *at-one-ment*. Moreover, with respect to the cross, all writers of the New Testament recognize in the event of the cross both the violence of rebellious humanity and the scandalous surprise of God wresting from that violence the means of making peace. The cross is God's turning of the cheek, surprising recalcitrant humanity with grace and forgiveness in Jesus taking all the violence on himself. God pays the price of our rejection of the one who is peace. The cross is, as Paul says, the power of God to save (1 Cor 1:18). That is why in the Bible atonement is never theory but news—gospel, rooted not in theory or transaction but in the event of human rejection and God's shockingly gracious response.

---

[27]For insightful discussion, see Hans Boersma, *Violence, Hospitality, and the Cross: Reappropriating the Atonement Tradition* (Grand Rapids, MI: Baker Academic, 2004); Darrin W. Snyder Belousek, *Atonement, Justice, and Peace: The Message of the Cross and the Mission of the Church* (Grand Rapids, MI: Eerdmans, 2012).

Any theory that does not make crystal-clear that atonement, and with it Jesus' giving of his life, is first and last the ingenious love of God at work "while we were still weak," "sinners," "enemies" (Rom 5:6-11) falls far short of the gospel of peace.

WRESTLING WITH THE BIBLE

It is evident from even such a small sample that reading the Bible with respect to violence is not simple. In an ancient biblical story, Jacob wrestles with "a man" in the night at the river Jabbok (Gen 32). In the morning, having both extracted a blessing and limping badly, he names the place *Peniel*, which means the face of God. In reading the Bible with an eye to violence we too struggle with "the man," the profoundly human aspect of the Bible as it is and has been used. Like Jacob, we must not let go until we are blessed, even if it leaves us limping. And like Jacob, in the morning we will call it Word of God.

The raw material of the Bible—testimonies, memories, passionate urgings and warnings, laws, songs and poems of both anger and celebration—is Word becoming words, *our* words, on *our* parchment, pages, and smartphones. And *we* live in a world ravaged by abused power, domination of the weak, and exploitation of privilege, whether of race, gender, or economic standing. That is the world in which we hear the gospel of peace articulated. We should seldom expect to use such a Bible like a manual and disparage it if it does not easily lend itself to such use. Its very nature and quality asks us rather to follow the story, to listen for the news, not as cool, critical, or even cynical observers, but as faith-full participants, as readers who are nonresistant to the summons to turn the cheek, to love enemies, to take up our cross, not to be conformed to this age, and to overcome evil with good. That is nothing less than following Jesus, nothing less than the imitation of God and thus participation in the gospel of peace.

Biblical scholars have noticed this aspect of participation within the Bible itself, dubbing it "intertextuality."[28] Texts, images, and metaphors are reread, reappropriated, and recast in light of new experience, whether in light of Babylon, Jesus, or the enthusiastic embrace of the gospel by Gentiles. The way the gospel of peace is expressed in the Bible is characterized by this mix of the familiar and the novel. Old language, some of it marked by the violence of its origin, serves to express the surprise of how the God of peace crushes Satan: a master who washes feet like a slave, a king with neither wealth nor army who liberates by dying, a community of sons and daughters of God who parade their exalted status by being slaves to each other and servants to the world, a community of militants who love their enemies. Every one of these elements is marked by contexts and expressed in vocabulary imbued with a legacy of violence. But each becomes witness to the wondrous irony of the gospel of peace.

We listen, wrestle, and demand a blessing together with this great cloud of biblical witnesses and each other.[29] The gospel of peace has always drawn and continues to draw together those who were once strangers and enemies of each other. Vigorous dispute is an entirely predictable outcome of the gospel doing its job, of the Spirit making peace. Most especially in relation to violence, we should always have in the hermeneutical community those who have experienced the text as lifegiving and those who have been hurt by it or its use. That will make interpretation wrenching, the wrestling painful, with the outcome quite

---

[28]See, e.g., Richard B. Hays, *Echoes of Scripture in the Letters of Paul* (New Haven, CT: Yale University Press, 1989); see also Willard M. Swartley, *Israel's Scripture Traditions and the Synoptic Gospels: Story Shaping Story* (Peabody, MA: Hendrickson, 1994); Thomas R. Yoder Neufeld, *"Put on the Armour of God!" The Divine Warrior from Isaiah to Ephesians* (Sheffield, UK: Sheffield Academic Press), 1997.

[29]For an imposing and masterful example of such wrestling with both Scripture and the community of interpreters, see Gregory A. Boyd, *Crucifixion of the Warrior God: Interpreting the Old Testament's Violent Portraits of God in Light of the Cross*, 2 vols. (Minneapolis: Fortress, 2017).

possibly leaving us with a limp. But that is how we hear God speak the gospel of peace. Such listening will thus always be a courageous act of faith, an exercise in what Richard Hays has called a "hermeneutic of trust"[30]—trust not in ourselves, each other, our hermeneutical skills, or our tradition, but in the one who is the Word speaking from within the words.

---

[30]Richard B. Hays, "Salvation by Trust? Reading the Bible Faithfully," *Christian Century* 114, no. 7 (February 26, 1997): 218-23.

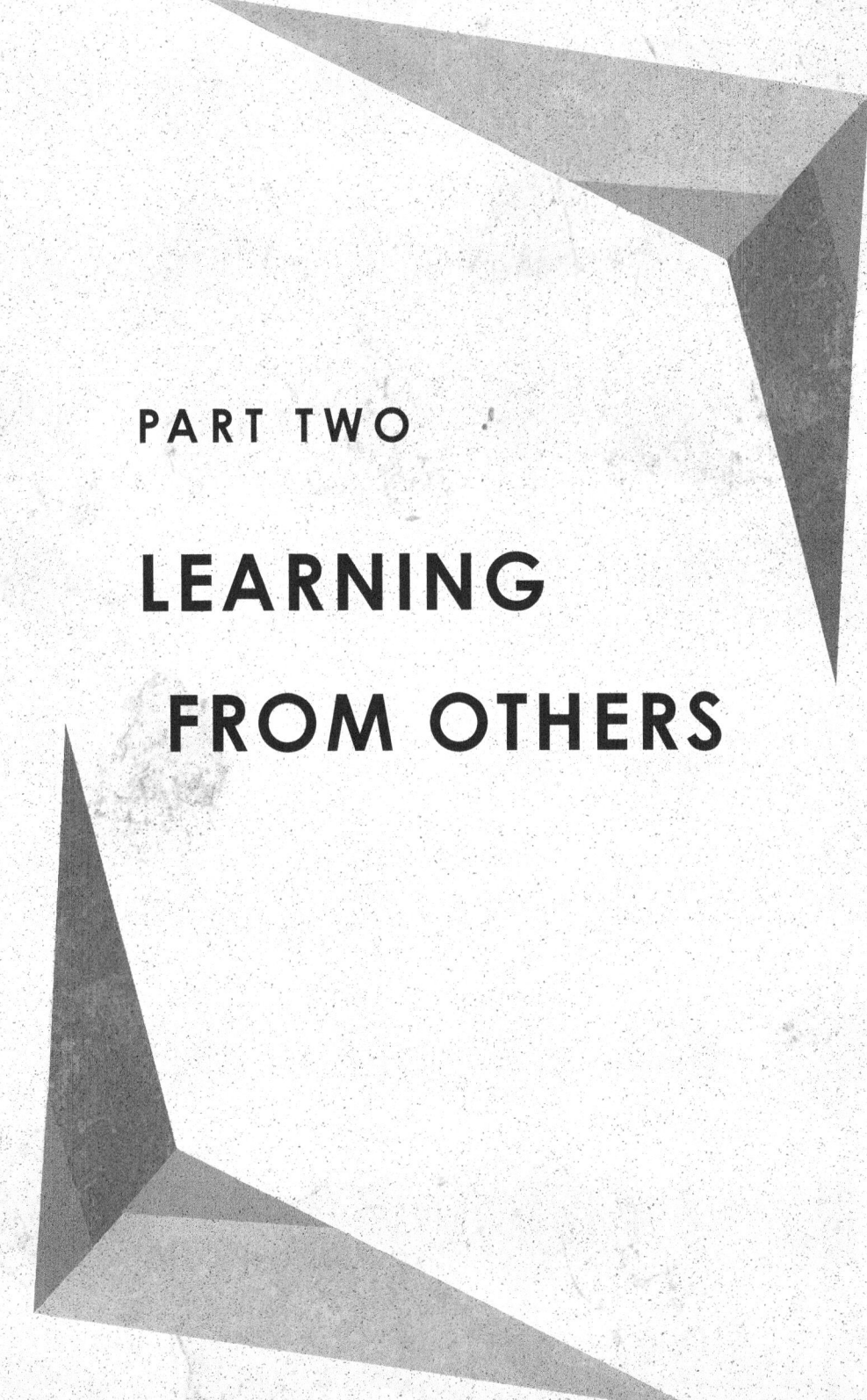

PART TWO

LEARNING FROM OTHERS

5

A PENTAGON FOR PEACE

WHAT AMERICA COULD LEARN FROM ITS OLDEST ENEMY

Randy S. Woodley

A RELATIVE OF MINE spent a number of years working in the nation's capital designing "war games." She (or he) sat for months, and eventually years, on end, devising strategies and counterstrategies for every "troops in battle" scenario imaginable. I don't have much else to say about the nature of that job except for the fact that it took many years for me to obtain that little bit of information. Of course, if I say too much here, he (or is it a she?) said they would have to kill me. I think the person was just kidding—or was he (or she)?

No doubt the US federal government keeps innumerable secrets concerning war strategies. In fact, I have no doubt the NSA could be reading this as I write. But can you imagine a whole top-level US government agency that didn't have to keep secrets? In fact, something like a "Pentagon for Peace" wouldn't need to protect secrets because it would *want* other nations, organizations, and agencies to become just as strategic as it is when it comes to peace efforts. Wouldn't it be great to be "outpeaced" by Iran, China, Syria, or Russia? When thinking of a Pentagon for Peace,

I can imagine the State Department and the Pentagon joining together with longtime civilian strategists who are experienced peacemakers to create an effective Department of Peace. I've been fantasizing about this idea, and even blogging about it, for years. And now, to my surprise, a Pentagon for Peace may actually become a reality!

Evidently I'm not the first person to conceive of such a thing. There are numerous groups who use the "Peace Pentagon" nomenclature or who are proposing to build a symbolic structure representing the Pentagon for Peace idea. After some research I discovered that a proposal for a type of Peace Pentagon has even been introduced in Congress on a number of occasions, including in 2005 when Congressman Dennis Kucinich (D-OH) introduced H.R. 3760 to create a Cabinet-level Department of Peace and Non-Violence. In 2013 Representative Barbara Lee (D-CA) introduced a similar bill, H.B. 808. According to Congresswoman Lee, "We invest hundreds of billions each year in the Pentagon, in war colleges, military academies, and our national defense universities all to develop war tactics and strategies. Now we need that kind of investment in peace and nonviolence here at home."[1]

Although the idea of a government agency for peacebuilding strategies has become official, regardless of how many times this type resolution is introduced to Congress, there remains a lack of support for it to pass. But we should be encouraged that momentum has begun. There is now even an organization called The Peace Alliance that lists the core of such a proposal. A Department of Peacebuilding, they say, which concerns itself both domestically and internationally, would work to

---

[1] Nathaniel Botwinick, "Democrats Propose Department of Peacebuilding," *National Review*, February 26, 2013, www.nationalreview.com/corner/341616/democrats-propose-department-peacebuilding-nathaniel-botwinick.

- Provide assistance to city, county, and state governments in coordinating existing programs
- Develop new programs based on best practices
- Teach violence prevention and mediation to US schoolchildren
- Treat and dismantle gang psychology
- Rehabilitate the prison population
- Build peacemaking efforts among conflicting cultures both here and abroad
- Support the military with complementary approaches to peacebuilding
- Create and administer a US Peace Academy, acting as a sister organization to the US Military Academy[2]

While it may seem stately for me to think I came up with the idea for a Peace Pentagon (like the time in the 1970s when I conceived of the "backpacker's guitar," only to find Martin Guitars beat me to it), I feel some kind of symbiotic ownership and pride to know that likeminded people have been active for a while in pushing for the idea. This is an idea whose time is long overdue. In fact, strategizing for peace on the North American continent has likely been happening for as long as North America has been inhabited.

ENEMY MYTHS

As a First Nations person I have always been impressed by the stories of our various tribal ancestors.[3] The stories that impress me most are not the war stories of popular books, television, and movies, which usually consist of bloodthirsty savages hiding behind a rock or a tree, waiting to

---

[2] "A Department of Peacebuilding Will Work To:," The Peace Alliance, copyright 2020, https://peacealliance.org/wp-content/uploads/2017/08/DoP-Will-...-full-text.pdf.

[3] I use terms such as First Nations, American Indian, Indigenous North American, Native American interchangeably.

wet their hatchets with the White man's blood and steal their women. No, there are better, truer stories among America's Aboriginal peoples than those Hollywood has told. But most of those stories have not been heard, and they certainly have not been popularized, because they would have had the opposite effect of what the propaganda intended. As we all have witnessed in recent history, the clarion call to war is laden with deception, expressed best in this proverb: *The first casualty of war is truth.*

Although the Europeans had a good deal of practice propagandizing war in the world they came from, they perfected the art on this continent when they used propaganda to justify mass land theft and attempted genocide against America's oldest enemy, the Native Americans. The Host People could easily have crushed the first fragile colonies in America if it had been their desire to do so. But that was not their normal practice. For instance, surrounding Jamestown, whose population at various points dwindled to mere handfuls of survivors, was the Powhatan Confederacy with an estimated population of thirteen thousand to thirty-four thousand people.[4] Those Hollywood and frontier novella images of the "red-skinned savages" lying in wait are nearly all patently false.[5] In fact, in most cases of Native American–Euro-American contact, the opposite was true.

On reading various accounts and monographs by explorers and anthropologists, what strikes one is the almost universal hospitality shown by Indian tribes, especially to their White visitors. It is remarkable, as described in David Bushnell's writings about explorers and missionaries among the Siouan, Algonquian, and Caddoan tribes west of the Mississippi, that there are practically no examples of inhospitality or harsh treatment of Whites. On the contrary, the tribal leaders went out of their

---

[4] Howard-Snyder, *Jesus and Pocahontas: Gospel Mission and National Myth* (Eugene, OR: Cascade, 2015), 8.
[5] The term "red-skin" has always been used to insult Native Americans. I use it in quotes to make that very point.

way to receive these visitors as special guests. There seems to have been a conviction among the Indians, at least until the middle of the nineteenth century, that they and the newcomers could share the land equally, even if the land was sometimes thought to be the tribe's sacred inheritance.[6]

President John F. Kennedy understood, at least tacitly, something of America's first great coverup when he wrote, "For a subject worked and reworked so often in novels, motion pictures and television, American Indians remain probably the least understood and most misunderstood Americans of us all."[7] Those debauched images of the bloodthirsty "red-skinned" savages were meant to create a myth for the purposes of a war that would justify wholesale land theft and the destruction of an entire race of people. Other myths surrounding these unfortunate circumstances surfaced as well, and because the indigenous people of America were dying at astonishing rates, there entered the myth of the "noble savage." Noble? I suppose that's a title the mythologizers add to your epitaph at your demise, a consolation prize in American enemy mythology. Among the manifold subaltern other, who have been mythologized by America into categories of savages, primitives, and terrorists, there remain many truths still covered by lies and mythologies. Of all those enemies of the state who became somehow less than human, American Indians have been stigmatized the longest. Says Seneca scholar John Mohawk,

> For the most part, contemporary historians have proceeded from the presumption that modern people are different from and superior to those who came before—especially those designated as "primitives." Distortions and incomplete and even dishonest renderings of the past are found

---

[6]Carl Starkloff, *The People of the Center: American Indian Religion and Christianity* (New York: Seabury, 1974), 88.

[7]John F. Kennedy, "Introduction," in Anne Terry White, *The American Indian* (New York: Random House, 1961).

in many modern accounts of ancient peoples and contemporary "primitive" peoples; these accounts serve to reinforce the sense of difference and to distance moderns from unflattering legacies of the past.[8]

In order for the European invaders to justify their permanent placement on stolen land, and especially for them to appear righteous in doing so, the myths about America's First Nations had to be thorough, pervasive, and sustainable enough to be passed down for generations. Often these myths were fraught with irony, using the political strategy of blaming one's enemy for the exact thing one is doing wrong. Take, for example, the phrase "dirty savages," which became mythologized in Western books and movies to describe American Indians. (Even in more contemporary movies you still see Indians looking tattered, with soot on their faces.) The facts bear out the reality that the Original People of this hemisphere led a life that was in many ways much cleaner and healthier than that of European peoples. The early Europeans, almost up until the twentieth century, recoiled from taking baths. Most First Nations people bathed daily. I have a feeling that if we could smell our way back through history, we would have a different idea of who the "sooty-faced savage" would be and who we would consider primitive.

I am a professor of history and theology, and when I teach about America before Columbus, it never fails that someone asks the question, "Why didn't I learn these things in college or high school?" Because we usually study this subject during the first class session of the course, I keep my answer short: "You were not supposed to learn about these things; they have been kept from you for a reason." Few of us were taught that prior to 1492, pre-invasion America was a densely populated continent filled with great civilizations such as those of Poverty Point,

---

[8]John C. Mohawk, *Utopian Legacies: A History of Conquest and Oppression in the Western World* (Santa Fe: Clear Light, 2000), 260.

Chaco Canyon,[9] Cahokia,[10] Hohokum,[11] and others. For example, in its time, the Poverty Point site in Louisiana, a great series of hand-built earthen mounds, featured the largest and most elaborate earthworks anywhere in the Western Hemisphere. No other known earthen construction approached the size of the Poverty Point site until the nineteenth century. Poverty Point is recognized today by the United Nations as one of three World Heritage sites in the continental United States, but who would know that unless they researched it? What type of mythologizing does it take to combat such extraordinary evidence? The following nineteenth-century reaction to a Canadian mound structure typifies the European settler mythology of the time:

> Whoever built the mounds had a faculty not possessed by modern Indians. . . . These require skill and adaptation un-possessed by the Indians. . . . Not only then by the ethnological, and other data cited do we conclude that the mound builders belong to a different race from the present Indians . . . they were preceded by a civilized race, well acquainted with the arts and science, knowing more art and astronomy in particular than they.[12]

What race could he be describing? Perhaps the mound builders were—I don't know, aliens? For a supposedly primitive people,

---

[9]Between AD 900 and 1150, Chaco Canyon was a major center of culture for the ancient Pueblo peoples. By AD 1115, at least seventy-five outlying cities had been built within the thirty thousand square miles consisting of agricultural communities, trading posts, and ceremonial sites in the San Juan Basin. They were connected to the central canyon and to one another by six major Chacoan roads. These thoroughfares extended to at least another sixty roads, well researched and surveyed, in generally straight routes, lit up at night with signal fires. Chaco also served as an astrological observatory.

[10]Cahokia was one of the largest urban centers in the world in its day (apex circa AD 1200). The city of Cahokia was surpassed in size in America only in 1800 by Philadelphia, long after it had declined. Cahokia featured a Stonehenge-type wooden "Woodhenge."

[11]Living in the Sonoran Desert since circa 2000 BCE, the Hohokam engineered in the seventh through fourteenth centuries a complex series of precise canals, weirs, and irrigation grids with genius, rivaling the sophistication of those used in the ancient Near East, Egypt, and China. Casa Grande, a notable structure, also served as an astrological observatory. The city of Phoenix uses many of these same canals to supply its own water today.

[12]George Bryce, *The Mound Builders* (Winnipeg, MB: Manitoba Free Press, 1885).

America's Indigene understood very well the plethora of relationships of the creation surrounding them to all other aspects of life, including the seasons, the stars, and medicines. For example, medicine formulations often came to indigenous peoples in their dreams. Native Americans utilized thousands of medicines and drugs, many of which are the basis of today's modern medicines. Much of Native American medicinal knowledge and practice has been lost due to the destruction of the cultures by settler colonialism, but even today, hundreds of medicines and herbal remedies are used in modern medicine that were initially developed by the First Peoples of America. Some of these include aspirin, quinine, petroleum jelly, ipecac, and digitalis.[13]

Other popular American myths the indigenous peoples of America have suffered include myths of underpopulation. I recall in fourth grade learning that the American Indian population at the time of Columbus was estimated to be between one and two million. Underreporting may have been used to corroborate low death tolls during the first centuries of contact. In actuality, in 1491 the indigenous North American population was considerably larger, with a high estimate of 160 million people; as much as 95 percent of the Indian population died shortly after contact with various European diseases, particularly smallpox.[14]

That would have amounted to about one-fifth of the world's total population at the time, a level of destruction unequaled before or since. These plagues wreaked havoc on traditional Indian societies. The "savages" the colonists saw, without realizing it, were usually the traumatized, destitute

---

[13]See Emory Dean Keoke and Kay Marie Porterfield, *Encyclopedia of American Indian Contributions to the World: 15,000 Years of Inventions and Innovations* (New York: Checkmark, 2003), and Jack Weatherford, *Indian Givers: How the Indians of the Americas Transformed the World* (New York: Crown, 1988).

[14]See Charles C. Mann, *1491: New Revelations of the Americas Before Columbus* (New York: Alfred A. Knopf, 2005), 147.

survivors of ancient and intricate civilizations that had collapsed almost overnight. In the end, the loss to us all was incalculable.[15]

America's Host People died in large numbers not just because of disease but because of deliberate genocidal treatment as well. Although the following estimate given by De Las Casas could be too high, his remarks help us understand the shock experienced by witnesses to such a population loss—one so great the number seemed unfathomable:

> As for the vast mainland, which is ten times larger than all Spain . . . we are sure that our Spaniards, with their cruel and abominable acts, have devastated the land and exterminated the rational people who fully inhabited it. We can estimate very surely and truthfully that in the forty years that have passed, with the infernal actions of the Christians, there have been unjustly slain more than twelve million men, women, and children. In truth, I believe without trying to deceive myself that the number of the slain is more like fifteen million.[16]

One of the reasons indigenous people continue to suffer from the myth of primitivism is that it is necessary to secure the Euro-American position of White superiority. The myth of White supremacy, though seldom acknowledged among Whites, is acute, particularly among missional Christians who learned to subjugate the role of Native Americans (at least in their own minds) to a people always in need of their rescue.[17] In order to be "good injuns,"[18] the First Nations of

---

[15]Mann, *1491*, 140.

[16]Bartolome De Las Casas, quoted in Denis Gainty and Walter D. Ward, *To 1600*, vol. 1 of *Sources of World Societies* (Bedford, MA: St. Martin's , 2011), 352. For a discussion of early population estimates, see Russel Thorton, "American Indian Population 1492," in *American Indian Holocaust and Survival: A Population History Since 1492* (Norman: University of Oklahoma Press, 1990), chap. 2.

[17]Refer to Hollywood films such as *Dances With Wolves*, *Last of the Mohicans*, and *Grey Owl*.

[18]"Good injun" is a phrase often used in Hollywood movies to depict the (sellout) Indian who sides with the White man and often says, in broken English, "me good injun." General Sheridan's response to a similar phrase used by one of his scouts was reported to be something like, "I always considered a good Indian to be a dead one."

America had to be poor, listless, uneducated, unruly, dirty, dying (or nobly vanishing), and in need of saving.

RECYCLED LIES

Many of the myths surrounding America's Aboriginal peoples have been used effectively from the earliest days of occupation until now. Often these old myths continue and are tested on all the new enemies the US encounters. These lies have been carefully devised, developed, calculated, implemented, and perfected over many years of practice on Native Americans, and they seem to work in other contexts as well. One of the many deceptions Thomas Jefferson used involved a strategy of indebtedness in order to create a needy people who would eventually assimilate and give up their lands. Jefferson wrote,

> To promote this disposition to exchange lands, which they have to spare and we want, for necessaries, which we have to spare and they want, we shall push our trading uses, and be glad to see the good and influential individuals among them run in debt, because we observe that when these debts get beyond what the individuals can pay, they become willing to lop them off by a cession of lands. . . . In this way our settlements will gradually circumscribe and approach the Indians, and they will in time either incorporate with us as citizens of the United States, or remove beyond the Mississippi. . . . Should any tribe be foolhardy enough to take up the hatchet at any time, the seizing the whole country of that tribe, and driving them across the Mississippi, as the only condition of peace, would be an example to others, and a furtherance of our final consolidation.[19]

Elsewhere Jefferson attempts to justify the near genocide of Native Americans: "This unfortunate race, whom we had been taking so much pains to save and to civilize, have by their unexpected desertion and

---

[19]Letter from Thomas Jefferson to William Henry Harrison, Indiana Historical Society, February 27, 1803, images.indianahistory.org/cdm/ref/collection/dc007/id/76.

ferocious barbarities justified extermination and now await our decision on their fate."[20] The practice of dehumanizing a potential enemy before going to war with them is used in almost every US military propaganda campaign.

Once a potential enemy is made to be just a fraction less human than us, it opens the door for all kinds of atrocities, including racism, sexism, and even genocide. Here President Monroe combines paternalistic concerns with claims of terrorism:

> The hunter or savage state requires a greater extent of territory to sustain it, than is compatible with the progress and just claims of civilized life, and must yield to it. Nothing is more certain, than, if the Indian tribes do not abandon that state, and become civilized, that they will decline, and become extinct. The hunter state, tho maintain'd by warlike spirits, presents but a feeble resistance to the more dense, compact, and powerful population of civilized man.[21]

Secretary of State Henry Clay probably reflects more accurately the popular sentiment of the government during the Jacksonian era of expansionism:

> There was never a full-blooded Indian that ever took to civilization. It is not in their nature. They are a race destined for extinction and I do not think that they are worth preserving. They are inferior to the Anglo-Saxon race which is now quickly replacing them on this continent. They are not an improvable breed, and their disappearance from the human family will be no great loss to the world. In point of fact, they are rapidly disappearing and if government should take proper action, in fifty years from this time there will not be any of them left.[22]

---

[20] Letter from Thomas Jefferson to David Bailie Warden, National Archives Founders Online, December 29, 1813, founders.archives.gov/documents/Jefferson/03-07-02-0046.
[21] Letter from James Monroe to Andrew Jackson, Library of Congress, October 5, 1817, www.loc.gov/resource/maj.01045_0360_0366/?st=text.
[22] Henry Clay, frontispiece, in William G. McLoughlin, *Champions of the Cherokees: Evan and John B. Jones* (Princeton, NJ: Princeton University Press, 1990).

President Jackson himself, known for his plain speech, captures the mood of the day, or at least the mood the US government was trying to promote when he said of America's First Nations:

> They have neither the intelligence, the industry, the moral habits, nor the desire of improvement which are essential to any favorable change in their condition. Established in the midst of another and a superior race, and without appreciating the causes of their inferiority or seeking to control them, they must necessarily yield to the force of circumstances and ere long disappear.[23]

Fortunately, it wasn't always the case in history that antagonistic voices were the loudest. In every era there have been people who put forward a voice of reason. Not all missionaries considered the Indians to be "devil worshipers" and "dumb as garden poles," which were two common phrases used for several centuries, but some missionaries were even leaders for indigenous rights.[24] Voices of reason could even be heard coming from the United States government, as in the case of Ben Franklin, who famously made this observation: "Savages we call them, because their manners differ from ours, which we think the perfection of civility; they think the same of theirs."[25] Says Franklin scholar Bruce Johansen,

> Franklin's writings on American Indians were remarkably free of ethnocentrism, although he often used words such as "savages," which carry

---

[23] Andrew Jackson, "Fifth Annual Message," The American Presidency Project, December 3, 1833, www.presidency.ucsb.edu/documents/fifth-annual-message-2.
[24] McLoughlin, *Champions of the Cherokees*.
[25] Benjamin Franklin, "Remarks Concerning the Savages of North America, [Before 7 January 1784]," National Archives Founders Online, 1784, founders.archives.gov/documents/Franklin/01-41-02-0280. "Franklin used the massacres to illustrate his point that no race had a monopoly on virtue, likening the Paxton vigilantes to 'Christian White Savages.'" "Franklin cried out to a just God to punish those who carried the Bible in one hand and the hatchet in the other: 'O ye unhappy Perpetrators of this Horrid Wickedness!'" "Franklin praised the Indian way of life, their customs of hospitality, their councils, which reached agreement by discussion and consensus, and noted that many white men had voluntarily given up the purported advantages of civilization to live among them, but that the opposite was rare" ("Noble Savage," Wikipedia, last updated October 18, 2021, en.wikipedia.org/wiki/Noble_savage).

more prejudicial connotations in the twentieth century than in his time. Franklin's cultural relativism was perhaps one of the purest expressions of Enlightenment assumptions that stressed racial equality and the universality of moral sense among peoples. Systematic racism was not called into service until a rapidly expanding frontier demanded that enemies be dehumanized during the rapid, historically inevitable westward movement of the nineteenth century.[26]

UNVEILING THE TRUTH

Having spent most of my life uncovering the myths surrounding the relationship of Native Americans to the United States, I have discovered that my own Keetoowah people, on a continent filled with other indigenous peoples who were by no means perfect societies, largely found ways to coexist with neighboring tribes. They were people who, like the great civilizations we learn about on other continents, thrived in America with unparalleled techniques in such areas as microagriculture and macroenvironmental management (including ecology, xeriscape landscape, agronomy, botany, forestry, raised beds, and naturally fertilized gardens), sustainable architecture (including passive solar heating, and water capture systems), the humanities (including psychology, philosophy, religion, rhetoric, languages, the arts, and ethics), and the sciences (including math, medicines, surgery [even brain surgery], dentistry, leeching poisonous foods to make them edible, and healthy waste disposal), in addition to urban planning, democratic government, educational systems, intercontinental economic trade, and the area I wish to focus on here, complex peacemaking strategies.[27]

---

[26]Bruce E. Johansen, *Forgotten Founders: Benjamin Franklin, the Iroquois, and the Rationale for the American Revolution* (Ipswich, MA: Gambit, 1982), www.ratical.org/many_worlds/6Nations/FFchp5.html.

[27]See Keoke and Porterfield, *Encyclopedia*; Weatherford, *Indian Givers*; Mann, *1491*.

I have over the years encountered thousands of Native American discoveries. These facts were somehow "missed" in my earlier education. Yet the stories about which I have been most impressed, especially in the past three decades, have been the ones that express amazing peacebuilding strategies among the indigenous peoples of what we often call Turtle Island or North America.

Why were the indigenous peoples of America so friendly? A primary reason for the customary practice of hospitality, including the desire for peace among Native Americans, was a widespread harmony-based worldview that is very much akin to biblical shalom.[28] This harmony way worldview also encompassed practical economic realities, to be sure. It has always been true economically that trade works better among friends than enemies. But in contrast to European countries, even when war was practiced in ancient America, it was invariably not about conquest, greed, or religion. For example, there is no record of there ever being a war among America's Indigene directed toward religious conversion. Most often Native American wars were a result of the need for obtaining more hunting lands during droughts or very lean years. The wars were never about "kill numbers" but more often used as a way for warriors to show their bravery. In many American Indian cultures, coming close to the enemy without killing him was considered the epitome of bravery.[29]

Why were there such different ideas of war and peacemaking on Turtle Island than in Europe during the same time period? Again, an

---

[28] For a comprehensive understanding of the harmony way worldview among Native Americans and how it compares to biblical shalom, see Randy S. Woodley, *Shalom and the Community of Creation: An Indigenous Vision* (Grand Rapids, MI: Eerdmans, 2012).

[29] For example, in March 1866 the Crow and Eastern Shoshone fought a four-day battle for a place now called Crow Heart Butte. Shoshone elders tell me that in spite of both armies having expert riders and marksmen, very few people in total were killed. The point being, war was often used to gain valor by brave deeds. To kill your opponent was easy. To come close to the enemy and touch him with a short stick, known as a "coup stick," was considered the height of courage.

indigenous worldview of harmony is different from a Western worldview, producing different values.[30] There are many differences we could examine, but here I will simply list a few to aid our understanding of the circumstances that produced the mythological propaganda used against America's First Nations:

- Physicality: When the first European newcomers arrived on the East Coast, the average sixteenth-century Native American was six inches taller than the Europeans whom they first encountered.
- Technology: The Indians knew not only how to survive but to thrive in what seemed like a hostile environment to European settlers.
- Religion: Native American religion was holistic, encompassing all of life, and not compartmentalized. Indigenous beliefs were congruous, not having a "secular" arena that allowed them to act out of character from their religion or spirituality. By this time the European worldview included both secular and spiritual components, which allowed them to act differently, depending on the arena. Indigenous people saw everything as spiritual.
- Land ownership: Often the only thing standing between the European settlers and their opportunity for prosperity (especially when one considers the options for land gain in Europe) was the Indians.
- Resource depletion: In much of Europe, especially England, the hardwood forests had been overharvested, land had been overused and exhausted, streams, rivers, and even ocean bays were being fished out and polluted. America offered a fresh supply of each of these vital resources.

---

[30] I realize there is a valid argument to be made for multiple Western worldviews. I am arguing not so much for subtleties among Western worldviews but the major differences between those and an indigenous worldview. For more, see Woodley, *Shalom,* 105-10, and Randy S. Woodley, "Where Pre-colonial and Postcolonial Thought Touch Jesus," *Geez,* Fall 2015, 14-15.

- Kindness: The hospitality and simplicity of the Indians were considered weaknesses by the Europeans, making the indigenous people seem savage and fearsome but also childlike and vulnerable, all of which were used commonly to typify Native Americans in popular literature.
- Tolerance: Native Americans hold a high level of tolerance in religious concepts and rarely argue about the Creator or matters of one's heart, as opposed to the Europeans' intolerance of other religions. In some tribes it is actually taboo to argue about another person's views of the Creator.

These difference in worldview produced marked differences in values on the part of the Europeans who came to Turtle Island and those of the people who were already present. A Western worldview, particularly the developed American expression of the Western worldview, results in a physical and moral dualism as contrasted with indigenous holism. It is ethereally spiritual as compared with a more tangible spirituality among the indigenous. Other Western values were built on individualism and hierarchical thinking, while many indigenous people held communal and egalitarian values. Western thinking was extrinsically categorical, not relationally categorized. Essentially, the Western European worldview was constructed on imperial standards of civilization using false binaries and a conquering mentality. The Western worldview is fundamentally competitive, not cooperative.

Both worldviews contain positive and negative characteristics and values. I do believe I am comparing apples to apples, and I think any honest rendering of American history will bear the fruit of my claims of an American tendency toward hierarchy and dualism. One of the consequences of a hierarchical, fundamentally competitive worldview is war. In an earlier writing I listed the long march of war in which

Europeans, and later Americans, have participated since they first arrived.[31] Since the time of that writing people have pointed out the many wars and conflicts I missed—so know that the list is even greater than I supposed.

Americans have been at war since they first entered the continent as European settlers. In fact, they say the Indians in those early days thought it strange that the Europeans, who were at war with one another in Europe, came all the way across the ocean to build forts just to fight against each other on this continent.

In the first decades of the twenty-first century Americans have been engaged in three wars, including the invasion of Afghanistan in 2001, the invasion of Iraq in 2003, and the Libyan conflict in 2011. In the 1990s Americans fought in Bosnia and Herzegovina and in the Persian Gulf War. The 1980s saw the American invasion of Grenada and Panama. In the 1960s and 1970s there was the Bay of Pigs invasion and, of course, Vietnam. In the 1950s Americans fought in Korea. The decades of the 1930s and 1940s saw us involved in World War II. In the 1920s (and most of the 1930s) America actually enjoyed an absence of conflict. But remember, just prior to this calm (maybe not so calm when we consider the domestic war on organized crime) was the storm of the First World War, from 1914 to 1918.

Looking back further at America's involvement in war in the nineteenth century, the 1890s saw the Spanish American War. The 1860s saw the Civil War. In the 1840s the Mexican-American War took place. The War of Texas Independence was fought in the 1830s. The War Against the Creek Indians, the Barbary War, and the War of 1812 were fought in the second decade of the nineteenth century; involvement in the Barbary War actually began in the earliest years of the century.

---

[31]Woodley, *Shalom and the Community of Creation*, 133-34.

The Franco-American Naval War was fought from 1798 to 1800. The American Revolution occurred in the 1770s and 1780s. The 1750s and 1760s witnessed the Cherokee War as well as the French and Indian War.[32] In the 1740s American colonists were involved in King George's War. Queen Anne's War took place from 1702 to 1713. King William's War spanned the decade of the 1680s and 1690s, and New England's reach for land saw war in the 1670s against the Wampanoag, Narragansett, and Nipmuck Indians as King Phillip's War.[33]

The United States of America is far from being a peace-loving or peacekeeping nation. Neither political party will consider serious cuts to the military, which by some estimations (although arguably so) is the largest single expenditure in the federal budget.[34] Americans are always in conflict because we are satisfied with our myths that have created a false sense of harmony when we prevail over others.[35] We cry "shalom, shalom when there is no shalom" (see Jer 6:14). The myth of American exceptionalism makes our citizenry feel justified in its righteousness. By some stretch of the American myth and imagination, we seem to think God is always on our side.

PEACEMAKING

The writer of Ephesians, speaking of Jesus, says, "For he is our [shalom]; in his flesh he has made both groups into one and has broken down the dividing wall, that is, the hostility between us" (Eph 2:14). My understanding is that Jesus actively becomes shalom, not just between

---

[32]In fact, there were periodic clashes with the Indians from first contact until the 1890s.
[33]See Woodley, *Shalom*, 133-5.
[34]Past and current military spending may take up 48 percent of the federal budget. See "Pie Chart Flyers—Where Your Income Tax Money Really Goes," War Resisters League, www.warresisters.org/pages/piechart.htm, accessed October 26, 2021.
[35]See Woodley, *Shalom*, and "America Has Been At War 93% of the Time—222 Out of 239 Years—Since 1776," Washington's Blog, February 23, 2021, washingtonsblog.com/america-has-been-at-war-93-of-the-time-222-out-of-239-years-since-1776.

Christians and Jews, but between all humanity and God. Those of us committed to transforming societal structures cannot ignore our nation's history on a land where God envisions shalom. The very fabric of Jesus' life and work demands our involvement in every area of life as shalom peacemakers.

Making peace is costly and requires a reorientation of thought and worldview. Because the "imagined Indian" is now indelibly part of the American mindset, it is necessary for me to quote a few examples that display the peacemaking principles of a harmony ethic. Even among those tribes that gained a reputation as warlike in the American experience, there existed striking counterbalances to war in their structure and philosophy. One such example is that of the Cheyenne peace chiefs.

According to the teachings of Sweet Medicine, the most revered Cheyenne teacher and prophet, all forty-four chiefs among them have to be peace chiefs, who are responsible for keeping the peace and reminding the people of their own harmony ways, including finding alternatives to war. I have known several Cheyenne peace chiefs in my life. These were men devoted to high moral standards, extreme forms of generosity, and the perpetuation of nonviolence. Even today Sweet Medicine's words are repeated at the inauguration of every new chief:

> Listen to me carefully ... and truthfully follow up my instructions. You chiefs are peacemakers. Though your son might be killed in front of your tepee, you should take a pipe and smoke. Then you should be called an honest chief. . . . If strangers come, you are the ones to give presents to them and invitations. When you meet someone, he comes to your teepee, asking for anything, give it to him. Never refuse.[36]

---

[36]Stan Hoig, *The Peace Chiefs of the Cheyenne* (Norman: University of Oklahoma Press, 1980), 7. In many Native American cultures tobacco is understood as a sacred plant that represents prayers. When smoked in the pipe, tobacco becomes a sacred medium, bringing together those around the circle in a covenant understanding together. It has often been referred to in history by the dominant American culture as a "peace pipe," because Native Americans insisted on sharing this act during the signing of treaties, usually under the semblance of peace. Generally,

He continues, "If you see your mother, wife, or children being molested or harmed by anyone, you do not go and seek revenge. Take your pipe. Go, sit and smoke and do nothing, for you are now a Cheyenne chief."[37] Among the Iroquoian peoples in upstate New York and Ontario is the story of a peacemaker who united the tribes during terrible times of tumultuous war. The peacemaker instituted a condolence ceremony that is still used to resolve grief and conflict today. The Six Nations still live according to the law and teachings of the peacemaker. Tadodaho Chief Leon Shenandoah comments,

> The teachings are very good. The most important thing is that each individual must treat all others, all the people who walk on Mother Earth, including every nationality, with kindness. That covers a lot of ground. It doesn't apply only to my people. I must treat everyone I meet the same. When people turn their thoughts to the Creator, they give the Creator power to enter their minds and bring good thoughts. The most difficult part of this is that the Creator desired that there be no bloodshed among human beings and that there be peace, good relations, and always a good mind.[38]

Native American understandings of balance and harmony can be helpful to Americans in the pursuit of peace. Our role on earth as people who restore harmony is very practical. Our ceremonies often require not only symbolic acts, but also practical restitution and full restoration. For example, the ancient Cherokee cementation ceremony occurred annually in the fall. At that time anyone with a grievance against another

---

North American indigenous people understand this act to mean an agreement concerning the process being undertaken, that there should be no lies or hidden agendas among those partaking, that everything is out on the table. So for Native Americans, smoking the pipe in such a process meant the parties were making an honest covenant. Unfortunately, the Americans understood it more as their seal of approval for peace, and as a result of that understanding, the process of treaty-making invariably lacked integrity on their part.

[37]Hoig, *Peace Chiefs*, 42.
[38]Paul Wallace, *The Iroquois Book of Life: The White Roots of Peace* (Santa Fe: Clear Light, 1994), 14.

person was required to participate in the ceremony. A fire was made and prayers spoken by the holy person. Then the families and friends on each side of the schism would face each other. Each would give their account of the offense, then they would go to the fire to pray for the ability to forgive. The two groups or individuals would then strip naked and exchange clothes with one another. They would speak words of forgiveness and vow never to bring the issue up again. The pipe was then passed back and forth, down the line so everyone could smoke. Then gifts were exchanged and a feast was made sponsored by both parties. The result was both ceremonial and practical.[39]

Also among the Cherokee, it was the women who made the final decision whether or not to go to war, because they often had the most to lose. I wonder how many wars America may have avoided if it dropped its commitment to paternalism and allowed women to decide on the importance of the war balanced against the possibility of losing their sons or daughters, husbands, fathers, and uncles.

The Cherokee and other Southeastern tribes had alternatives to war. In Cherokee it was called *A-ne-jo-di,* meaning "little brother to war." This stickball game, similar to modern-day lacrosse, may have been developed in ancient times as an alternative to war. Although the game could get violent, resulting in injury and even, on occasion, death, it served as a determinant for conflict among the tribes. Stickball is still played today for recreation among Southeastern Indian tribal cultures.

Another peacemaking practice among America's First Nations was adopting a relative who might serve to prevent or resolve a conflict. Such adoptions were also good for trade purposes, one of many strategies employed in the great expanse of Turtle Island's ancient trade networks.

---

[39]The three preceding paragraphs are based on material from Randy Woodley, "The Harmony Way:" Integrating Indigenous Values Within Native North American Theology and Mission (2010): *Faculty Publications - Portland Seminary,* 72 https://digitalcommons.georgefox.edu/cgi/viewcontent.cgi?article=1071&context=gfes&httpsredir=1&referer=.

Often these adoptions involved sending people from one tribe to live with another. Many indigenous tribes would never think of attacking a village where one of their relatives lived. The following story recorded by nineteenth-century anthropologist James Mooney illustrates this strategy:

> Ga'na' was a Seneca war chief. He called a council and said, "We must go to the Cherokee and see if we can't agree to be friendly together and live in peace hereafter." The people consented, and the chief said, "We must go to water first before we start." So they went, a great party of warriors, far away into the deep forest by the riverside. There were no women with them. For ten days they drank medicine every morning to make them vomit and washed and bathed in the river each day.
>
> Then the chief said, "Now we must get the eagle feathers." They went to the top of a high hill and dug a trench there the length of a man's body, and put a man into it, with boughs over the top so that he could not be seen, and above that they put the whole body of a deer. Then the people went off out of sight, and said the words to invite Shada'ge'a, the great eagle that lives in the clouds, to come down. . . . They had to trap a good many eagles in this way, and it was two years before they could get enough feathers to make a full tail, and were ready to start for the Cherokee country.
>
> They were many days on the road, and when they got to the first Cherokee town they found there was a stockade around it so that no enemy could enter. They waited until the gate was open, and then two Seneca dancers went forward, carrying the eagle feathers and shouting the signal yell. When the Cherokee heard the noise they came out and saw the two men singing and dancing, and the chief said, "These men must have come up on some errand." The Seneca messengers came up and said, "Call a council; we have come to talk on important business." All turned and went toward the townhouse, the rest of the Seneca following the two who were dancing. The townhouse was crowded, and the Seneca sang and danced until they were tired before they stopped. The Cherokee did not dance.

After the dance the Seneca chief said, "Now I will tell you why we have come so far through the forest to see you. We have thought among ourselves that it is time to stop fighting. Your people and ours are always on the lookout to kill each other, and we think it is time for this to stop. Here is a belt of wampum to show that I speak the truth. If your people are willing to be friendly, take it," and he held up the belt. The Cherokee chief stepped forward and said, "I will hold it in my hand, and tomorrow we will tell you what we decide." He then turned and said to the people, "Go home and bring food." They went and brought so much food that it made a great pile across the house, and all of both tribes ate together, but could not finish it.

Next day they ate together again, and when all were done the Cherokee chief said to the Seneca, "We have decided to be friendly and to bury our weapons, these knives and hatchets, so that no man may take them up again." The Seneca chief replied, "We are glad you have accepted our offer, and now we have all thrown our weapons in a pile together, and the white wampum hangs between us, and the belt shall be as long as a man and hang down to the ground."

Then the Cherokee chief said to his people, "Now is the time for any of you that wishes to adopt a relative from among the Seneca to do so." So some Cherokee women went and picked out one man and said, "You shall be our uncle," and some more took another for their brother, and so on until only Ga'na,' the chief, was left, but the Cherokee chief said, "No one must take Ga'na,' for a young man is here to claim him as his father." Then the young man came up to Ga'na' and said, "Father, I am glad to see you. Father, we will go home," and he led Ga'na' to his own mother's house, the house where Ga'na' had spent the first night. The young man was really his son, and when Ga'na' came to the house he recognized the woman as his wife who had been carried off long ago by the Cherokee.[40]

Sometimes, as in the case of Ga'na,' the peacemaker gains back what was lost. Others of us have mostly lost at the hands of America, the

---

[40] James Mooney, *Myths and Formulas of the Cherokees* (Nashville: Elder's Bookstore, 1982), 367-70. I have edited the story for brevity's sake.

warmonger, but America has also lost much in its pursuit of perpetual violence. We have all lost much, including a portion of our souls. We have lost the ability to understand the sacredness of all life and the dignity of every human being. To gain back our harmony way, the shalom way of Jesus, the way of indigenous Americans, will take work. Here are a few suggestions:

1. Remythologize America through education and policy, replacing the myth of freedom through violence. In its stead, include the greater truth of the cost to the offended, with reparations made by the offender, and the reasons for wars. I propose that a national curriculum be developed as a resource for public schools that tells the whole American story, including those minority voices from ethnic, racial, and gendered views that have been excluded. I propose a campaign to erect, revise, or replace state and national historic markers that reflect the new, more inclusive stories. Our markers often tell a different story than the actual history because the story is usually only told by the victor. Could we at least have a synthesis or even two accounts listed? By retelling the American story by those who bore the burden of the blood that is said to have created American freedom—the same people who now have also spilled their blood for this nation—we can begin to see a new kind of American myth surface for all of us, one that need not always spill blood and one that is inclusive of all our citizenry.

2. Create a process whereby the Pentagon, in full cooperation with the State Department and civilian senior peacemakers, adds a new branch under its auspices that spends as much time, human expertise, and money developing peace strategies and peace contingencies around the world as it does developing war strategies. Along with this I propose new incentives for the video game

manufacturers that create war titles such as *Call of Duty* to make peace strategy games that reward effective peacemaking as the way to win the game and the war.

3. Create a more stringent democratic process for going to war by creating women's councils that have representation at local, state, and federal levels and make decisions concerning going to war. For too long women have been left out of decision-making in national decisions. Certainly, at minimum, the violence in our nation has taken its toll on our conscience and on our children. The price we are now paying is too high. We must begin again. Uplifting the role of women—mothers and grandmothers—will guide us in a different way than in our past.

I would like to end by sharing an email from a friend who asked that I withhold her name. To end a long era of warmaking and become peacemakers will take a new way of living. In my friend's email she points out how our Cherokee people prepared for the green corn ceremony. The following are her words:

> A festival among many Eastern Woodland tribes, including the Cherokee, is green corn. . . . The Cherokee Ceremonial Festival of the Green Corn Moon (which coincides with when the first, thinnest crescent of the moon appears after the "new" or dark moon) will fall August 20th this year. Celebration in the southeastern nations traditionally includes a lot of preparation.
>
> - Houses are cleaned but so are lives.
> - Gifts of your extra or excess are given away.
> - If you have more than one of anything—any duplicated item—you would give it away before green corn starts, preferably to someone who doesn't have that item.
> - Extra food is also shared with those who need it.

- Debts are paid, and those who have grudges seek to end them before green corn begins.
- Weddings are planned—and divorces become final before green corn's first day.
- It [is] a time of celebration—so to make room for that, it [is] preceded by a time of reflection and contemplation. . . .
- We are to prepare our calendars—clear time off to celebrate it correctly by planning ahead.
- We are to prepare our minds—start choosing to do what is right.
- We are to prepare our hearts—begin shedding ourselves of all that might tempt us to be miserly.
- We are to prepare our bodies—medicine is taken, bad habits dropped.
- We are to prepare our home—so our clan may visit and be welcomed.
- It is solemn now—but the feast is coming![41]

Peace must be something for which we prepare ourselves. Peace will not occur through a tacit approach or lazy lifestyle. We must seek peace daily by preparing ourselves, our children, our communities, and our nation. Our Native American nations knew how to make war, and many of us were good at it. But making peace was always much more important to indigenous peoples. We prepared for peace all year round and with special ceremonies throughout the year. Perhaps this lesson can be learned today, while we are still able to welcome peace.

---

[41]Personal correspondence, name withheld.

PREACHERS, PROPHETS, AND PHILOSOPHERS

MARTIN LUTHER KING JR.'S MORAL REASONING ON NONVIOLENCE

Aaron James

[Some views] take as the root of morality in human nature a capacity for attention to things imagined or perceived; what I think it would be fair to call a loving and respectful attention.

CORA DIAMOND, *THE REALISTIC SPIRIT*

A CRUCIAL MOMENT in the Montgomery bus boycott of 1955–56 was the bombing of Martin Luther King Jr.'s house. King was speaking at the local First Baptist Church, but his family was home.[1] Hearing of the bombing, King rushed back to find a crowd of Blacks already there, some with crude weapons, growing angry as a result of the bombing and

---

[1] For a biographical account of that night see Harvard Sitkoff, *King: Pilgrimage to the Mountaintop* (New York: Hill and Wang, 2008), 38-39. For King's own autobiographical account, see Martin Luther King Jr., *Stride Toward Freedom: The Montgomery Story* (San Francisco: Harper & Row, 1958), 135-38.

barely restrained by White police officers. After confirming that his family was safe and those in the crowd unhurt, he said to the people assembled, "He who lives by the sword shall perish by the sword. I want you to love your enemies. Be good to them. Love them and let them know you love them." He insisted that they hear and follow Jesus' message: "Jesus still cries out in words that echo across the centuries: 'Love your enemies; bless them that curse you; pray for them that despitefully use you.'"[2]

Instead of rioting, the crowd broke out in song. Coretta King recalled, "This could well have been the darkest night in Montgomery's history." By King's own assessment it turned out instead to be "a majestic group demonstration of nonviolence."[3] Throughout the bus boycott of 1955–1956, and then later throughout his ministry until his death, King was constantly imploring Blacks not to hate racist Whites but to love them and to forgive them. Loving them meant Blacks could not use violence against Whites. King called for justice by advocating nonviolently for an end to segregation not only for the sake of Blacks, but also for the sake of White southerners and for the sake of reconciliation between Blacks and Whites.

For King, the insistence that Blacks love their White oppressors was rooted in the baptist vision as described by James Wm. McClendon Jr.[4] McClendon argues that the baptist vision, the organizing principle and animating vision for all of life for baptists, is essentially a way of reading Scripture. Baptists read Scripture with a "this is that" hermeneutic,

---

[2] King, *Stride*, 137-8.
[3] King, *Stride*, 138.
[4] McClendon argues that King's religion was the "organizing principle" for his life. See James William McClendon Jr., *Biography as Theology: How Life Stories Can Remake Today's Theology* (Nashville: Abingdon, 1974), chap. 3. Sitkoff likewise argues that King's faith was central to his work and in particular to his "radicalism" (*King,* xii-xiv). In his graduate studies King was influenced by various philosophical and theological sources, but if McClendon and Sitkoff are right, those sources were disciplined by King's prior habituation to Christian faith.

hearing the call of Jesus in the Gospels to his disciples as a call to *us*, hearing Peter's sermon to the crowds in Acts as a sermon preached to *us*.[5] We might say it is a way of reading the world through the Bible, rather than a way of applying the Bible to the world. In this sense, it is vision more akin to eyesight—a way of seeing—than vision in the sense of what is seen. The baptist vision is an acquired eyesight that sees the biblical world as our world. It is a hermeneutic embodied in King's words to the angry crowd gathered at his bombed home: "Jesus still cries out"—Jesus still cries out to *us*. King learned to read the Bible in this way from his immersion in the Black church.[6]

It is important for what I argue below to grasp at least a sense of the breadth and depth of what McClendon has in mind here. The baptist vision does not primarily involve doctrinal propositions, though the vision no doubt generates them. Nor is the vision reducible to values, though no doubt values are operative. Nor is it a mere technique for interpreting the Bible—naive biblical literalism or the historical-critical method as just two examples. Nor is the baptist vision merely the sum total of all the bits—doctrines, propositions, values, and so on. Rather, it is "the guiding pattern by which a people . . . shape their thought and practice as that people . . . the continually emerging theme and tonic structure of their common life."[7] It is, to borrow a couple of illuminating

---

[5]McClendon reserves "Baptist" (capital "B") for denominational Baptists. However, the "baptist vision" (lowercase "b") is shared by some other Christian groups beyond denominational Baptists. See James William McClendon Jr., *Ethics*, rev. ed., vol. 1 of *Systematic Theology* (Nashville: Abingdon, 2002), 33-34. I will follow McClendon's convention and use "Baptist" only for denominational Baptists. For McClendon's account of the baptist vision see *Ethics*, 26-34, and *Doctrine*, vol. 2 of *Systematic Theology* (Nashville: Abingdon, 1994), 44-46.

[6]For a different though complementary focus on King's religious context and its application to the civil rights movement, see Charles Marsh, "The Civil Rights Movement as Theological Drama—Interpretation and Application," *Modern Theology* 18 (2002): 231-50. Marsh argues that a theological analysis of the movement suggests not only that King's convictional Christian beliefs are fundamental to his approach, but furthermore that interpreting the movement through those convictions opens up new ways of understanding the movement as a whole.

[7]McClendon, *Ethics*, 27.

phrases from Iris Murdoch, "their total vision of life" and "the texture of [a community's] being."[8]

Applied now to ethics, the baptist vision as King's organizing principle and animating vision suggests that the moral reasoning behind such a difficult teaching—forgive those who beat and kill you; protest them and their actions in ways that leave open a path to reconciliation and friendship—was infused in him through his life in the Black Baptist church. It is rooted not so much in direct doctrinal or propositional claims about nonviolence (though there were no doubt doctrines and propositions involved) than it is a matter of vision.

It is this insight—that King's nonviolence is as much about vision as argument—that I want to explore. The quote from Cora Diamond that serves as the epigraph of this essay suggests a fruitful way to do so. It suggests a focus on the kind of attention that is at the root of King's nonviolence, a theological or even scriptural attention, if McClendon is right about the baptist vision—perceiving Whites as redeemable sinners rather than enemies to be destroyed. The capacity to see them this way was a capacity instilled and nurtured by the Black Baptist church, a capacity developed in terms of the baptist vision—the "this is that" reading strategy of Scripture.

What fruit grows from seeing King's nonviolence in terms of attention? Potentially there are many, but I will focus on two. First, understanding King in these terms, if true to King, has the benefit of better understanding a Christian pacifism—a pacifism rooted not so much in argument but in vision or attention.[9] This is important because if

---

[8]Iris Murdoch, *Existentialists and Mystics: Writings on Philosophy and Literature* (New York: Penguin, 1997), 80-81. Of the second quote, Murdoch's original reads "the texture of a man's being." Here I have applied the insight to a community instead of an individual.

[9]I intentionally leave pacifism, nonviolence, and the like imprecise and undefined, for as Yoder observed, "There is no such thing as a single position called pacifism, to which one clear definition can be given and which is held by all pacifists. Instead, there are varied kinds of opposition

King's nonviolence has the character I suggest, then the first step in engaging it—whether for support or criticism—is not to seek out the moral principles or rules that define it but to listen to what McClendon calls the "continually emerging theme and tonic structure" of the life that inhabits the vision.

Second, seeing King's nonviolence in terms of attention and perception exercises our own capacities of attention and perception. Exercising these capacities may lead us to recognize that habits of attention, vision, and perception are the roots of at least some kinds of *rejections* of pacifism, and if that is true, there are apologetic and evangelistic reasons to be aware of it. The nonpacifist of this sort would need not to be convinced of certain arguments (moral principles that provide reasons that can be applied to the "facts" of war and peace) but to experience some kind of leading toward or development of new, expanded, or redirected capacities of attention and perception. In fact, I think this is one helpful way of seeing what King is doing: his sermons, speeches, and actions are not so much arguments but rather presentations of alternative habits of attention and imagination, together with an invitation—and also prophetic challenge—to take up those habits of attention and perception as one's own.

All of this suggests that the way to engage—to argue—with and about King's nonviolence is not first within the space of moral principles or theory, but rather within the space of vision. Furthermore, such a move engages the sort of normative evaluation that characterizes much of modern philosophical ethics. But in order for us to get there, it will be helpful to contrast what I've suggested so far with the dominant way in which contemporary analytic Anglo-American ethics tends to operate and how that approach shapes arguments about war and nonviolence.

---

to war." John Howard Yoder, *Nevertheless: The Varieties and Shortcomings of Religious Pacifism* (Scottdale, PA: Herald Press, 1992), 12.

Making this contrast will help us gain a clearer picture of what I think King is doing and to see the narrow conception of ethical reasoning that may obscure our ability to see various ways of reasoning about violence and nonviolence.[10]

MORAL PHILOSOPHY ACCORDING TO MORAL PHILOSOPHERS

The epigraph at the beginning of this chapter contrasts with the usual way of characterizing moral philosophy, at least in the analytic tradition, which is still the dominant tradition in Anglo-American philosophy.[11] Post-Enlightenment moral philosophy has generally insisted that, while there are countless ways to state a position and even to persuade a person of that position, there is really only one way to legitimately justify a moral position. That way is the articulation and testing of moral principles or rules and their application to various actions by means of argument. This process of argumentation defines the area of philosophical ethics—action judged according to rationally defensible moral principles.

Consider as an example Peter Singer, one of the most influential moral philosophers working today. Singer says that what defines ethics or moral reasoning is the activity of giving reasons, or justifications, for one's actions—but, more so, justifications of a particular kind. Singer's language is pointed: "the justification *must be* of a certain kind."[12] For an act to be justified, "it *must be* shown to be compatible with more broadly

---

[10]The contrast I draw in this essay should not be taken as a refutation of the manner of philosophical ethics described. Rather, the contrast is meant to evoke a different picture of moral reasoning for the purposes of bringing to the surface hidden assumptions taken by many to be given or obvious, but from the perspective of the alternative picture controvertible. I mean only to offer possible fruits that grow from considering King and nonviolent moral reasoning more broadly under this aspect.

[11]For Diamond's description of the dominant form of reasoning along these lines, see Cora Diamond, *The Realistic Spirit: Wittgenstein, Philosophy, and the Mind* (Cambridge, MA: MIT Press, 1991), 292-97, 309-12.

[12]Peter Singer, *Practical Ethics*, 3rd ed. (Cambridge: Cambridge University Press, 2011), 10, emphasis added.

based ethical principles."[13] But what justifies the ethical principles? After citing a long list of religious and nonreligious figures (including Moses and Jesus on the so-called golden rule), he suggests that though vastly different in many important respects, they all have in common a universal perspective: "They agree that the justification of an ethical principle cannot be in terms of any partial or sectional group."[14] He continues, "Ethics goes beyond 'I' and 'you' to the universal law, the universalizable judgment, the standpoint of the impartial spectator or ideal observer, or whatever we choose to call it."[15] This, according to Singer, is what *must be* the case. An action is legitimately morally justified only if it can be shown to be compatible with an ethical principle that itself is justified only from this neutral, impartial, ideal perspective.

The same basic argumentative structure applies no matter one's ethical theory. Singer is himself a utilitarian, but a deontological argument, though the principles are different, runs formally more or less the same: the relevant general moral principle is applied to the particular act under consideration. So too for someone operating on a rights-based theory of ethics and so on. It is the general form of the argument that matters: a universal ethical principle is brought to bear by means of argumentation on particular cases or actions, and this and only this can legitimately, *rationally*, justify an action.

MORAL ARGUMENTS AND NONVIOLENCE

All of this is relevant to issues of war and peace because this form of argument is common in those debates as well. Consider just one

---

[13] Singer, *Practical Ethics*, 10, emphasis added. One aspect of Wittgenstein's work that Diamond emphasizes is Wittgenstein's rejection of metaphysics. By "metaphysics" Wittgenstein (as Diamond understands him) meant illegitimate and fictitious philosophical requirements laid over questions and issues by philosophers. Singer's "must be" language is an example of this. For more, see Diamond, *Realistic Spirit*, 13-38.
[14] Singer, *Practical Ethics*, 11.
[15] Singer, *Practical Ethics*, 11.

contemporary example. David Kinsella and Craig Carr introduce pacifism as a moral position by stating what pacifism must do in order to be "coherent."[16] In order for pacifism to be coherent—*coherent* is their word, repeated more than once—the pacifist must "advance moral reasons that justify the conclusion that under no circumstances should wars be fought."[17]

Why must pacifists do this? Kinsella and Carr connect the process of advancing moral reasons to justify conclusions directly with "a moral point of view."[18] Ordinarily in ethics, "the moral point of view" defines a viewpoint that is impartial and universal—that others' dignity, interests, rights, and so on count just as much as mine and, relatedly, that what is right or wrong for me is right or wrong universally (at least for anyone in exactly the same circumstances).[19] Singer's description of moral justification above is essentially justification from "the moral point of view." Moral principles—be they utilitarian, deontological, or some other—are what do the work of constructing this impartial, universal point of view. When we act according to moral principles—and not according to particular desires, emotions, and so on—then we are acting morally, that is, impartially and according to the standards of universality. This is because it is the impartial and universal principle governing our actions, not some particularity about us.

So it is no surprise that when Kinsella and Carr describe pacifism, they identify "two strategies open to pacifists" for advancing the moral reasons that justify the conclusion that war is always morally wrong. The

---

[16] David Kinsella and Craig L. Carr, "Pacifism: Introduction," in *The Morality of War: A Reader*, ed. David Kinsella and Craig L. Carr (Boulder, CO: Lynne Rienner, 2007), 33-34.
[17] Kinsella and Carr, "Pacifism," 34.
[18] Kinsella and Carr, "Pacifism," 33
[19] Kinsella and Carr don't directly define what they mean by "a moral point of view." However, it is clear from their argument that they presume the ordinary account of it. For just one articulation of how "the moral point of view" is ordinarily understood in philosophical ethics, see Barbara MacKinnon and Andrew Fiala, *Ethics: Theory and Contemporary Issues,* 8th ed. (Stamford, CT: Cengage Learning, 2015), 76.

two strategies? Deontological moral reasoning and consequentialist moral reasoning.[20] They identify the deontological form of argument as one "premised upon certain principles that are presumed to obligate persons regardless of any concern for the greater good."[21] They identify the consequentialist form of argument as one premised on the principle that an action is "morally wrong if doing it would make people worse off than not doing it."[22] So here is an instance of Singer's insistence that when doing ethics there is one way, and apparently only one way, to proceed that legitimately (and for Kinsella and Carr coherently) justifies moral conclusions: universal moral principles applied to particular actions.

What does any of this have to do with King's advocacy of nonviolent resistance? Just this: *it appears to define Martin Luther King Jr. out of the activity of moral reasoning.* If McClendon is right that King's nonviolence is rooted fundamentally in the baptist vision, then the philosopher who adopts the view that there is only one legitimate form of moral reasoning will not see King's religious nonviolent advocacy as moral reasoning. King's actions are certainly within the realm of morality insofar as they are actions and choices available to moral evaluation, and King no doubt regularly uses the language of moral principles.[23] But King's preaching and the vision that animates it are morally justified only if they can be shown to be at least consistent with the form of moral reasoning identified above. We don't need to expect King to be a philosopher, but we should hope that the positions he preaches are, when appropriately "translated," defensible by philosophical argument. After all, so the philosopher would say, there is preaching, and then there is moral reasoning.

---

[20]Kinsella and Carr, "Pacifism," 34-36.
[21]Kinsella and Carr, "Pacifism," 34.
[22]Kinsella and Carr, "Pacifism," 35.
[23]Marsh argues that King's theological convictions are fundamental and supplemented by other philosophical and religious traditions. "Civil Rights Movement," 233.

The problem with the modern analytic view of moral philosophy is that it unnecessarily narrows the scope of moral reasoning, and in such a way that it obscures the ways in which attention and perception are inextricably bound up with morality—at least in a view of morality suggested by the epigraph at the beginning of this chapter.[24] The dominant philosophical view seems to presume that there is a fixed range of actions available to any person, fixed by moral principles and facts on the ground (war, nonviolence, and so on). Yet King's preaching and witness seem to presume that the range of possible actions is not merely made evident but, perhaps more strongly, *created anew* out of new modes of attention, that "the facts" are not definable apart from a particular vision, and if this is so, then what is needed is not first or principally argument—at least not argument of the philosophical kind—but the development of new capacities for seeing.[25]

MORAL REASONING ACCORDING TO THE BAPTIST VISION

One example where we see King employ baptist-vision-patterned moral reasoning to inform the exhortation for Blacks to love Whites and to resist them nonviolently is his sermon "Love in Action" on the text of Luke 23:34.[26] King reflects on Jesus, humiliated and suffering on the cross, as he forgives those who crucified him. Jesus crucified and forgiving his crucifiers is the axis around which the moral instruction in the sermon turns. King's point isn't that we should forgive our enemies because Jesus shows us that the general moral principle "forgive your

---

[24]For Diamond's argument for this see *Realistic Spirit*, 291-308.

[25]I am aware that this way of writing—"facts" are not definable apart from a particular vision—cannot help but raise the ugly specter of relativism, both ethical and epistemological. There is much to be said here, but it is far beyond the scope of this essay. So I'll simply note without argumentation that it need not necessitate any sort of pernicious relativism. I say this only to ask readers who wonder about this to bracket the worry out for now.

[26]Martin Luther King Jr., *Strength to Love* (New York: Harper & Row, 1963), 25-33.

enemies" is true (even if it is). Nor does it generate a general moral principle that can then be applied apart from the narrative—as in, "Jesus shows us that this moral principle is true, so now we should apply the principle."[27] Rather, for readers and hearers whose vision is shaped by the baptist vision, the appeal to Jesus' suffering and humiliation does a number of other things, all of which contribute to a kind of moral justification for treating enemies this way—forgiving them instead of attacking them. In fact, for most of the sermon the extension of Jesus' forgiveness of the soldiers to Blacks' forgiveness of Whites in the South is implicit, yet it is obvious in King's immediate context to those schooled in the same vision as he is.[28]

For example, the appeal to Jesus' forgiveness of those who crucified him invites the hearers, schooled already in the baptist vision, to identify with Jesus in such a way that they see the intimate relationship between his suffering at the hands of his crucifiers and his response to those same crucifiers—that he does not suffer on the cross and then along with that forgive his enemies, but rather, to suffer as the Jesus portrayed in the Gospels suffers is to forgive those who cause the suffering. Animated by the baptist vision, the hearers are brought to see their own suffering inside the gospel story. Such seeing opens up the possibility of a new or renewed attention to the character of their own suffering: to be the people who follow Jesus, suffering occasions forgiveness of those who are the source of the suffering.

That the White persecutor cannot see his mutual inclusion in the story, at least not in the way the suffering Black does, raises another function of the appeal to Jesus on the cross. Jesus forgives because, as Jesus says,

---

[27] King does seem to think such a moral principle is indeed true, and the sermon says as much. But conceptually it is not the moral principle that does the work. It is the account of Jesus on the cross, the image brought to bear on the contemporary situation, that does the work.

[28] Even so, he does explicitly make the connection between Jesus and race relations when discussing the reasons for Jesus' forgiveness. See below, as well as King, *Strength*, 29-31.

"They do not know what they are doing." King makes an explicit connection here between the blindness of the soldiers and the blindness of White southerners.[29] They—both soldiers and southern Whites—are not evil, or at least not especially evil. They are blind. They cannot see what they do, and they cannot see the character of what they do. While characterizing their actions as sinful, King creates a space in which attention is brought to bear on Jesus' forgiveness of the blind soldiers as a medium or frame for attending to the blindness of White southerners.

But there is another way the appeal to blindness works, a way left unaddressed explicitly in King's sermon but open to those schooled in the baptist vision. It does more than include the Whites in the story of Jesus along with the Blacks. It implicitly invites Blacks to see their own blindness in terms of the soldiers' blindness. Blinded perhaps by the genuine evil perpetrated against them, they do not initially or instinctively see White persecutors as objects of love and reconciliation—until they see that they also are like the soldiers. They are blind and must see anew in order to recognize their White persecutors as objects of love and forgiveness.

Understanding the appeal to Jesus on the cross in this way suggests that, for King, though his appeal may be extended toward something like a moral justification for nonviolence, its cumulative effect does more the work of something like concept formation.[30] In a sense, the inclusion of the Black persecuted and the White persecutor into the same Jesus story by means of the baptist vision is itself an identification of the *kinds* of beings involved.[31] In other words, the concept of common humanity, a concept that might do some work in justifying the extension

---

[29]King, *Strength*, 29-31.
[30]Diamond makes a similar claim for some of the work that moral reasoning may do. See *Realistic Spirit*, 301-4, 321-26.
[31]Diamond uses this phrase in a different context (moral vegetarianism) but to the same general end about concept formation. *Realistic Spirit*, 323.

of forgiveness to a White segregationist, is not constituted by a fact of common sentience or a fact of equal possession of rights, for example—common options within contemporary moral philosophy. Those notions do not figure into the concept of humanity employed here.[32]

Rather, that both Whites and Blacks are identifiable in terms of the narrative of Jesus on the cross and Jesus' extension of forgiveness even to his crucifiers—this is what "makes them human." The spade turns on reading both Whites and Blacks in terms of the story, as seen through the baptist vision, not on either's capacities or inherent rights or any other general moral principle. But, then, King's sermons are not only examples of rhetorically powerful persuasive discourse. They are indeed *moral* discourse, a part of the task of learning new modes of response by exercising new capacities for attention brought into focus by the baptist vision, and consequently of tracing and then reshaping the moral texture of a person and of a community. For the philosopher then to say, "Well and good so far as it goes, but what we still do not have in these sermons is a reasoned justification of the moral appropriateness of extending forgiveness to the one who unjustly causes suffering" is simply a failure on the part of that philosopher to see the pattern of reasoning present and to make the unwarranted assumption that philosophical justification is the only legitimate justification, the only possible means of transcending our own narrow and inconsistent self-interest.

MORAL REASONING, APOLOGETICS, AND EVANGELISM

Perhaps we are willing to grant that these sermons are moral discourse, not just persuasive discourse on nonviolence—for Black Baptist Christians in the South, at least. But then they are insiders to this shared vision. So in what sense can we call this "witness" if (presumably) outsiders are in view? In other words, is any of this amenable to outside

---

[32]Though it is still possible they are compatible.

criticism, appropriation, questioning, and so on? A central context for any moral evaluation, philosophical or otherwise, is persuasion that amounts to more than mere power or influence. But can the baptist vision be something other than parochial and hence furnish a nonviolent moral vision for others?

I suggest that this thoroughly insider language is precisely what is needed to communicate with outsiders. If it is true that we can come to reconsider and reform our moral views, responses, and characters by means of a whole host of complicated and interweaving comparisons, arguments, attention, imagination, and the like, then it is just the particulars of one's moral texture that must be on offer. Consider Diamond's arguments on ethics and literature. How, for example, could the novels of Dickens or Henry James (two examples raised by Diamond) possibly inform moral discourse? Whatever exactly it looks like, it can't be by leaving behind the novel itself, otherwise it wouldn't be a question about literature and moral discourse. To try to "translate" Dickens into abstract philosophical language and then evaluate its worth to moral discourse is exactly what will make the work the novel is thought to do impossible. Focusing on the development of capacities for attention and imagination would be a more fruitful way of approaching them. I am arguing that something analogous is at work in King's sermons. It is precisely its insider particularities that make it available for genuine moral engagement with others.

On another level, the argument so far suggests that the question about insiders and outsiders is obfuscated by unnoticed assumptions about the allowable sort of answer—namely, a kind of theoretical account of moral justification apart from the moral texture of those who are involved in the complicated interweaving processes of moral justification—and the failure to see this as a symptom of what has been challenged, that the only possible or legitimate or allowed response must be in terms of general theoretical principles available to anyone from a neutral or impartial perspective. But the purpose of putting this alternative view of moral reasoning alongside the dominant philosophical one is to challenge the assumed hegemony of just such a theoretical account of moral justification.

My hunch is that I simply cannot give a general theoretical response to the question "What about outsiders?" without betraying the very insights I am trying to employ. I imagine that a better approach would be to take a series of cases—the modes of moral reasoning present in the struggle for civil rights would be a good one; various ways literature shapes moral evaluation (as Diamond does) might be another—and attend as closely as possible to discern where communication and transformation are happening and where they are not. This would allow us to trace as closely as possible the various textures of moral discourse and justification and to see as clearly as possible the concepts employed and their place in "the texture of a man's being."[33] If we attend in that way, I think we would find a whole host of complicated and interweaving patterns of discourse and moral justification that would not be reducible to general moral principles, though perhaps they would be inclusive of them—but, then, we would just have to look and see. I would also not be surprised if we found the communication most effective, and hence moral expansion occurring most effectively, when communicants make genuine offerings of themselves and their moral vision to one another and receive the other without imposing any demands for philosophical generality. If this is right, then the best prospects for successful witness to nonviolence is along these lines, and this suggests that the best argument for nonviolence may be nonviolent lives animated by a nonviolent vision.

---

[33] Murdoch, *Existentialists*, 81.

LISTENING FOR PEACE

NONVIOLENCE IN WILLIAM STAFFORD'S WRITING AND TEACHING

Sarah Azaransky

WILLIAM STAFFORD (1914–1993) was an American writer, professor, and poet laureate in 1970. He taught composition and literature at Lewis and Clark College, where he developed a pedagogy of open engagement—of being a "listener-reader," as he called it.[1] Stafford was a sought-after leader of writing workshops, where his focus on process and practice rather than technique earned him a reputation as a champion of everyone's capacity to write. Stafford touted writing as "one of the great free human activities," one that was also a means for people to access their deepest selves.[2]

Nonviolence grounds Stafford's poetry as both topic and method. Certainly Stafford's poems warn against violence, but just as importantly they proffer communication and attention as antidotes to dominating

---

[1] This chapter builds on and extends a blog post written by the author: Sarah Azaransky, "Listening in Our Disasters," February 29, 2018 on *The Immanent Frame*, https://tif.ssrc.org/2018/02/28/listening-in-our-disasters/ under Creative Commons License CC BY-NC-ND 3.0 US.
[2] William Stafford, *Writing the Australian Crawl: Views on the Writer's Vocation* (Ann Arbor: University of Michigan Press, 1978), 20.

social patterns. In "A Ritual to Read to Each Other," Stafford suggests that paying attention to another has implications for social justice, for "if you don't know the kind of person I am / and I don't know the kind of person you are / a pattern that others made may prevail in the / world."[3] Stafford sought new ways of being in relationship, in part through a new way of being grounded by a fifty-year practice of solitary early morning writing in which he honed his capacity to listen, to sense what he called "impulses and nudges."

I chanced upon Stafford's writing last year. While researching the history of education for a larger project about school desegregation campaigns in New York city, I found a few references to William Stafford's work. They grabbed my attention, so I followed Stafford through most of his essays and much of his poetry. I was inspired by his conviction about the intellectual and ethical significance of listening. As a professor of social ethics I was struck by the idea of listening as a moral commitment; it was an apt description of what I aimed for in my own teaching and research. I surprised myself by how engrossed I became in Stafford's work, that of a White man and a poet, given that my research focuses on midcentury African American Christian intellectuals and activists. A cornerstone of my research is a conviction that Black intellectuals and activists provide us with compelling models of moral reflection and moral action, a result, in part, of their critical reflection from their social locations.[4] They knew more than their White contemporaries did about racism and White supremacy, about whether White churches could confront injustice. Yet in reading Stafford I experienced something akin to what it was to read about Pauli Murray, Bayard Rustin,

---

[3]William Stafford, "A Ritual to Read to Each Other," in *Stories That Could Be True: New and Collected Poems* (New York: Harper & Row, 1977), 52.

[4]Sarah Azaransky, *This Worldwide Struggle: Religion and the International Roots of the Civil Rights Movement* (New York: Oxford University Press, 2017), and *The Dream Is Freedom: Pauli Murray and Democratic Faith* (New York: Oxford University Press, 2011).

or Ella Baker for the first time, what Stafford himself once called a "way of living that recognizes more than we know."[5] I added Stafford to my list of moral sages, people who help us rethink who we are and what the world is like.

A force in Stafford's work is his steadiness and capacity to engage, without flinching, with complex social and political issues. Throughout his forty-year career, a repeated theme among his reviewers and interlocutors was how trenchant his insight was for *this* moment, whether "this" was early protest against American involvement in Vietnam, the crisis of Watergate, Reagan's militarism, or, in retrospectives after his death, during the post-9/11 "war on terror."[6] Stafford's poetry, prose, and writing practice inspired the composure and instilled the confidence people needed in order to face their particular political contexts. In my own reading I found how Stafford may speak to us in this moment of deep political and spiritual crisis. Stafford's writing and teaching, and his self-conscious attention to the practice of both, provide a variety of resources for contemporary readers who are looking for alternative responses to violence. This chapter focuses on three: nonviolence as an ongoing practice, reflection as a ground for activism, and a capacious sense of history.

---

[5] William Stafford, *The Answers Are Inside the Mountains: Meditations on the Writing Life*, ed. Paul Merchant and Vincent Wixon (Ann Arbor: University of Michigan Press, 2003), 27.
[6] For how Stafford's work addresses various moral conflicts, see John K. Roth, *The Failure of Ethics: Confronting the Holocaust, Genocide, and Other Mass Atrocities* (New York: Oxford University Press, 2015), 1, 3-4; for how it was received during the US war in Vietnam, see Kim Stafford, *Early Morning: Remembering My Father, William Stafford* (Minneapolis: Graywolf Press, 2003), 48, 52; for how it addressed Reagan's militarism, see *Every War Has Two Losers: William Stafford on Peace and War*, ed. Kim Stafford (Minneapolis: Milkweed Editions, 2003), 129; for how it spoke to the 1990s Persian Gulf War, see Philip Metres, "William Stafford's *Down in My Heart*: The Poetics of Pacifism and the Limits of Lyric," *Peace and Change* 29, no. 1 (January 2004): 22; for people reading Stafford in response to 9/11, see "More Than Words," *The Baltimore Sun*, September 25, 2001, www.baltimoresun.com/news/bs-xpm-2001-09-25-0109260120-story.html; for how Stafford's poetry continues to speak to contemporary political crises, see Jerry Harp, "On Political Poetry and William Stafford's 'At the Bomb Testing Site,'" *Kenyon Review*, April 6, 2017, www.kenyonreview.org/2017/04/political-poetry-william-staffords-bomb-testing-site.

PRACTICING NONVIOLENCE: JUSTICE WILL TAKE US MILLIONS OF INTRICATE MOVES

William Stafford was born in Hutchinson, Kansas, and during his early years his family moved frequently to follow his father's jobs. He grew up in a peace household, part of "a worldwide fellowship" of people who looked for alternative ways of being in relationship.[7] His family's peace commitment inspired Stafford's activism at the University of Kansas in the late 1930s, when he joined sit-ins to protest the campus policy of separating Black students and White students in the cafeteria. Stafford became a witness, then, to what James Farmer would later call the "race logic of pacifism," that American pacifists should prioritize dismantling a primary source of violence, antiblack racism.[8] Stafford's life story is punctuated by the three and a half years he was consigned to Civilian Public Service (CPS) camps during World War II. Stafford was one of the twelve thousand conscientious objectors (COs) who were stationed around the country to undertake strenuous physical labor, such as building roads and fighting forest fires, often without pay.

Stafford's earliest publication was a memoir of his experiences as a CO, which explored frankly the lonely choice of refusing to participate in what almost every American agreed was a good war. In one chilling vignette, Stafford recounts how he and a group of COs, on leave for the day, were surrounded by a group of townspeople who berated them for being cowards, reproached their lack of patriotism, and condemned them as a threat to American democracy. As the men from the town took the shape of a mob, when it started to look as if the COs might be hanged, Stafford recalls,

> During all of this heckling and crowding we were merely quiet and respectful. We didn't know what else to do. We learned then rapidly what we later learned about other provokers—including policemen—that

---

[7]Stafford, *The Answers Are Inside the Mountains*, 26.
[8]James L. Farmer Jr., "The Race Logic of Pacifism," *Fellowship* 8, no. 2 (February 1942): 24-25.

almost always the tormentor is at a loss unless he can provoke a belligerent reaction as an excuse for further pressure of violence.[9]

Stafford underscores a pacifist conviction in being "quiet and respectful," an alternative to what nonpacifists accept as a binary choice between fighting back or running away. Stafford's portrayal also contains a more complicated moral lesson; he explains how "it takes such an intricate succession of misfortunes and blunders to get mobbed by your own countrymen—and such a close balancing of good fortune to survive."[10] Peace, or in this case avoiding violence, requires a series of careful and precise—one might say *conscientious*—steps. In a poem written a decade later, he concludes, "We live in an occupied country, misunderstood; / justice will take us millions of intricate moves."[11] The memoir is an early witness to Stafford's moral and spiritual poise and his conviction that nonviolence involves an ongoing practice of deliberative, receptive, and sensitive engagement.[12]

---

[9] William Stafford, *Down in My Heart: Peace Witness in War Time* (Corvallis: Oregon State University Press, 1998), 19-20.
[10] Stafford, *Down*, 15.
[11] William Stafford, "Thinking for Berky," in *Stories That Could Be True*, 65.
[12] In later poems, Stafford broadened and developed pacifist insights from this experience. For example, "A Ritual to Read to Each Other" warns, "If you don't know the kind of person I am / and I don't know the kind of person you are / a pattern that others made may prevail in the world" (89). Stafford asserts the agency and moral significance of an individual's decision to foster relationships on her own terms and not be swayed by foreign policy initiatives of that moment. During the Trump administration, many Americans may have cultivated the distinction between a people and their leader, a political and moral move that builds solidarity with people around the world who do not identify closely with their national leadership. For example, just as "the United States" does not aptly describe how Americans think and feel about particular policies of their government, so "North Korea" does not aptly describe how North Koreans think and feel about particular policies. While forms of government are, of course, meaningful here—"their national leadership" much more readily describes the government of people living in a democracy with an opposition party than it does people living in a dictatorship—Stafford consistently underscores how at odds a person can be even, or especially, in a democracy. For instance, in "Objector," Stafford stresses the significance of an individual's decision: "In a line at lunch I cross my fork and spoon / to ward off complicity—the ordered life / our leaders have offered us." Stafford insists also on a different focus in international relations, for example, "At the Un-National Monument Along the Canadian Border," Stafford notices that "this is the field where the battle did not happen" and "where no monument stands / and the only heroic thing is the sky." *Every War*, 87.

After the war, when COs were freed from the CPS camps, Stafford returned to school, finished a graduate degree in writing, and secured a job teaching composition and literature in Oregon, where he would remain for the rest of his life. But being a CO inculcated what Stafford later called a "fortress mentality and of being part of a little group that's apart from society."[13] Stafford's experience of being set apart—literally when he was in the camps, but also spiritually and existentially as he was separated from mainstream American cultural and religious life—gave him a vantage point that was independent of dominant and dominating cultural and religious influences. He and other COs risked social, political, and economic alienation to maintain integrity of their peace witness. COs were paid little, and sometimes not at all, for their public service and were often derided as cowards and unpatriotic. Stafford and other COs exemplified a vocation of Christians to be "truly oppositional to public culture"—in other words, to be "countercultural."[14] If Christians today prioritize nonviolence, if we want to live differently, nonviolence requires us to have the moral acuity to perceive dominating patterns of social power *and* the wherewithal to live in such a way that we resist violence. Stafford sustained his orientation to nonviolence through a daily practice of listening and waiting.

REFLECTION: THE SILENCES ARE IMPORTANT

Listening, waiting, and expectation thrum through Stafford's work. The world is waiting to be understood, not quantified or even qualified; rather, the world is waiting to be met in its integrity. In order to cultivate his capacity to listen, Stafford awoke before dawn:

---

[13]Stafford, *Every War*, 130.

[14]Traci C. West, *Disruptive Christian Ethics: When Racism and Women's Lives Matter* (Louisville, KY: Westminster John Knox, 2006), xviii; Lisa Cahill, *Family: A Christian Social Perspective* (Minneapolis: Fortress, 2000), 83. Many Christian theologians and ethicists call for the church to oppose the dominant culture, to be countercultural; for example, see Michael L. Budde and Robert W. Brimlow, eds., *The Church as Counterculture* (Albany, NY: SUNY Press, 2000).

Those quiet mornings bring the feeling there is a tide, or what makes the tide, something you miss if people interrupt, or if there is noise where you live or in the kind of life you live. Even the kindest friend would jar that faint, delicious message you are receiving: something is offering you a guidance available only to those undistracted by anything else.[15]

Stafford began his habit of writing before dawn when he was a CO. He found that if he woke up before breakfast, he had the time and stamina to listen and write ahead of the hours of physical labor. Readers are right to wonder if Stafford's daily listening and waiting, this time "undistracted from anything else," is available to others who are subject to racial domination and economic exploitation. Queer Chicana cultural theorist and author Gloria Anzaldúa recognizes that the primary obstacle to writing faced by poor people and minoritized women is "to focus, to concentrate." Anzaldúa admits that "the body distracts, sabotages with a hundred ruses. . . . The solution is to anchor the body to a cigarette or some other ritual." Had Stafford read Anzaldúa's essay, a collection of letters she wrote to Third World women writers, he would have resonated with this call for ritual in light of his own repeated practice of early morning writing. Later in Stafford's career, when he was an English professor and living in Portland, Oregon, getting up early to write did reflect his privilege. But when we recognize that the practice began when he was imprisoned in government work camps, we see connections between his insistence on the role of writing for his political resistance and Anzaldúa's call for women of color to "forget the room of one's own—write in the kitchen, lock yourself up in the bathroom. Write on the bus or the welfare line, on the job or during meals, between sleeping or waking."[16]

---

[15] William Stafford, *You Must Revise Your Life* (Ann Arbor: University of Michigan Press, 1986), 21.
[16] Gloria Anzaldúa, "Speaking in Tongues: A Letter to Third World Women Writers," in *The Gloria Anzaldúa Reader,* ed. AnaLouise Keating (Durham, NC: Duke University Press, 2009), 31.

Stafford's writing practice, which he continued for fifty years, was always rooted in his nonviolence, his noncooperation with dominant moral and political traditions. In Stafford's CO service and in his writing is evidence of an ongoing process of self-reflection. In pacifism, Stafford lived out a commitment to internal transformation, to learn about himself so that he could better engage ethically in the world. At first glance Stafford's solitary predawn practice seems at odds with a robust worldly engagement. But to bracket the world was, paradoxically, a way for him to grasp his place in it. "I felt my morning writings as maintenance work or repair work on my integrity," he once explained.[17]

Stafford's writing practice affirms an integral connection between an individual and her social world. In this way Stafford's nonviolence was part of a larger tradition that asserts the moral significance of a person coming to see herself differently, of how social transformation is inherently linked to an individual's capacity to know herself, which enables the moral courage necessary to live nonviolently.[18] In this way an individual's self-knowledge is intimately linked to the larger social structures of which she is a part, thus her coming to understand herself initiates the possibility of structural analysis and change.

---

[17]Stafford, *You Must Revise*, 12.

[18]For Christians this tradition is wide and deep, from the Jesuit spiritual exercises of Ignatius Loyola (1548) to Quaker Rufus Jones, *The Inner Life* (New York: MacMillan, 1916). For an overview of how spiritual practices may provide "the wellsprings necessary live morally," see William C. Spohn, "Spirituality and Ethics: Exploring the Connections," *Theological Studies* 58 (1997): 109-23. Howard Thurman may also be helpfully placed in an American theological tradition of personalism, sharing with King, whom he mentored, a conviction that people are agents, beloved by God, and they have a responsibility to take an active role in history. See, for example, Rufus Burrow Jr., *God and Human Dignity: The Personalism, Theology, and Ethics of Martin Luther King, Jr.* (Notre Dame, IN: University of Notre Dame Press, 1992). Personalism underscores the relationship between individuals and the social order; it holds that people's spirituality and faith are sources of insight about political, social, and economic structures that foment injustice in people's daily lives; see Gary Dorrien, *The Making of American Liberal Theology: Crisis, Irony, and Postmodernity* (Louisville, KY: Westminster John Knox, 2006), 9-57. Dorothy Day was also inspired by personalism and it shaped her leadership of the *Catholic Worker*; see James J. Farrell, *The Spirit of the Sixties: The Making of Postwar Radicalism* (New York: Routledge, 1997), 21-50.

Howard Thurman made a similar argument in *Jesus and the Disinherited* when he associated Jesus' personal transformation with the possibility of social change. According to Thurman, Jesus was able to overcome fear, deception, and hate through a spiritual practice that grounded Jesus in love for God. Thurman argued that it is crucial for a person to perceive his participation in the wider river of life, what Thurman also called the "ethical field," in order to live justly.[19] Thurman underscored how an individual's spiritual transformation has potentially larger social significance. Thurman and Stafford agree, then, that an individual's consistent practice sparks "the spiritual force to act effectively" and has the potential to transform communities toward justice.[20]

I hesitate to characterize Stafford's daily writing as a spiritual practice because of Stafford's own caution that readers are apt to "distort and impose rather than discover," whether it be a poem's meaning or in this case an author's religious orientation.[21] Furthermore, Stafford's religious identity is not straightforward but surfaces in and through the witness of historic peace churches. When he was a CO, he was imprisoned in camps administered by the Church of the Brethren, and, in the midst, he married the daughter of a Brethren minister; his first job after the war was at a Brethren service agency. But Stafford's pacifism was not the result of family membership in a peace church; instead he came from a "peace household," which Stafford points out was not rare in the 1930s, when there was a vibrant peace movement in the United

---

[19] Howard Thurman, *Jesus and the Disinherited* (Boston: Beacon, 1996), 102.
[20] Jean Toomer, a poet and novelist of the Harlem Renaissance, was also a Quaker who wrote about social transformation arising from spiritual practice. When describing the Quaker practice of centering down in silence, Toomer recognized that some would see silently waiting for spirit as anathema to action, but Toomer pointed out, "We say we are activists, but we often lack the spiritual force to act effectively." Jean Toomer, "Keep the Inward Watch," in *Black Fire: African American Quakers on Spirituality and Human Rights*, ed. Harold D. Weaver Jr., Paul Kriese, and Steven W. Angell (Philadelphia: Quaker Press, 2011), 55.
[21] Stafford, *Writing the Australian Crawl*, 43.

States and around the world. When asked why he became a CO, he replied that he had always been one; he wondered at all the people who had opted, against their former opposition to war, to enlist.[22]

Stafford has been identified as Quaker. Indeed, throughout Stafford's poetry and essays is Quaker vocabulary of messages, leadings, and listening. For instance, to illustrate his aim in writing, he once said, "Think of a person centered in a life and ready to follow leads into creating something."[23] This slight sentence may be read as thoroughly Quaker: "centering down" describes how Quakers ready themselves for worship by seeking a calm, quiet, and receptive attitude. "Leadings" refers to God-given guidance in a particular direction, typically toward an ethical stance.[24] "Creative" is a term used repeatedly by Quakers to denote the moral possibility that emerges from right practice, particularly noncooperation and nonviolence. Quakers are not alone, of course, in advocating for "creative" responses to social and political injustice; Gandhi used the term "experimental" to describe his forays into new kinds of activism, and Americans who emulated him adopted it also.[25] But it is distinctly Quaker to have faith in the possibilities of creating new things, including new ways of being, as a result of listening, waiting, and paying attention to others and to God.[26]

Stafford neither affirmed nor denied a particular religious identity. For example, in an interview with a Quaker journal, when asked if he were Quaker, Stafford said, "That's as good a way as any to identify me," and confirmed that he and his wife had often attended Quaker meeting

---

[22]Stafford, *The Answers*, 26.
[23]Stafford, *The Answers*, 39.
[24]Jackie Leach Scully, "Quakers and Ethics," in *The Oxford Handbook of Quaker Studies*, ed. Stephen W. Angell and Pink Dandelion (Oxford: Oxford University Press, 2013), 538.
[25]Azaransky, *Worldwide Struggle*, 94.
[26]It is distinctly but not exclusively Quaker. Other kinds of religious writers have extolled the virtues of attention and waiting; see, for example, Simone Weil, *Waiting for God* (New York: Harper Classics, 2009), and "Attention and Will," in *Gravity and Grace* (New York: Routledge Classics, 2002), 116-22.

for worship (though he was not a member of the meeting; this is one more way Stafford's example has resonated with me: I attend but am not a member of my local meeting). He admitted that "wider Quaker fellowship would be more accurate than any other label." Stafford underscored how the word *quiet* appeared frequently in his poems, likely because he felt that only in conditions of quiet might he apprehend the "still small voice," a phrase Quakers commonly use to describe how silence may enable people to perceive how God or Spirit is at work in the world.[27]

Stafford's refusal to embrace or confirm his denominational identity may have been one more way for him to clear space to see and hear what was truly of God. In a lovely, small poem titled "On a Church Lawn," Stafford credits dandelions with theological insight: "They surround a church and outside the window / utter their deaf little cry: 'If you listen / well, music won't have to happen.'" The dandelions, "little light saviors," announce, "God is not big; He is right."[28] Stafford worries what churchgoers miss when they do not listen well, when their faith is not as discerning as a dandelion's.

Stafford's primary faith seems to be in the capacity of people to come to know themselves and in the power of daily practice to develop new viewpoints. Stafford was once asked why his poetry struck such a different tone from his contemporaries', including the so-called confessional poets such as Sylvia Plath, John Berryman, and Anne Sexton, who wrote often about sin and evil. Stafford replied, perhaps surprisingly, that he believed "even the conviction of sin is too presumptuous for a human being."[29] Certainly Stafford knew about sin, he who had refused to cooperate in the war, he who had protested racism in the

---

[27]David Elliott, "A Priest of the Imagination," *Friends Journal*, November 1991, 27.
[28]Stafford, "On a Church Lawn," in *Stories That Could Be True*, 14.
[29]Stafford, *Writing the Australian Crawl*, 130.

1930s. Yet in his poetry he resisted "the repeating of formulas already arrived at by others." In an interview about the role of Christian values in his poetry, Stafford ventured that "if you simply assert something, you are likely to forget a reader, a worthy reader, needs not just your random speaking out, but an experience of sharing the source of values, the evidence for values, the adventures inherent in the finding and maintaining of values."[30] Stafford practiced listening in his daily writing and modeled it in his published work. Instead of telling his readers what to think, Stafford used "quiet forensics" in his poems, for its value "over the loud kind, is that it incorporates those silences and gives each side a time to think. The silences are important."[31]

Listening also guided his teaching. In listening to his students, Stafford developed a pedagogy of accompaniment, in which he was a reader who could give responses and ask questions. Instead of acting as an authority from on high, Stafford encouraged a solidarity with his students in their shared endeavor of coming to know themselves and in making meaning. "I began to treat each encounter with a student as an occasion for learning as well as possible where the student was," Stafford said, "but this procedure required my listening in class or in conference, and my readiness to adjust my next move as a result of what I found out." Stafford's teaching was connected also to his pacifism, for, he insisted, "imposing my will on language—or on a student, or on the citizens of a country—was not my style. I wanted to disappear as teacher, as writer, as citizen—be 'the quiet of the land,' as we used to designate ourselves in CO camps."[32]

Throughout his writing Stafford underscored the moral and literary significance of encounter with experience, and he encouraged this disposition in his students. As a teacher of writing, Stafford minimized

---

[30]Stafford, *You Must Revise*, 68.
[31]Stafford, *You Must Revise*, 61.
[32]Stafford, *You Must Revise*, 21.

praise, blame, and other typical forms of evaluation. He wanted students to learn to write out of their own practice of listening, of sensing impulses and following little nudges. While criticism of form or technique could certainly derail a student who was making early forays into finding her voice, Stafford worried that praise could also hinder her development, for a student might learn from it to write toward the teacher's goals for what constituted good writing. By resisting praise and blame, Stafford tried to nurture in his students the equanimity to enable understanding and justice work: "I'm trying to locate . . . that condition of a being who is not distorted from the receptive, accurate encounter with experience." In a metaphor for what he wanted for himself and his students, he affirmed how "an individual's intellect and emotions should be like a good seismograph: sensitive enough to register what happens but strong enough not to be wrecked by the first little things that happen. . . . So I just try to get into the readiness and be receptive, not stampeded, not overly trustful."[33] Stafford sought sensitivity in himself and his students so they might apprehend themselves, in spite of sociopolitical tumult, in the midst of the vastness of creation. Stafford's writing practice, his daily ritual of listening and waiting, was a way to ready himself so that he might understand what the world was actually like and what his place was in it.

HISTORY: THERE MAY BE GREATER THINGS THAN CIVILIZATION

Stafford did not trust dominant versions of the past, and he admonished Americans to broaden their sense of history. When he was a CO, Stafford experienced firsthand the martial nature of authoritative versions of American history, the way they accepted and encouraged war. Our historiographical imagination is anemic in who we presume to be heroes,

---

[33]Stafford, *You Must Revise*, 79.

and we neglect to chart absence of conflict. In "At the Un-national Monument Along the Canadian Border," Stafford quietly commemorates how "no people killed—or were killed—on this ground / hallowed by neglect an air so tame / that people celebrate it by forgetting its name."[34] Stafford advocates versions of the past that offer alternatives to history as a nationalizing force.

Stafford's poems broaden and deepen American history to centuries before European settlers arrived. Depicting Native American communities' engagement with each other and the land, and later with European terror, Stafford calls on White Americans to see our occupation of the United States as merely one moment in a much larger historical drama. "There is even a sense" in Stafford's poems "that the fastmoving European way may only be a passing thing," writes Robert Bly, poet and dear friend to Stafford.[35] In this way Stafford implicitly questions Euro-American ways of life and wonders whether they ought to be preserved. Stafford's attitude calls on us to be clear on why we are committed to maintaining our ways of life, to be clear on what our commitments are. When describing how he approached his morning writing, the openness he aspired to foster in himself, he once said, "I do not have any commitments, just opportunities," for his aim was "not the learning of methods, not the broadening of culture, not even the preserving of civilization (there may be greater things than civilization)."[36] His parenthetical, sly and astute, catches a reader off guard and stimulates moral imagination so that she thinks beyond what would seem to have been an outer limit. If we are not preserving this civilization, what else might be possible?

Stafford's venture that there may be greater things than civilization anticipates what Jane Anna Gordon and Lewis Gordon have called the

---

[34]Stafford, *Every War*, 87.
[35]Robert Bly, "William Stafford and the Golden Thread," *American Poetry Review* 23, no. 1 (January/February 1994): 19.
[36]Stafford, *Writing the Australian Crawl*, 22.

"pedagogical imperative," that "teaching and learning requires the constant articulation of reality's vastness."[37] They situate this imperative as emerging importantly from Black studies, where professors have undertaken to teach what "dominant educators claimed either did not exist or wasn't relevant."[38] Jane Anna Gordon underscores the ethical significance of a kind of scholarship that "treats people as ends rather than as means, or with dignity."[39] Stafford's writing and teaching share this moral commitment to treat readers and students as ends in themselves, as worthy of attention.[40] Stafford's ongoing practice of listening was also then a way to resist narcissism. It was a way, in Jane Anna Gordon's terms, to bring "the world . . . more fully into view," so he might sense his place in the vastness of creation.[41] To treat a student as an end in herself means valuing her as a person and not merely as a future worker and consumer. Stafford and Gordon share a commitment that their teaching counter dominant ways of understanding, prevalent epistemological frames, that leave hierarchy and exploitation uninterrogated.

---

[37] Lewis R. Gordon, "Theory in Black: Teleological Suspensions in Philosophy of Culture," *Qui Parle* 18, no. 1 (Spring/Summer 2010): 203.

[38] Lewis R. Gordon and Jane Anna Gordon, "Introduction: On Working Through a Most Difficult Terrain," in *A Companion to African-American Studies*, ed. Lewis R. Gordon and Jane Anna Gordon (New York: Blackwell, 2005), xxii.

[39] Jane Anna Gordon, "Beyond Anti-elitism: Black Studies and the Pedagogical Imperative," *Review of Education, Pedagogy, and Cultural Studies* 32, no. 2 (Spring 2010): 137.

[40] Most of us who teach would likely (or at least, like to!) see ourselves in the call to treat students as ends in themselves. Yet the Gordons' and Stafford's critiques should encourage us all to lay bare what education is for. From the perspective of Black studies, for example, the challenge is to create kinds of content and pedagogy that do not reinscribe racial domination and economic exploitation that sustain the status quo in the United States. Inherent in Black studies is the challenge to create different kinds of knowledge, different ways of learning that resist dominant and dominating values. Similarly, Stafford is suspicious of teaching that endorses dominant views of history that empower a national project that depends on war. The Gordons' appeal to Kant's categorical imperative—that we are to treat people always as ends in themselves, never as mere means—is also simultaneously tongue-in-cheek and reclaiming of an ethical tradition that was imbricated in Kant's highly influential "anthropological" assertions of racial hierarchy. For example, see James Samuel Logan, "Immanuel Kant on Categorical Imperative," in *Beyond the Pale: Reading Ethics from the Margins*, ed. Stacey Floyd-Thomas and Miguel de la Torre (Louisville, KY: Westminster John Knox, 2011), 69-80.

[41] Jane Anna Gordon, "Beyond Anti-elitism," 137.

Understanding our place in the world is particularly crucial for White professors and White students, whose enjoyment of unearned power and privilege may dissuade them from confronting violence abetted by structural sin.⁴² If we want to generate the moral insight necessary to practice nonviolence, to be countercultural, it matters *whose* insights we prioritize. For those of us who research and teach in universities and seminaries, this is about whom and what we write, about how we teach. Some ways of teaching, some focus of study, may get us closer to what Stafford called the "hidden meanings written closely / inside the skins of things."⁴³ Stafford was not naive that this was difficult work. Dominant patterns of social power make compelling cases for what is right and good, who is authoritative. These dominant patterns, as well as atrocity and violence in every corner of the world, can overwhelm us. But we can develop better understanding of ourselves and our communities with insight from better sources.

And yet a greater likelihood is that many of us don't understand ourselves because we live in an "invented delusional world," one of the many ways philosopher Charles Mills describes "white supremacy" as the "unnamed political system that has made the modern world what it is today."⁴⁴ Now more than twenty years old, Mills's account in *The Racial Contract* becomes more urgent by the day: we live in a "cognitive and moral economy" premised on "white misunderstanding, misrepresentation, evasion and self-deception."⁴⁵ For people like me, then, a White professor who researches and teaches, the work is to listen to many others who know more than I do so that I learn to see myself more clearly and undertake work that is more just, that is accountable to my students and their humanity.

---

⁴²As Christian ethicist Cristina Traina asserts, "Those who have the most to gain from leaving [structural evil] undisturbed see it least." Cristina L. H. Traina, "'This Is the Year': Narratives of Structural Evil," *Journal of the Society of Christian Ethics* 37, no. 2 (2017): 5.
⁴³William Stafford, "Sophocles Says," in *Stories That Could Be True*, 144.
⁴⁴Charles M. Mills, *The Racial Contract* (Ithaca, NY: Cornell University Press, 1997), 1, 18.
⁴⁵Mills, *Racial Contract*, 19.

William Stafford provides us with a model of how to listen: a cornerstone of nonviolence must be a consistent contemplative practice that helps us understand ourselves in light of our location to existing social structures and that readies us to be in right relationship. Stafford's writing practice affirms the integral connection between an individual's spiritual practice and her capacity to analyze and work to dismantle structural injustice.

LIVING NEXT DOOR TO THE BRONZE LADY

Michael Jimenez

*Where are you going, Bronze Lady, with your
quick blue sky and slow shepherd's staff?*

EUNICE ODIO

THE FIRST ACADEMIC CONFERENCE I ever attended was in Bluffton, Ohio. Recently married to my wife Lluvia, we decided to fly together for a weekend trip. Luckily, I asked my wife to join me since there were only about four other people there to hear my paper. This was my first experience with a truly small-town atmosphere in the United States outside of California. We walked around the town, admiring the photos of the cheerleaders and soccer and football players in the windows of the local supermarket, diner, and other businesses. We thought the whole place was just quaint. On Friday night, it looked like the entire community left their homes and walked to the stadium to attend the football game.

That night we got lost heading back to our hotel since we decided to check out the local mall, which I recall featured a Sears. These were the days when you printed out your map from MapQuest before hitting the road and did not simply listen to the directions from the voice coming from your smartphone. We were surrounded by fields with no lights around. It was pitch-black. We were totally out of our element. Luckily, my wife had the patience to navigate us back to the route home. However, no matter how lost we were, I never felt in danger.

My paper for my tiny audience was about welcoming the other. I opened with a discussion of the recent harassment of Latin American immigrants in the American Southwest. Then I used the theology of the neighbor by Protestant theologian Karl Barth and the philosophy of hospitality by French postmodern thinker Jacques Derrida to make the case for openness to the "non-American other."[1] This paper was an effort to engage with the ideas of the theorists I was learning about in my studies.

In retrospect, I see a problem in attempting to address the issue of immigration without once quoting someone from Latin America. Never mind the lack of discussion of anyone from the United States either. This problem has a name: *Eurocentrism*. Nothing against Europe, but those of us who take the plunge into higher education often spend most of our time studying solely the works of Europeans.

Our fixation on writings from another place hampers our ability to hear the voices next door, especially if they speak Spanish. Groups of people are made to feel separate even though they grow up with each other. Rigid isolation showcases an attitude very different from hospitality and neighborliness. Barth, without thinking about the Americas, talks about how languages have the power to unite rather than divide.[2] Learning the language and culture of another person is a way to build

---

[1] See Jacques Derrida, *On Cosmopolitanism and Forgiveness*, trans. Mark Dooley and Michael Hughes (New York: Routledge, 2001). See also Michael Jimenez, *Remembering Lived Lives: A Historiography from the Underside of Modernity* (Eugene, OR: Cascade, 2017), 32-47, for an analysis of Barth's concept of the far and near neighbor.
[2] See Jimenez, *Remembering Lived Lives*, 35.

bridges in the community. In fact, this reminds me of how Mexican-American author Richard Rodriguez describes English as the public language and Spanish as the private language, which reinforces the idea that Spanish is a *foreign* language.[3] The problem with Rodriguez's binary logic is that Spanish has been spoken for centuries on American soil—it is not historically foreign. Even if we buy into the nationalist myth, what actually prevents us from learning the language of our neighbors? The pragmatic solution is a commitment to recognizing that Spanish was, is, and will be a public language in the United States.

Barth's and Derrida's theories are fine for their time and place. They appeal to ideas we are familiar with and ideas we define as Western values. However, the roots of their ideas flow out of a European social-historical context that is somewhat foreign to the Americas. There are contemporary writers from all over the Americas who better understand their historical situation. My paper's fatal flaw was that I was discussing an Americas problem but did not include anybody from the Americas! My own paper is an unfortunate example what is typical of academia, including Christian academic institutions.

For example, philosophically inclined Christian theologians frequently advocate their choice of thinker as a corrective to what they determine to be a deficiency within the churches. Whether it is classical modern masters of suspicion Marx, Freud, and Nietzsche or the postmodern options Foucault, Lyotard, and Derrida, there seems to be an attempt to use these mostly anti-Christian voices against their own wishes—as a soft critique meant to make churches more Christlike. Reader, let's take Derrida to church on Sunday, they suggest.

Appealing to Derrida or someone like Barth is fine. What is missing is an insistence on taking seriously contemporary American figures

---

[3] See Richard Rodriguez, *Hunger of Memory: The Education of Richard Rodriguez* (New York: Bantam, 1983).

within the church. For example, Martin Luther King Jr. is often quoted but seldom read (especially his lesser known non-"Dream" speeches). Rather than the latest imported French intellectual, what would it mean to take Cesar Chavez or Dolores Huerta to church? Given the current sociopolitical turmoil surrounding migration of our neighbors and the violence that often fuels their movement, what would it mean to actually read writers from Latin America?

LITERATURE TEACHES US HISTORY

> *Terror is the given of the place.*
> JOAN DIDION

One of the major ways of addressing twentieth-century Latin American history is through literature, especially the magical realism best seen in the work of Gabriel García Márquez and Isabel Allende. In Latin America, writers are celebrities. Europeans and North Americans read and enjoy their stories. Some of the literature has a historical streak where, in short, the writer creates a fictional account out of a historical narrative. This is a dynamic way to learn about the ups and downs of Latin American history and culture. A common type of this historical fiction is the "dictator novel."

A quick glance at a sample list of famous books that focus just on Rafael Trujillo, one of the most famous dictators of Latin America, illustrates the popularity of this form of writing: Mario Vargas Llosa's *The Feast of the Goat*, Junot Díaz's *The Brief Wondrous Life of Oscar Wao*, and Julia Alvarez's *In the Time of the Butterflies* are just a few examples. Literature has a robust way of conveying the fear and violence associated with living under the Trujillo regime. It is much better than a thirty-second remark in a world civilization class. And yet many of my students have never been exposed to Latin American history or literature.

Leave it to the American writer Joan Didion, one of the masters of New Journalism, to rely on Gabriel García Márquez's *The Autumn of the Patriarch* to make sense of the military dictatorship in El Salvador.[4] She finds the bloody violence incomprehensible, so she relies on what she knows best: fiction. Maybe more bureaucrats in the Reagan administration should have read Latin American novelists to gain an understanding of the shady characters they were dealing with.

The United States has its different schools of philosophy and its own great novelists, but to be perfectly honest, they are often found lounging around in the shade of Europe's shadow. Even the most American of our novelists, Hemingway and Fitzgerald, fled to Europe to master their craft after World War I.

Like Didion, we can pick up a translated novel by one of the Latin American masters to gain insight into the situation down south, where the banana trees sway in the tropical breeze. Yet how many of us have Didion's attention span to read the Latin American boom novels, applying them as a lens to the historical situation?

LITERATURE, THE SALVADORAN CIVIL WAR, AND DRUG VIOLENCE

The whole story is an absurd, circular nightmare.
VALERIA LUISELLI

The Salvadoran Civil War should be a great historical-theological moment, one of the most important international tragedies of recent memory. Alas, it is not. Oscar Romero, four American nuns, Ignacio Ellacuria, and Jon Sobrino give us a picture of the liberating Christ from inside a hellish war zone in the backyard of the United States. Our

---

[4]Joan Didion, *Salvador* (New York: Vintage, 1983), 52-59.

country was, in fact, indirectly responsible. Many do not know. Many do not care.

The United States supported the brutal military dictatorship in El Salvador for the sake of anticommunism. Didion described El Salvador as the most dangerous, terrifying place she had ever seen. These were not just the words of a frightened writer from Sacramento. This was real terror.

I grew up in the 1980s, the era of North American evangelical culture end times videos. The scenario of a violent future attack based simply on our belief in Jesus Christ hung over our heads constantly. This fiction played out on many a TV screen in Christian youth group rooms across the United States, portraying a dystopian nightmare. Simultaneously, real violence and terror were being executed on Christians in El Salvador. It was the last stages of the communist utopian failure of the twentieth century. Didion learned this lesson well. She came to the conclusion that "I must understand: the Church was dangerous," because it was perceived as linked with the socialist dream.[5] The wars in El Salvador represent the most violent examples of terror in the United States' backyard (see the story of El Mozote if you want the most infamous spectacle).[6] Derrida's language of hospitality and Barth's language of neighborliness do not extend to this region in a way that fits the historical situation.

Salvadoran civil war violence transformed in the blink of an eye to international gang violence. After the fall of the Soviet Union in the early 1990s, support for communist-sponsored guerilla wars fell by the wayside. However, the violence of this region prepared it to inherit the drug wars.

---

[5] Didion, *Salvador*, 78.
[6] Didion, *Salvador*, 37. See Mark Danner, *The Massacre at El Mozote* (New York: Vintage, 1994) for the most famous study of this event.

Mexican novelist Valeria Luiselli gives a succinct account of the current drug war situation.[7] She narrows in on a subject matter invisible in these types of stories: children. Young boys and girls are often forced to enlist in one of the rival drug gangs at the point of a pistol. One particular teenage boy's harrowing story made an impact on Luiselli. Spoiler alert: the plot twist of the story is that when she checks up on this boy, who was approved for asylum in the United States, he informs her that the same gang that harassed him in Honduras, murdered his friend, and forced him to run for his life to the US border is now antagonizing him at school in New York. So exactly how big do we make that wall?

Nobody claims that politics isn't a messy business. The past century has seen utopian dreams transform into dystopian nightmares. When religion enters the political arena, it often claims to represent the voice of the innocent. Who will speak up for the right of life if those who believe we are all made in God's image are suddenly silent? Real flesh-and-blood kids are fleeing one war zone only to arrive in another. Luiselli poignantly declares, "Children chase after life, even if that chase might end up killing them. Children run and flee."[8] The heightened screams of anti-immigration in the United States betray a long history of nostalgic nativism that privileges only those they approve of as neighbors. Who is speaking up for their right to life?

When the threat of communism loomed over the planet, the United States exerted its will over the globe. Now with ubiquitous drug and gang violence, US voices want to retreat behind a wall. Luiselli declares the reality of our globalized world: "It's urgent that we begin talking about the drug war as a hemispheric war, at least—one that begins in the Great

---

[7]Valeria Luiselli, *Tell Me How It Ends: An Essay in Forty Questions* (Minneapolis: Coffee House Press, 2017), 70-83.
[8]Luiselli, *Tell Me How It Ends*, 19.

Lakes of the northern United States and ends in the mountains of Celaque in southern Honduras."[9] It is a great feat of the imagination when we in the United States can, like Pontius Pilate, wash our hands of problems that originate in our own backyard. There would be no drug gang violence without US drug consumers. What exactly does Bluffton, Ohio, have to do with Celaque, Honduras?

THE LAND OF THE KENNEDYS AND CHAVEZ

Nonviolence supports you if you have a just and moral cause.
CESAR CHAVEZ

I became interested in Latin American/Hispanic theology at the tail end of my doctoral work. One of the tricky parts of this is that I was raised Protestant and still identify as one, while much of Hispanic theology has its roots in Roman Catholicism. In addition, each country and each writer has a particular story, a particular frame of reference. In other words, one cannot read a single theologian from Peru or El Salvador and take that work to represent all of Latin America.

Recently I visited Costa Rica with my father, who was born and raised there. One part of the tour that surprised me was the discussion of President John F. Kennedy's visit to San Jose in 1963, specifically to El Teatro Nacional de Costa Rica. It was a monumental event for the country, symbolized by the naming of a nearby park after him. This story has a personal dimension as well. While the tour guide showed the group a picture of the youthful and energetic US president confidently entering the theater gates, my dad turned to me and said, "I was there that day. I remember everything the tour guide is saying." Even the minute detail of volcanic ash from a recent eruption lying on the shoulders of JFK's

---

[9]Luiselli, *Tell Me How It Ends*, 86.

coat was not lost to my father's memory. More importantly, during his visit Kennedy granted the type of visas that would eventually lead my father to come to the United States in 1968. In Costa Rica, JFK represents a president who practiced diplomacy and neighborliness with at least one Latin American country.

Kennedy actually joked that, based on the enthusiasm with which he was greeted in Costa Rica, if he could have brought Costa Ricans, or "Ticos," to Ohio, he might have won that state in the election. Did he really say "Ohio"? I wonder how welcoming the community I visited in Bluffton, Ohio, would have been to a bunch of Ticos.

There is something to the Kennedy magic in Latinx history. The most famous Latino in US history is arguably Cesar Chavez. He is best known for being a labor organizer for farm workers in California. He openly admitted that all the success he gained in activism was due to his spirituality and his commitment to nonviolent protest. At one crucial point in the labor strike, he fasted for twenty-five days for his own sins, for the collective sins of the farm workers, and to recommit the movement to nonviolence. The fast ended with a visit from Senator Robert F. Kennedy, who took Mass along with Chavez for what was the most famous photo-op of the farm workers movement. Those who were closest to Chavez noted the sincerity of his core beliefs. Why did he choose nonviolence as a principle, especially at a time when it seemed a bit passé? Chavez declared, "I am not a nonviolent man. I am a violent man who is trying to be nonviolent."[10] This was a common response he gave about nonviolence throughout his life. It was through the spiritual practices of his Christian faith that he had any success. This is what RFK celebrated with him. Robert Kennedy would be murdered by violence just like his brother Jack. The assassin's bullet is a fixture in the history books

---

[10] Mario T. García, ed., *The Gospel of César Chávez: My Faith in Action* (New York: Sheed & Ward, 2007), 64.

of 1968, the year my father came to the United States. Violence is on both sides of the wall. Always has been. Probably always will be.

Chavez was accused of being a communist, which was a common threat to anyone challenging the status quo. This scenario was true in both North and South America, with the horror of the Vietnam War becoming the proverbial egg on the United States' face. As Didion's husband, John Gregory Dunne, who was covering the Delano grape strike, pointed out, "It was Robert Kennedy who legitimated Chavez."[11] These charges of communism retreat as nonsense into history, and now in California and throughout the United States large groups of people celebrate Cesar Chavez's birthday on March 31 as a commemorative holiday. However, he may in the future also be little studied. Of course, it made good political sense at the time for the Kennedy brothers to reach out to the Latinx community both inside and outside US borders. It unfortunately does not seem so commonsense nowadays to extend the open arms of hospitality. Are we now betraying the sense of civic and spiritual unity symbolized in the Mass between Kennedy and Chavez?

Sometimes, every now and then, a Tico travels to the United States, the land of the Kennedys and Chavez. The poet Eunice Odio memorialized her time here with a poem about the Statue of Liberty called "The Bronze Lady."[12] Her words have tragic beauty that speaks to many travelers' experiences. There is something about US ideals of democracy and liberty that many in the Americas find fascinating. However, the inconsistencies of these ideals in our practices are troubling. Still, throughout all of the ups and downs of history, we remain neighbors. The Kennedy

---

[11] John Gregory Dunne, *Delano: The Story of the California Grape Strike* (Berkeley: University of California Press, 2008), 181.

[12] Eunice Odio, *Territory of Dawn: The Selected Poems of Eunice Odio*, trans. Keith Ekiss, Sonia P. Ticas, and Mauricio Espinoza (New York: Bitter Oleander Press, 2016), 98-103. The book includes both the Spanish original and the English translation. Odio is one of the major Costa Rican writers to be translated into English.

brothers, Chavez, and Odio were not perfect people by a longshot. Neighbors can sometimes be upsetting and messy. We sometimes find the violence we hear about in one region of the Americas suddenly in our own front yard. No one demagogue can magically make it go away, no matter what kind of protection he or she promises.

The neighborhood of the Americas is diverse and rich. It is important for us in the United States to start treating it this way rather than with the paternalism it is usually known for. Perhaps we will begin to be good neighbors and learn about the various cultures that surround us rather than retreating behind a wall of ignorance. And maybe we'll stop being so Eurocentric in academia and begin reading writers from the Americas—both North and South.

A UNIVERSAL LOVE ETHIC

NONVIOLENCE AND HUMAN RIGHTS ADVOCACY

Shawn Graves

THERE ARE COMPELLING REASONS for thinking that the fundamental moral imperative is to love everyone without exception. The moral mandate is universal, fully inclusive love. Given the theological claims they hold, Christians in particular have additional reasons for embracing a universal love ethic. As Howard Thurman writes, "The religion of Jesus makes the love-ethic central."[1] In this essay, I'll begin with some clarifying comments about the nature of love within the context of a universal love ethic. Next, I'll present and briefly explain an argument to support a universal love ethic. Finally, I'll offer brief references to some examples of how a universal love ethic has motivated and fueled nonviolent human and civil rights advocacy.

---

[1] Howard Thurman, *Jesus and the Disinherited* (Boston: Beacon, 1976), 89. For textual support from the New Testament, see Mt 22:34-40; Mk 12:28-31; Lk 10:25-28; see also Rom 13:8-10; Gal 5:13-14; Jas 2:8; 1 Jn 4:7-12.

A UNIVERSAL LOVE ETHIC: THE NATURE OF LOVE

The language of love is found in a wide variety of contexts. For example, people use "love" to describe their posture toward romantic partners, family members, friends, neighbors, fellow faith adherents, colleagues, celebrities, cultural icons, religious leaders, political figures, companion animals, countries, cities, neighborhoods, workplaces, professions, theories, frameworks, systems and ideologies, restaurants, museums, shopping centers, sports and leisure activities, music, the visual and performing arts, movies, series, shows, food, sports teams, technology, gadgets, and trinkets. And it's not at all clear that "love" is picking out the same thing in each of those occurrences. If one insisted that one meant exactly the same thing—was referring to exactly the same posture—when one uttered "I love my family" and "I love strawberry jam," one would no doubt cause considerable confusion and face searing scrutiny, at least from one's family. Consequently, it's worth exploring briefly here what "love" means within the context of a love ethic.

We can get some direction from the relevant literature, from which a few common themes emerge. Martin Luther King Jr. states, "The meaning of love is not to be confused with some sentimental outpouring. Love is something much deeper than emotional bosh."[2] For assistance, King goes to the Greek language, noting the distinction between *eros*, *philia*, and *agape*. King opts for *agape*:

> The third word is *agape*, understanding and creative, redemptive goodwill for all men. . . . When Jesus bids us to love our enemies, he is speaking neither of *eros* nor *philia*; he is speaking of *agape*, understanding and creative, redemptive goodwill for all men.[3]

---

[2]Martin Luther King Jr., "Loving Your Enemies," in *Strength to Love* (Minneapolis: Fortress, 2010), 46.
[3]King, "Loving Your Enemies," 46-47.

In the same vein, Thomas Merton writes, "Love seeks one thing only: the good of the one loved.... To love another is to will what is really good for him."[4] Thomas Oord claims that "to love is to act intentionally, in sympathetic/empathetic response to others... to promote overall well-being."[5] Nicholas Wolterstorff contends, "The understanding of love that we need... is an understanding of love as seeking both to promote the good in a person's life and to secure that she be treated as befits her worth."[6] C. S. Lewis asserts,

> He communicates to men a share of His own Gift-love. This is different from the Gift-loves he has built into their nature. These never quite seek simply the good of the loved object for the object's own sake. They are biased in favor of those goods they can themselves bestow, or those which they would like best themselves, or those which fit in with a pre-conceived picture of the life they would want the object to lead. But Divine Gift-love—Love Himself working in a man—is wholly disinterested and desires what is simply best for the beloved.[7]

Elsewhere, Lewis adds, "Love is not affectionate feeling, but a steady wish for the loved person's ultimate good as far as it can be obtained."[8]

Others provide similar insights on the nature of love within the context of a love ethic or love command. William Frankena, in discussing a love ethic, claims, "The clearest and most plausible view, in my opinion, is to identify the law of love with what I have called the principle of benevolence, that is, of doing good."[9] Eleonore Stump, following Thomas Aquinas, offers, "On Aquinas's account of the nature of

---

[4]Thomas Merton, *No Man Is an Island* (Boston: Shambhala, 1955), 3.
[5]Thomas Oord, *Defining Love: A Philosophical, Scientific, and Theological Engagement* (Grand Rapids, MI: Brazos, 2010), 29.
[6]Nicholas Wolterstorff, *Justice in Love* (Grand Rapids, MI: Eerdmans, 2011), 93.
[7]C. S. Lewis, *The Four Loves* (New York: Harcourt Brace, 1960), 128.
[8]C. S. Lewis, "Answers to Questions on Christianity," in *God in the Dock: Essays on Theology and Ethics*, ed. Walter Hooper (Grand Rapids, MI: Eerdmans, 1970), 49.
[9]William Frankena, *Ethics*, Foundations of Philosophy Series, ed. Elizabeth and Monroe Beardsley (Englewood Cliffs, NJ: Prentice-Hall, 1963), 44.

love, love requires two interconnected desires: (1) the desire for the good of the beloved, and (2) the desire for union with the beloved."[10] Frances Howard-Snyder asserts,

> To tell someone to love his neighbor is, among other things, to tell him to care about his neighbor's welfare, and to give that neighbor's welfare a fairly significant place in his system of priorities. The commandment implies, then, behavior which results, or can reasonably be expected to result, in improvements in the welfare of others.[11]

She adds that "it makes sense that our love for other people should not be simply benevolence or sheer concern for their well-being, but should also involve desires to be related to them, and an appreciation of what is valuable in them, and enjoyment of them."[12] Jim Forest remarks,

> As used in the Bible, love has first of all to do with action and responsibility, not about your emotions or liking someone. To love is to do what you can to provide for the well-being of another whether you like that person or not.[13]

According to Harry Frankfurt,

> As with every type of love, the heart of it is that the lover cares about the good of his beloved for its own sake. He is disinterestedly concerned to protect and pursue the true interests of the person whom he loves.[14]

Moreover, bell hooks gives us the following:

> I spent years searching for a meaningful definition of the word "love," and was deeply relieved when I found one in psychiatrist M. Scott

---

[10]Eleonore Stump, "The Nature of Love," in *Wandering in Darkness: Narrative and the Problem of Suffering* (Oxford: Clarendon Press, 2010), 91.
[11]Frances Howard-Snyder, "Christianity and Ethics," in *Reason for the Hope Within*, ed. Michael J. Murray (Grand Rapids, MI: Eerdmans, 1999), 391.
[12]Howard-Snyder, "Christianity and Ethics," 387-88.
[13]Jim Forest, *Loving Our Enemies: Reflections on the Hardest Commandment* (Maryknoll, NY: Orbis, 2014), 14.
[14]Harry Frankfurt, *The Reasons of Love* (Princeton, NJ: Princeton University Press, 2004), 85.

Peck's classic self-help book *The Road Less Traveled*, first published in 1978. Echoing the work of Erich Fromm, he defines love as "the will to extend one's self for the purpose of nurturing one's own or another's spiritual growth."[15]

We get additional comments touching on similar themes. John Rawls tells us, "Now love clearly has among its main elements the desire to advance the other person's good as this person's rational self-love would require."[16] Elsewhere Rawls adds, "In general, to love another means not only to be concerned for his wants and needs, but to affirm his sense of the worth of his own person."[17] Martha Nussbaum comments, "When we love people, we want to be good to them, and this typically means being better than we sometimes, even usually, are."[18] On Robert Nozick's account, "What is common to all love is this: Your own well-being is tied up with that of someone (or something) you love."[19] And Alan Soble remarks, "A quite ordinary (and true) thought is that when *x* loves *y*, *x* wishes the best for *y* and acts, as far as he or she is able, to pursue the good for *y*."[20] Finally, J. David Velleman elaborates:

> In my view, appreciation for someone's value as a person is not distinct from loving him: it is the evaluative core of love. I do not mean that love is a value judgment to the effect that the beloved has final value as an end in himself. Love is rather an appreciative response to the perception of that value. And I mean "perception" literally: the people we love are the ones whom we succeed in *perceiving* as persons, within some of the human organisms milling about us. . . . A sense of wonder

---

[15]bell hooks, *All About Love: New Visions* (New York: William Morrow, 2018), 4.
[16]John Rawls, *A Theory of Justice* (Cambridge, MA: Harvard University Press, 1971), 190.
[17]Rawls, *Theory of Justice*, 464.
[18]Martha Nussbaum, *Political Emotions: Why Love Matters for Justice* (Cambridge, MA: Belknap, 2013), 384.
[19]Robert Nozick, "Love's Bond," in *The Examined Life: Philosophical Meditations* (New York: Simon & Schuster, 1989), 68.
[20]Alan Soble, "Union, Autonomy, and Concern," in *Love Analyzed*, ed. Roger E. Lamb (Boulder, CO: Westview, 1997), 65.

at the vividly perceived reality of another person is, in my view, the essence of love.[21]

Velleman continues, "I have tried to describe the feeling of love by saying that it is an arresting awareness of value, similar to other arresting responses such as wonder and awe, and that it arrests our emotional defenses, so that it results in an opening of the heart."[22] We "have to *see* the person in him,"[23] "see *someone there*,"[24] as Velleman puts it, and space within us is created for the other. Commenting on Jesus' command to love our enemies, including our political enemies, Howard Thurman notes, "To love the Roman meant first to lift him out of the general classification of enemy. The Roman had to emerge as a person."[25] Marlena Graves draws the connection between our desire for love and being seen as follows:

> We all, every one of us, want our God-given dignity affirmed by others. We want to receive attention. We want to be valued, appreciated, admired, and sought after. We want to feel cherished and adored—to be "in" with others. We want to know that our lives matter. We want to be loved.[26]

The unloved are the unseen, rendered invisible, cast to the margins where they can't be noticed. On being seen, one gets the sense that one is loved. No doubt this is why Hagar names God "the God Who Sees" (Gen 16:13 HCSB).[27] This is in line with Gustavo Gutierrez's observation: "The God of Jesus is none other than the God of the forgotten

---

[21]J. David Velleman, "Beyond Price," *Ethics* 118 (January 2008): 199.
[22]Velleman, "Beyond Price," 203.
[23]J. David Velleman, "*Really Seeing* Another," in Alex Voorhoeve, *Conversations on Ethics* (Oxford: Oxford University Press, 2011), 245.
[24]Velleman, "Beyond Price," 203.
[25]Howard Thurman, *Jesus and the Disinherited* (Boston: Beacon, 1976), 95.
[26]Marlena Graves, *A Beautiful Disaster: Finding Hope in the Midst of Brokenness* (Grand Rapids, MI: Brazos, 2014), 131.
[27]See Amy R. Buckley, "In the Midst of the Mess: Hagar and the God Who Sees," CBE International, June 5, 2013, www.cbeinternational.org/resource/article/mutuality-blog-magazine/midst-mess-hagar-and-god-who-sees.

and excluded, of those whom people want to silence."[28] Commenting on the plight of the poor, Dallas Willard states,

> The overarching biblical command is to love, and the first act of love is always the giving of attention. Therefore the poor are not to be avoided, forgotten, or allowed to become invisible. We are to *see* them as God's creatures, of equal significance with anyone else in the divine purpose.[29]

Rebecca Konyndyk DeYoung writes, "Couldn't knowing and acknowledging another *itself* be an expression of love? Attentiveness to others can be a gift that love expresses."[30] There's a good reason Bryan Stevenson emphasizes proximity. Speaking at Boston College, Stevenson asserts, "We cannot change global injustice today if we isolate ourselves on BC's campus, if we isolate ourselves in places that are safe and removed and disconnected. To change the world, we are each going to have to find ways to get closer to people who . . . are living on the margins of society."[31] And there's a good reason Terence Lester's book articulating his work with the poor and homeless is titled, *I See You: How Love Opens Our Eyes to Invisible People*.[32]

There are several things worth noting about these accounts of love. First, one clear theme that emerges from the above is the following: at minimum, when one loves another, one seeks to promote the flourishing of the beloved for the sake of the beloved. There is a striving and straining to see to it that things go well for the beloved, to improve the welfare or

---

[28]Gustavo Gutierrez, *Gustavo Gutierrez: Spiritual Writings*, ed. Daniel G. Groody (Maryknoll, NY: Orbis, 2011), 103.

[29]Dallas Willard, *The Spirit of the Disciplines: Understanding How God Changes Lives* (New York: HarperOne, 1988), 210.

[30]Rebecca Konyndyk DeYoung, *Vainglory: The Forgotten Vice* (Grand Rapids, MI: Eerdmans, 2014), 21.

[31]See Megan Kelly, "Stevenson Counsels 'Proximity' to the Marginalized," *The Heights*, October 14, 2019, www.bcheights.com/2019/10/14/stevenson-counsels-proximity-others.

[32]Terence Lester, *I See You: How Love Opens Our Eyes to Invisible People* (Downers Grove, IL: InterVarsity Press, 2019).

enhance the well-being of the beloved. When one loves another, one labors to ensure that the beloved has a genuinely good life.

If I claim to love another and yet I am hostile to or otherwise indifferent to their well-being, then I have demonstrated that my claim to love them is false. Hostility and indifference to well-being, even if packaged in pleasing language or accompanied by clever public relations and marketing campaigns, is antithetical to love. After all, "suppose a brother or a sister is without clothes and daily food. If one of you says to them, 'Go in peace; keep warm and well fed,' but does nothing about their physical needs, what good is it?" (Jas 2:15-17 NIV). If I claim to love another and yet any effort to promote, advance, improve, or sustain their ultimate good is easily and consistently outweighed or overwhelmed by other matters on my agenda, then I have significantly undermined my claim to love them. It would be cold comfort to Lazarus to hear that the rich man considered going out to the gate to attend to him but other matters kept coming up (Lk 16:19-22). If I claim to love another and yet have eyes only for how contributing to their welfare might serve to advance my own cause, then I have effectively negated my claim to love them. It is for my sake alone that I act, not theirs, and this is not the posture of love. If I claim to love another and yet my treatment of them when compared to my treatment of the rich and powerful is dismissive and degrading, then I make it clear that I do not love them. Such favoritism, while ubiquitous and typically regarded as savvy and strategic, runs counter to love (Jas 2:1-9).

So, as can be discerned from the above, loving another entails seeking to promote the beloved's flourishing. Second, it's worth rehearsing at this point, as noted above, that loving another does not entail liking the beloved. As Martin Luther King Jr. comments,

> Now we can see what Jesus meant when he said, "Love your enemies." We should be happy that he did not say, "Like your enemies." It is almost

impossible to like some people. "Like" is a sentimental and affectionate word. How can we be affectionate toward a person whose avowed aim is to crush our very being and place innumerable stumbling blocks in our path? How can we like a person who is threatening our children and bombing our homes? That is impossible. But Jesus recognized that *love* is greater than *like*.[33]

Nor, for that matter, does loving another entail a positive assessment of the beloved's character or behavior. Otherwise, given the reasonable assumption that we don't hold our enemies in high regard from the moral point of view, the very idea of loving one's enemies would make little sense.

Appealing to self-love may help make both these points clearer. There may be a great deal that I don't like about myself—various habits, idiosyncrasies, physical features, intellectual deficits, emotional tendencies, vices, personality traits, and so on—such that I confess to myself and others, in a moment of candor and vulnerability, that I really don't like myself. And I may grade myself quite poorly from the moral point of view as well, noting with dismay my vices and with regret the many times I've mistreated others and neglected to do the right thing for the right reasons. And yet, even in the face of all this—a strong dislike and harsh moral assessment—I may nevertheless persist in loving myself. C. S. Lewis puts it this way:

> How do you love yourself? When I look into my own mind, I find that I do not love myself by thinking myself a dear old chap or having affectionate feelings. I do not think I love myself because I am particularly good, but just because I am myself and quite apart from my character. I might detest something which I have done. Nevertheless, I do not cease to love myself.[34]

---

[33] King, "Loving Your Enemies," 46-47.
[34] "Answers to Questions on Christianity," in *God in the Dock: Essays on Theology and Ethics*, ed. Walter Hooper (Grand Rapids, MI: Eerdmans, 1970), 49.

So, the above accounts of love yield, first, that loving another entails seeking to advance the beloved's well-being and, second, that this does not entail liking the beloved or holding the beloved in high regard from a moral point of view.

Third, some of the above accounts of love maintain that loving another entails seeking or desiring union with the beloved, to be related to the beloved, to experience intimacy or closeness with the beloved. Surely this will resonate in typical cases of love—people ordinarily long to be with dear family and friends. And countless others would say the same thing about their love of God—it manifests as a yearning for communion with God:

> As the deer pants for streams of water,
>> so my soul pants for you, O God.
>
> My soul thirsts for God, for the living God
>> When can I go and meet with God? (Ps 42:1-2 NIV)

And while there will no doubt be moments, even long stretches, of friction and frustration, there remains an underlying desire to be united with the beloved.

Difficulties arise, however, when considering others besides God and those dear family and friends—others such as the "lepers, criminals, enemies, morons, the sulky, the superior and the sneering," as C. S. Lewis identifies them.[35] Looking inward, the challenge continues: there seems to be no desire for union with such people even when taking seriously the command to love. To seek to promote the ultimate good of the decidedly despicable is one thing, but, one might press, to desire union or intimacy with them is another thing altogether. Velleman expresses this worry:

> But, surely, it is easy enough to love someone whom one cannot stand to be with. Think here of Murdoch's reference to a troublemaking relation.

---

[35]Lewis, *Four Loves*, 128.

> This meddlesome aunt, cranky grandfather, smothering parent, or overcompetitive sibling is dearly loved, loved freely and with feeling: one just has no desire for his or her company.[36]

Some things can be offered in reply here, thereby sharpening this notion of desiring union with the beloved. Eleonore Stump, elaborating on Aquinas's account, clarifies that "whatever exactly the union is which is desired in love on Aquinas's account, the desire for it is not equivalent to the desire to be in the company of the beloved."[37] Stump continues:

> Other philosophers have remarked that one can love a person without desiring to be in that person's company, and being in someone's company is obviously not equivalent to being united to her. It is manifestly possible to be in the company of someone when one is alienated from her, rather than united to her. So desiring union with a person might not include a desire to be in that person's company, at least not now, as that person currently is.[38]

In addition, Stump notes that in Aquinas's view, the desire for the good of the beloved and the desire for union with the beloved are interrelated. This makes a difference here. For, as Stump writes, "if the desire for union is to be a desire of love, what is sought in this desire has to be compatible with the true good of the beloved."[39] She offers this example:

> If a mother tries to prevent her son from ever leaving home, when leaving home is necessary for his flourishing, then she is not in fact desiring the good for her son. Her desire for what she takes to be union with him will, therefore, also not be a desire of love.... To count as a desire of love, the mother's desire to be united with her son therefore has to allow for his being at some physical distance from her if that is, in fact, what is good for him.[40]

---

[36]J. David Velleman, "Love as a Moral Emotion," *Ethics* 109 (January 1999): 353.
[37]Stump, "Nature of Love," 91.
[38]Stump, "Nature of Love," 92.
[39]Stump, "Nature of Love," 95.
[40]Stump, "Nature of Love," 95-96.

There are countless cases demonstrating that physical distance between a person and the beloved is precisely what contributes to the ultimate good of both. Whether it's physical distance due to strong dislike, diverging life vocations, abuse, exploitation, oppression, humiliation, otherwise threatening circumstances, overpowering temptations, or infectious disease, significant physical distance and, in many such cases, relational distance is precisely what's needed for all to flourish. Loving one's enemies, as L. Gregory Jones acknowledges, "might well include a recognition that one's, or one's people's, survival may require not being able, or even desiring, to be in those enemies' presence anymore."[41] The command to love one's enemies is not a command to live with one's enemies.

So the desire for union with the beloved doesn't always take the form of a desire for physical and relational intimacy or proximity. Once again, reflecting a bit on self-love might help clarify things here. Surely one ought to love oneself, and so, given the above, one ought to desire union with oneself. That is, one ought to desire internal, subjective integration—a mind, heart, and will that come together in cooperation to form a coherent whole, absent division, inconsistency, tension, and friction. As Stump notes, "A person can be divided against herself. She can lack internal integration in her mind, and the result will be that she is, as we say, double-minded. She can also lack whole-heartedness or integration in the will."[42] Stump concludes, "There is no union with herself for such a person."[43]

These reflections point to union as integration, wholeness, and cooperation. Desiring union with the beloved, then, is a desire, minimally, for social integration, wholeness, and cooperation—a desire for

---

[41]L. Gregory Jones, *Embodying Forgiveness: A Theological Analysis* (Grand Rapids, MI: Eerdmans, 1995), 264.
[42]Stump, "Nature of Love," 100.
[43]Stump, "Nature of Love," 100.

community, even if that is not, cannot, or ought not be reflected in physical and relational proximity. It's a desire for being "on the same page" with the beloved—sharing a life's agenda—regarding ultimate ends, values, and projects. And it seems clear that one can desire this sort of union even with one's enemies—in this way, loving one's enemies need not, and likely does not, involve a desire for physical proximity and relational intimacy, but it does involve desiring their moral transformation, an upending of their moral framework, a reassessment of their life's projects, and a thoroughgoing change of their life's orientation. In this way one must repudiate the original, entirely understandable yet decidedly unloving, impulses of Jonah, who dreaded the repentance, redemption, and resulting salvation of Nineveh—indeed, "who would rather die than face a gracious God and the Ninevites as potential friends," as L. Gregory Jones put it.[44] It is with this powerful impulse to desire the enemy's destruction in mind that King urges us to say to our "most bitter opponents":

> We shall match your capacity to inflict suffering by our capacity to endure suffering. We shall meet your physical force with soul force. Do to us what you will, and we shall continue to love you. We cannot in all good conscience obey your unjust laws, because noncooperation with evil is as much a moral obligation as is cooperation with good. Throw us in jail, and we shall still love you. Send your hooded perpetrators of violence into our community at the midnight hour and beat us and leave us half dead, and we shall still love you. But be ye assured that we will wear you down by our capacity to suffer. One day we shall win freedom, but not only for ourselves. We shall so appeal to your heart and conscience that we shall win *you* in the process, and our victory will be a double victory.[45]

---

[44] Jones, *Embodying Forgiveness*, 265.
[45] King, "Loving Your Enemies," 50-51.

His confidence was driven by the conviction that "love is the only force capable of transforming an enemy into a friend."[46] To be sure, the love in question here is a sobering love, a love "that compels us to face the truth about others," a love that is perhaps often learned by "engaging in lament, by prophetically calling them to account, by showing them an alternative way of life."[47] It is, as Oscar Romero insists, a love that "ought not to turn away from honorable conflict."[48] Of course, one cannot presume that sustained prophetic love directed toward truthful transformation will, without fail and in one's lifetime, result in a thoroughgoing reorientation toward the good of deeply corrupt institutions, systems, and individuals. Even so, whether or not one's love accomplishes this transformation, love is what is called for here. Love's aim and love's prospect for success are not equivalent to love's foundation and love's justification.

Yet transformation remains the aim. And this is precisely where Martin Luther King Jr. and others would direct one's attention to the final goal of love—and of nonviolent resistance, for that matter—the creation of that "beloved community" as he, following Josiah Royce, called it. This gesturing toward the beloved community was repeated throughout King's life and work. King acknowledged that "it would be nonsense to urge men to love their oppressors in an affectionate sense."[49] Yet decrying "hatred and violence" as "the so-called practical way" that "has led inexorably to deeper confusion and chaos," King states, "While abhorring segregation, we shall love the segregationist. This is the only

---

[46] King, "Loving Your Enemies," 48.
[47] Jones, *Embodying Forgiveness*, 264.
[48] See Marie Dennis, Renny Golden, and Scott Wright, *Oscar Romero: Reflections on His Life and Writings* (Maryknoll, NY: Orbis, 2000), 51.
[49] Martin Luther King Jr., "'Facing the Challenge of a New Age,' Address Delivered at the First Annual Institute on Nonviolence and Social Change," Martin Luther King, Jr. Research and Education Institute, Stanford University, December 3, 1956, kinginstitute.stanford.edu/king-papers/documents/facing-challenge-new-age-address-delivered-first-annual-institute-nonviolence.

way to create the beloved community."⁵⁰ Speaking to "the victims of the evil system of segregation," King urges,

> As you press on for justice, be sure to move with dignity and discipline using love as your chief weapon. Let no man pull you so low that you hate him. Always avoid violence. If you sow the seeds of violence in your struggle, unborn generations will reap the whirlwind of social disintegration.⁵¹

The way of violence leads to social fracturing and fragmentation; the way of love leads to social integration and cooperation. The final goal of love and nonviolence is interrelatedness, being bonded together, wrapped up with each other, in union, experiencing social integration and cooperation. Here's a description of this beloved community:

> Dr. King's Beloved Community is a global vision, in which all people can share in the wealth of the earth. In the Beloved Community, poverty, hunger and homelessness will not be tolerated because international standards of human decency will not allow it. Racism and all forms of discrimination, bigotry and prejudice will be replaced by an all-inclusive spirit of sisterhood and brotherhood. In the Beloved Community, international disputes will be resolved by peaceful conflict resolution and reconciliation of adversaries, instead of military power. Love and trust will triumph over fear and hatred. Peace with justice will prevail over war and military conflict.⁵²

King insisted that this is not a "sentimental fantasy—an idealized vision of living happily ever after," as Velleman expressed the objection to what he referred to as "care and share" and "benefit and be with" views of love.⁵³ On the contrary, for King, it was a "a realistic, achievable goal that could be attained by a critical mass of people committed to and

---

[50] King, "Loving Your Enemies," 50.
[51] King, "Paul's Letter to American Christians," in *Strength to Love*, 150-51.
[52] "The King Philosophy—Nonviolence365," The King Center, thekingcenter.org/about-tkc/the-king-philosophy, accessed October 31, 2021.
[53] Velleman, "Love as a Moral Emotion," 353.

trained in the philosophy and methods of nonviolence."[54] Indeed, for King, though we are clearly not living in a fully realized beloved community, interrelatedness and dependency are already features of our social reality. King insists,

> In a real sense, all life is interrelated. All men are caught in an inescapable network of mutuality, tied in a single garment of destiny. Whatever affects one directly affects all indirectly. I can never be what I ought to be until you are what you ought to be, and you can never be what you ought to be until I am what I ought to be. This is the interrelated structure of reality.[55]

Too often in the present sociopolitical and economic reality, people insist on rugged individualism and declare with pride that their good fortunes are the work of their hands alone and condemn with scorn the poverty of others as entirely their own fault. People celebrate those mythical bootstraps as the means of their own prosperity and deride those tattered social safety nets as political mechanisms for cultivating dependence. There is a myopic focus on personal responsibility coupled with a demonic neglect of social responsibility. By contrast, in the beloved community there is delight in mutual dependency and glory in social cooperation for the common good. On this point Eddie Glaude Jr. directs our attention to neoliberalism, which, in his view, "undergirded the outright attack on the success of the civil rights movement." He continues:

> The economic philosophy of neoliberalism not only involved a rethinking of the role of the state—the state was to be merely the guarantor of the proper functioning of markets and to provide for our national defense—it also resulted in a particular idea of who we take ourselves to be as Americans. Neoliberalism narrowed the idea of citizen. Any concept of the

---

[54]"King Philosophy."
[55]King, "The Man Who Was a Fool," in *Strength to Love*, 69.

public good or responsibility for our fellows (those at the heart of Dr. King's notion of the Beloved Community) was displaced by the idea that human beings ought to engage in the rational pursuit of self-interest. A robust idea of citizenship gave way to a crude notion that Americans are simply individual entrepreneurs and consumers.[56]

David Schwartz elaborates:

> In today's economy humans are nothing if not consumers. Consuming has become a primary function of human beings, essential for our survival, entertainment, and general flourishing. For some, consumerism is a major component of their very identities. Furthermore, many academic and policy studies routinely assume that the primary social function of humans is that of ("rational") consumer, and many legislators, economists, and policy makers seem to conceive of the public as consumers even more than citizens.[57]

Adopting Cain's stance, many people seem to have forsaken their status as citizen of a larger collective and abandoned the corresponding concern for the common good, opting instead for individual consumption and the corresponding pursuit of an individual agenda. This runs counter to the spirit of the beloved community.[58]

One can hear in Carlo Carretto's work the same emphasis on love of one's enemies being aimed at union through transformation:

---

[56]Eddie Glaude Jr., *African American Religion: A Very Short Introduction* (Oxford: Oxford University Press, 2014), 87.

[57]David Schwartz, *Consuming Choices: Ethics in a Global Consumer Age* (Lanham, MD: Rowman and Littlefield, 2010), 83.

[58]It's worth noting that King was quite aware of this regrettable reality that we function principally as consumers. Commenting on his time in Watts in the aftermath of the August 1965 riots in Los Angeles, he writes, "When all is finally entered into the annals of sociology; when philosophers, politicians, and preachers have all had their say, we must return to the fact that a person participates in this society primarily as an economic entity. At rock bottom we are neither poets, athletes, nor artists; our existence is centered in the fact that we are consumers, because we must first eat and have shelter to live. This is a difficult confession for a preacher to make, and it is a phenomenon against which I will continue to rebel, but it remains a fact that 'consumption' of goods and services is the raison d'être of the vast majority of Americans." *The Autobiography of Martin Luther King, Jr.,* ed. Clayborne Carson (New York: Grand Central Publishing, 1998), 295.

> When Jesus tells me, "Love your enemy," he indicates the maximum possibility and capacity for loving; and at the same time he offers me the maximum hope of having peace on earth. By besieging my enemy with love and not with weapons, I facilitate in him and in myself the possibility of seeing that day dawn when "calf and lion-cub will feed together and a child will put his hand into the viper's lair, and none will harm the other" (see Isa. 11:6-9).[59]

In this description of the final aim of love another familiar concept is invoked, that of shalom. One might say the final aim of love is shalom and that the command to love directs us to create a community marked by shalom. The temptation is to invoke "peace" here, but, as Jim Forest remarks, "The word *peace* has been on the receiving end of a great deal of political smoke."[60] He notes that "in America, the Strategic Air Command, one of the world's principal instruments for waging nuclear war, has as its motto, 'Peace is our profession.'"[61] But the sort of peace brought about by drones, where there is rampant destruction, devastation, disillusionment, and discord, seems more akin to war-in-waiting—there is merely a break in the conflict until depleted resources are replenished, political will is restored, and enemy vulnerabilities are revealed. As Robert Holmes puts it,

> We know that resort to war and violence for all of recorded history has not worked. It has not secured either peace or justice to the world. The most it has brought are brief interludes in which the nations of the world regroup, catch their breath and prepare for the next war.[62]

Forest offers a remedy for this corruption of the word *peace*: "One way to restore the word is to see how *peace* is used in the Bible. In Hebrew, it

---

[59] Carlo Carretto, *Carlo Carretto: Essential Writings*, ed. Robert Ellsberg (Maryknoll, NY: Orbis, 2007), 101.
[60] Jim Forest, *The Ladder of the Beatitudes* (Maryknoll, NY: Orbis, 1999), 108.
[61] Forest, *Ladder of the Beatitudes*, 108-9.
[62] Robert Holmes, *Pacifism: A Philosophy of Nonviolence* (London: Bloomsbury Academic, 2017), 312.

is *shalom*, meaning a condition of perfect welfare, serenity, prosperity, happiness, and peaceful relations among people."[63]

Walter Brueggemann characterizes shalom as follows:

> The central vision of world history in the Bible is that all of creation is one, every creature in community with every other, living in harmony and security toward the joy and well-being of every other creature. ... That persistent vision of joy, well-being, harmony, and prosperity is not captured in any single word or idea in the Bible; a cluster of words is required to express its many dimensions and subtle nuances: love, loyalty, truth, grace, salvation, justice, blessing, righteousness. But the term that in recent discussions has been used to summarize that controlling vision is *shalom*.[64]

Noting that Brueggemann's "understanding of shalom and the Native American constructs of harmony ... have numerous points in common,"[65] Randy Woodley adds,

> Shalom is communal, holistic, and tangible. There is no private or partial shalom. The whole community must have shalom or no one has shalom. As long as there are hungry people in a community that is well fed, there can be no shalom. Where there are homeless and jobless people amidst the employed and wealthy, shalom cannot exist. Shalom is not for the many, while a few suffer; nor is it for the few while many suffer. It must be available for everyone. In this way, shalom is everyone's concern. Shalom very much defines the common good.[66]

Lengthened border walls and strengthened border patrols are powerless to bring about shalom so long as migrant children continue to be separated from their families, kept in cages, neglected and abused, and adopted away by perfect strangers or expelled unrepresented and

---

[63] Forest, *Ladder of the Beatitudes*, 109.
[64] Walter Brueggemann, *Peace* (St. Louis: Chalice, 2001), 13-14.
[65] Randy Woodley, *Shalom and the Community of Creation: An Indigenous Vision* (Grand Rapids, MI: Eerdmans, 2012), 19n9.
[66] Woodley, *Shalom*, 21.

unaccompanied to other countries.⁶⁷ The same goes for bloated, outsized law enforcement presence and duties and military budgets in the face of crumbling infrastructure, prohibitively expensive health care, a tattered social safety net, a growing housing crisis, overburdened and insufficiently resourced schools, targeted voter suppression and gerrymandering, and a corrupted criminal justice system.⁶⁸ Woodley's

---

⁶⁷See "UN Rights Chief Slams 'Unconscionable' US Border Policy of Separating Migrant Children from Parents," UN News, United Nations, June 18, 2018, news.un.org/en/story/2018/06/1012382; "Neglect and Abuse of Unaccompanied Immigrant Children by U.S. Customs and Border Protection," International Human Rights Clinic, University of Chicago Law School, May 2018, www.dropbox.com/s/lplnnufjbwci0xn/CBP%20Report%20ACLU_IHRC%205.23%20FINAL.pdf; Matthew Haag, "Thousands of Immigrant Children Said They Were Sexually Abused in U.S. Detention Centers, Report Says," *New York Times,* February 27, 2019, www.nytimes.com/2019/02/27/us/immigrant-children-sexual-abuse.html; Nick Cumming-Bruce, "Taking Migrant Children from Parents Is Illegal, U.N. Tells U.S.," *New York Times,* June 5, 2018, www.nytimes.com/2018/06/05/world/americas/us-un-migrant-children-families.html; Camilo Montoya-Galvez, "Migrant Kids to Be Expelled Under Virus Order Not Entitled to Attorneys and Other Safeguards, DOJ Lawyers Say," CBS News, August 6, 2020, www.cbsnews.com/news/migrant-children-expelled-not-entitled-to-safeguards-doj-lawyers; Nomaan Merchant, "Migrant Kids Held in US Hotels, Then Expelled," Associated Press, July 22, 2020, apnews.com/c9b671b206060f2e9654f0a4eaeb6388; Garance Burke and Martha Mendoza, "Separated from Parents, Some Migrant Children Are Adopted by Americans," *Christian Science Monitor,* October 19, 2018, www.csmonitor.com/USA/2018/1009/Separated-from-parents-some-migrant-children-are-adopted-by-Americans.

⁶⁸See Jon Schuppe, "What Would It Mean to 'Defund the Police'? These Cities Offer Ideas," NBC News, June 10, 2020, https://www.nbcnews.com/news/us-news/what-would-it-mean-defund-police-these-cities-offer-ideas-n1229266; George Gascón and Todd Foglesong, "Making Policing More Affordable: Managing Costs and Measuring Value in Policing," U.S. Department of Justice, Office of Justice Programs, December 2010, https://www.ncjrs.gov/pdffiles1/nij/231096.pdf; Taylor Miller Thomas and Beatrice Jin, "As U.S. Crime Rates Dropped, Local Police Spending Soared," Politico, https://www.politico.com/interactives/2020/police-budget-spending-george-floyd-defund/, May 10, 2020; William D. Hartung and Mandy Smithberger, "America's Defense Budget Is Bigger Than You Think," *The Nation,* May 7, 2019, https://www.thenation.com/article/archive/tom-dispatch-america-defense-budget-bigger-than-you-think/; Mallory Simon and Rachel Clarke, "America's Infrastructure Is Crumbling and These People Are Suffering Because of It," CNN, June 21, 2019, https://www.cnn.com/2019/06/17/us/crumbling-american-infrastructure/index.html; "U.S. Health Care Spending Highest Among Developed Countries," Johns Hopkins Bloomberg School of Public Health, January 7, 2019, https://www.jhsph.edu/news/news-releases/2019/us-health-care-spending-highest-among-developed-countries.html; Steven Ross Johnson, "Despite ACA Coverage Gains, More People Can't Afford Care," Modern Healthcare, January 27, 2020, https://www.modernhealthcare.com/insurance/despite-aca-coverage-gains-more-people-cant-afford-care; Shawn M. Carter, "Over Half of Americans Delay or Don't Get Health Care Because They Can't Afford It—These 3 Treatments Get Put Off Most," CNBC Make It, April 3, 2019, https://www.cnbc.com/2018/11/29/over-half-of-americans-delay-health-care-becasue-they-cant-afford-it.html; "The Problem," National Low Income

observation brings to mind Martin Luther King Jr.'s claim: "Injustice anywhere is a threat to justice everywhere. We are caught in an inescapable network of mutuality, tied in a single garment of destiny. Whatever affects one directly affects all indirectly."[69] It's why Bryan Stevenson, recalling his life-changing visit with a death row inmate as a young law student, says, "All of a sudden I knew I wanted to help condemned people get to higher ground. But more than that I knew that *my* journey to higher ground was tied to *his* journey to higher ground. If he didn't get there, I wouldn't get there either."[70]

Nicholas Wolterstorff adopts the view that love's ultimate aim is shalom.[71] He comments,

> There is in the Bible a vision of what it is that God wants for God's human creatures—a vision of what constitutes human flourishing and

---

Housing Coalition, https://nlihc.org/explore-issues/why-we-care/problem, May 10, 2020; Elle Reeve, "The US Already Had a Housing Crisis. Covid-19 Has Only Made It Worse," CNN Business, May 20, 2020, https://www.cnn.com/2020/05/20/success/rent-housing-crisis-coronavirus-covid-19/index.html; Abigail Johnson Hess, "Widespread School Closures Mean 30 million Kids Might Go Without Meals," CNBC Make It, March 14, 2020, https://www.cnbc.com/2020/03/14/widespread-school-closures-mean-30-million-kids-might-go-without-meals.html; "Block the Vote: How Politicians Are Trying to Block Voters from the Ballot Box," ACLU, August 18, 2021, https://www.aclu.org/news/civil-liberties/block-the-vote-voter-suppression-in-2020/; Rev. Jesse L. Jackson and David Daley, "Voter Suppression Is Still One of the Greatest Obstacles to a More Just America," *Time*, June 12, 2020, https://time.com/5852837/voter-suppression-obstacles-just-america/; "UN Experts Condemn Modern-Day Racial Terror Lynchings in US and Call for Systemic Reform and Justice," United Nations Human Rights Office of the High Commissioner, June 5, 2020, https://www.ohchr.org/EN/NewsEvents/Pages/DisplayNews.aspx?NewsID=25933&LangID=E; "Report to the United Nations on Racial Disparities in the U.S. Criminal Justice System," The Sentencing Project, April 19 2018, https://www.sentencingproject.org/publications/un-report-on-racial-disparities/; "US: Criminal Justice System Fuels Poverty Cycle," Human Rights Watch, June 21, 2018, https://www.hrw.org/news/2018/06/21/us-criminal-justice-system-fuels-poverty-cycle

[69] Martin Luther King Jr., "Letter from a Birmingham Jail," April 16, 1963, Online King Records Access, Stanford University, okra.stanford.edu/transcription/document_images/undecided/630416-019.pdf.

[70] Bryan Stevenson, "Attorney Bryan Stevenson Found His Calling When He Visited Death Row," Oprah Winfrey Network, YouTube, November 2, 2015, www.youtube.com/watch?v=gOKyzpQOd6s.

[71] Nicholas Wolterstorff, "Jesus' Love Command and Shalom—Nicholas Wolterstorff," Biola University Center for Christian Thought, YouTube, May 30, 2017, www.youtube.com/watch?v=IxVdHOuml4U.

of our appointed destiny. The vision is not that of disembodied individual contemplation of God; thus it is not the vision of heaven, if that is what one takes heaven to be. It is the vision of shalom—a vision first articulated in the poetic and prophetic literature of the Old Testament, but prominent in the New Testament as well under the rubric of *eirene*, peace.[72]

Wolterstorff elaborates on shalom:

> To dwell in shalom is to find delight in living rightly before God, to find delight in living rightly in one's physical surroundings, to find delight in living rightly with one's fellow human beings, to find delight even in living rightly with oneself.[73]

"Justice is the ground floor of shalom," Wolterstorff continues, where "each person enjoys justice, enjoys his or her rights," and "God's laws for our multifaceted existence are obeyed."[74] Moreover, and importantly, "it is shalom that we are to work and struggle for. We are not to stand around, hands folded, waiting for shalom to arrive. We are workers in God's cause, his peace-workers. The *missio Dei* is *our* mission."[75] Lewis Smedes delivers a similar sentiment, asserting that love "enriches justice by keeping the biblical vision of righteousness and *shalom* alive."[76] Smedes continues:

> Love wants more for people than what they have coming to them within a secular social order. Love envisions a community in which people care for one another and help each other find joy in life. Love seeks a society in which people flourish together as children of God.[77]

---

[72]Nicholas Wolterstorff, *Educating for Shalom: Essays on Christian Higher Education*, ed. Clarence W. Joldersma and Gloria Goris Stronks (Grand Rapids, MI: Eerdmans, 2004), 22-23.
[73]Wolterstorff, *Educating for Shalom*, 23.
[74]Wolterstorff, *Educating for Shalom*, 23.
[75]Nicholas Wolterstorff, *Until Justice and Peace Embrace* (Grand Rapids, MI: Eerdmans, 1983), 72.
[76]Lewis Smedes, *Mere Morality: What God Expects from Ordinary People* (Grand Rapids, MI: Eerdmans, 1983), 56.
[77]Smedes, *Mere Morality*, 56.

Love propels people to move beyond mere anticipation, mere desire for shalom. Rather, love propels people to labor for the universal common good as realized in a fully inclusive, fully integrated global community. Woodley writes,

> As a social construct, shalom is also dynamic. Shalom is not a utopian destination; it is a constant journey. One does not wait on shalom; one actually sets about the task of shalom. This active, persistent effort takes place at every level, from personal relationships to societal and structural transformation.[78]

This is all in line with the views of Gustavo Gutierrez, who contends that "peacemaking is an essential task of Christians," where shalom, as opposed to a mere "absence of war or conflict" (or "negative peace," as it is called)[79] is the ultimate aim of peacemaking.[80] Gutierrez writes, "*Shalom* is opposed to all that militates against the well-being and rights of persons and nations" and involves "the establishment of authentic justice and salvation."[81] One can detect clearly the relationship between love and the resulting cultivation of shalom right here, right now, in one's particular social, political, and economic context:

> The word "solidarity" has been used among the poor of the Latin American continent for the action that follows upon their new awareness of their situation of exploitation and marginalization, as well as of the role they must play in the building of a new and different society. For Christians this action is an efficacious act of charity, of love for neighbor and love for God in the poor. Christians thus realize that the question is not

---

[78] Woodley, *Shalom*, 21-22.
[79] Andrew Fiala writes, "At any rate, peace scholarship has long emphasized the distinction between *negative peace* and *positive peace*: negative peace is the absence of violence or war while positive peace encompasses cooperative, tranquil, and harmonious relations and the broader concerns of human flourishing and integration." Andrew Fiala, "Pacifism," Stanford Encyclopedia of Philosophy Archive, Stanford University, Fall 2018, plato.stanford.edu/archives/fall2018/entries/pacifism.
[80] Gutierrez, *Spiritual Writings*, 212.
[81] Gutierrez, *Spiritual Writings*, 212.

simply one of personal attitudes. The issue is the solidarity of the entire ecclesial community—the church—with movements of the poor in defense of their rights.[82]

Or, as Oscar Romero puts it,

> The world of the poor teaches us what the nature of Christian love is, a love that certainly seeks peace, but also unmasks false pacifism—the pacifism of resignation and inactivity. It is a love that should certainly be freely offered, but that seeks to be effective in history.[83]

A UNIVERSAL LOVE ETHIC: WORTH AND DIGNITY OF HUMAN PERSONS

With these reflections in mind, it would now be helpful to consider briefly an argument to support a universal love ethic. The argument begins with the claim that all human persons have equal worth and dignity.[84] Dignity may be understood here as Kant does—namely, as "an unconditioned and incomparable worth"[85] such that whatever "has a dignity" is "above all price, and therefore admits of no equivalent"[86] and is "infinitely beyond any price, with which it cannot in the least be brought into competition or comparison without, as it were, violating its holiness."[87] As Velleman puts it, "Kant says the value of a person is

---

[82] Gutierrez, *Spiritual Writings*, 172.

[83] Oscar Romero, as quoted in Dennis, Golden, and Wright, *Oscar Romero: Reflections*, 51.

[84] The argument is framed with "human persons" being the chief subject, in contrast to other familiar ways of framing the issue, with subjects such as "persons" or "humans." This is deliberate. Using "persons" brings in other persons, such as divine persons and any persons found among nonhuman animals. Using "humans" invites questions about whether all humans—including human fetuses (particularly at early stages of development), anencephalic infants, and humans with higher-brain death—are rightly counted as persons and, if not, whether and upon what basis such humans have incalculable worth and dignity. To simplify this particular discussion, and in a way that takes no position at all on those sorts of issues, I've restricted the discussion to human persons. This is not intended to diminish the significance of sorting out these other issues.

[85] Immanual Kant, *Foundations of the Metaphysics of Morals: Text and Critical Essays*, trans. Lewis Beck White, ed. Robert Paul Wolff (Indianapolis: Bobbs-Merrill, 1969), 61.

[86] Kant, *Foundations*, 60.

[87] Kant, *Foundations*, 61.

different in kind from the value of other things: a person has a dignity, whereas other things have a price."[88] For Kant, according to Thomas Hill, "the dignity of humanity" is "an unconditional and nonquantitative value attributed to everyone with the potential capacities to be a moral agent" such that "as a human being, everyone has an equal worth, independent of social standing and individual merits."[89] Or, as Arthur Holmes puts it, "differences in race, religion, sex, politics, or social and economic status" are "ethically irrelevant and do not affect the essential nature and worth of a person."[90]

The worth and dignity of a human person is not tied to their skill, talents, intelligence, character, appearance, age, physical or mental health, strength, body type, criminal record, gender identity, sexual orientation, race, ethnicity, citizenship, religious affiliation, socioeconomic status, political leanings, family background, popularity, contributions to society, workplace productivity, and so on. Given that a human person's worth and dignity are tied entirely to their status as a human person, *any* arbitrarily selected human person whatsoever has this worth and dignity. Consequently, *every* human person has this worth and dignity. And given that there are no degrees of being a human person—that is, given that one human person cannot be more of a human person than any other—every human person has this worth and dignity equally.

The premise gets additional theological support in taking seriously the claims that each and every human person is a beloved child of God who is made in the image of God and that, morally, one ought to act as though any encounter with a human person is an encounter with

---

[88] Velleman, "Love as a Moral Emotion," 364.
[89] Thomas E. Hill Jr., "Respect for Humanity," Tanner Lectures on Human Values Delivered at Stanford University, April 26 and 28, 1994, tannerlectures.utah.edu/_resources/documents/a-to-z/h/Hill97.pdf.
[90] Arthur Holmes, *Ethics: Approaching Moral Decisions*, 2nd ed. (Downers Grove, IL: IVP Academic, 2007), 83.

Jesus—God the Son—himself (see Gen 1:27; 9:6; Mt 25:31-46; Jn 3:16; Acts 17:29; 1 Jn 4:20-21). These claims powerfully express just how valuable each human person is, the standing that each human person has in the eyes of God. Nicholas Wolterstorff accounts for the worth and dignity of human beings by explicitly appealing to how humanity is related to God.[91] Specifically, on Wolterstorff's account,

> Suppose that one is chosen by God as someone with whom God wants to be friends. That is to be honored by God. And to be honored by God is to have worth bestowed upon one. Add now that every human being has the honor of being chosen by God as someone with whom God wants to be friends. Then every human being has the worth that being so honored bestows on one.[92]

Wolterstorff regards this as a type of love—namely, friendship love. So, it's being friendship-loved by God that, in Wolterstorff's view, bestows worth and dignity on all human beings. But one might think being loved by God in the way understood above—not friendship love as such but as seeking to promote the flourishing of the beloved and desiring transformative union or cooperative community with the beloved—is up to the task of bestowing incalculable worth and dignity on all human beings.[93]

One shouldn't pass too quickly over this first premise, thereby missing its practical, political significance. As Martha Nussbaum points out, "Equality is a cherished political value in modern democracies. It is often associated with the idea of human worth or dignity, and also with questions of political entitlements and rights (including the right to vote, the

---

[91]The move in terminology here from "human person" to "human being" is entirely because this is how Wolterstorff frames the discussion, as can be seen below.

[92]Wolterstorff, *Justice in Love*, 155.

[93]It's worth noting that having incalculable worth and dignity bestowed on one by being the beloved of God is consistent with having incalculable worth and dignity for other, perhaps nontheological, reasons.

right to education, and many others)."⁹⁴ Noting that equality talk is a reaction against political systems such as feudalism and the Indian caste system, Nussbaum claims, "To assert, against this, that human beings are equal is, most fundamentally, to assert that all human beings have a worth or dignity that is basically equal, and that they are not inherently, naturally, ranked above and below one another in a hierarchical ordering. The hierarchies we observe are the creation of social forces."⁹⁵

Elizabeth Anderson makes similar remarks. She notes,

> Inegalitarianism asserted the justice or necessity of basing social order on a hierarchy of human beings, ranked according to intrinsic worth. Inequality referred not so much to distributions of goods as to relations between superior and inferior persons. Those of superior rank were thought entitled to inflict violence on inferiors, to exclude or segregate them from social life, to treat them with contempt, to force them to obey, work without reciprocation, and abandon their own cultures. . . . Such unequal social relations generate, and were thought to justify, inequalities in the distribution of freedoms, resources, and welfare. This is the core of inegalitarian ideologies of racism, sexism, nationalism, caste, class, and eugenics.⁹⁶

Anderson continues, "Egalitarian political movements oppose such hierarchies. They assert the equal worth of persons."⁹⁷

Furthermore, one can find appeal to human dignity in landmark international documents. As Jane Kotzmann and Cassandra Seery say, "The concept of dignity is foundational to modern international human rights law."⁹⁸ Thus, for example, in the preamble to the Charter of the

---

⁹⁴Martha Nussbaum, "Political Equality," in *The Norton Introduction to Philosophy*, 2nd ed., ed. Gideon Rosen et al. (New York: W. W. Norton, 2018), 1146.
⁹⁵Nussbaum, "Political Equality," 1149.
⁹⁶Elizabeth Anderson, "What Is the Point of Equality?" *Ethics* 109, no. 2 (January 1999): 312.
⁹⁷Anderson, "What Is the Point?" 312.
⁹⁸Jane Kotzmann and Cassandra Seery, "Dignity in International Human Rights Law: Potential Applicability in Relation to International Recognition of Animal Rights," *Michigan State International Law Review* 26, no. 1 (2017): 9.

United Nations, we read that the member states aim to "reaffirm faith in fundamental human rights, in the dignity and worth of the human person, in the equal rights of men and women and of nations large and small."[99] In the preamble to the Universal Declaration of Human Rights, we get reference to "recognition of the inherent dignity and of the equal and inalienable rights of all members of the human family" as well as "faith in fundamental human rights, in the dignity and worth of the human person."[100] Article 1 of the Universal Declaration of Human Rights holds, in part, that "all human beings are born free and equal in dignity and rights."[101] Both the International Covenant on Civil and Political Rights and the International Covenant on Economic, Social and Cultural Rights affirm "recognition of the inherent dignity and of the equal and inalienable rights of all members of the human family" and that "these rights derive from the inherent dignity of the human person."[102] Meanwhile, the International Convention on the Elimination of All Forms of Racial Discrimination maintains "the dignity and equality inherent in all human beings" and that "all human beings are born free and equal in dignity and rights."[103]

Denying this first premise seems deeply problematic. Not only does it amount to the denial of a core conviction of modern liberal democracies and signal a clear departure from an integral component of pivotal

---

[99] "United Nations Charter: Preamble," United Nations, www.un.org/en/about-us/un-charter/preamble, accessed October 31, 2021.

[100] "Universal Declaration of Human Rights," United Nations, www.un.org/en/universal-declaration-human-rights, accessed October 31, 2021.

[101] "Universal Declaration."

[102] "International Covenant on Civil and Political Rights," United Nations Human Rights, Office of the High Commissioner, December 16, 1966, www.ohchr.org/en/professionalinterest/pages/ccpr.aspx; "International Covenant on Economic, Social and Cultural Rights," United Nations Human Rights, Office of the High Commissioner, December 16, 1966, www.ohchr.org/en/professionalinterest/pages/cescr.aspx.

[103] "International Convention on the Elimination of All Forms of Racial Discrimination," United Nations Human Rights, Office of the High Commissioner, December 21, 1965, www.ohchr.org/en/professionalinterest/pages/cerd.aspx.

international documents, it's equivalent to affirming that some human persons do not have equal worth and dignity, that some human persons have greater or lesser worth or dignity than other human persons, or, using Kantian language, that all human persons have a price and some would command a greater or lesser price than others. In addition, this invites scrutiny over the basis of their greater or lesser worth relative to other human persons, and whatever is selected as the basis would have to be nonessential to being a human person since the comparison is between human persons. Is the basis the presence or absence, or greater or lesser measure, of some capacity, power, function, or ability? Moral superiority or inferiority? More or less of a human person? More or less of a rational nature or will? More or less the image of God? Loved more or less by God? Nothing here suggests itself that is philosophically, theologically, legally, and politically satisfying.

The second premise in the argument asserts that, morally, as a fitting response to the worth and dignity of a human person, one ought to love that human person. From the moral point of view, the incomparable and priceless worth of a human person demands a particular type of response from those who encounter the human person. According to this premise, that response is love, the sort of love articulated above where one seeks to promote the flourishing of the beloved and desires a transformative and cooperative union characterized as shalom. It's the sort of response one detects in the Good Samaritan, who encounters a human person of incomparable and priceless worth and dignity left for dead, beaten and battered, by the side of the road to Jericho. Martin Luther King Jr. commends the Samaritan for, among other things, his "universal altruism," for rejecting the "limiting of neighborly concern to tribe, race, class, or nation."[104] King continues,

---

[104] Martin Luther King Jr., "On Being a Good Neighbor," in *Strength to Love*, 23.

> The real tragedy of such narrow provincialism is that we see people as entities or merely as things. Too seldom do we see people in their true *humanness*. A spiritual myopia limits our vision to external accidents. We see men as Jews or Gentiles, Catholics or Protestants, Chinese or Americans, Negroes or whites. We fail to think of them as fellow human beings made from the same basic stuff as we, molded in the same divine image. The priest and the Levite saw only a bleeding body, not a human being like themselves. But the good Samaritan will always remind us to remove the cataracts of provincialism from our spiritual eyes and see men as men.[105]

One can hear the Kantian language here, of treating people as mere things, but instead of the Kantian punchline where the Samaritan *respected* the beaten and battered man, Jesus tells us that the Samaritan *loved* the man and serves as our model for loving our neighbors as ourselves. The prescription seems to be that, morally, one ought to respond to any human person with love, for that is what counts as a fitting response to the infinite worth and dignity of the human person.

Given the theological claims offered above in support of premise one—that each and every human person is a beloved child of God who is made in the image of God and that, morally, one ought to act as though any encounter with a human person is an encounter with God the Son incarnate, Jesus himself—one can now reason theologically in defense of this second premise as follows. Each and every human person is a dearly beloved child of God such that every interaction with a human person ought to be regarded, from the moral point of view, as an interaction with Jesus himself—God the Son. Having this status—being the beloved of God—bestows incalculable worth and dignity on each and every human person. As love is the fitting response to God, as love is the fitting response to Jesus whom we are in effect encountering, so love is

---

[105]King, "On Being a Good Neighbor," 24.

the fitting response to human persons bearing incalculable worth and dignity. To withhold love from, to remain indifferent to, any human person is to express an objectionable lack of love for God. Oscar Romero paints a vivid portrait here:

> Each time we look upon the poor, on the farmworkers who harvest the coffee, the sugarcane, or the cotton, or the farmer who joins the caravan of workers looking to earn their savings for the year . . . remember, there is the face of Christ. . . . The face of Christ is among the sacks and baskets of the farmworker; the face of Christ is among those who are tortured and mistreated in the prisons; the face of Christ is dying of hunger in the children who have nothing to eat; the face of Christ is in the poor who ask the church for their voice to be heard. How can the church deny this request when it is Christ who is telling us to speak for him?[106]

Indifference to the plight of the downtrodden, the marginalized, the neglected, the exploited, the oppressed, the caged, the deported, the turned-away, the excluded, the swept-under-the-rug constitutes indifference to the plight of Christ himself.

The third and final premise functions as a linking premise: if it really is true that all human persons have equal worth and dignity, and if it really is true that morally, as a fitting response to the worth and dignity of a human person, one ought to love that person, then it follows that, morally, one ought to love all human persons. This seems true. Assume, as argued above, that from the moral point of view an encounter with a human person, in light of their worth and dignity, is an encounter where love is the fitting response. Assume also, as argued above, that all human persons have this worth and dignity and have it equally. Consequently, an encounter with any human person at all is an encounter where, from the moral point of view, love is the fitting response. That is, morally, one

---

[106]See Dennis et al., *Oscar Romero*, 35.

ought to love all human persons. That's just what this premise holds, so this premise is true. And from these three premises, the conclusion follows: morally, one ought to love all human persons.

I turn now to consider how a universal love ethic has inspired and fueled human and civil rights advocacy.

A UNIVERSAL LOVE ETHIC: HUMAN AND CIVIL RIGHTS ADVOCACY

According to William Frankena, "There is one ethical theory which has been and still is widely accepted, especially in Judaic-Christian circles—namely, the ethics of love. This holds that there is only one basic ethical imperative—to love—and that all others are to be derived from it."[107] Even though, as Frankena notes, this view is "generally neglected in philosophical introductions to ethics,"[108] the moral mandate to love has shaped powerfully and profoundly the leaders and inspirers of various local and global nonviolent campaigns against pervasive oppression, exploitation, discrimination, marginalization, and dehumanization. Indeed, some see this moral mandate to love as essential to dismantling systems and structures of domination. As bell hooks claims,

> Without love, our efforts to liberate ourselves and our world community from oppression and exploitation are doomed. As long as we refuse to address fully the place of love in struggles for liberation we will not be able to create a culture of conversion where there is a mass turning away from an ethic of domination.[109]

For hooks, a love ethic is necessary to motivate the oppressed and marginalized to move beyond a particular concern for oneself and one's immediate group and toward a broader, general concern for the

---

[107]Frankena, *Ethics*, 42.
[108]Frankena, *Ethics*, 42.
[109]bell hooks, *Outlaw Culture: Resisting Representations* (New York: Routledge, 1994), 289.

well-being of *all* who suffer from these systems and structures of domination.

Unfortunately, there isn't space here to rehearse how love has featured prominently among key figures past and present in their tireless and persistent nonviolent advocacy for human rights.[110] But looking at a few examples will prove instructive and illustrative.

There is little doubt that the moral mandate to love played a significant role in the struggle for human and civil rights for Black Americans during the mid-twentieth century. As bell hooks observes, the "civil rights movement transformed society in the United States because it was fundamentally rooted in a love ethic."[111] Efrem Smith puts it this way:

> Another gift is a biblically rooted strategy for loving your enemy and seeking reconciliation, which the Black church cultivated through the civil rights movement. At the core of the movement was nonviolence, which was fueled by the agape love shown to us by Jesus in the scriptures.[112]

Rev. James Lawson Jr. had an especially profound effect on the movement from its early days. Martin Luther King Jr. called Lawson "the leading theorist and strategist of nonviolence in the world."[113] Among many other things, Lawson organized and led regular workshops on the theory and practice of nonviolence in Nashville, Tennessee. These workshops attracted many university students who then went on to lead test sit-ins in downtown Nashville prior to the sit-ins in Greensboro, North Carolina, and then, on a larger scale, after the Greensboro sit-ins. Diane

---

[110]Beyond those mentioned here, consider, for example, Gandhi, Tolstoy, Badshah Khan, Howard Thurman, Thomas Merton, Dorothy Day, Thich Nhat Hanh, Cornel West, Martha Nussbaum, John Dear, Yoriko Yasukawa, Ibram X. Kendi, Michael Lerner, Valarie Kaur, and Bryan Stevenson.

[111]hooks, *Outlaw Culture*, 290.

[112]Efrem Smith, *The Post-Black and Post-White Church: Becoming the Beloved Community in a Multi-ethnic World* (San Francisco: Jossey-Bass, 2012), 109.

[113]See "The Reverend James M. Lawson, Jr.," Martin Luther King, Jr. Research and Education Institute, Stanford University, kinginstitute.stanford.edu/reverend-james-m-lawson-jr, accessed November 2, 2021.

Nash was a major leader among these students. She noted that through Lawson's workshops, "I discovered that practical and real power of truth and love."[114] C. T. Vivian, another important leader among the students who first participated in a lunch counter sit-in in 1947, well before such sit-ins became a well-known strategy in the movement, declared that "radical loving is needed to defeat radical evil. If you love the world enough, you'll find a way."[115]

Congressman John Lewis was another significant leader among these students. Lewis observed, "The movement created what I like to call a nonviolent revolution. It was love at its best. It's one of the highest forms of love. That you beat me, you arrest me, you take me to jail, you almost kill me, but in spite of that, I'm gonna still love you."[116] It makes sense that workshop participants would see love as being at the heart of nonviolence. According to Jenifer Stollman, "Strongly impressed and guided by the teachings of Jesus Christ, Lawson employed Christian notions of love as a foundational political, social, and legal strategy by which to effect change."[117]

---

[114] See "James Lawson," Digital SNCC Gateway, snccdigital.org/people/james-lawson, May 10, 2020. Nash continues to emphasize love, or what she calls "agapic energy," in her addresses and interviews. See, for example, Colton Williams, "Civil Rights Leader Diane Nash Lectures on Agapic Energy, Social Justice," *The Sewanee Purple*, April 23, 2018, thesewaneepurple.org/2018/04/23/civil-rights-leader-diane-nash-lectures-on-agapic-energy-social-justice; Kevin Allen, "Civil Rights Pioneer Says Love Fueled the Movement," The Law School, University of Notre Dame, March 9, 2017, law.nd.edu/news-events/news/civil-rights-pioneer-says-love-fueled-the-movement; Kathryn Flagg, "Civil Rights Leader Diane Nash Recounts Life at the Forefront of Social Change," Middlebury, April 4, 2018, www.middlebury.edu/newsroom/archive/2018-news/node/570375; Amber Bemis, "Legendary Civil Rights Activist Delivers Martin Luther King, Jr. Keynote," Feinberg School of Medicine, Northwestern, January 27, 2016, news.feinberg.northwestern.edu/2016/01/legendary-civil-rights-activist-delivers-martin-luther-king-jr-keynote; Mary O'Leary, "Civil Rights Icon Diane Nash Talks Nonviolent Action, Continuing Struggle, in New Haven Event," Yale University, January 25, 2017, mlk.yale.edu/news/civil-rights-icon-diane-nash-talks-nonviolent-action-continuing-struggle-new-haven-event.

[115] See "2010 Martin Luther King Jr. Celebration Featuring Rev. C.T. Vivian," Gustavus Adolphus College, gustavus.edu/events/mlk/2010.php, May 10, 2020.

[116] See "John Lewis: Love in Action," *On Being with Krista Tippett*, March 28, 2013, onbeing.org/programs/john-lewis-love-in-action-jan2017.

[117] "Diane Nash, "'Courage Displaces Fear, Love Transforms Hate'": Civil Rights Activism and the Commitment to Nonviolence," in *The Human Tradition in the Civil Rights Movement*, ed. Susan M. Glisson (Lanham, MD: Rowman & Littlefield, 2006), 203.

Lawson drafted the statement of purpose for the Student Nonviolence Coordinating Committee, an influential organization within the movement conceived and organized by veteran activist Ella Baker in 1960. In that statement, we read the following:

> We affirm the philosophical or religious ideal of nonviolence as the foundation of our purpose, the pre-supposition of our faith, and the manner of our action. Nonviolence as it grows from Judaic-Christian traditions seeks a social order of justice permeated by love. . . . Love is the central motif of nonviolence. Love is the force by which God binds man to himself and man to man. Such love goes to the extreme; it remains loving and forgiving even in the midst of hostility. It matches the capacity of evil to inflict suffering with an even more enduring capacity to absorb evil, all the while persisting in love.[118]

Ansley Quiros claims that this love ethic and nonviolence amounted to a way of living out "a powerful countertheology to white supremacist religion."[119] Commenting on the Black American struggle for liberation, Quiros elaborates:

> In the twentieth century, the "love ethic" and the praxis of Christian nonviolence gave the struggle concrete expression. Men like Martin Luther King Jr. and James Lawson, both ministers nurtured in the black church, fused their theological training with the ideas of Bayard Rustin, A. Phillip Randolph, and Gandhi to create a protest movement designed for black Christians in the South. The way to live theology, they declared, was to demonstrate it in love and nonviolence, as Christ himself did.[120]

Similarly, while holding that, in general, "love is a key concept in the theory and history of civil disobedience," Alexander Livingston

---

[118] See "The Student Voice (SNCC)," Freedom Summer Digital Collection, Wisconsin Historical Society, content.wisconsinhistory.org/cdm/ref/collection/p15932coll2/id/50058, accessed November 2, 2021.

[119] Ansley Quiros, *God with Us: Lived Theology and the Freedom Struggle in Americus, Georgia, 1942-1976* (Chapel Hill: University of North Carolina Press, 2018), 72.

[120] Quiros, *God with Us*, 72.

more specifically sees "love as a key concept in a vernacular black political theology."[121]

This provocation to justice through love seen in the human and civil rights movement of the mid-twentieth century continues in the ongoing contemporary struggle for human and civil rights for Black Americans. For example, consider Black Lives Matter, "founded in 2013 in response to the acquittal of Trayvon Martin's murderer"[122] as "a hashtag that reignited a movement" which has now "grown into a global community working toward Black liberation and freedom."[123] All three cofounders of Black Lives Matter have attested to the central place of love in their global work. Alicia Garza professes, "Our movement is grounded in love."[124] Opal Tometi elaborates: "When we say 'Black Lives Matter,' we're not saying that any other life doesn't matter. That has never, ever been our message. Our message has always been from a place of love. Love for our people, a love for even our society and our brothers and sisters."[125] Elsewhere, Tometi states, "Ultimately, we are fueled by love and fueled by a hope that things can be different."[126] Finally, Patrisse Cullors explains,

> It's both rage and love at the center of our work, I think. From the beginning, Alicia Garza's "Love Note" to black people that ended with, "Our lives matter, black lives matter," it was from a place of rage, but also from a place of deep love for black people. And I think that—when we show

---

[121] Alexander Livingston, "'Tough Love': The Political Theology of Civil Disobedience," *Perspectives on Politics* 18, no. 3 (September 2020): 1-16.

[122] See "About," Black Lives Matter, https://blacklivesmatter.com/about/, May 10, 2020.

[123] See "8 Years Strong," Black Lives Matter, July 13, 2021, https://blacklivesmatter.com/8-years-strong/.

[124] Alicia Garza, "Black Lives Matter (BLM) Has a Message You Don't Hear," Fusion, YouTube, September 22, 2016, www.youtube.com/watch?v=KIUnz3cfo-w.

[125] See Stephen Dinan, "Opal Tometi: Black Lives Matter Is Message of 'Love' for All," *Washington Times*, September 30, 2015, www.washingtontimes.com/news/2015/sep/30/opal-tometi-black-lives-matter-message-love-all.

[126] See Angelica Euseary, "Opal Tometi Addresses Black Lives Matter and Police Brutality at BGSU," Falcon Media, Bowling Green State University, March 27, 2019, www.bgfalconmedia.com/campus/opal-tometi-addresses-black-lives-matter-and-police-brutality-at-bgsu/article_19feccac-5100-11e9-8a9d-f7c674eaefde.html.

up on the freeway, when we chain ourselves to each other, that's an act of love. That act of resistance is an act of love, that we will put our bodies on the line for our community and really for this country.[127]

As with others, Cullors testifies to the role love plays in inspiring, motivating, and sustaining courageous, active resistance against longstanding injustices and in building that beloved community referred to by Josiah Royce, founder of the Fellowship of Reconciliation, and popularized by Martin Luther King Jr.[128] It's a proactive, sacrificial, resisting love immediately directed toward securing justice for Black people but ultimately accomplishing the common good.

Michelle Alexander locates love at the locus of our collective holistic liberation. Indeed, she sees love at work in recent nonviolent uprisings:

> And it's also true that we need much more than a political revolution; we also need a moral, cultural, and spiritual revolution—an awakening to the dignity and value of each and every one of us no matter who we are, where we came from, or what we've done. We saw this revolutionary spirit on the streets of Ferguson, Baltimore and beyond when signs were held high saying "Black Lives Matter" even as tear gas flowed. We saw this revolutionary spirit when undocumented students literally risked everything by coming out of the shadows to protest mass deportation. We saw this revolutionary spirit when thousands flooded the streets in solidarity with Occupy Wall Street, calling for an end to corporate exploitation and greed—greed that not only caused a global economic crisis but that is driving climate change and threatening life on the planet itself. It is this revolutionary spirit—a revolutionary love for all people and for life itself—that will ultimately determine our collective fate.[129]

---

[127]See "Patrisse Cullors + Robert Ross: The Spiritual Work of Black Lives Matter," *On Being with Krista Tippett*, February 18, 2016, onbeing.org/programs/patrisse-cullors-and-robert-ross-the-spiritual-work-of-black-lives-matter-may2017.

[128]For more on the beloved community, see "The Beloved Community," The King Center, https://thekingcenter.org/about-tkc/the-king-philosophy/, December 17, 2021.

[129]Michelle Alexander, Facebook, February 18, 2016, www.facebook.com/Michelle-Alexander-168304409924191.

In the immediate aftermath of the murder of George Floyd, people took to the streets around the globe in the midst of a viral pandemic to protest the pandemic of police brutality, overreach, and deeply entrenched social, political, cultural, and economic racism. Taking it all in, Alexander repeated her call for a unifying, liberating, transforming, agitating, all-encompassing political love: "Our only hope for our collective liberation is a politics of deep solidarity rooted in love."[130]

With the above, we get good reasons for thinking that a universal love ethic features prominently among key figures who have commended nonviolent resistance grounded in love in their tireless work to put an end to oppression, exploitation, discrimination, marginalization, and dehumanization and in their courageous, persistent advocacy for human rights. Society-shaping, indeed, world-altering movements and campaigns have been grounded in a universal love ethic. In this vein Bryan Stevenson reflects, "I think I've increasingly recognized that we have to be intentional and explicit in our affirmation of the power of love."[131] As we have seen, there is great power in this love to motivate, animate, and sustain our individual and collective laboring for the beloved community, for the universal common good as realized in a fully inclusive, fully integrated global community.

---

[130]Michelle Alexander, "America, This Is Your Chance," *New York Times*, June 8, 2020, www.nytimes.com/2020/06/08/opinion/george-floyd-protests-race.html.

[131]Bryan Stevenson, "Love Is the Motive," December 3, 2020, in *On Being with Krista Tippett*, onbeing.org/programs/bryan-stevenson-love-is-the-motive.

PART THREE

WAR AND VIOLENCE

10

WAR, TERROR, AND PEACE

Lisa Sharon Harper

Blessed are the meek, for they will inherit the earth.

MATTHEW 5:5

Put your sword back into its place; for all who take the sword will perish by the sword.

MATTHEW 26:52

IT WAS 8:30 A.M. IN LOS ANGELES. My apartment mate, Donna, banged on my door, ran into my room, and woke me out of a deep sleep, yelling, "The World Trade Center is gone and America is at war!"[1]

In the aftermath of the horror—after people fell from the sky, black clouds of dust filled with steel, concrete, and flesh pushed screaming New Yorkers out of downtown Manhattan and across the iconic Brooklyn Bridge, and after one-fifth of the Pentagon was destroyed by an airplane

---

[1] This chapter previously appeared in David Gushee, ed., *Evangelical Peacemakers: Gospel Engagement in a War-Torn World* (Eugene, OR: Cascade Books, 2013). Used by permission of Wipf and Stock Publishers, www.wipfandstock.com.

strike and another plane went down over Shanksville, Pennsylvania—after it all, America went on lockdown. Airports across the country shut down. No one could get into or out of the United States. And no one knew when or where or *if* there would be another attack.

Two thousand nine hundred and ninety-six people died on September 11, 2001, including the nineteen hijackers who carried out the attacks.

That day was a hinge point in the history, trajectory, and very culture of the United States of America. 9/11 changed everything.

Thomas Hammarberg, commissioner for human rights for the Council of Europe, has said, "The problem is not whether or not we will react to terrorists, but how."[2]

How does Jesus answer terror? The author of the Fourth Book of Ezra describes the empire of Rome as a terrorist state, the last of four occupying beasts:

> You, the fourth that has come, have conquered all the beasts that have gone before; and you have sway over the world with much terror, and over all the earth with grievous oppression; and for so long you have dwelt on the earth with deceit. And you have judged the earth, but not with truth; for you have afflicted the meek and injured the peaceable; you have hated those who tell the truth, and have loved liars; you have destroyed the dwellings of those who brought forth fruit, and have laid low the walls of those who did you no harm.[3]

In 63 BC Pompey conquered Judea and claimed it as a client kingdom of Rome. In AD 6 Augustus Caesar made Judea a Roman province. In the days when Jesus walked the earth, the Zealots bore arms to free the Jews of their Roman occupiers. They were considered terrorists by the

---

[2]As reported by Gerald Staberock (deputy secretary general, World Organization Against Torture) in Skype interview with author, February 3, 2011.
[3]Lee Griffith, *The War on Terrorism and the Terror of God* (Grand Rapids, MI: Eerdmans, 2002), 21.

Roman state. In *The War on Terrorism and the Terror of God*, Lee Griffith explains that in both Matthew's and Luke's accounts of the Sermon on the Mount, "Jesus admonished his followers to turn the other cheek, to love enemies, and to do good to persecutors."[4]

In the chapter "War and Terror" in my book *Left Right and Christ: Evangelical Faith in Politics*, which serves as the basis of these reflections, I ask the reader to "imagine being Simon, the Zealot (the terrorist) who believes in the use of violence to fight violence and the poverty caused by Israel's Roman occupation. Imagine being Simon, who Jesus just chose to be his follower a few verses ago."[5] Can you see it? Now see Jesus. He sits Simon down with the other eleven disciples and says,

> "Blessed are the poor in spirit, for theirs is the kingdom of heaven.
>
> "Blessed are those who mourn, for they will be comforted.
>
> "Blessed are the meek, for they will inherit the earth.
>
> "Blessed are those who hunger and thirst for righteousness, for they will be filled.
>
> "Blessed are the merciful, for they will receive mercy.
>
> "Blessed are the [shalom-]makers, for they will be called children of God.
>
> "Blessed are those who are persecuted for righteousness' sake, for theirs is the kingdom of heaven.
>
> "Blessed are you when people revile you and persecute you and utter all kinds of evil against you falsely on my account. Rejoice and be glad, for your reward is great in heaven, for in the same way they persecuted the prophets who were before you." (Mt 5:3-12)

Griffith explains, "The admonitions of the Sermon on the Mount were understood as literal ethical guidance."[6] Jesus serves as the great rabbi and demonstrates what it looks like to live according to his own ethical

---

[4]Giffith, *War on Terrorism*, 23.
[5]Harper and Innes, *Left Right and Christ*, 186.
[6]Griffith, *War on Terrorism*, 23.

teachings when he himself is faced with the Roman Empire's primary instrument of terror—the cross.

Judas betrayed Jesus with a kiss in the Garden of Gethsemane. A detachment of Roman soldiers along with police from the chief priests and Pharisees moved to seize Jesus. Just then, in a bold act of defiance, Peter took out his sword and sliced off the right ear of a man named Malchus, a slave of one of the chief priests. Jesus commanded, "Put your sword back into its place; for all who take the sword will perish by the sword." And he touched the slave's ear and it was healed (Mt 26:52; Lk 22:51; Jn 18:1-11).

Then, as I explain in *Left Right and Christ*, "Jesus stared into the faces of people who considered him their enemy and he turned his other cheek. Jesus allowed himself to be whipped. He allowed spikes to be driven into his wrists and ankles. He allowed a terrorist state to use his death as a horrifying warning to any who dare follow him from this point on."[7] Allegiance to Jesus would be a direct challenge to the deity of Caesar and to the ultimate authority of occupying Rome. Do so and die.

Why didn't Jesus fight? The people had been waiting for a messiah to overthrow Caesar by force. If it was going to happen, it had to happen in that very moment. Why did Jesus rebuke Peter? And, further, why did Jesus heal the slave's ear? Why did he walk the path of silence and nonviolent resistance with Pilate rather than lashing out or arguing his case? (Mt 27:11-14). Why did Jesus turn the other cheek? Why did he exercise meekness, which means disciplined power, while staring terror in the face?

I believe it was because in the faces of the chief priests and their slaves and the Roman soldiers, even Caesar himself, Jesus saw the image of

---

[7]Harper and Innes, *Left Right and Christ*, 174.

God. I ask, "How could Jesus strike down the image of God? He came to redeem and restore the image of God on earth, to set the slaves, and the soldiers, and the priests free from the violent reign of men. He came that Caesar himself might be brought back to life by the dominion of God."[8] From the picture of creation in Genesis 1–2 to the establishment of Israel in Exodus, Deuteronomy, Leviticus, and Numbers to the cries of the prophets Isaiah, Jeremiah, Micah, and Ezekiel, Scripture paints a picture of God's kind of dominion. It is characterized by disciplined power, servant leadership, truth telling, just dealing, reconciliation, reparation, and above all else love. I believe Jesus did not fight because Jesus believed in redemption.

Considering the effect of ethical dualism on the paradigms we draw in times of conflict, Griffith reflects, "Conquest comes through the infliction of suffering. Redemption comes through the Suffering Servant."[9] D. C. Innes, my *Left Right and Christ* coauthor, states, "God authorizes the sword, a fearsome weapon of deadly consequence, because there are cruel beasts at the city gates who will not depart unless they are either destroyed or credibly threatened with destruction."[10] This is not my worldview. I and my nation are not inherently good and those who might come against me or my nation are not automatically cast as evil. Rather, the entire world and all relationships in it suffer under the repercussions of the Genesis 3 fall.

We are all fallen. We all suffer the consequences of the choices we make to exercise a human kind of dominion rather than God's kind of dominion. We suffer the consequences of our bids to secure our kind of peace—the kind of peace that comes at the expense of the peace of others. Griffith illuminates the key distinction between my paradigm

---

[8]Harper and Innes, *Left Right and Christ*, 185.
[9]Griffith, *War on Terrorism*, 76.
[10]Harper and Innes, *Left Right and Christ*, 174-75.

and that of my coauthor: "These are sharply contrasting views of the world: a world filled with evil in need of conquest, or a suffering creation groaning for redemption."[11]

Gerald Staberock, the deputy secretary general of the World Organization Against Torture in Switzerland, explains the effect of the ethical dualism embedded in the paradigm of war: "The war paradigm works on an 'us versus them' framework. . . . If you speak in the terms of war you only have friends and enemies."[12]

The United States is a nation founded on core values: the rights of the individual, the protection of the rights of minorities, the rule of law, free and fair elections, and due process all make up the pillars of our democracy. In a legal paradigm, Staberock explains, you have the law, the courts, and time-tested processes, and you protect your values. In a war paradigm all bets are off. Individual liberties are severely limited or sacrificed, minorities are vulnerable to scapegoating, and the rule of law is limited because laws change under the wartime paradigm. For example, killing is forbidden in all circumstances in a legal paradigm. In a war paradigm it is not only excusable, but states are expected to kill "the enemy."

Consider the results of President George W. Bush's "global war on terror." First, according to international law, wars can be declared only against nation states, not against individual actors or networks. The declaration unleashed a new norm with no end in sight in American life—the norm of dehumanization and disregard for the rule of law. The era has no end because how can we name an end point in a "global war on terror"? Bush's use of the war paradigm led to the adoption of dehumanizing tactics such as torture and the detention of US citizens and residents at Guantanamo Bay. A national commission recently confirmed

---

[11]Griffith, *War on Terrorism*, 76.
[12]Staberock, interview.

that the United States did, in fact, break international law with the use of torture tactics during the Iraq war.[13]

The United States answered the horror of 9/11 with the paradigm of war—conquest, not redemption, "us versus them," and "friends versus enemies"—not law. One might argue that the terrorists won on 9/11. Terror laid hold of the American soul and, under the guise of strength, America weakened its grip on its fundamental values: due process, the rule of law, and protection of the rights of minorities and of individuals. As a result, we are all less safe today than we were on September 10, 2001. Also as a result, the police state and the pervasive presence of the mechanisms of war have become normative in everyday American life.

On September 10, 2001, military personnel were not a regular part of the landscape of every airport and train station. At airports, friends could meet flyers at their flight gate. On September 10, it had been more than twenty-five years since America's last major war, and the most popular television shows were *Sex in the City*, *ER*, *Moesha*, and *Friends*. After September 11 the police state was established and violent images permeated our culture. For everyday entertainment people turned to *24*, *CSI*, *Breaking Bad*, *The Wire*, and a plethora of military video games. According to a recent report by MotherJones.com, there were thirty-three mass shootings from 1982 to 2002 (twenty years). There were almost as many mass shootings (twenty-nine) in almost half that time (twelve years) after 9/11.[14]

President Obama inherited the legal chaos created by Bush's war paradigm, tolerance of torture, and a culture where violence had become normative. In the first years of his presidency he systematically

---

[13]Scott Shane, "U.S. Engaged in Torture After 9/11, Review Concludes," *New York Times*, April 16, 2013, A1.

[14]Mark Follman, Gavin Aronsen, and Deanna Pan, "US Mass Shootings, 1982-2012: Data from *Mother Jones*' Investigation," *Mother Jones*, updated May 26, 2021, www.motherjones.com/politics/2012/12/mass-shootings-mother-jones-full-data.

strengthened our cooperation with and accountability to the United Nations and international and human rights law bodies. Yet President Obama has a long way to go to live up to his stated value for the rule of law and due process. To reconcile his promises with his policies he must close the Guantanamo Bay prison.

As I stated in *Left Right and Christ*, "War is not inevitable. We have choices. We can choose the licentiousness of war and terror or the disciplined power of law and meek redemption of broken international relationships. War does not ultimately save us from evil-doers; it transforms the principled into perpetrators. We must do everything within our power to find another way."[15]

---

[15]Harper and Innes, *Left Right and Christ*, 192.

CHRISTIAN PACIFISM AND THE "GOOD WAR"

Ted Grimsrud

Does Christian pacifism make the claim that everyone should be pacifist?[1] Or is pacifism only a calling for those who affirm Jesus as Lord? This issue can—and should—be addressed on a theological and philosophical level. However, it may also be addressed on a more pragmatic level. Are there wars that can be considered legitimately justifiable? If no actual war can be justified, is that a basis for claiming that everyone should be pacifist (defining pacifism here as the conviction that one should never take part in or support warfare)? This chapter aims to investigate these questions and propose a possible answer.

THE ONE CERTAIN "JUST WAR"?

One way to ask how widely we should advocate pacifism is to look closely at a war most Americans, including many American pacifists,

---

[1] This chapter is adapted from two previously published blog posts: Ted Grimsrud, "Christian Attitudes Toward War: Rethinking the Typology," ThinkingPacifism.net (April 9, 2012) and Ted Grimsrud, "Christian Pacifism and the 'Good War,'" PeaceTheology.net (May 30, 2015). Used with permission.

believe was just—World War II. Catholic pacifist Robert Brimlow draws such a conclusion:

> The war against Hitler, Nazism, and the atrocities they perpetuated certainly satisfies all the requirements for a just war: even if no other war was justifiable, even if every other dispute could have been settled by nonviolent means, that dispute could only have been solved through violence."[2]

The kind of nonviolence Brimlow advocates is based on faithfulness, not on the expectation that it might practically be the best way to deal with conflict.

Methodist Stephen Long makes a similar argument. Long also suggests that World War II may be seen as a just war, where it was shown that "violence and war do sometimes work."[3] Long argues for what he calls "christological pacifism," an approach that "only makes sense because of the christological convictions we hold about what God has done in Christ."[4]

World War II was perhaps as true a test of pacifist convictions as could be imagined. Because of the widespread popularity of that war, only those with clear pacifist convictions would have chosen to be legal conscientious objectors (CO). If Long is correct about the link between a high Christology and pacifism, you would expect people who affirmed that Christology to tend toward pacifism. As it turned out, about twelve thousand young American men took the CO route, and something more than twelve million entered the military (so the number of pacifists was about 0.1 percent). The traditions that tended to emphasize doctrine

---

[2] Robert Brimlow, "What About Hitler?" in *A Faith Not Worth Fighting For: Addressing Commonly Asked Questions About Christian Nonviolence*, ed. Tripp York and Justin Bronson Barringer (Eugene, OR: Cascade, 2012), 51.
[3] D. Stephen Long, "What About the Protection of Third-Party Innocents?" in *A Faith Not Worth Fighting For*, 25.
[4] Long, "What About," 24.

more (e.g., Roman Catholics, Lutherans, and evangelical Protestants) had few if any conscientious objectors.[5]

To respond to a phenomenon such as World War II as a Christian pacifist, it seems to me, requires a broader sense of how pacifism works than that provided by Brimlow and Long. To affirm pacifism without condemning World War II as an unjust war weakens the case for pacifism significantly. That Christian pacifists today won't challenge that war's moral validity reflects a failure to see the necessary connection between pragmatic and principled (or confessional) factors that support pacifism. I propose that Christian pacifists should be willing to challenge the myth of World War II as a just war—and to use pragmatic grounds to do so.

In general, reflection on war and peace tends to repeat the general typology introduced by historian Roland Bainton in *Christian Attitudes Toward War and Peace*.[6] Bainton saw three categories: pacifism, the just war, and the crusade. This typology leaves too much out and oversimplifies what is left. As an alternative, I propose a revised typology that has two main types: (1) negatively disposed toward war and (2) positively disposed toward war. Each of these two types has three subtypes, as I will explain below.

Negatively disposed toward war. What unites the three "negatively disposed" approaches is the conviction that, morally, the benefit of the doubt is always against war.

1. Principled pacifism. This view is against war based on starting principles. One example would be how many Mennonites have said that they cannot fight due to their understanding of Jesus' commands such as

---

[5]See Theodore G. Grimsrud, "An Ethical Analysis of Conscientious Objection to World War II" (PhD diss., Graduate Theological Union, 1988).

[6]Roland H. Bainton, *Christian Attitudes Toward War and Peace: A Historical Survey and Critical Re-evaluation* (Nashville: Abingdon, 1960).

"love your enemies." Hence, the relative justice of particular wars is irrelevant.

Most World War II COs fit in this category. They refused military service, for the most part, simply because they believed any war was wrong due to their moral principles. Even in the case of a "just war," they would still have refused to fight. In this view someone could even affirm that at times warfare has improved overall human welfare while still refusing to fight.

2. *Pragmatic pacifism.* This view is against war due to conclusions based on the evidence of how warfare works in the world. These conclusions follow from using just war criteria to determine that all actual wars are certain to be unjust; that is, the pacifism is based on evidence. This view suggests that each war has violated some if not all the standard just war criteria.

These two views may reinforce each other. One could start with a principled pacifism view. However, with sensitized moral perceptions, one could recognize that wars in actuality do not ever work for human well-being in practice. Or one could start with an evidence-oriented analysis and, after concluding that no known wars have ever been just, begin to start with that conclusion when reflecting on the morality of warfare.

3. *Skeptical just war.* This view differs from pragmatic pacifism in that it is open to the possibility that just war criteria may be met. Still, this view starts with the assumption that any particular war is not just unless proved otherwise. The logical conclusion for those holding this view is that wars that do not overcome that burden of proof should be opposed. Something like this was, in fact, a common view in the United States during the Vietnam War for many prospective draftees who went to Canada or prison.

My description of the skeptical just war view is close to the way many describe the just war position in general. They assume that this is the main alternative to pacifism in the Christian tradition. However, this is actually an unusual view in terms of actual adherents. Notice that this view has no legal standing in the United States; those opposed to particular wars are still required to enter the military in the case of a draft or stay in the military if they are already there. You would think if this view actually were common, there would have been more effort to make it legally viable in this country.

Positively disposed toward war. What unites the three "positively disposed" approaches that follow is the conviction that war is inevitable and therefore we should not imagine a world without war. We should not assume that wars need to overcome an antiwar benefit of the doubt.

4. Just war as restraint. This view accepts the inevitability of war and believes it is dangerous to seek to do away with war. Such a negative attitude toward war hinders preparedness efforts and jeopardizes national interests by weakening the ability to respond appropriately with military force when necessary. This view also asserts that when citizens imagine doing away with war, this may ironically reinforce the interests of those who believe in total war. If you focus on stopping war and fail (which will almost certainly happen), you will miss the chance to influence efforts to restrain the violence of war.[7]

5. Blank check.[8] Though this view has not been named or studied by students of the history of war, it is by far the most common view held by Christians since the fourth century. The core conviction here is that citizens by definition have the responsibility to go to war when their nation calls on them to.

---

[7]Key thinkers advocating this view include Paul Ramsey (*War and the Christian Conscience: How Shall Modern War Be Conducted Justly?* [Durham, NC: Duke University Press, 1960], James Turner Johnson (*Can Modern War Be Just?* [New Haven, CT: Yale University Press, 1984]), and Jean Bethke Elshtain (*Just War Against Terror: Ethics and the Burden of American Power in a Violent World* [New York: Basic, 2003]).

[8]I have struggled to come up with a name for this view. "Blank check" may be too pejorative. However, terms such as "patriotic duty" or "nationalistic obedience" don't capture the sense of uncritical acceptance I see as central here.

Though the influential fourth-century bishop Augustine has been called the founder of Christian just war thought, his influence in undergirding the blank check approach has been probably his more important legacy. Augustine argued that citizens should leave the reasoning concerning a war's justness to the government. A citizen's responsibility is simply to obey one's government.[9] Christian citizens do not undertake just war reasoning prior to deciding to go to war, nor do they engage in just war reasoning in the course of the conflict as to whether the tactics are too unrestrained. They simply obey orders.

6. *Crusade.* This view differs from the blank check view by having a more positive view of the goodness of war. If there are transcendental values at stake, when one has a clear sense of calling to fight, then one must do so. Since for a crusade the war serves an absolute good, one need not be concerned with just war concerns for proper procedures. In a crusade, the calling is to fight, all-out.

This typology helpfully separates two general approaches to pacifism. In practice, most pacifists probably combine the principled and pragmatic approaches. It also helps us see how pacifism and certain approaches to just war philosophy actually have a great deal in common and are part of one continuum that includes all those who are disposed against war.

Also, this typology draws a dividing line between two distinct just war approaches. The skeptical just war view has much more in common with pacifism than with the just war as restraint view (and likewise the just war as restraint view links more closely with the blank check view). This typology lifts up the blank check view as not only a distinctive view rarely noticed in most discussions on this topic, but actually as by far the dominant view among Christians (and other citizens).

---

[9]Augustine, *Contra Faustus*, 22.75, in *The Political Writings of St. Augustine,* ed. Henry Paolucci (New York: Gateway, 1962), 164.

WHAT ABOUT WORLD WAR II?

The moral legacy of World War II has been devastating for the United States and for the world—and for Christianity as well.[10] For Americans, this war stands not as the war that ended other wars so much as the war that justified other wars.

Seeing war as sometimes the best option leads to empowering the societal structures that are needed to prepare for war. In the past the nation inclined toward seeing war as a last resort. Now it sees many conflicts that require a militarized first response. Hence the extraordinary American military presence around the world.

Borrowing from social critic Naomi Klein, we could say that the "shock" of total war in the early 1940s led directly to the takeover of the United States by advocates of the American national security ideology.[11] That point of vulnerability led to the creation of permanent structures such as the Pentagon, the Central Intelligence Agency, and the nuclear weapons program. As a consequence of the transformative influence of these entities, in the United States, "all politics is a politics of war."[12]

To seriously doubt the justness of World War II is almost unheard of. Even historians who raise questions about the war's justness almost invariably conclude that it indeed ultimately was just.[13] And for many American historians, simply to raise moral questions about the war is unacceptable. As historian Eric Bergerud wrote, "I find it almost

---

[10] This assertion is the burden of my recent book, from which much of what follows in this essay is drawn. See Ted Grimsrud, *The Good War That Wasn't—and Why It Matters: World War II's Moral Legacy* (Eugene, OR: Cascade, 2014), especially the conclusion, 244-65.

[11] Naomi Klein, *The Shock Doctrine: The Rise of Disaster Capitalism* (New York: Metropolitan, 2007).

[12] Walter Wink, *Engaging the Powers: Discernment and Resistance in a World of Domination* (Minneapolis: Fortress, 1992), 27.

[13] See, for example, Michael Bess, *Choices Under Fire: Moral Dimensions of World War II* (New York: Knopf, 2006), 338-45, and Kenneth D. Rose, *Myth of the Greatest Generation: A Social History of Americans in World War II* (New York: Routledge, 2008), 251-54.

incomprehensible that anyone would claim to discover moral ambiguity in World War II. . . . If World War II was not necessary, no war has been."[14]

However, the just war tradition has at its core claims that should lead to a rejection of Bergerud's assertion that a war stands as a just war simply because it is deemed "necessary." Just war analysis should establish stable criteria for moral evaluation and then apply those objectively to the actions of one's enemies, oneself, and one's friends and allies. Norman Davies, a rare historian who does apply this approach in his account of World War II, expresses it this way: "All sound moral judgments operate on the basis that the standards applied to one side of the relationship must be applied to all sides."[15]

JUST CAUSE DOUBTS

When we use the two basic categories of just war analysis, cause and conduct, we find evidence (decisive, in my view) that this was not a just war for the United States. It is true that the official entry of the United States into World War II as a full-fledged protagonist came about due to two events that did provide just cause: (1) the Japanese attack on the American naval base at Pearl Harbor on December 7, 1941, and (2) the German declaration of war on the United States a few days later.

However, neither of these events initiated US involvement in the war. The United States was already strongly on the side of Great Britain in the conflict with the Germans and on the side of China in the conflict with the Japanese. The events in early December 1941 only accelerated an ever-growing conflict between the United States and the Axis powers.

So we should ask if the American entry into the conflict prior to the overt declarations of war had just causes. The "good war mythology"

---

[14]Eric Bergerud, "Critique of *Choices Under Fire*," *Historically Speaking: The Bulletin of the Historical Society* 9 (2008): 41.

[15]Norman Davies, *No Simple Victory: World War II in Europe, 1939–1945* (New York: Penguin, 2006), 63.

tends to cite three main reasons for US involvement: (1) the need to protect the United States from a direct invasion by Germany or Japan, (2) the moral imperative to stop the domination of the tyrannies of Nazi Germany and imperial Japan in the cause of furthering democracy, and (3) the need to rescue Jews who were being annihilated by the Nazis.

In the actual event, though, none of these three reasons likely played a major role in American involvement. We have no evidence that either the Japanese or the Germans seriously imagined invading the United States. It would simply not have been possible to cross either the Pacific or Atlantic Ocean with invasion forces.

Many Americans surely opposed the tyrannies of Japan and Germany. However, the United States and Britain joined in alliance with a regime as equally tyrannical as Hitler's Germany—the Soviet Union. Insofar as this alliance actually sustained and advanced Soviet tyranny, we can scarcely say the cause for the United States' engaging in the conflict was to defeat tyranny.

Many Americans looked positively on the Nazis in 1933 as a bulwark against communism. When the Nazis came into power they immediately began implementing anti-Jewish policies. As the violence toward Jews increased, humanitarian voices were raised on behalf of beleaguered Jews; however, humanitarian efforts were thwarted by US leaders. When World War II actually began and the genocidal violence increased, these leaders continued to resist efforts to offer help. The Western Allies were not motivated by a desire to directly save Jewish lives.[16] In fact, the war's expansion likely made the lot of Europe's Jews even worse.[17]

---

[16] See Theodore S. Hamerow, *Why We Watched: Europe, America, and the Holocaust* (New York: Norton, 2008). Hamerow writes in support of the Allied leaders in face of charges they were anti-Semitic. However, in arguing that these leaders were constrained by circumstances from effectively saving Jewish lives, he also confirms that saving Jewish lives was *not* part of the purpose of the war for Americans.

[17] Doris L. Bergen, *War and Genocide: A Concise History of the Holocaust*, 2nd ed. (Lanham, MD: Rowman and Littlefield, 2009): "War provided killers with both a cover and an excuse for

Why then did the United States act to make war inevitable and then fight a "total war"? Partly, the United States had been involved in a clash of imperialisms with Japan dating back decades. The war with Japan happened because of a series of escalating moves taken by both sides in the conflict. As well, the United States' close ties with Great Britain led to aid to the British after the outbreak of war in Europe. This aid took an ever more overtly militaristic cast and involved the United States in the conflict as a partisan ally of the British. The British war with the Germans began due to a British war alliance with the Polish dictatorship based on imperial concerns (not noble motives such as self-determination and disarmament).

In time, it became clear that the United States would benefit greatly from this war and that the forces within the United States that would benefit the most were the military and business elites. The war was an opportunity for the military to gain power and influence within the federal government and for American corporations to profit immensely.

None of these dynamics satisfies traditional criteria for just cause for going to war (e.g., self-preservation, defending innocent victims, serving the interests of the entire county, leading to a better peace than existed before the war).

JUST CONDUCT?

Many who write about World War II seem to assume that since the causes were just, we need not go further with moral discernment. Even if the causes were clearly just, the just war tradition *should* insist that moral discernment is only beginning. The second area of concern for just war thought, after reflection on whether the cause is just, is to reflect

---

murder; in wartime, killing was normalized, and extreme, even genocidal measures could be justified with familiar arguments about the need to defend the homeland. Without the war, the Holocaust would not—and could not—have happened" (vii).

morally on how the war is conducted. The two main criteria used to judge conduct are proportionality (the damage of the fighting should not outweigh the good the war accomplished) and noncombatant immunity (those not engaged as soldiers should not be attacked).

In relation to both of these criteria, the conduct of the US military crossed the line into immoral behavior. Most obviously, the United States provided support when the British attacked the inner city of Hamburg and intentionally created a firestorm that killed tens of thousands of noncombatants. Then came the February 1945 attack on the defenseless German city of Dresden, a city with no military significance, killing well over fifty thousand noncombatants.

The first of a series of attacks on Japanese cities, carried out March 9, 1945, on Tokyo, created another firestorm that surpassed the deaths caused by the bombing of Dresden. The climax of the American attacks on Japanese civilian populations came in August 1945 with the use of atomic bombs. Any pretense of adhering to standards of proportionality and noncombatant immunity ended.

We might also add the practices of America and Britain's key ally in the war, the Soviet Union. The Soviets' conduct was extraordinarily brutal. In allying with the Soviets the United States actually empowered a spirit as vicious as the spirit of Nazism. As the Soviets turned back the German invasion and moved toward Berlin, their tactics were some of the most brutal violations of just conduct criteria ever—murder, rape, destruction of civilian infrastructure, and more.

WHY THIS UNJUST WAR WAS A MORAL DISASTER FOR THE UNITED STATES

When I apply the just war criteria to American involvement in World War II, I conclude that it was not a just war. Though the Axis powers were guilty of aggression and many atrocities, it does not appear that the Allies were motivated by the need to stop the atrocities—and in fact one of the three main Allies (the Soviet Union) had itself engaged in extraordinary atrocities in the years prior to the war.

As well, the Axis powers' egregious violation of just conduct standards did not justify violations by the Allies. What's more, the moral legacy of the war does not have to do only with what had happened through August 1945. We also need to consider the impact of prosecuting the war on American society and the aftermath of the war in relation to American foreign policy. I suggest we broaden our sense of how we use critical just war analyses—not only just cause and just conduct, but also just consequences over time.

What if World War II was an unjust war? Obviously that judgment cannot change the past. The main issue related to how we now think about World War II is how this might impact our current disposition toward American military policies and toward warfare in general.

To conclude that World War II was unjust, and to affirm that we should never act unjustly or support unjust actions, leads to rejecting use of the war as a basis for arguing for the necessity of warfare. If we can't use World War II as such a basis, we will have a much more difficult time making such an argument in general.

At the end of World War II, the United States stood with unprecedented economic power and unmatched international prestige as the bearer of the ideals portrayed to great effect in statements such as the Atlantic Charter and the initial declaration by the United Nations.[18] These statements rallied people to defeat forces in the world that stood implacably against ideals such as self-determination and disarmament.

---

[18]"The Atlantic Charter," August 14, 1941, NATO, www.nato.int/cps/en/natolive/official_texts_16912.htm; "Preparatory Years: UN Charter History," United Nations, www.un.org/en/about-us/history-of-the-un/preparatory-years, accessed November 4, 2021.

The generations that followed have shown that the United States was not a good steward of the power it possessed in 1945. The war actually pushed the country in deeply problematic directions. It (1) corrupted the American democratic polity, (2) empowered the forces of militarism in the country that have since 1945 led the United States into foreign policy disaster after foreign disaster,[19] and (3) shifted the economic center of gravity in the country toward the corporate sector, setting the country on a long path of corruption and economic self-immolation.

The basic moral lesson we should learn from World War II is to find ways to resist the lure of trust in military action. Certainly the rise of the Axis powers created the need for decisive resistance to their politics. But the path of resistance that America took, while in a short-term sense victorious, actually itself led to the long-term victory of fascist-like nationalistic brute power and nihilism. If even this "good war" led to such a moral disaster, then Americans must find ways to resist the evils of aggressive militarism that do not rely on the use of aggressive militarism.

Pursuing an unjust war had numerous long-term morally devastating consequences. When a democracy pursues such a war, inevitably democratic processes will be corrupted. In theory, a just war approach should enhance democracy because if the benefit of doubt is against going to war, it will take clear and persuasive evidence to justify the war. This evidence should be publicly presented, with open debate, and if the case is *not* made, the decision that follows should be not to enter the war. And just causes should be factors that are consistent with genuine national security and the best interests of the nation.

In the lead-up to World War II, though, the US government did not give an honest account of the factors for and against intervention, nor did it illumine the democratic values at stake. Rather, a pro-war

---

[19] William Blum, *Killing Hope: U.S. Military and C.I.A. Interventions Since World War II* (Monroe, ME: Common Courage, 2004).

propaganda campaign distorted the facts and fanned unwarranted fears of American national security being breached through the dangers of invasion. When the war did come, the stage was set for ongoing policymaking that paid little heed to democratic practices and would long outlast the "emergency" that initially justified it. The most notable examples are the creation of the atomic weapons program and the insistence on unconditional surrender as a nonnegotiable war goal.

The prosecution of World War II permanently transformed the American way of fighting. Before 1941, American air warfare followed a doctrine of reluctance to target civilians. This reluctance was completely gone by the end of the war; witness the firebombing of Tokyo and the use of atomic bombs on Hiroshima and Nagasaki. The ensuing wars—Korea and Vietnam most notably—saw unrestrained air warfare that cared little about proportionality and noncombatant immunity.[20]

The continued development of and willingness to deploy ever more destructive nuclear weapons witnesses to such a disregard for just war constraints.[21] Many times major policymakers in the United States actively advocated the use of nuclear bombs. That they were in the end not used does not change the reality that they easily could have been.

In 1937, the US military was small and peripheral to the society as a whole. It ranked in size sixteenth in the world, between Portugal and Romania. Today we cannot imagine the United States as such a nonmilitarized society. In the late 1930s, advocates of military "preparedness" took advantage of the deteriorating international order to move the country toward an extraordinary reorientation of priorities that moved the American military from the periphery to the center of society—permanently.

---

[20] Sven Lindqvist, *A History of Bombing*, trans. Linda Haverty Rugg (New York: New Press, 2001).
[21] Joseph Gerson, *Empire and the Bomb: How the US Uses Nuclear Weapons to Dominate the World* (London: Pluto, 2007).

Three months before the United States formally entered the war, ground was broken for the Pentagon. The huge physical structure was completed with remarkable speed. The stage was set for the American military to gain a measure of freedom from the constraints of the democratic checks and balances of governmental oversight.[22] Then, the next month, Roosevelt approved the establishment of a program to create atomic weapons. The Manhattan Project remained top-secret but soon absorbed tremendous resources and inexorably moved the country into a future of tremendous peril.

World War II provided the shock that empowered those supportive of the armed forces to establish these key engines for ongoing militarization. The Pentagon and the nuclear weapons program gained their sense of legitimacy from the "needs" of total war—and then, when the war was over, devoted their energies to retaining and actually expanding their domination of the American body politic.

Then, the National Security Act of 1947 established the Central Intelligence Agency and consolidated the various branches of the military. It also created the National Security Council as a top leadership group to guide the nation's policies. Around this same time, President Truman delivered his famous speech that delineated the Truman Doctrine, asserting, in effect, that any resistance to American hegemony anywhere in the world would be seen as a communist threat and a basis for military intervention. The die was cast.

So World War II was a test of whether war in fact can ever serve the moral good. It in effect tested the hypothesis that war might occasionally be necessary and even good. After all, we may point to many reasons why this war was necessary. We probably cannot overstate the moral corruption of Nazi Germany and its aggressive efforts to spread that

---

[22]James Carroll, *House of War: The Pentagon and the Disastrous Rise of American Power* (Boston: Houghton Mifflin, 2006).

corruption. Imperial Japan was almost as bad. And, for the United States, at least, the war was won at relatively low cost and led to unprecedented prosperity and power in its aftermath—that is, the world's pioneering democracy was in position to further its ideals of freedom and self-determination.

Yet look what happened. The very effort of prosecuting this most terrible of all wars led directly to a transformation of the United States from a nonmilitarized, relatively free and democratic nation to a global imperial power. This global imperial power evolved to a point at which it became impossible to turn away from a devastatingly self-destructive path of empire as a way of life.

CONCLUSION

I believe that pacifists should actively critique World War II—not because our pacifism is valid only if we can prove the war was unjust, but because part of the pacifist calling is to work for a more peaceable world. The myth that World War II was just, necessary, and even good has continued to underwrite much violence down to our present day.

Our critique, at least in part, may draw heavily on just war reasoning, as I have done in this essay, because our rejection of warfare is best based on both principled (or confessional) and pragmatic grounds. These two sources of moral reasoning are complementary, not mutually exclusive.

The line of disagreement in relation to war is not between pacifist and just war views nearly so much as between what I call "negatively disposed to war" and "positively disposed to war" views. The most fundamental issue is whether we assume war is necessary or we assume that the benefit of doubt should be against war. Among the "negatively disposed" views,

I believe that the principled/confessional elements and the pragmatic elements are not in opposition but actually complement each other.[23]

One consequence of affirming both principled and pragmatic moral resources in relation to war is that we may then recast the role of World War II in our thinking. It becomes a site of moral reflection rather than serving as the war to end all our moral reflection about war. Pacifists need not cede to war supporters the assumption that World War II proves that war can be just, necessary, and even good—an assumption that powerfully undermines just about all arguments for pacifism (even the christological ones).

---

[23]For an argument for Christian pacifism that emphasizes confession and principled elements, see Ted Grimsrud, *Arguing Peace: Collected Pacifist Writings,* vol. 3 of *Biblical and Theological Essays* (Harrisonburg, VA: Peace Theology Books, 2014).

PROBLEMATIC PACIFISM

PURSUING BIBLICAL JUSTICE
TOWARD EFFECTIVE CHANGE

Mae Elise Cannon

CHRISTIANS AROUND THE WORLD worship the person of Jesus Christ as the Prince of Peace and the epitome of biblical justice in a broken world. The trajectory of Christian history, in large part, has been formed on the theological and ideological backbone of just war theory. From Augustine and Aquinas to Martin Luther and John Calvin to more contemporary Christian thinkers such as Paul Ramsey and Jean Bethke Elshtain, Christians have wrestled with moral questions about violence and war. These thinkers and others have contributed nuanced components to our Christian understanding of when it might be morally permissible to use state-imposed violence to right wrongs in the world.

Other followers of Jesus throughout the centuries have pursued pacifism as a manifestation of their biblical worldview. There are many historic examples of successful nonviolent movements that have embraced principles of pacifism as a means of bringing about societal change. According to Ron Sider, Christian theologian and activist who founded Evangelicals for Social Action (now known as Christians for Social

Action), at least seven Latin American dictators in the twentieth century have been overthrown by nonviolent general strikes.[1] However, what is an appropriate Christian response when nonviolent resistance to injustice does not yield the most effective results? What happens when peaceful actions do not provoke the desired and necessary change? Are there circumstances that demand a response other than pacifism? This chapter wrestles with both the problems of pacifism and the limitations of just war theory. As Christians committed to advocating for justice, we must ask whether or not there are limitations to nonviolent effectiveness in provoking societal change.

My work in the past decade or so has focused on evangelical engagement in what the gospel of Christ teaches us about biblical justice. I wrote extensively about issues of justice in my first book, *Social Justice Handbook: Small Steps for a Better World*, and the subsequent volume on the integration of justice and spiritual formation in *Just Spirituality: How Faith Practices Fuel Social Action*.[2] In the Bible, themes of justice are core to the foundation of God's engagement in the world. Throughout the Hebrew Scriptures and the New Testament, the key Hebrew and Greek words for justice appear more than one thousand times.[3] Biblical justice is the manifestation of the kingdom of God and its principles in the world as an expression of the way God originally intended his creation to be. Wrongs are made right. Justice is realized through biblical shalom once an ultimate and complete peace is established.

We see glimpses of God's intention and the integration of both peace and justice in the laws of Leviticus. The people of God are commanded

---

[1] Ron Sider, *Nonviolent Action: What Christian Ethics Demands but Most Christians Have Never Really Tried* (Grand Rapids, MI: Brazos, 2015), 12.
[2] Mae Elise Cannon, *Social Justice Handbook: Small Steps for a Better World* (Downers Grove, IL: InterVarsity Press, 2009), and *Just Spirituality: How Faith Practices Fuel Social Action* (Downers Grove, IL: InterVarsity Press, 2013).
[3] Glen H. Stassen, ed., *Just Peacemaking: The New Paradigm for the Ethics of Peace and War* (Cleveland: Pilgrim Press, 2008), 23.

to live according to the laws and principles of *shalom* according to the Sabbath, every seventh year, and ultimately the Year of Jubilee, the year after seven times seven. The Year of Jubilee, in the fiftieth year, declared on the Day of Atonement and liberty, was to be proclaimed throughout the land to all its inhabitants. Jubilee is a manifestation of peace and restoration. Leviticus 25 lays out the plan for this Sabbath year in which both people and land are restored and equipped to thrive. People were commanded to return to "their own property" (Lev 25:13 NIV). Business was to be conducted honestly and fairly (Lev 25:16-17). The land was to be "redeemed" and acknowledged as belonging to the Lord (Lev 25:23-24). The losses of the poor were to be alleviated by the wealthy (Lev 25:25-28). Strict rules were to be followed for the Israelites who had become slaves or indentured servants; they were to be set free and released of their obligations during the Year of Jubilee (Lev 25:39-43). Jesus made reference to this declaration of peace, the Year of Jubilee, when he preached from the words of the prophet Isaiah at the launch of his ministry:

> The Spirit of the Lord is upon me,
> > because he has anointed me
> > > to proclaim good news to the poor.
> He has sent me to proclaim release to the captives
> > and recovery of sight to the blind,
> > > to let the oppressed go free,
> to proclaim the year of the Lord's favor. (Lk 4:18-19)

Scholars debate whether or not the Year of Jubilee as described in Leviticus ever came to be. Nonetheless, the laws of the Hebrew Scriptures in Leviticus make clear God's intent that ultimate peace, *shalom*, is expressed when God's justice and laws are applied to God's people. These laws of justice mandated right treatment of the land, foreigners, and the poor and ultimately instructed the Israelites, the chosen people of God, in the ways they should conduct their affairs. In Luke 4, Jesus declares himself to be the fulfillment of these laws. His declaration in proclaiming the "year of the Lord's favor" clearly makes reference to what the Jewish people of the day would have known as the Year of Jubilee. Christ's ministry and incarnational presence on earth, ultimately culminating in his death on the cross, completely encapsulates God's demand for righteousness and justice and marks the penetration of the kingdom of God here on earth. The Prince of Peace, by embracing the horrific act of violence perpetrated against him during the crucifixion, experiences the just punishment for the sinfulness of humankind and thus creates an opportunity for the true peace of the kingdom to reign on earth as it does in heaven.

PACIFISM

It is imperative that we understand the foundational principles of both biblical justice and shalom as we seek to understand and pursue an end to earthly violence. Pacifism is the belief that all wars and state violence are unjustifiable, regardless of the circumstances. For pacifists, the only morally acceptable response to violence and disputes is through peaceful, nonviolent means. Christian pacifists undergird their religious convictions with scriptural passages such as the prophet Isaiah's imagery that God will teach us his ways. In God's way, disputes will be settled as swords are beat into plowshares and spears converted into pruning hooks: "Nation shall not lift up sword against nation, neither shall they learn war any more" (Is 2:3-4).

In the New Testament, pacifists esteem Jesus as the ultimate witness of nonviolent resistance. Many of Jesus' followers, including Judas Iscariot, desired for him to take up the sword and revolt against the unjust policies of the Roman emperor and occupation. Jesus responded by demanding the disciples put their swords away, for "all who take the sword will perish by the sword" (Mt 26:52). Christ had the power and authority to respond victoriously through violence to his arrest in the Garden of Gethsemane but chose rather to submit and sacrifice himself, bearing unjust treatment, humiliation, suffering, and death. He reminded his disciples, "Do you think that I cannot appeal to my Father, and he will at once send me more than twelve legions of angels?" (Mt 26:53). Even though Jesus had the power and authority to overcome his arrest and imprisonment with violence, he reminded his followers that his way was a different way.

To some degree, the strengths of a pacifist perspective are obvious. Pacifism employs a response to human violence and evil that transcends the natural emotional and physiological inclination to respond with force or to retaliate and seek revenge. In the words of academic ethicist and philosopher Jean Bethke Elshtain, pacifism puts "violence on trial."[4] Pacifism shows a willingness toward self-sacrifice for the sake of righting a wrong, deescalating a violence, or responding to an injustice. J. Daryl Charles writes of the merits of pacifism in *Between Pacifism and Jihad: Just War and Christian Tradition:*

> [Pacifism] is keenly sensitive to the distortions of faith that come with an uncritical view of the state—a continual problem throughout the history of the church. Pacifists help sensitize nonpacifists to an all too human tendency to rationalize violence in the service of nationalism, reminding us of the relative norms of politics and "social justice."[5]

It is worth pondering the merits of pacifism particularly in the twenty-first century world, where state violence, the rise of religious extremism, and civil unrest seem rampant. Pacifism offers valuable

---

[4]Jean Bethke Elshtain, *Women and War*, rev. ed. (Chicago: University of Chicago Press, 1995), 123, 132.
[5]J. Daryl Charles, *Between Pacifism and Jihad: Just War and Christian Tradition* (Downers Grove, IL: InterVarsity Press, 2009), 126.

responses that are often rooted in the teachings of Jesus and cannot be ignored as one considers an ethic of responding to evil in the world.

THE DIFFICULTIES OF PACIFISM

One of the main criticisms of pacifism is that in the face of global tyrants and despots such as Hitler, Stalin, Mao, and others, pacifists cannot sit idly by and watch murder, mayhem, ethnic cleansing, and genocide without being willing to risk pain, suffering, and even death as a means of combating violence and injustice. On one hand, pacifism asserts an alternative to violence. Ron Sider issues a loud and compelling challenge to the pacifist community:

> Only pacifists ready to risk death by the thousands will have credibility after a century that has witnessed the greatest bloodshed in human history. Costly pacifist involvement in successful nonviolent campaigns is perhaps the most effective way to convince doubting contemporaries that there is an alternative to war.[6]

Is the call to pacifists to be willing to face the cost enough? If the pacifist community were to be mobilized as Sider describes and to carry the burden of self-sacrifice and even death, would evil be deterred? Many—in fact most—Christian academics think not.

Pacifists often fail to distinguish between church and state. According to Christian ethicist David Gushee, the requirements of believers must be distinguished from the expectations and obligations of the body politic that governs a society.[7] Some, such as Lisa Sharon Harper, founder and president of Freedom Road (see freedomroad.us), express concern about an unhelpful dualism and overly exemplified separation

---

[6]Ron Sider, *Nonviolent Action: What Christian Ethics Demands but Most Christians Have Never Really Tried* (Grand Rapids, MI: Brazos Press, 2015), 167.
[7]David Gushee, "Evangelical Peacemakers: A Critical Analysis," in *Evangelical Peacemakers: Gospel Engagement in a War-Torn World,* ed. David Gushee (Eugene, OR: Cascade, 2013), 116.

between the responsibilities of individual faith communities and the responsibilities of government. Still, as Gushee points out, one must be willing to ask the questions about functionality and purpose of the church while distinguishing those expectations and requirements from those imposed upon the rule of government and the state. Most assume nation states have not only the requirement but also the obligation to protect and provide self-defense for the people they govern. This notion of security is often not adequately addressed in pacifist ideology.

Another weakness of pacifism, according to J. Daryl Charles, is "an exceptionally apocalyptic view of governing authorities" that assumes some type of inherent evil or systemic injustice in bodies politic.[8] Charles argues that a society without coercive powers is an impossibility, but those elements of coercion need not be corrupt. He believes power and coercion can be used for the good of society and that an inherent assumption of evil in governing authorities and political institutions is unwarranted.

Many just war theorists and critics of pacifism agree in the identification of one of pacifism's greatest weaknesses. They assert pacifism underestimates the necessity and moral requirement to defend the weak and protect those within society who are underprivileged or powerless. Pacifists reject the notion that their refusal to bear arms is a "callous or cowardly disregard of their obligations to defend the weak and defenseless against bullies and tyrants."[9] To some degree the ideological difference between pacifists and adherents of interventionism is a matter of where one places the moral imperative. Is it more important to not impose violence toward another human being or society, or is it more important to offer protection, safety, and security against external enemies?

---

[8] Charles, *Between Pacifism and Jihad*, 127.
[9] Sider, *Nonviolent Action*, 167.

INTERVENTIONISM AND THE RESPONSIBILITY TO PROTECT

Certainly all of us desire the utopic ideal of a world without war and violence. But how do we embrace the core tenets of pacifism in a less than ideal world? As World War II progressed and the German Third Reich increased its geographic and political control, Reinhold Niebuhr, leading American theologian and ethicist, wrestled with these questions. Niebuhr wrote extensively for the influential Protestant liberal magazine *The Christian Century* until his opinions about the necessity of intervention and his delusions of pacifism caused him to leave the journal. In 1940 Niebuhr attacked the merging of Christian pacifism and American isolationism and developed strong arguments against pacifism in the church.[10] As a result, in 1941, Niebuhr launched *Christianity and Crisis,* a periodical reflective of his changing views on how American Christians should respond to the German Nazis' treatment of the Jewish people in Europe. Biographer Richard Fox says that *Christianity and Crisis* was a "conscious clone" of *The Christian Century,* down to the double C alliteration, and that the *Century* was both target and model for *Christianity and Crisis.*[11] Niebuhr's new journal and views on interventionism created a rift between him and C. C. Morrison, editor of the *Century.*[12] Niebuhr argued that moral responsibility requires the resistance of evil with force. In the years he wrote for the *Century,* Niebuhr was a pacifist. However, he came to believe that Christians should be "interventionist," standing up for the Jews and actively opposing the wrongs being committed against them by the Nazis.

In large part, Niebuhr used *Christianity and Crisis* to propagate his interventionist views. In the first issue of the journal, Niebuhr writes,

---

[10]Ronald H. Stone, *Professor Reinhold Niebuhr: A Mentor to the Twentieth Century* (Louisville, KY: John Knox Press, 1992), 102.
[11]Richard Wightman Fox, *Reinhold Niebuhr: A Biography* (New York: Pantheon, 1985), 196.
[12]Fox, *Reinhold Niebuhr,* 196.

"We intend this journal to . . . combat what seems to us false interpretations of our faith, and consequent false analyses of our world and our duties in it."[13] Niebuhr goes on to specify what he means in relation to current world events: "We think it dangerous to allow religious sensitivity to obscure the fact that Nazi tyranny intends to annihilate the Jewish race."[14] In the third issue of *Christianity and Crisis*, an article with no byline states,

> While the immediate occasion for the appearance of this journal is the impact of the war, our main purpose is to contribute to a better understanding of Christianity in relation to moral struggle. The deepest issue before us is not who should win the war, but what in the time of moral crisis does Christianity mean?[15]

For Niebuhr, and other interventionists such as Dietrich Bonhoeffer, in the face of the most obtuse evil manifested in the world, pacifism just wasn't enough. Rather, the use of violence and state-inflicted war was justifiable because of the injustices it would prevent, the lives it would ultimately save, and the evil that would be rectified by such intervention.

As exemplified in the account on Niebuhr, one of the key principles in support of an interventionist approach is the notion of the "responsibility to protect." This says that someone or some system of power and influence has a moral obligation to protect those with less access to power and resources. In Brazil in 2006, the World Council of Churches (WCC) issued a statement on this responsibility. On one hand, the WCC sought to shift the emphasis of the debate from a viewpoint of the intervener to that of people who need assistance. Ultimately, the statement concluded that intervention at times may be an appropriate response to

---

[13]Reinhold Niebuhr, "The Christian Faith and the World Crisis," *Christianity and Crisis* 1, no. 1 (Feb 10, 1941): 4.
[14]Niebuhr, "Christian Faith," 6.
[15]"Quest Not Conflict," *Christianity and Crisis* 1, no. 3 (March 10, 1941): 2.

injustice: "The fellowship of the churches is not prepared to say that it is never appropriate or never necessary to resort to the use of force for the protection of the vulnerable."[16]

The Rev. Dr. H. Martin Rumscheidt, an ordained United Church minister and retired professor of theology, wrestled with questions of interventionism and reframed the question by saying, "It is the neighbor in need who matters, and not the quandary of intervention or nonintervention."[17] His academic contributions focused on the church in the former German Democratic Republic and the Holocaust, with particular specialization in Karl Barth and Dietrich Bonhoeffer. Rumscheidt says, "The people crying for protection have ethical priority over the ethical principles of those who may or may not intervene."[18] He believes the Bible prioritizes love for neighbor in response to the "cries of the vulnerable" over strongly affirmed principles such as those of nonviolence.[19] Rumscheidt connects this love of neighbor to Bonhoeffer's "view from below." In Bonhoeffer's words, "It remains an experience of incomparable value that we have for once learned to see the great events of world history from below, from the perspective of the outcasts, the suspects, the maltreated, the powerless, the oppressed and reviled, in short from the perspective of the suffering."[20]

It is interesting to note that a perspective of sensitivity toward the suffering of the oppressed could be used, as it is here, both to justify interventionism and also to discredit it. One could argue that an

---

[16]"Vulnerable Populations at Risk—the Responsibility to Protect," Statement of the World Council of Churches 9th Assembly, February 14-23, 2006, www.oikoumene.org/en/resources/documents/commissions/international-affairs/responsability-to-protect/vulnerable-populations-at-risk-the-responsibility-to-protect.

[17]Martin Lukens-Rumscheidt, "To Intervene or Not to Intervene: Is That the Question?" *Conrad Grebel Review* 28, no. 3 (September 1, 2010): 57.

[18]Lukens-Rumscheidt, "To Intervene," 58.

[19]Lukens-Rumscheidt, "To Intervene," 64.

[20]Dietrich Bonhoeffer, *Letters and Papers from Prison*, Dietrich Bonhoeffer Works, vol. 8 (Minneapolis: Fortress Press, 2010), 52.

interventionist approach denies individual agency and autonomy to the individuals or segment of society that is in "need of protection." Interventionism is similarly in danger of a paternalistic perspective that ignores the subaltern voices and their own perspective and agency toward liberation from oppression. Nonetheless, Rumscheidt holds to the belief that one is ultimately responsible to care for and intervene on behalf of one's neighbor: "This issue is that radical openness to God and willingness for responsibility for the neighbor materializes itself in liberation by accepting culpability."[21]

Mennonite Gerald W. Schlabach argues for a "just policing" view.[22] For him, this is a form of interventionism that comes before the "exceptional last resort" of true just war theory and as an acceptable answer to pacifists who do not currently have concrete plans for how to intervene nonviolently. In his words, "In some cases [pacifists] may need the honesty and fortitude to be silent, admitting that for some situations they do not now (right now!—in time to save *these* lives) have operationalized nonviolent solutions ready to roll out."[23] For Schlabach, this "just policing" could be "conflict resolution" or a "Gandhian interventionist model." As Sider also asserts, the major roadblock to these ideals is not that they are utopian but that we lack "the critical mass of courageous soldiers of nonviolence needed for such a venture."[24]

JUST WAR THEORY

When one studies the New Testament in light of passages regarding peace, it soon becomes clear that a mere pacifist reading isn't enough; the teachings of Jesus regarding violence and war and the relationship

---

[21]Lukens-Rumscheidt, "To Intervene," 69.
[22]Gerald W. Schlabach, "Just Policing, Responsibility to Protect, and Anabaptist Two-Kingdom Theology," *Conrad Grebel Review* 28, no. 3 (September 1, 2010): 73-88.
[23]Schlabach, "Just Policing," 78.
[24]Schlabach, "Just Policing," 77.

between disciples, the community of believers, and the state are more complex and deserve more in-depth attention than a mere passing glance. Certainly Christians who acknowledge Jesus as the Messiah maintain him worthy of the title "Prince of Peace" (Is 9:6), but for adherents of just war theory that does not necessitate a lack of virtue in justified warfare and violence to right the world's wrongs. Jesus himself said, when giving his disciples instructions for their ministry in the world, "Do not think that I have come to bring peace to the earth; I have not come to bring peace, but a sword" (Mt 10:34). For many first-century followers of Jesus, these words would have been welcomed in the spirit of the Zealots, a Jewish movement of people who believed the Messiah would come to physically deliver the Jewish people from their position under the thumb of the Roman Caesar. For others, a reading of this passage would justify the use of the sword as a last resort when the appropriate conditions applied. For Christians, just war theory addresses whether or not state-sanctioned violence or war is just or unjust. According to Sider, one can adhere to just war theory, and even believe in the maintaining and possession of nuclear weapons, and still hold the "fervent desire to substitute nonviolent strategies for violent ones whenever possible."[25]

Peter Kreeft—Christian philosopher, author, and speaker—strongly advocates and claims that "just war is in the service of peace." Kreeft cites Jesus' model as the good shepherd: "The Good Shepherd fights the wolves because He loves the sheep. Not to fight the wolves is not to love the sheep."[26] One of the questions in just war theory is who gets to make the determination about who are sheep and who are wolves. What guarantees a fair and righteous attribution of intent and qualification of individuals and communities in this paradigm? In response Kreeft says,

---

[25]Sider, *Nonviolent Action*, xv.
[26]Peter Kreeft, *Ecumenical Jihad: Ecumenism and the Culture War* (San Francisco: Ignatius Press, 1994), 50.

God is raising an army, forging a new alliance of all who hate evil.... You cannot demonize a demon, any more than you can personalize a person. Our enemies *are* demons. We have been clearly told that in Scripture. The theme of supernatural spiritual warfare runs from Genesis through Revelation. It is on every page.[27]

Kreeft, and other just war theorists, rest on a Christian tradition that has been rooted in the teachings and philosophies of the church since the fourth-century writings of Augustine of Hippo. Augustine's *City of God* theologically shaped and provided the foundational intellectual framework for Christian understanding of just war theory, which always included the notion that war could be morally permissible and even required but that killing must always be employed as a last resort. Augustine's theory held the concepts of two dwelling places—a heavenly city of God, where life was blessed in the presence of God, and a city of earth, which consisted of the political community of humankind and its history. The earthly city could be defined by temporal order, justice, and peace with the responsibility to govern held by temporal authorities. According to James Turner Johnson, professor of religious ethics, the city of God was not a rival political entity to the city of Earth, but rather the church within the imperfect and unfulfilled earthly city represented the potential of the heavenly society manifested on this earth.[28] For Augustine, just war was openness to the use of armed force, or "force employed by the ruling authority in the political order for the purpose of protecting justice and punishing injustice, with the aim of maintaining, establishing, or restoring peace, the ultimate securing of peace between and among communities rested on the creation of just order within

---

[27]Kreeft, *Ecumenical Jihad*, 49.
[28]James Turner Johnson, "Debates over Just War and Jihad: Ideas, Interpretations, and Implications Across Cultures," in *Debating the War of Ideas*, ed. Eric D. Patterson and John Gallagher (New York: Palgrave MacMillan, 2009), 87.

them individually and in their relations with one another."²⁹ Just war, as established by Augustine and adhered to for centuries following, provides justification for the use of armed forces and limitations that apply to the use of such force.

As Eric Patterson, adherent to just war theory and executive vice president of Religious Freedom Institute, recounts, Augustine pensively considered how Christianity should engage and inform the use of force in political life. Patterson emphasized the notion that a core tenet of Christian belief is the idea to "love your neighbor as yourself," which includes implementing *caritas*, "protecting one's neighbor when he or she is attacked, even if one is forced to employ violence to protect that individual."³⁰ Another key contribution of Augustinian thought is the emphasis of order over disorder, *jus ad bellum*; thus, violence can justifiably be applied for the purpose of maintaining civil order within society.

Aquinas, leading thirteenth-century Christian thinker and philosopher, inherited Augustine's views regarding just war theory. He believed three requirements were necessary to justify the use of violence in response to lawlessness and disorder: sovereign authority, just cause, and right intent. These three principles are foundational components for adherents of just war theory today.

James Turner Johnson, professor of religious ethics at Rutgers University, presents a classical parsing of the key tenets of just war theory, including the following:

- Just cause: the protection and preservation of value (e.g., defense of the innocent against armed attack; retaking of persons, property, or other values wrongly taken; punishment of evil)

---

²⁹Johnson "Debates over Just War," 88.
³⁰Eric Patterson, "Just War Theory: Christian Teaching on Justice and Security," in *Evangelical Peacemakers: Gospel Engagement in a War Torn World,* ed. David Gushee (Eugene, OR: Cascade, 2013), 17.

- Right authority: the person sanctioning use of force must be the duly authorized representative of a sovereign political entity.
- Right intention: in accordance with just cause and not territorial expansionism, intimidation, or coercion
- Proportionality of ends: the overall good achieved by the use of force must be greater than the harm done.
- Last resort: force must only be employed when no other means can achieve the desired outcome.
- Reasonable hope of success: a prudent calculation of the likelihood of success determines the level, type, and duration of force employed.
- The aim of peace: the goal of intervention is stability, security, and peace, which may include nation building, disarmament, and other peacemaking measures.[31]

In addition to Johnson's critical work, in 2010, authors J. Daryl Charles and Timothy J. Demy published *War, Peace, and Christianity: Questions and Answers from a Just-War Perspective* in order to more holistically address the application of historical notions of just war toward more contemporary geopolitical challenges and contemporary incidents of violence and conflict.

Some contemporary scholars, like Richard Mouw, former president of Fuller Theological Seminary, assert that if just war theory were rightly applied, there would be far fewer campaigns than our military record currently shows.[32] Leaning on the teachings of late Mennonite ethicist John Howard Yoder, Mouw reminds us that the "real divide concerning the use of violence was not between pacifists and Just War defenders"; rather it is necessary to "insist that it is extremely important to subject questions about the legitimacy of violence to strict

---

[31]Patterson, "Just War Theory," 15-16.
[32]Sider, *Nonviolent Action*, ix.

moral examination."³³ Does moral examination ever permit the use of military violence? This is the question that provokes such great debate.

Mouw is not the only one who thinks Christian history has been wrought with wars and violence that, on reflection and analysis, might be deemed as less than just. In his famous essay "The Moral Equivalent of War," William James argues that the struggle for nonviolent alternatives is an uphill battle because "history is a bath of blood" and notions of war are deeply embedded in the human heart.³⁴ War, when viewed from an idealistic perspective, can be attractive. It provokes notions of bravery and courage, sacrifice and discipline; victory triumphs over evil for the sake of humanity and a better world. This brings to mind the crusade ethic, which was used to justify and inspire holy wars in the name of God. Certainly this includes the brutal Crusades of Christian history, but this ethic reemerged in contemporary discourse in some modern faith communities in response to the events of September 11, 2001, and the rise of religious terrorist groups in the twenty-first century.

Despite some of the critiques of just war, Eric Patterson reminds Christians to approach questions of the legitimate use of violence, pacifism, and just war with a posture of humility that gives appropriate credence and deference to the thousands of years of church history that have lauded the merits of just war.³⁵ Patterson rightly asserts, in large part, that just war theory was normative for Christians over the trajectory of human history. He writes, "Christianity has two millennia of teaching on government and use of force and modern evangelicals should start their deliberations with modest and intent study on what the great churchmen of the past have to say on these issues."³⁶

---

³³Sider, *Nonviolent Action*, ix.
³⁴Sider, *Nonviolent Action*, 175.
³⁵Patterson, "Just War Theory," 15.
³⁶Patterson, "Just War Theory," 17.

Patterson is right to encourage humility and diligent study of past Christian thinkers and leaders. There is much to be learned from their insight and teachings. This doesn't outright dismiss the merits of pacifism but should influence the posture by which pacifist activities are embraced. Certainly there is some merit to be had in the tomes of Christian history that have leaned toward just war as a credible theory providing moral justification of the use of state violence in protection of society.

It is important to note, however, that the argument of "history being on our side" doesn't quite hold water when, in hindsight, the politicization of Christianity has arguably justified gross violations of human rights and grotesque violence against various segments of human society. One could argue that segments of contemporary Christian society continue to justify unnecessary violence by weak application of just war theory. Historically, there are numerous examples of abusive use of force seeking to justify the moral legitimacy of violence by an abuse of just war theory. Consider Constantine's exploitation of political authority for territorial expansionism in order to extend the influence of both church and state,[37] the brutality and violence of Christian crusades of the Middle Ages, Hitler's appropriation of Christianity to justify the pursuit of a pure race in carrying out the eugenics of the Holocaust toward Jews and other minority communities, and more recently the American campaign of violence on the Middle East to win the war on terror. One could argue the legitimacy of some of these campaigns or even argue that just

---

[37]It is important to note that some contemporary scholars disagree that Constantine's appropriation of Christianity as the state religion of his empire was a shift from "Christianity to Christendom." Historians and Christian scholars question whether or not the early church of antiquity was pacifist in nature and how Constantine's use of political authority may or may not have shifted the praxis of the early church and its views toward violence and just war. See Peter Leithart, *Defending Constantine: The Twilight of an Empire and the Dawn of Christendom* (Downer's Grove, IL: InterVarsity Press, 2010). See also David Swartz, "Debating Constantine," *Patheos*, September 18, 2013, www.patheos.com/blogs/anxiousbench/2013/09/debating-constantine.

war theory was unduly applied. Nonetheless, the evidence of human history too often seems to paint Christianity with a brush of war and violence. *Abusus non tollit usum.* The abuse does not take away the proper use. The misapplication of just war theory does not mean it must be altogether dismissed. Even so, abuses must be critically observed, studied, and considered in future practice.

Twentieth-century Christian ethicist Paul Ramsey is credited by many as having reintroduced just war theory into "Protestant ethical reflection."[38] Ramsey supported the limited permission of the war in the 1960s during the height of loud pacifist voices decrying America's ongoing military engagement in Vietnam. He was one of the most prominent contemporary theologians to begin to look at just war through a Christian lens. Academics Caner and Feryal Taslaman write of Ramsey's contribution,

> The importance of Ramsey for the modern just war theory lies in his support of war and limited use of nuclear weapons in an era when the threats of nuclear weapons and total war were at their peak. . . . According to him, the prescripts of love and charity derived from Christian ethics made it the social responsibility of a good Christian to protect the life and property of one's neighbor against a threat or an aggression, and limited force should be used for this purpose.[39]

Ramsey saw war not as an "exception" but as a necessary "expression" of "Christian understanding of moral and political responsibility."[40] He did not believe in war for war's sake but prioritized the ability of war to bring about justice and argued war as not only a necessary but a critical intervention in order to right wrongs in global society. For Ramsey, force is

---

[38] Oliver O'Donovan, "Obituary: Paul Ramsey (1913–88)," *Studies in Christian Ethics* 1, No. 1 (1988): 82-90. http://sce.sagepub.com/cgi/pdf_extract/1/1/82.
[39] Caner Taslaman and Feryal Taslaman, "Contemporary Just War Theory: Paul Ramsey and Michael Walzer," *Journal of Academic Studies* 15, no. 59 (November 2013): 5-6.
[40] Taslaman and Taslaman, "Contemporary Just War," 6.

used not for self-preservation or self-defense but for the sake of others and "to protect those who are in need of defense or who have suffered wrongs needing to be righted and is a moral obligation for good Christians to resort to armed force for neighbors being treated unjustly. For an intervention to be just it has to be either a counter intervention or intervention with invitation."[41]

Ramsey did not impose a legalistic paradigm of criteria for just war, but rather required Christian sensitivity as an expression of what it means to "love one's neighbor." According to Ramsey, even preemptive wars can be just if there is an enemy endangering a neighbor. Political theorist Michael Walzer has a similar view. For Walzer, if just war doctrine only allows defensive wars, then it is shallow and nationalistic rather than exhibiting a love for one's neighbor.[42] He supports interventionism for humanitarian purposes but does not consider intervention just simply for purposes of "regime change, free enterprise, economic justice or democracy."[43] The Taslamans critique Ramsey's hermeneutic of just war theory by claiming it privileges an interpretation in favor of powerful states. Powerful states, according to Taslaman, can simply choose to intervene by using the rhetoric of "helping their neighbor in need" as long as they are powerful enough to do so.

One of the main concerns with just war theory is the application of criteria. Who determines legitimate political authority? Who measures whether or not all legitimate alternatives have been duly exercised? How can one determine whether or not military intervention has a reasonable chance of success? And who defines what "success" looks like when war is used as a mechanism of seeking to bring about peace or at least absence of physical unrest? Many liberal scholars would assert that one of

---

[41]Taslaman and Taslaman, "Contemporary Just War," 8.
[42]Taslaman and Taslaman, "Contemporary Just War," 8-9.
[43]Taslaman and Taslaman, "Contemporary Just War," 9.

the primary weaknesses of just war is its privileging of the powerful, even when benevolent intentions are present, to the dispossession of those who play more subaltern roles within society.

JUST PEACEMAKING

It is clear that misapplied praxis of both pacifist ideologies and just war theory neglect to holistically address the desperate need for peacemaking measures in a war-torn world. As scholars such as Sider and other have noted, pacifists often fail to diligently apply nonviolent activism and frequently are unwilling to pay the price of injury or even death when such sacrifice may be necessary and even required for effective peacemaking to occur. Just war adherents may, in principle, have moral virtue on their side justifying interventions to prevent abuse and oppression; but can it truly be argued that all attempts are made to avoid war at all costs? Or have the modern economic engines of militarization and other political motivations caused a biased leaning in favor of war instead of a desperate pursuit of all other possible interventions? It would seem there are significant weaknesses with both a pacifist and a just war perspective.

Perhaps there is a third way. Just peacemaking advocates David Gushee and Glen Stassen claim that simply focusing on just war and pacifism isn't enough. Stassen writes, "Just to say no to war is always a losing position" because of its impracticalities, overemphasis on idealism, and inability to provide positive, constructive, and effective solutions to the problems at hand.[44] Just peacemaking includes such practices as sustainable economic development; advancement of human rights, democracy, and religious liberty; working with emerging cooperative forces in the international system; and cooperative conflict

---

[44] Glen Stassen, "Learn and Teach Practices That Make for Peace," in Gushee, *Evangelical Peacemakers*, 26.

resolution.[45] The theory of just peacemaking seeks to answer the questions "When, if ever, are war and military force justified?" and "What practices of war prevention and peacemaking should we be supporting?"[46] Under the principles of just peacemaking, the focus first and foremost is on nonmilitary preventive action, with attention to the root causes of impending crises. However, there are examples, such as in cases where military action could stop a massacre, where the use of military force is affirmed.[47]

Thirty scholars of both just war and pacifist traditions from diverse backgrounds and Christian faith traditions came to consensus and identified ten principles of just peacemaking. Furthermore, they broke these principles into three priority categories: initiatives, justice, and love (including enemies in the community of neighbors). The principles of just peacemaking that require initiative include supporting nonviolent direction action, taking independent initiatives to reduce threat, using cooperative conflict resolution, acknowledging responsibility for conflict and injustice, and seeking repentance and forgiveness.[48] The principles of just peacemaking that emphasize themes of justice, based on Matthew 6:19-33, include advanced democracy, human rights and religious liberty, and fostering just and sustainable economic development.[49] Finally, just peacemaking principles that emphasize the love of neighbors, including one's enemies, include working with emerging cooperative forces in the international system, strengthening the United Nations and international efforts for cooperation and human rights, reducing offensive weapons and weapons trade, and encouraging grassroots

---

[45]Glen H. Stassen, ed., *Just Peacemaking: The New Paradigm for the Ethics of Peace and War* (Cleveland: Pilgrim, 2008), 3-4.
[46]Stassen, *Just Peacemaking*, 9.
[47]Stassen, *Just Peacemaking*, 10.
[48]Stassen, "Learn and Teach," 31-32.
[49]Stassen, "Learn and Teach," 32-33.

peacemaking groups and voluntary associations.⁵⁰ Convinced of the effectiveness of these principles, Glen Stassen and other adherents to just peacemaking believe that "no discussion of evangelical engagement with issues of peace and war is adequate without serious consideration of just peacemaking."⁵¹ Proponents of just peacemaking issue this invitation: "We *appeal to all people of good will* to adopt these practices and work for them, grounding themselves in a commitment to change our world (or at least their own little briar patch) to peace rather than war and oppression."⁵²

Stassen, in his own translation of Isaiah 32:16, says the biblical text is the foundation of effective peacemaking:

> Then justice will dwell in the wilderness,
> And delivering justice abide in the fruitful field;
> The effect of delivering justice will be peace,
> And the result of delivering justice quietness and trust forever.⁵³

It would seem just peacemaking takes the best of just war theory, including its historical legitimacy and moral justification for military action when certain conditions are met, but demands that war not be pursued unless rigorous application of pacifist ideology and goals are first pursued and applied. Ron Sider calls people to just peacemaking by more diligent, fervent, and courageous pursuit of nonviolent action. He defines nonviolent action as "an activist confrontation with evil that respects the personhood even of the 'enemy' and therefore seeks both to end the oppression and to reconcile the oppressor through nonviolent methods."⁵⁴ Sider believes that both pacifists and adherents to just

---

⁵⁰Stassen, "Learn and Teach," 33.
⁵¹Stassen, "Learn and Teach," 33.
⁵²Stassen, *Just Peacemaking*, 17.
⁵³Stassen, "Learn and Teach," 26.
⁵⁴Sider, *Nonviolent Action*, xv.

war tradition must "demand a commitment to nonviolent action" in order to have any integrity.[55]

IN PURSUIT OF KINGDOM JUSTICE AND BIBLICAL SHALOM

Just peacemaking is a pursuit of both kingdom justice and biblical shalom. Three theological convictions undergird an ideology of just peacemaking: initiatives informed on the biblical concept of discipleship and the peacemaking modeled in the "life, teachings, death, and resurrection of Jesus Christ"; justice pursued by seeking the peace of the city, not withdrawal or quietism, to further God's reign; and, finally, love and community where the body of Christ can together "seek to discern together what just peacemaking means and to model peacemaking practices in corporate and individual lives."[56]

Peter Kreeft writes in *Ecumenical Jihad* that the most powerful and unique weapon possessed by Christians is that of "suffering love." Kreeft reminds readers that the struggles of the universe are "not of this world" but also spiritual in nature. He says, "Most Christians in America today also fail to understand the Christian paradox that suffering love *is the most powerful of all weapons in spiritual warfare.*"[57]

Christ modeled perfect suffering love through his death on the cross. Certainly one could morally justify the violent response of Peter and the disciples to the arrest of Jesus because of Judas's betrayal. The anger of the disciples was righteous and justified. And yet Jesus called them to put their swords back in their place (Mt 26:52). He pursued a response of overwhelming love and forgiveness, even through his words on the cross to the very ones who had perpetuated the violence against

---

[55]Sider, *Nonviolent Action*, 166.
[56]Stassen, *Just Peacemaking*, 18-19.
[57]Kreeft, *Ecumenical Jihad*, 43.

him: "Forgive them; for they do not know what they are doing." (Lk 23:34).

Ron Sider speaks analogously of the power of love: "Self-sacrificial love has innate power. It often weakens even vicious opponents—though not always, of course. People ready to suffer for others sometimes get crucified. But often, too, they evoke a more human, loving response, even from brutal foes."[58] Might the overwhelming transformational power of Christ's love be applied even to the choices of the political authorities when decisions are wrought about what mechanisms of intervention should be employed? David Gushee shares similar ideas: "We are called to follow the trail that Christ blazed, and to embrace reconciliation, love, and peacemaking. This is Christ's way, and it is the only way to redemption."[59]

Walter Wink, esteemed biblical scholar and progressive theologian, also famously equates the Christian life with struggles against principalities and powers. Wink believes it is an imperative to call Christ-followers into battle—but a spiritual one rather than earthly military campaigns. He asserts, "There is a whole host of people simply waiting for the Christian message to challenge them for once to a heroism worthy of their lives."[60] Nonviolent direct action, as a manifestation of just peacemaking, provides just such opportunity. May we each, when presented with the opportunities to diligently pursue peace and advocate for justice, be willing to pay the ultimate sacrifice for the sake of the gospel of Christ.

---

[58] Ron Sider, *Nonviolent Action: What Christian Ethics Demands but Most Christians Have Never Really Tried* (Grand Rapids, MI: Brazos Press, 2015), 173.
[59] Gushee, "Evangelical Peacemakers," 114.
[60] Sider, *Nonviolent Action*, 177.

LIGHTS IN THE DARKNESS

CHRISTIAN PEACE PRACTICE IN THE VIOLENCE OF CENTRAL AMERICA

Willi Hugo Perez Lemus and Adrienne Wiebe

How can the gospel of peace be lived out in places of violence and suffering in the world today? This reflection explores the role of churches and followers of Jesus in the midst of the various forms of violence currently engulfing Central America.[1] Violence touches everyone in everyday life in Central America: a family from the church is forced to pay extortion to a local gang and feels unsafe in their home; a Christian businessman's children are threatened if he does not transport illegal goods; a young unemployed father risks the dangers of migrating north to look for work to support his family; a woman in the church is frequently beaten by her husband; a church is offered a generous monthly donation by a criminal organization if it stays silent about its illegal activities; everyone has experienced at least one assault and robbery in a public place. How can Christians and church communities live fully and fearlessly the gospel of peace in this dark context of everyday violence?

---

[1] Central America lies south of Mexico, and consists of Guatemala, Belize, Honduras, El Salvador, Nicaragua, Costa Rica, and Panama.

THE NEED FOR TRANSFORMATION: VIOLENCE IN CENTRAL AMERICA

Spanish theologian Juan José Tamayo reminds us that "peace is one of the most precious and sought-after goods; but at the same time, it is one of the most fragile and threatened."[2] These words are very true in the current Central American reality. This is a land that longs for peace, yet Central Americans have grown accustomed to living with violence, an endemic evil that has been entrenched in this region for the last fifty years causing suffering, pain, and destruction.

There were times that Central Americans envisioned a horizon of peace, but then reality returned in an even more overwhelming way. Many remember how, in the 1990s, it seemed that there would dawn a new era of peace with the end of the armed conflicts in Guatemala, El Salvador, and Nicaragua. The decades of repression and civil war had left hundreds of thousands dead and missing, millions of widows and orphans, economic and ecological destruction, and a devastated social fabric. But the joyful celebration of the signed peace accords soon collapsed in disillusionment that the promises of peace would remain as unrealized utopias and truncated dreams.

Reality returned, and with it other, even more cruel and devastating forms of violence appeared. In the words of the Nicaraguan theologian José María Vigil, "The violence we live today . . . makes the violence we lived in the revolutionary decades look pale in comparison."[3] Today it is impossible to determine the extent of the damage, victims, human losses, and costs caused by the various forms of violence that are perpetrated in every corner of our society: organized crime, drug trafficking,

---

[2]Juan José Tamayo, *Otra telogía es posible: Pluralismo religioso, interculturalidad y feminismo* (Barcelona: Editorial Herder, 2011), 52.
[3]José María Vigil, *Aunque es de noche: La hora espiritual de América Latina en los Noventas,* 2nd ed., (Managua, Nicaragua: Editorial Envio, 1996), 32.

gang violence, and violence against migrants, as well as gender-based, domestic, structural, and political violence.

Until about twenty years ago, most violent conflicts in the world, including those in Central America, were largely based on ethnic and racial divisions and were associated with intergroup conflict and unresolved issues of nationhood. Most often there were two identifiable armed bellicose groups in conflict with each other. Usually the conflicts were concerned with political power, although they always had social and economic dimensions as well. However, in the last couple of decades, new forms of violence and conflict have become prominent, particularly in Latin America, the most urbanized and unequal region of the Global South.

This type of violence is not a struggle for political power; rather, it is an expression of social and economic inequality and conflict.[4] And unlike previous armed conflicts that were more often fought in rural areas, these mainly take place in cities, in the marginal, segregated, and excluded sectors.

In these urban contexts, conflict is not between two identifiable antagonistic social groups but rather the interaction of a complex, embedded set of forces, usually linked to delinquent gangs and organized crime. While there is frequent intergang warfare, considerable violence, both physical and symbolic, is directed against nonparticipatory community members. This is lateral violence between people of the same socioeconomic class. People from the middle class may feel afraid and be occasional victims; however, in reality, most of the violence is experienced by residents of the poorest and most marginalized neighborhoods.[5]

---

[4] Briceño-León Roberto, "La nueva violencia urbana de América Latina," *Sociologías* 4, no. 8 (July–Dec. 2002): 34-51.
[5] Roberto, "La nueva violencia."

Research has identified some of the factors that create fertile conditions for this type of urban violence. These factors include impoverishment (getting poorer), inequality, exclusion from educational and work opportunities, a second generation of urban residents that fail to meet expectations for advancement, easy accessibility of firearms, a culture of toxic masculinity, and weak police and justice systems.[6]

These factors have contributed today to making Central America one of the world's most violent places, particularly the countries of the Northern Triangle: Guatemala, El Salvador, and Honduras. In 2016, the murder rate in El Salvador was eighty-three homicides per 100,000 inhabitants, in Honduras it was 56, and in Guatemala it was 27.[7] In comparison, the rate in Canada was 1.8 and in the United State it was 5.3 that same year. The majority of deaths by homicide are young men between eighteen and thirty years of age.

As part of the strategic overland route for the drug trade between South America and North America, the Central American countries have become quasi-narco states. Since the 1990s, organized crime has gained enormous power and control over state structures, political powers, and even churches and religious institutions. There has been an increase in political corruption, arms trafficking, money laundering, and illegal drug production and trafficking.

Marginalized young men living in poverty and lacking opportunities are attracted to easy money and a sense of status and belonging offered by gangs, leading them to become entangled in the distribution of drugs, contract killings, extortion, and other crimes. More than nine hundred gangs with more than seventy thousand members operate in Central America, with the largest presence in Guatemala, El Salvador,

---

[6]Roberto, "La nueva violencia."
[7]United Nations Office on Drugs and Crime, *Global Study on Homicide* (Vienna: United Nations, 2019), www.unodc.org/unodc/en/data-and-analysis/global-study-on-homicide.html.

and Honduras.[8] These complex and rapidly growing groups create insecurity and fear, especially in urban areas, through assault, rape, robbery, extortion, killings, and drug distribution.[9]

Central and South America have the highest levels of physical assaults and violent robberies in the world. The average for the regions is 365 reported robberies per 100,000 people; this is compared to 70 per 100,000 in North America.[10]

Violence against women is also a serious problem in the region. Patriarchal and sexist social patterns persist in these countries. Various types of abuse and violence affect thousands of women in culture, the family, and society. Based on biased forms of biblical interpretation, the teachings of some churches foster dynamics that violate women, urge women to resign themselves to domestic violence, and prevent them from realizing their full potential. Among the four countries in the world with the highest numbers of women murdered, or femicides, are Honduras, El Salvador, and Guatemala, in which more than eight homicides occur per 100,000 women each year.[11] Widespread domestic violence impacts thousands of women. Many children also suffer abuse, neglect, abandonment, or denial of care and affection. The violence suffered within the home impacts society, destroys families, and creates intergenerational trauma.

Structural violence is both a form of violence and a root cause of interpersonal and social violence, evident in this region in the extreme inequalities of human and social development. In Central America,

---

[8] C. Ribando Seelke, *Gangs of Central America* (Washington, DC: Congressional Research Services, 2016).

[9] United Nations Development Programme, *Guatemala: A Land of Opportunities for Youth? National Human Development Report 2011/2012* (Guatemala City: Don Quixote, 2012), 176.

[10] R. Muggah and K. Aguirre, *Citizen Security in Latin America: The Hard Facts* (Rio de Janiero: Igarape Institute, 2018).

[11] Mireille Widmer and Irene Pavesi, "A Gendered Analysis of Violent Deaths," Small Arms Survey, November 2016, www.smallarmssurvey.org/resource/gendered-analysis-violent-deaths-research-note-63.

22 percent of young people between fifteen and twenty-nine neither study nor have gainful employment because of a lack of jobs, accessible education, and government leadership.[12] Fifty percent or more of the populations of the Central American countries live on incomes of less than two dollars per day per person.[13]

Given the inability to provide for their families, millions of people are migrating to other countries in search of better life chances, leaving holes in their families and communities. Outmigration is driven largely by poverty, lack of economic possibilities, and violence. Central American outmigration has increased from 2.6 million migrants in 2000 to 4.2 million in 2015, and 80 percent of these migrants are destined for the United States.[14] The migrant journey itself is a form of violence, including high risk for assault, exploitation, injury, and death.

This overview of data provides a profile of the current Central American context, but the statistics do not capture the magnitude of impotence, despair, and suffering experienced by the human beings behind the numbers. Yet this is the reality that we as Central American Christians are called to confront and to transform.

THE BIBLICAL CALL TO PEACEMAKING: SHALOM AND THE MESSAGE OF JESUS

The current reality being lived in Central America is not the life that God wants for people. God wants peace for Central Americans, as for the whole world. But peace is not merely the absence of conflict and war (negative peace). Nor is peace restricted to the individual spiritual realm. So what is peace? The peace that is offered in the Bible is

---

[12]Comisión Económica para América Latina y el Caribe, *Panorama Social de América Latina 2014* (Santiago, Chile: Naciones Unidas, 2014), 27.
[13]Comisión Económica, *Panorama Social*, 17.
[14]M. Orozco, *Recent Trends in Central American Migration* (Washington DC: InterAmerican Dialogue, 2018).

rooted in the concept of shalom and in the teachings and example of Jesus.

There is an urgent need for a renewal of the message of shalom within the violence of Central America at this moment. The Hebrew word *shalom* has a wealth of meaning that is not adequately reflected in other visions of peace, such as Greek *eirēnē* or the Latin *pax*. Shalom is not only the absence of conflicts and wars, the establishment of order by the rigorous application of the law, or individual spiritual peace. Biblical shalom transforms thoughts, attitudes, behaviors, actions, and relationships so that all people can live a life characterized by love, sanctification of life, truth, justice, the common good, and harmony.

Shalom is expressed in right relationships with God, neighbors, and all creation. It is the experience of healthy, inclusive, and equitable relationships between people that overcome barriers of culture, nationality, gender, and social status. It fosters an attitude of abundance in human relationships, of coexistence in the family and community, and justice in the economic, political, and ecological realms. Holistic and collective well-being is central to shalom peace.

Shalom peace cannot be dissociated from justice; on the contrary, justice is a condition for peace. It is impossible to have peace on earth as long as there are circumstances and structures that promote injustice, inequality, and exclusion. That's why the biblical prophets proclaimed that the fruit of justice would be peace (Is 32:17), that it is important to love and practice justice (Mic 6:8), and that peace, justice, love, and truth must go hand in hand (Ps 85:10-11). Peace is the presence of justice in life and in human and social relations.

It is only possible to achieve shalom peace through nonviolence. Violence cannot be the way, because violence leads only to more violence, enmity, and death. True peace involves dismantling ideologies, means, and mechanisms of violence, war, and destruction (Is 2:4).

Genuine peace is reached through love and the power of the Spirit of God (Zech 4:6).

The promises of God's peace are fulfilled and updated in Jesus, the Prince of Peace. According to John Driver, "In Jesus, the Messiah, the Messianic prophetic vision of *shalom*, the expected peace in the Old Testament is fulfilled. Therefore, the message of God through Jesus Christ is called the 'Gospel of Peace' (Acts 10:36)."[15]

Jesus' teachings are a message of peace. The Sermon on the Mount (Mt 5–7), the ethical core of the Christian faith, and Jesus' parables and sayings communicate the meaning of peace and how to achieve it. They reveal the conditions and values for organizing life and channeling attitudes, actions, and relationships: justice, integrity, honesty, brotherly and sisterly love, love of enemies, forgiveness, reconciliation, the value of life, and solidarity. He invites his followers to embody these values, to proclaim and promote them in the world they live in.

Jesus began his ministry by announcing that the kingdom of God had come (Mk 1:14-15). The announcement was revolutionary for those affected by sin, injustice, human suffering, oppression, and violence. A new era began in the fulfillment of the messianic promises that the Prince of Peace would come bringing a kingdom whose distinctive features would be lasting peace, justice, righteousness, and good (Is 9:6-7). In contrast to earthly kingdoms, this kingdom is configured according to God's character and promises fullness of life for all through the grace, love, and power of nonviolence (Lk 1:46-55).

The good news of salvation and peace is holistic, affecting all dimensions of life. Jesus says he has come to give abundant life (Jn 10:10). Therefore Jesus' ministry was marked by his deeds of love, compassion, and restoration to all people. Beginning in Nazareth, Jesus traveled to

---

[15]Juan Driver, *Una teología bíblica de la paz* (Ciudad de Guatemala: Ediciones Semilla, 2003), 102.

villages and cities taking this message to those living under various forms of human, spiritual, structural, religious, or social oppression (Mt 18:1-5; 23:24; Mk 9:37; 10:14-15; Lk 4:17-21; 6:17-19; Jn 4). The outcasts of society, the young and those oppressed by violent social structures, such as children, women, enslaved people, and migrants, were touched by his gospel of love and salvation in a way that radically changed their lives.

The peace of Jesus is based on an ethic of nonviolence. Jesus faced persecution and attacks with firmness and courage and without violence or weapons. When arrested in Gethsemane, Jesus refused to be defended by the sword (Mt 26:50-54). When dying, Jesus forgave his enemies and prayed for them (Lk 23:34). On this basis, his disciples are called to make nonviolence and love their principles for faith and practice (Mt 5:38-48). But the nonviolence of Jesus does not passively accept evil and injustice. Rather, Jesus responds with active nonviolence to transform structures and powers that violate the most vulnerable of society. Of course, that led him to the cross. But the cross did not mean defeat. His resurrection was a paradigmatic fact that demonstrated the power of love, nonviolence, and life over hatred, violence, and death.

This biblical and christocentric vision of peace gives us guidance as to God's vision for Central America and what work we need to do. Central America is a beautiful but damaged land that is yearning for life, justice, and peace. Working for peace in this violent and suffering context is, beyond doubt, a healing, liberating, and transforming pastoral task.

GLIMMERS OF HOPE: THE WITNESS AND WORK OF THE FOLLOWERS OF JESUS IN CENTRAL AMERICA

This reflection is written from the context of violence in Central America, but we do not offer only a lament of the seemingly overwhelming darkness that engulfs us. We want to recognize that there are lights that glow in the darkness and transmit hope. These lights are followers of Jesus who, in response to his call (Mt 5:9), work for this peace of God. Countless believers, churches, and communities work with faith and enthusiasm to counteract the violent and unjust situations and build another reality. Here are a few examples of how these Christians are practicing nonviolent peacemaking in Central America today.[16]

Accompaniment of victims of violence. Ministries of comprehensive pastoral care offer help for victims of violence. The violence these victims experience leaves untold levels of suffering, fear, insecurity, damaged self-esteem, and psychosomatic wounds that are difficult to heal. Here holistic pastoral care is vital to help the victims in their grief and recovery so that they can free themselves from their traumas, heal their wounds, and recover a sense of life. Some churches have facilitated groups in which people can share their stories with others who have also suffered various forms of violence and trauma, leading to comfort and healing.

Supporting women victims. There are also Christians who focus on working with women who have suffered violence, providing pastoral and emotional accompaniment, helping to break the cycles of violence and supporting women to be empowered and find alternatives for a better life. For example, the Peace and Justice Project of the Mennonite

---

[16] The experiences and practices referred to are the result of the event "The Churches Before the Violence in Central America: Models and Experiences of Peace," held in Guatemala in July 2013 and involving practitioners of peace (Anabaptists, evangelicals, and Catholics) from Mexico, Central America, and Colombia. It was organized by the Center for Latin American Studies from American University in Washington, DC, and the SEED Seminar. It also includes learnings from the "Consultation on Urban Violence and Peacebuilding in Latin America" facilitated by the Mennonite Central Committee in 2014 and various experiences of the authors. Claudia Dary Fuentes, "Las Iglesias Ante Las Violencias En Latinoamérica: Modelos Y Experiencias De Paz En Contextos De Conflicto Y Violencia (Churches in the Face of Violence in Latin America: Models and Experiences of Peace in Contexts of Conflict and Violence)," *CLALS Working Paper Series*, no. 3 (December 2013). See https://ssrn.com/abstract=2412771 or http://dx.doi.org/10.2139/ssrn.2412771

Church in La Ceiba, Honduras, operates a program to support survivors of domestic violence. Other churches have answered the call to work with women prisoners or women caught in prostitution. In these ministries of peace, many women have found safe spaces, trust, and care that they need to change their lives.

Solidarity with migrants. Peace work on migrant issues seeks to foster an attitude of welcome and solidarity with migrants to help alleviate the suffering and dangers they encounter on their journeys. It also provides pastoral accompaniment to families left behind when someone migrates. For example, the Mennonite Commission for Social Action (CASM) implements programs to support migrants deported back Honduras from the United States to gain employable skills and to provide social, emotional, and financial support for their families.

Reconciliation. Individual Christians, institutions, and faith communities are working to support healing and reconciliation among people and communities damaged by conflict, hatred, and discord. They create conducive spaces for people to meet, discuss, and analyze their conflicts and together find solutions. People are given a space where they can feel safe to meet, speak freely, reconcile, and build new relationships.

Restorative justice. In countries like Nicaragua and Honduras, restorative justice initiatives aim to support victims of violence to heal wounds and overcome traumas. At the same time offenders are offered the opportunity to repent and change their lives. As fruits of this work, there are testimonies of people who suffered traumatic violence who have managed to heal and restore themselves to wholeness. There are cases of offenders and criminals who have changed violent behavior and now live different lives as a result of beautiful stories of forgiveness and reconciliation. In Honduras, there are projects with people in the jails, and the Semilla Latin American Anabaptist Seminary has trained members of the judicial system in Nicaragua on restorative justice approaches.

Reintegrating gang members. Some churches, such as the Mennonites, Pentecostals, and Catholics, are working to rescue and restore members of gangs, mostly in Honduras, Guatemala, and El Salvador. Through methods such as pastoral accompaniment, psychological and medical assistance, removal of tattoos with gang identification, and education, these churches are helping young people leave the gangs, build new lives, and reintegrate into their families and communities. There are inspiring stories of young people who found the strength to leave gangs, change their lives, and contribute to the transformation of other children and youth.

Peace education. Christian peace practitioners know that education is a fundamental means of awareness raising and training of values, attitudes, habits, and skills. Using the awareness-reflection-action cycle builds capacity and promotes individual, social, and environmental change. As one Guatemalan practitioner of peace described it, "Through education, we sow seeds in the hearts of the people and then reap the fruits of peace in this land." Through teaching in schools, community groups, and churches, these peace practitioners prepare participants to be peace promoters and conflict mediators who then teach others. Semilla, the Latin American Anabaptist Seminary in Guatemala City, is an example of a church institution providing peace education throughout the region with distance education and workshops tailored to the needs of particular church communities.

Educating children to develop attitudes, skills, and values for conflict transformation and holistic peacebuilding builds capacity for the future at both the local and societal level. Community education projects with children aimed at building a "culture of peace" are another very common area of work for churches throughout Central America.

Gender justice. Important efforts are being made to address the rights and roles of women in the family, church, and society. This is intended to change the attitudes, social structures, and cultural patterns that repress and marginalize women and prevent their full, happy, and effective fulfillment in life. This has evolved from a deeper study of the Scriptures to rediscover the liberating message for women in the gospel of Jesus and, from there, propose changes for life, justice, and gender equality.

Prophetic voices building shalom. From a critical reading of social reality, prophetic voices are raised in defense of life, the rights of individuals and peoples, and the environment. There is active participation in nonviolent actions to address threats to human, environmental, and social life, such as political and social corruption, mining operations that damage creation and communities, injustices against migrants, and neoliberal economic policies that lead to further impoverishment.

Transformative community development. Many Christians address the root causes of violence through transformative social action and community development. Churches and faith-based organizations put the gospel of love, compassion, and solidarity of Jesus into practice by promoting various initiatives and projects to alleviate and transform the lives of people. There are initiatives in education, literacy, health, community development, agricultural projects, solidarity, economy, humanitarian and pastoral support during natural disasters, housing, and alternative technologies. These seek to go beyond charity to train and empower people and communities to move toward a sustainable transformational development. This includes creating safe and secure places for community building such as daycares, community kitchens and lunch programs, afterschool programs, youth programs, family support classes, and women's income-generation projects.

LIGHTING THE DARKNESS: PROPOSALS FOR A PEACE MINISTRY

We need to continue the work that God has begun. In this world damaged by human and social sin, by injustice and violence, we need to announce and build peace based on the biblical concept of shalom and on the teachings of Jesus. Here are some proposals of how we can do this as individuals, as Christian communities, and as citizens of Central America today.

	Actions for a Peace Practice in Central America
As individual Christians	Strengthen our spirits to resist evil and violence.
	Place our confidence in God to overcome fear.
	Build our knowledge and capacity of peace practice.
As church communities	Model shalom.
	Invite conversion.
	Create safe spaces.
As participants in society	Be in the world but not of the world.
	Work for just peace.
	Be prophetic communities.

As individual Christians

Strengthen our spirits to resist evil and violence. Paul says, "Be strong in the Lord and in the strength of his power. Put on the whole armor of God, so that you may be able to stand against the wiles of the devil. For our struggle is not against enemies of blood and flesh, but against the rulers, against the authorities, against the cosmic powers of this present darkness, against the spiritual forces of evil in the heavenly places" (Eph 6:10-12). These words are an exhortation to strengthen the spirituality of resistance to evil. The problems facing societies affected by violence can be overwhelming, and we can succumb to the temptations of evil and corruption or feel powerless in the face of the brutal reality. Therefore, it is crucial to cultivate a strong spirituality to be able to resist, and Paul provides a list of the resources available to us to do this: truth, justice, peace, faith, prayer, preparedness, the Word, and the power of the Spirit (Eph 6:13-20).[17]

Place our confidence in God to overcome fear. As followers of Christ we can have confidence that God is watching over us and will protect and care for us (Ps 5:11; 55:22; 1 Pet 5:6-7). This does not mean nothing bad will ever happen to us and our loved ones, but it does mean God is with us in everything and we can live our lives with confidence instead of fear.

Build our knowledge and capacity for peace practice. In order to work building God's kingdom of shalom, we need to prepare ourselves with the appropriate knowledge and skills. We need to be "equipped for every good work" (2 Tim 3:17). Church members in the region have asked for more training on peace theology, conflict transformation, conscientious objection, accompaniment of victims, leadership, and law.

As church communities

Be communities that model shalom. Our churches and faith communities should be alternative spaces where God's peace is alive. These should be peace communities where people can see and experience the ethical values of Jesus: love, forgiveness, reconciliation, nonviolence, just relations, the sanctity of life, kindness, mutual assistance, and solidarity. For people damaged and suffering because of injustice and violence, peace communities can be sites of healing, restoration, inspiration, and hope.

---

[17] Pablo Richard, "Crítica teológica a la globalización neoliberal," in *Globalizar la Esperanza: Reflexiones desde América Latina en la autora del tercer milenio* (Ciudad de México: Ediciones Dabar, 1988), 53.

Be communities that invite conversion. Ours must be communities that invite people to an encounter with the God of peace, to follow Jesus, and to live the values of the kingdom of justice and peace in all its radicalism. This is a call to conversion, that is, the renunciation of other domains, behaviors, patterns, and structures in order to live a life of reconciliation, communion, and peace.

Create safe spaces. Church buildings and community program spaces can provide places of hope and safety for children, youth, and adults and be a physical beacon of light in darkness. As one Honduran pastor said, churches can "maintain a quiet constant presence in neighborhoods"—a presence that does not come and go like some other institutions and organizations—creating stability in a context of vulnerability and insecurity.

As Christians and churches participating in society

Be in the world but not of the world. Praying for his disciples, Jesus said, "I have given them your word, and the world has hated them because they do not belong to the world, just as I do not belong to the world. I am not asking you to take them out of the world, but I ask you to protect them from the evil one" (Jn 17:14-15). What does it mean to live in this world without being of the world? In the case of Central America, Christians live in a world prone to violence, inequality, hatred, and injustice. But Christians should not get caught up in the values of this world, nor be indifferent to reality, nor escape by taking refuge in a very introverted spirituality. Rather, followers of Jesus are called to accept the challenge of being in this world but living in a spirit that is completely different (Jn 14:17).

Work for just peace. Churches that have credibility and history in their communities can use this social capital to work for peace. If churches are seen as nonpartisan and without self-interest, they can use this power to support what is good for the community as a whole. Violence destroys confidence and trust within communities and creates fear and isolation. Ideally, the church can provide a sense of community, of acceptance, and of being part of a trusted, extended family. The church can initiate and nurture projects that address the root causes of violent conflict, such as poverty, discrimination, and inequality. Churches can also work in violence prevention, conflict transformation, and the construction of a new society based on the principles of shalom.

Be prophetic communities. Like Jesus and the prophets, Christians must critically read their reality to expose all forms of violence that threaten life and well-being in the world. The church cannot remain silent but must make its voice heard in defense of life, justice, rights of the people, and freedom. The church must also rekindle hope. In Central America, millions of human beings live burdened by conflict, danger, and despair. There is an urgency to bring relief, comfort, and hope through the proclamation of the virtues of the kingdom.

As Spanish philosopher Ortega y Gasset points out, "If war is something that is made, then peace is also something that has to be made, with all the effort of human potential."[18] The ultimate desire of God is to bring healing, reconciliation, hope, and peace to our world (Col 1:19-20). As Christians in Central America and other parts of the world suffering from violence and oppression, we are called to a renewed commitment to God's purpose to redeem and transform the world. Christians who proclaim, embody, and model biblical shalom and the message of Jesus are instruments of God in building a reconciled, more just, and peaceful world. People who are lights that illuminate life and anticipate the bright future that God has promised.

---

[18]José Ortega y Gasset, *La rebellion de las masas* (Madrid: Editorial Tecnos, 2009), 35.

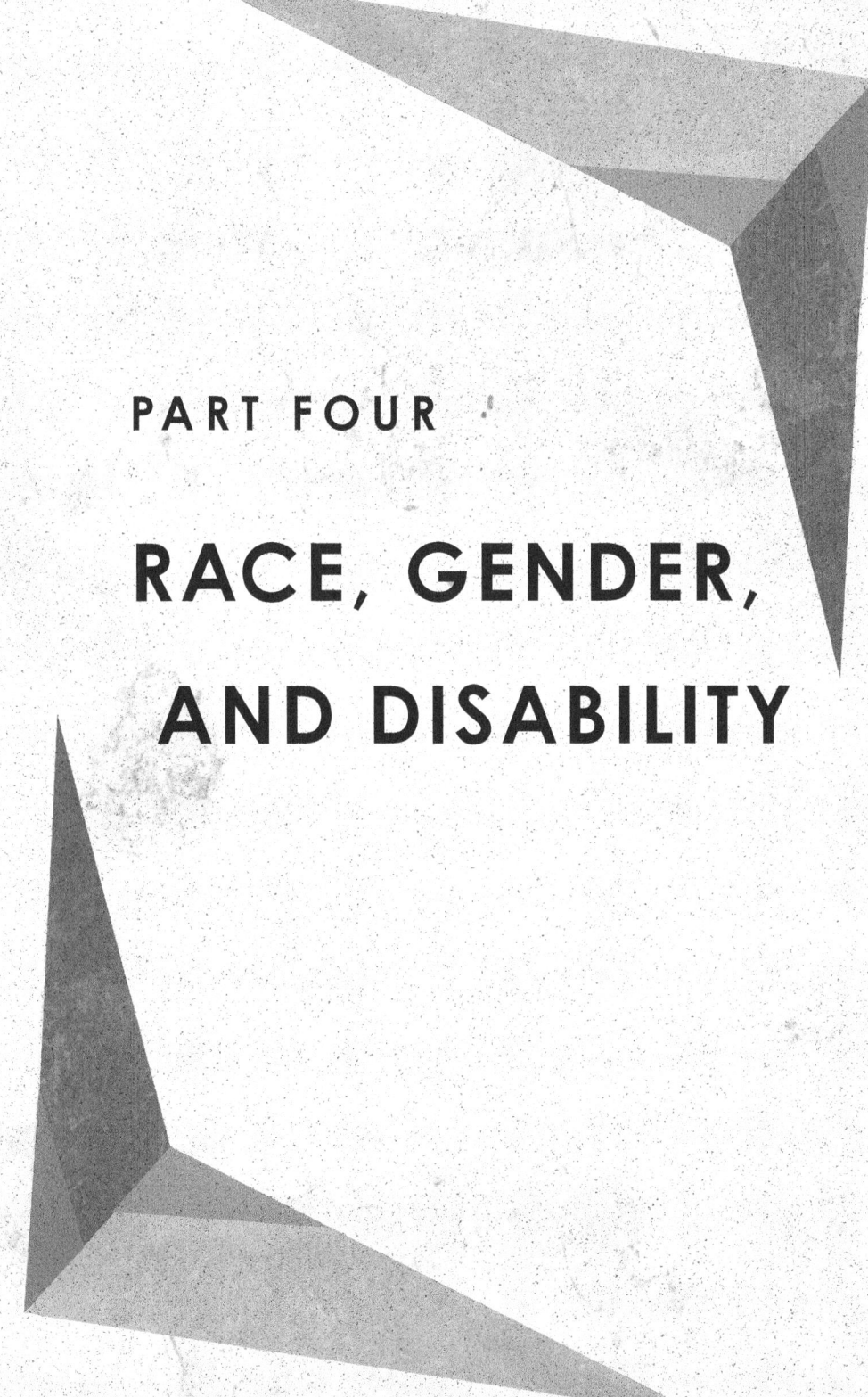

PART FOUR

RACE, GENDER, AND DISABILITY

SHALOM AND WHITE SUPREMACY

Drew G. I. Hart

WHITE SUPREMACY IS IN RESISTANCE to God's shalom. Most followers of Jesus today would easily agree with such statements on the surface. However, such a statement needs further clarification. Few people reflect on the full scope of these two social phenomena or comprehend what they mean for their own practice. Particularly problematic is that many who are committed to the peacemaking of Jesus have also neglected the implications of White supremacy as a form of systemic violence that rejects the way of God's shalom.

White supremacy and shalom, when fleshed out fully, are both intended to be all-encompassing social realities. Though each is manifested in the world in contrasting and opposing ways, both desire to be comprehensive social realities. Both want alignment of our lives, bodies, and even the social order so that everything synchronizes together toward their complete materialization. There is no mode of being or social space these two visions don't desire to form and pattern in alignment to their eventual consummation. Everything finds its appropriate role in social realities such as these.

For those who follow Jesus in faith and hold on to the fulfillment of God's kingdom, shalom is, according to Walter Brueggemann, the "central vision . . . that all of creation is one, every creature in community with every other, living in harmony and security toward the joy and well-being of every other creature."[1] This vision of wholeness not only includes a reconfiguring of social relationships but, more specifically, shalom also defines the nature of those relationships. It includes the entire cosmos living in harmony with God and creation. More concise and to the point, Brueggemann summarizes that shalom is "the substance of the biblical vision of one community embracing all creation."[2]

This vision of shalom permeates throughout the biblical narrative, reminding us that our Creator is shepherding humanity and history toward this end. The theme of shalom in Scripture offers repeated glimpses into God's ongoing deliverance and hope-filled future. A brief sample consideration of this theme will aid us in comprehending the voluminous intentions of the triune God for creation.

SHALOM

Peace is a gift from God, but it is also expected to be actively pursued. We are commanded, "Depart from evil, and do good; seek peace, and pursue it" (Ps 34:14). We are urged to diligently strive for peace. In the New Testament we are called to be a people who "make peace" (Jas 3:18). Or, more popularly, out of the mouth of Jesus in the Sermon on the Mount we are simply given the term *peacemakers* as one of the central characteristics of God's people (Mt 5:9). In contrast, Jesus lamented the coming destruction of Jerusalem because the people didn't know "the things that make for peace" (Lk 19:42).

---

[1] Walter Brueggemann, *Peace* (St. Louis: Chalice, 2001), 13.
[2] Brueggemann, *Peace*, 14.

Pursuing peace is a central way of life for God's people. Even during exile in Babylon God's people were expected to both work and pray for the peace of the foreign city in which they resided (Jer 29:4-7). They were to embody shalom and work toward its realization. This was a practical desire for well-being, wholeness, and prosperity for the entire society. God's people have constantly been reinvited back into "a covenant of peace" that we are expected to faithfully embody (Num 25:12; Ezek 34:25; 37:26; Hos 2:18; Mal 2:5; Heb 13:20; Eph 2:11-22).

We must realize that shalom is ultimately a divine intervention. We can't bring it to fruition on our own. Jesus told his disciples, "Peace I leave with you; my peace I give to you. I do not give to you as the world gives" (Jn 14:27). The establishment of peace will not come through the efforts of the powers that be or through the execution of "law and order," which normalize and mask all sorts of systemic violence. In contrast, shalom breaks into our space, offering deliverance despite the hegemonic structuring of our society. The frequent calls for "peace and quiet" from those in control or benefiting from our social order have nothing to do with the kind of shalom God delivers.

We are referring to a divinely inaugurated revolutionary reality. Shalom is a subversive disruption to this present age. God's peace includes the presence of justice (Ps 72:2), righteousness (Jas 3:18), fairness (Is 32:17), and deliverance (Ps 85:9). Ultimately, the peace that Jesus established breaks down the hostility between Jew and Gentile and therefore dismantles all walls of hostility based in violent hierarchy that exist for the purpose of domination instead of forming a new humanity. There is solidarity in Christ that grows out of oppressors repenting and turning away from domination and coming alongside those who have been oppressed. It's seen in Zacchaeus's encounter with Jesus, resulting in a subversive reorientation of Zacchaeus's life that straightened his crooked past and unjust lifestyle as he made reparations to victims so they might encounter jubilee-shaped restoration (Lk 19:1-10). This is the subversive gift of peace. Experiencing the inbreaking of God's shalom means a radical reconfiguring of social relationships and power dynamics. The existence of God's shalom is the end of a system of categorizing human value sustained in violent concentrated power. Jesus renounced lording over others within his kingdom (Mt 20:20-28).

A crucial passage to consider when getting a handle on shalom is Isaiah 11:1-9. This passage explains that from Jesse will sprout "a shoot" that the Lord will rest upon. This one will judge rightly, fairly caring for the poor and providing justice for "the downtrodden of the earth" (Is 11:1-4 NET). Then we receive a beautiful sketch of the kind of well-being and harmony that all creation will experience:

> Justice will be like a belt around his waist,
> integrity will be like a belt around his hips.
> A wolf will reside with a lamb,
> and a leopard will lie down with a young goat;
> an ox and a young lion will graze together,
> as a small child leads them along.
> A cow and a bear will graze together,
> their young will lie down together.
> A lion, like an ox, will eat straw.
> A baby will play
> over the hole of a snake;
> over the nest of a serpent
> an infant will put his hand.
> They will no longer injure or destroy
> on my entire royal mountain.
> For there will be universal submission to the LORD's sovereignty,
> just as the waters completely cover the sea. (Is 11:5-9 NET)

Two things are worth mentioning. First, notice this is not solely about humanity. All of creation is brought into shalom. All of creation finds its balance and harmony together. There is a new kind of belonging and life together. Everyone and everything experiences the goodness of shalom together. Second, this eschatological sketch includes "universal submission" to the Lord, offering an all-encompassing scope of shalom's reach. All of creation experiences deliverance into God's peace. All of creation is reordered within the cosmos under the Lord's sovereignty, meaning no more domination and violence. Revelation 21:1-5 reminds us the former age of suffering under violence will pass and a new age will begin where all of humanity and creation are reconciled to God. This peace is experienced only in part right now but will eventually incorporate all things.

WHITE SUPREMACIST REALITIES

One could easily get lost in the awe-inspiring vision of shalom while the death-dealing realities of White supremacy continue to pattern our current society. Consequently it's necessary that the average American awaken to how their life operates congruently with White supremacy, even without their awareness. I imagine using the language of "white supremacy" in the twenty-first century seems exaggerated for some.

Many misunderstandings remain around the existence of White supremacy today. Its usage is often limited to participation in overt KKK-like rhetoric and practices commonly enacted sixty or more years ago. Many believe White supremacy has been fading away, receiving its fatal blow following Martin Luther King. Our present task, many assume, is to passively wait for the remaining racial residue to dissipate. That is, except for exposing "the few bad apples." Considered to be a marginal issue, White supremacy is assumed to be highly individual. Many also tend to perceive racism only from a horizontal angle, unable to conceptualize the hierarchical component present in routine interaction.[3] Hence it is assumed that the solution is always more frequent interaction. That may at times be helpful, but it doesn't get at the root issue. With those misconceptions and others, most people do not engage in critical examination of our White supremacist social order.

Moving forward, we must stop evaluating White supremacy according to the norms of a different era. We ought not to judge ourselves against the slaveholding era of 1850, or 1950 during the Jim Crow era, but must understand how racism operates in the twenty-first century. Changes in White supremacy from 1850 to 1950 never meant that racial hierarchy was gone. The routine lynching of thousands of Black men, women, and children became routine *after slavery*, with White Christians either leading such violence or refusing to intervene. After slavery Black churches and homes were regularly bombed or threatened by White terrorism, as Black Christian leaders in the southern freedom movement were regularly attacked, assaulted, or assassinated. After slavery the governing order was still operated by an overt principle of White supremacy. For example, Governor George Wallace didn't blush when he proclaimed "Segregation now, segregation tomorrow, segregation forever!" After slavery, enforced racial segregation shaped all spheres of life, humiliating Black people with antiblack laws that denied their humanity. The forms of church life, education, business, and civil life during Jim Crow were different from the antebellum slavery era, but there is no question that after the emancipation of slaves all the way up to the 1960s there existed a new White hierarchy. White supremacy has never been static. It has always been dynamic and slippery, now growing

---

[3]A good historical example to deconstruct the idea that racism is primarily a gap in geographical proximity or lack of interaction is the master and enslaved relationship. Households often held both slaveholders and slaves in the same space. Regular interaction did not solve the race problem. The hierarchical framing of race was able to remain intact despite such encounters. These human touch points were perceived as inherently carrying a differential in status, power, and worth.

even more sophisticated, covert, and malleable in its twenty-first century manifestation.

Therefore people seeking to be peacemakers today must awaken to our twenty-first-century society still organized by racial power and control in the United States. Joe Feagin, a sociologist, calls the "framework of white supremacy" in America "the central organizing principle of society."[4] Eduardo Bonilla-Silva, a leading scholar in race theory, argues that "white supremacy (racially based political regimes that emerged post-fifteenth century) and racial ideology are the most important sociological variables to explain the status of racial minorities."[5] Yet few pacifists connect their ways of peacemaking with these racially based regimes.

Racism is more than the taken-for-granted definition that most Americans operate by. White supremacy is an all-encompassing reality in our society that operates systemically and hierarchically in our everyday lives. It permeates our lived experience and organizes the societal patterns that shape life experiences for both the White majority and racial minority groups. Joe Feagin explains:

> In the United States, racist thought, emotion, and action are structured into the rhythms of everyday life. They are lived, concrete, advantageous for whites, and painful for those who are not white. Each major part of the life of a white person or person of color is shaped directly or indirectly by this country's systemic racism. Even a person's birth and parents are often shaped by racism, since mate selection is limited by racist pressures against intimate interracial relationships and intermarriage. Where one lives is frequently determined by the racist practices of landlords, bankers, and others in the real-estate profession. The clothes one wears and what one has to eat are affected by access to resources that varies by position

---

[4] Joe R. Feagin, *Racist America: Roots, Current Realities, and Future Reparations*, 3rd ed. (New York: Routledge, 2014), 237.
[5] Eduardo Bonilla-Silva, *White Supremacy and Racism in the Post-Civil Rights Era* (Boulder, CO: Lynne Rienner, 2001), 11.

in the U.S. racial hierarchy. When one goes off to school, one's education is shaped by contemporary racism—from the composition of the student body to the character of the curriculum. Where one goes to church is often shaped by racism, and it is likely that racism affects who one's political representatives are. Even getting sick, dying, and being buried may be influenced by systemic racism. Every part of the life cycle, and most aspects of one's life, are shaped by the racism that is integral to the foundation and continuing operation of the United States.[6]

It is also vital to stay particularly attentive to systemic violence against Black and Brown people. Mainstream awareness of mass incarceration has grown because of Michelle Alexander's *The New Jim Crow*.[7] After the civil rights movement in the early seventies, the prison population was about 300,000 inmates, but in about three decades it exploded to around two million inmates! This disproportionately impacts Black and Brown youth who are routinely convicted for nonviolent drug offenses. Studies nonetheless reveal that Black youth and White youth are using (and selling) marijuana at similar rates.[8] This deconstructs the antiblack assumptions of criminality commonly used to explain away these issues. Alexander's highly researched argument reveals the racial discrimination impacting poor Black and Brown communities at every stage in the judicial system. It results in disproportionate Black and Brown policing, stop-and-frisks, and arrests, along with stiffer sentencing handed out for the same offense as compared to White counterparts. The war on drugs is waged with racially selective execution. And people with convictions are legally discriminated against after release. They are legally discriminated against in housing and employment, and in many states they have their right to vote taken away. One of three

---

[6]Feagin, *Racist America*, x.
[7]Michelle Alexander, *The New Jim Crow: Mass Incarceration in the Age of Colorblindness* (New York: New Press, 2012).
[8]Alexander, *The New Jim Crow*, 7.

African American males will go through the judicial system at some point in their life, mostly for nonviolent drug offenses. White supremacy turns its claims of an American dream into an American nightmare for those living on its racialized underside.

More could be said about racialized patterns in education, in access to employment, or in wages—the scarcity of affordable housing, ongoing redlining, negligent preventive healthcare for minorities, and food deserts in many poor neighborhoods of color are all issues minorities across the country have struggled with for generations. The ongoing problem of police brutality against Black men, women, and children, highlighted of late by the Black Lives Matter movement, is also an old problem. Feagin notes that "during the years 1920–1932 substantially more than half of all African Americans killed by whites were killed by white officers." In addition, the police regularly participated in "the estimated 6,000 bloody lynchings of black men and women from the 1870s to the 1960s."[9] The danger of Black bodies maneuvering in our White supremacist society is spotlighted by Tamir Rice and Rekia Boyd's blood spilled on the ground, along with that of countless others over the last four hundred years. The Black church continues to pray for "a coming king" who brings deliverance and affirms that their lives matter:

> For he will rescue the needy when they cry out for help,
> and the oppressed who have no defender.
> He will take pity on the poor and needy;
> the lives of the needy he will save.
> From harm and violence he will defend them;
> he will value their lives. (Ps 72:12-14 NET)

Our society has never been indifferent to race despite the emergence of colorblind rhetoric in the White majority since the civil rights

---

[9]Feagin, *Racist America*, 156.

movement. Many White people claim to merely "see people as people" because "we are all Americans," but their deeply racialized lives undermine such sentiments.[10] Some refute personal racism by claiming that their best friend is black, a false equivocation for why they aren't racist. However, the evidence suggests that the initial claim itself is grounded in either complete fiction or deep exaggeration for most. According to the Public Religion Research Institute, 91 percent of White people's closest friends are actually White and only 1 percent of their closest friends are Black, suggesting most White claims of a Black best friend are disingenuous. White people have remained fairly steadily in segregated intimate social networks despite common contrary sentiments. American lives reveal a uniquely racialized character that is shaped predominantly by one's own racial group. Consider the neighborhoods people choose to live in, the authors filling up their bookshelves, the stores they frequent, and the neighborhoods they don't spend much time in. Who regularly sits and eats with you around your table? Who do you intimately confide in? Most people are immersed in relationships and places that reflect their own racial group. Even in neighborhoods that are racially and ethnically diverse one typically finds racial distinctiveness in the social relationships that matter most for the majority of Americans.

For Christians, racialization typically increases rather than decreases.[11] The White church has mostly continued in patterns of White supremacist segregation through not only homogeneous White leadership and White decision-making power but also through nondialogical White theology and dominant cultural influence. If Whiteness is a social construct created to sustain societal power, then the church has a problem.

---

[10] Eduardo Bonilla-Silva, *Racism Without Racists: Color-Blind Racism and the Persistence of Racial Inequality in America*, 3rd ed. (Lanham, MD: Rowman & Littlefield Publishers, 2009).

[11] Michael Emerson, *Divided by Faith: Evangelical Religion and the Problem of Race in America* (New York: Oxford University Press, 2000).

Consider what conferences one attends and who is creating and designing the shape and focus of these conferences and organizations. It matters which preachers you are not exposed to and the curriculum you will never consider. How about the people of color who are selected solely because they thoroughly adhere to the White-dominant cultural logics of your particular group? This reflects an unwillingness to be transformed by the broader wisdom, conversations, and traditions among racialized minority groups in the church. Followers of Jesus must wrestle through these issues impacting the larger church within White supremacist society.

We have sketched how the United States is thoroughly shaped by White supremacy in structure and character because it is thoroughly racialized (encompassing all of society) and hierarchical (Whiteness is positioned at the top of the ladder of power). White people dominate a racially structured society that offers material advantage to some while giving only psychological and perceived advantages for others.[12] That many White females and White poor often align themselves with White identity rather than with the masses of people of color who might actually share a closer lived experience with them demonstrates the power, lure, and perceived benefits of White identification in society.

White followers of Jesus need to seriously reflect on a marred Christian witness in relation to the racialized oppression in general and the denial of centuries of Black suffering in particular, which opens up the possibilities for a new trajectory. There is always the invitation to turn away from being saviors to the dark peoples of the world, assuming superiority in perspective, culture, and values, and instead taking a posture of learner with those who know a deeper meaning of Christ

---

[12]Consider poor White people and persistent classism within our capitalist society, as well as White women facing patriarchy in the United States. Each experience is impacted by marginalization despite the choice of identification with White society.

crucified because of having lived as "strange fruit" in a strange land while following Jesus out of that experience.

How does one practice Christian pacifism in the United States while not resisting White supremacy? Some redefinitions around violence might help answer this question. Drawing from Glen Stassen and Michael Westmoreland-White, Mennonite theologian J. Denny Weaver shares this definition: "Violence is destruction to a victim by means that overpower the victim's consent."[13] This definition makes room for physical violence as well as systemic violence. Weaver explains further that "although systemic violence is clearly distinguishable from physical violence such as lynching or war, it is important to acknowledge the real harm done to people by the systemic violence of unjust structures and policies. Social structures and tax policies that enforce poverty do real harm to people."[14] Many White Christian pacifists focus exclusively on bodily harm and military action while only incidentally dealing with racism, but not as central to the peace question. But can a life thoroughly sustained by White supremacist social patterns and blind to its widespread systemic violence still be peacemaking?

James Cone, a pioneer in modern Black theology, has frequently written about the hypocrisy of White pacifism in the church. He insists that White pacifists needed to expand their definition of violence and ought not be surprised when Black Christians aren't quick to join their nonviolent protests. Operating out of a thin definition of violence, he notes, White people are usually more concerned about Black people's responses to White violence than about challenging White supremacist violence. Cone says, "The problem of violence is not the problem of a few black revolutionaries but the problem of a whole social structure which outwardly appears to be ordered and respectable but inwardly is

---

[13]J. Denny Weaver, *The Nonviolent God* (Grand Rapids, MI: Eerdmans, 2013), 192.
[14]Weaver, *Nonviolent God*, 193.

'ridden by psychopathic obsessions and delusions'—racism and hatred."[15] White pacifist framings of violence flow out of White-dominant culture, and it's taken for granted that their reasoning has "accepted the oppressor's definitions."[16] Usually it would appear foolish to allow perpetrators to define what constitutes violence and what does not. However, violence and pacifism today have too often been defined in such a way that people can claim peacemaking while feeling no obligation to resist racialized systemic violence. Cone, for that reason, explains why Black Christians have been skeptical of White pacifist causes:

> That is why blacks, unfortunately, are seldom found in the crowds protesting nuclear arms. We have lived with white violence for nearly four hundred years, faced slave ships, auction blocks, lynchings, ghettos, inadequate education, and medical care, indecent housing, chronic unemployment, and constant police brutality. When physical survival is a daily task in which the odds are against you, because the nation in which you are a citizen has defined you as the enemy, there is little motivation to protest against a nuclear crisis that your enemies have created, especially when the people protesting look like your oppressors and do so little to connect justice with peace issues.[17]

The contradiction of a sincere pacifism shaped by a vision of shalom while thoroughly implicated in a way of life organized by one of the most historically devastating forms of systemic violence in the modern era is the problem being slowly untangled in this essay. To get even closer to the root of the problem we should consider Jon Pahl's concept of "innocent domination" from his book *Empire of Sacrifice*.[18] In his book he teases out a theory describing how a highly religious country like

---

[15]James Cone, *God of the Oppressed* (New York: Seabury, 1975), 200.
[16]Cone, *God of the Oppressed*, 201.
[17]James Cone, *Speaking the Truth: Ecumenism, Liberation, and Black Theology* (Grand Rapids, MI: Eerdmans, 1986), 66.
[18]Jon Pahl, *Empire of Sacrifice: The Religious Origins of American Violence* (New York: New York University Press, 2010), 2.

America can perceive itself through a lens of innocence and thereby never implicate itself in the violent domination central to its original founding and ongoing practices. As he describes it, innocent domination involves the "patterns or systems of domination, hegemony, or power over others that are largely absent of malice on the part of the perpetrators."[19] As a scholar in American religion Pahl has as his book's ultimate goal to initiate a dialogue that differentiates religious practice that is indeed peacemaking from religious life caught up in the web of violence. His "claim is that we can, and must, differentiate reasonably (and contingently) among *types of religion*: those that legitimize or produce systemic violence and those that can help prevent it."[20] The problem, as Pahl points out, is that we trick ourselves into believing in our own innocence.

The life of John Howard Yoder brings these concerns concretely to the forefront. Yoder was a gifted writer and thinker on peace and nonviolence while simultaneously embroiled in a life of violence. In an article titled "Defanging the Beast," Rachel Waltner Goossen offers a clarifying historical record unveiling Yoder's violent sexual experiments that he performed on his "sisters" for decades while framing it as theological exploration. Using his power, status, and influence as a world-renowned peace ethicist, he violated women at his local seminary as well as overseas in places as far away as Africa, all while using his gifts of reasoning and explanatory power as weapons to continue slipping out of the grip of those who tried to hold him accountable.[21] Yoder continued to be one of the most influential Christian ethicists on peace in the late twentieth and early twenty-first centuries after his untimely death. Yet his ongoing practice of ignoring the power dynamics inherent

---

[19]Pahl, *Empire of Sacrifice*, 4.
[20]Pahl, *Empire of Sacrifice*, 7.
[21]Rachel Waltner Goossen, "'Defanging the Beast': Mennonite Responses to John Howard Yoder's Sexual Abuse," *Mennonite Quarterly Review* 89, no. 1 (January 2015): 7-80.

in his life while leaving a path of violence and survivors behind his callous "experiments" raises the question of what it means to be peacemaking. Certainly Yoder's "revolutionary subordination" concept in *The Politics of Jesus* lacks the necessary power differential analysis to be truly revolutionary, therefore failing to prevent his own "innocent domination" of women.[22] Exploring the realities of White supremacy, we find that Yoder's record is only slightly better. Yoder was aware that race was an issue and that it related to peace. Yoder nonetheless seemed to broach the subject only incidentally and sparingly. He mostly conformed to White patterns of avoidance, frequently writing as though such realities were not vital to the subject of violence. However, he did address White hypocrisy on peace directly once, contending that African American communities embodied nonviolence more than any White group had. He stated, "Most white Christians are not, and since the fourth century, never have been, against all violence." Then said, "Black Christians, past and present, though often not by choice, have often been closer to Christian nonviolence than whites have been." Finally he declared, "In terms of objective cultural history, the idea of violence in the cause of justice is European, and the idea of nonviolent direct action is nonwhite."[23] Despite that brief peripheral commentary, Yoder overall exemplified the ways White pacifism has regularly been supervised by White supremacy, rarely resisting such warped theological imaginations and praxis.

CONCLUSION

In summary, I have contended that White supremacy is an all-society-encompassing form of violence. It desires complete conformity in how we structure our lives. White supremacy has morphed and changed over

---

[22]John Howard Yoder, *The Politics of Jesus: Vicit Agnus Noster* (Grand Rapids, MI: Eerdmans, 1994).

[23]John Howard Yoder, Glen Harold Stassen, and Matt Hamsher, *The War of the Lamb: The Ethics of Nonviolence and Peacemaking* (Grand Rapids, MI: Brazos, 2009), 162.

time with inertia not dependent on a single generation's awareness of it, because "after a society becomes racialized, racialization develops a life of its own."[24] Likewise it is hierarchical and "structured in dominance."[25] In contrast, shalom seeks to include all of life, repatterning our relationship with God, one another, and creation. More specifically, shalom is about God's vision for deliverance and reconciliation that encompasses the whole order. It marks the end of lording over others. "*Shalom* is the end of coercion. *Shalom* is the end of fragmentation. *Shalom* is the freedom to rejoice. *Shalom* is the courage to live an integrated life in a community of coherence."[26] Shalom and White supremacy cannot coexist without tension, for they are both competing visions about what organizing norm will pattern humanity and creation.

Unfortunately, the church has too often allowed White supremacy to filter its vision of peace, allowing its rhetoric concerning shalom to be molded by systemic violence of this present age. Even Jesus was pressed through White supremacist molds with his blond flowing hair, deep ocean blue eyes, and Western identity that denied his Jewish particularity. Such misrepresentation of Christ was not deemed profane for realigning Jesus with oppressive social dominance. It ought to remind all Christians that the first source to turn to for understanding Christian peacemaking might not be those with well-turned phrases and compelling arguments created comfortably within dominant culture, but those concretely following Jesus through the underside of White supremacy's violence. Don't get me wrong, we must learn from the entire church, but it must be done through mutual dialogue as an exilic people living, belonging, and standing in solidarity with the oppressed from below the imperial violence and oppression.

---

[24]Bonilla-Silva, *White Supremacy*, 45.
[25]Bonilla-Silva, *White Supremacy*, 47.
[26]Brueggemann, *Peace*, 51.

For these reasons Martin Luther King's nonviolence becomes more than academic explanatory power. In his words, as he practiced the Sermon on the Mount, "Nonviolence became more than a method" and more than "intellectual assent" but "it became a commitment to a way of life."[27] There is a lived nonviolence tradition in America that is rarely gleaned from, though existing for centuries and able to aid the church's embodiment of peace. I would like to turn pacifist attention toward the Black church, which is full of men who practiced transformative love instead of retribution, and the women, as Karen Baker-Fletcher reminds us, "like Mother Mamie Till-Mobley, Mother Rosa Parks, Mother Ella Baker, and First Lady Coretta Scott King [who] could have hated, but walked in love. They could have sunk to violent rage, but instead they walked in holy indignation and holy dignity. They led others as they followed Christ in the comforting, encouraging, and healing power of the Holy Spirit."[28] May we all begin to learn from and imitate the witness of these saints that pursued the deliverance of shalom while living in the ditch of White supremacy.

---

[27]Martin Luther King Jr., *Strength to Love* (Minneapolis: Fortress, 2010), 160.
[28]Karen Baker-Fletcher, *Dancing with God: The Trinity from a Womanist Perspective* (St. Louis: Chalice, 2006), 168.

HEALING FROM RACIAL TRAUMA

Sheila Wise Rowe

A LARGE CROWD FOLLOWED and pressed around Jesus. A woman with an issue of blood was there. She had been hemorrhaging for twelve years and suffered under the care of incompetent doctors. The woman spent all she had, and instead of getting better, she grew worse. She made her way through the crowd and came up behind Jesus and touched his cloak, because she thought, "If I but touch his clothes, I will be made well" (Mk 5:24-28). Every day in America and across the world, Black, indigenous, and other women, men, and children of color experience spiritual and emotional hemorrhaging because of racism. We have endured traumatic histories and are told we need to just get over it. In Jeremiah 6:14 we read, "They have treated the wound of my people carelessly, saying, 'peace, peace' when there is no peace." This verse reminds us that in a rush to reconciliation, the past and present wounds and profound pain of people of color are often unacknowledged. Some people of color have endured by praying about the racism or have acted out their feelings. Others have taught themselves to minimize or deny the constant flow of blood, saying "peace, peace," when there is no peace.

When God acknowledges that "they have treated the wound of my people carelessly," he is telling us that he sees and knows that our wounds are untreated.

ALTERNATIVE FACTS

We live in a time when "alternative facts" are presented that deny the truth about racism and its impact. Alternative facts are half-truths. There is a whole story, but significant portions are missing, overlooked, or minimized, or it is all a flat-out lie. They will say it's not true, didn't happen, and will judge our experience or reaction. In reality they have simply formed an opinion based on their biases and then blindly acted on it. Some celebrate their alternative facts, saying, "I just don't believe white people should socialize or marry outside their race." While others say, "We are all the same. I don't see color or ethnicity; I just don't." Whether they do or don't see color or ethnicity, their responses imply that racism and xenophobia are inconsequential or nonexistent. Alternative facts can seem benign, but the reality is that they can be dangerous.

One survey revealed that almost 80 percent of Black Christians believe police-involved killings are part of a larger pattern of police treatment of African Americans. In contrast, over 70 percent of White Christians, including White evangelical Protestants, Catholics, and mainline Protestants, believe the opposite to be true, that these were simply isolated incidents.[1] People of color often ask how these two versions of reality can coexist. It became more apparent during the 2016 election cycle and after the inauguration of President Trump. The fact is that we live in different worlds. In one world there is the proclamation

---

[1]Robert P. Jones, Daniel Cox, Betsy Cooper, and Rachel Lienesch, "Anxiety, Nostalgia, and Mistrust: Findings from the 2015 American Values Survey," Public Religion Research Institute, November 17, 2015, www.prri.org/research/survey-anxiety-nostalgia-and-mistrust-findings-from-the-2015-american-values-survey.

of peace, peace even as the vitriol flowed from the White House and society in general. The rise in White supremacy and microaggressions against people of color did not seem to matter much. While in the other world where people of color live, the impact of bias and racism is titanic and traumatic.

When White folks rush toward reconciliation proclaiming "peace, peace," they are failing to engage in true racial reconciliation. White folks are not the only ones with alternative facts; people of color also have alternative facts. In our rush to reconciliation, my sisters and brothers of color often don't take our wounds seriously either. There are times when our response to racism is similar to the disciples on the road to Emmaus; on some level, we believe Jesus is dead, at least in regard to this issue. We may respond to issues of race and racism by raging against, ignoring, or minimizing racial trauma until it becomes our alternative fact, and we also neglect to acknowledge our trauma.

A few years ago I taught a class in Johannesburg, South Africa, titled Trauma Awareness, Healing, and Reconciliation. My students were peacebuilders from across the African continent and a Canadian. They were advocates for racial and ethnic reconciliation, social justice, and peace. They served on the front line in their home countries of Northern Nigeria, Swaziland, Rwanda, Zambia, Mozambique, Kenya, Canada, Angola, Uganda, and South Africa. A couple of my students worked with the families of the kidnapped Chibok, Nigerian schoolgirls, and the traumatized Christian and Muslim students and families affected by the massacre at Garissa University College in Kenya. Others were involved in ethnic and racial reconciliation, youth ministry, and outreach to sexually trafficked women and children. The intensity of spending that week together, learning and sharing our stories, was profound. When I taught on trauma healing, I shared as a metaphor the story of how a friend survived the 9/11 terrorist attack on the twin towers in New York.

As she ran down sixteen flights of stairs and finally exited, the twin tower ash gently clung to her hair and clothing. She raced toward her apartment, and along the way, she passed people sitting at café tables sipping their cappuccinos, unaware that the towers were falling. She arrived home safely and told her family she was okay. But as time passed, it became apparent that all was not well. One morning she sat on her sofa and watched a TV special on the 9/11 attack. She sat in front of the screen transfixed for hours, and when the day passed unaccounted for, she realized it was time to come out of denial and process her grief and trauma.

There are many ways that people of color are transfixed or stuck. Sometimes it's historical, transgenerational, interpersonal, or physical racism, microaggression, or gaslighting. All of these experiences can inflict racial trauma, which impairs our minds, bodies, souls, spirits, and communities. Some research shows that "our minds may forget, but our bodies don't and deep inside of every cell a memory trace is stored of every event we ever experienced and the sensations and feelings that occurred with them."[2] Other research has shown that historical racism may weaken our DNA, causing racial trauma to be passed down to future generations.

Recently people of color were rocked by the racism and racially biased murders of two people in their own homes. Atatiana Jefferson was shot by a police officer in her own home while playing video games with her nephew. Botham Jean was shot while sitting in his apartment in front of his TV, eating a bowl of ice cream. We were told there must be some reason why they deserved this. It is hard to live in Black and Brown bodies when we are so often viewed as suspects. It doesn't matter if we have an advanced degree or are a teenager in a hoodie, a member of the Senate, a janitor, or a celebrity. At some point many of us have

---

[2]Satsuki Ina, "Tule Lake Reunion Symposium," Children of the Camps Project, June 1998, www.pbs.org/childofcamp/project/remarks.html.

experienced microaggression and have been racially profiled. Each incident of personal or vicarious racism has inflicted racial trauma even if we aren't aware of it. As we watch footage of children kept in cages on the southern border, we remember our ancestors enslaved in pens or forced into boarding schools or internment camps. As we learn of White supremacists destroying Black and Brown bodies in churches and shopping malls, everywhere starts to feel unsafe.[3] The pain of loss is felt more intensely by people of color. Although an incident may not have happened to us or a member of our family, we feel it vicariously because we know it could have been us. Many of us spend our lives running as if from a house on fire. Some of us experience gaslighting, and now we also minimize or deny our wounds and believe the lie that everything is okay. We have just dusted ourselves off and taken a seat at a café table sipping our cappuccinos. We've made a false peace and have not addressed the severity of our wounds.

RACIAL TRAUMA

Racial trauma can be defined as the physical and psychological symptoms that people of color experience after a racist incident. When we experience a racist threat, our brains are wired to prepare our bodies to fight or flee. When microaggressions or personal or vicarious racial incidents happen repeatedly, racial trauma accumulates, which contributes to a more insidious, chronic stress.[4] The result is that our brain and body don't fully stand down. We remain racially traumatized, which triggers a physical and emotional response, which in turn feeds our racial trauma. So we are in an endless trauma loop.[5] According to a report titled "The

---

[3]See Sheila Wise Rowe, "Transcending Racial Trauma," *The Art of Taleh*, August 8, 2019, www.theartoftaleh.com/transcending-racial-trauma/.
[4]Robert T. Carter, "Racism and Psychological and Emotional Injury: Recognizing and Assessing Race-Based Traumatic Stress," *Counseling Psychologist* 35, no. 1 (2007): 13-105.
[5]See Rowe, "Transcending Racial Trauma."

Impact of Racial Trauma on African Americans," the effects of racial trauma include fear, aggression, depression, anxiety, low self-image, shame, hypervigilance, pessimism, nightmares, difficulty concentrating, substance abuse, flashbacks, and relational dysfunction. Other people of color also bear these symptoms in addition to physical issues such as hyperactivity, heart disease, headaches, and poor concentration.[6]

People of color pray, yet still battle with the symptoms. We are exhausted from silently carrying racial trauma and the burden of White people's fears. We urgently need Christ-centered healing where the Lord meets, heals, and helps us to better love our neighbor and ourselves.[7]

THE WHOLE STORY

As the woman with the issue of blood touched the hem of Jesus' garment, immediately her bleeding stopped, and she felt in her body that she was free from her suffering. When Jesus realized that power had gone out from him, he turned around in the crowd and asked, "Who touched my clothes?" "You see the crowd pressing in on you," his disciples answered; "how can you can say, 'Who touched me?'" (Mk 5:30-31). But Jesus kept looking around to see who had touched him. Then the woman, knowing what had happened to her, came and fell at his feet and, trembling with fear, told him the whole truth (Mk 5:32-33). Jesus allowed the woman to show herself and to share her story. If we apply the law written in Leviticus 15:19, the woman would be considered unclean, so Jesus' interaction with her would make him ceremonially unclean until the evening. Regardless of the consequences, Jesus stopped and waited for the woman to share her whole story. Sharing our whole story is central to the healing process.

---

[6]Walter Howard Smith Jr., "The Impact of Racial Trauma on African Americans," Heinz Endowments, February 16, 2010, www.heinz.org/userfiles/impactofracialtraumaonafricanamericans.pdf.
[7]See Rowe, "Transcending Racial Trauma."

Once I shared my friend's 9/11 story with my students, they began to open up. They shared how they also carried trauma from the past, and although they had chosen to forgive their abusers, their trauma persisted. For my students, the symptoms came in different forms. For some it was fear of impending disaster, a fear of intimacy, or a refusal to visit the part of town where the trauma occurred. Some students were suspicious of "the other" or reluctant to tell their story for fear they wouldn't be believed. A safe space was created in our classroom. Many of my students recognized for the first time that they carried unprocessed, unhealed racial and ethnic trauma. Christians and Muslims shared stories they'd never shared.

One story that struck me deeply was that of a Muslim student. She shared how, after an incident of violence at Garissa University in Kenya, people were eager to attend to the trauma of the Christian students while the Muslim students were bypassed. There was no recognition that the Muslim students also suffered profound losses that day. They had witnessed the gunmen walk up to Muslim and Christian friends and asked which was a Christian, and then their Christian friend was shot dead at point-blank range. After the massacre, the Muslim students were not allowed to return to the university. That day they lost everything, and in the days and months that followed, they were left to deal with their grief and trauma on their own. Some turned to self-medicating their pain and trauma with alcohol or drugs, some were just idle or engaged in crime. Others left confused and angry and were easily radicalized. As my students listened to one another, many wept and afterward prayed for one another. For some, there was a degree of closure, yet for others, their healing journey had just begun.

THE HEALING JOURNEY

There are several essentials in our journey of healing racial trauma: soul care, lament, support, forgiveness, reconciled relationships, and action. Let's look at each in turn.

Soul care. Although soul care sounds suspiciously like an excuse for selfishness, it is the opposite. Racism is relentless, so people of color have to be relentless in engaging our faith and caring for our souls. Even if our faith is smaller than a mustard seed, it is enough to commit to cultivating a deeper relationship with the Lord through his Word, prayer, and worship. When we engage in soul care, we are more available to God, a blessing to others, and we feel more fully alive and present rather than living in detached numbness. Soul care involves knowing when and how to go slow, destress, rest, and know when and how to expose injustice. It also includes knowing when to engage in activities that advocate for our needs and those of others.

There are three critical biblical principles related to soul care for us to consider. First, our healing, our recovery, our pilgrimage is from beginning to end God's work, God-inspired and God-sustained. He is the one who keeps things intact for us and who is our rest and the ultimate source of care. Second, we live in this tension: it's not all about us; our healing journey is also outward-focused. We are healing so that when we are ready, we can help "bear one another's burdens, and in this way . . . fulfill the law of Christ" (Gal 6:2). At the same time, the Lord is teaching us how to say no. We can learn and discern how to extend ourselves safely and not be manipulated by others. Finally, memory is crucial, founded in practices such as keeping a journal or simply sharing with others the highs and lows of our journey. This is crucial because it's easy to forget how far we've come, where we are going, and that the Lord loves us unconditionally.

There are some basic soul care routines to consider in light of the principles mentioned above. We need to take time for our closest relationships, our family, friends, and church community (Heb 10:25). One of the benefits of healing is that our ability to hear the still small voice of the Holy Spirit is gradually restored. Then we begin to notice if an interaction or event is troubling our mind or body and needs attention. It's vital that we cultivate healthy routines and take care of our health. We are vulnerable to being sidetracked by racism simply because we aren't eating, sleeping well, or getting exercise. The resilient walk by faith; we don't deny the situation, but we get help and seek new ways of being that will help us heal and keep moving forward. These new ways of being deepen our love for God, our families, and our neighbors, and they help us celebrate life with all its beauty and complexities.

Lament. We need the Lord to show us what we have been carrying for so many years and to no longer minimize how recent events have retraumatized many of us. Some of us need professional counseling to work through the trauma, and there is no shame in that. All of us can bring our feelings to the Lord and allow the Comforter, the Holy Spirit, to come and treat our wounds. Our genuine emotions of sadness, anger, indifference, or weariness must be brought into the light. Bessel van der Kolk writes, "It takes tremendous energy to keep functioning while carrying the memory of terror, and the shame of utter weakness and vulnerability."[8] Healing from racial trauma starts with remembering and then being honest with God about how we really feel, about what we saw, felt, and heard. We cry out in lament, not just for ourselves but also for our community. Lament is described by Soong-Chan Rah as "an act of protest as the lamenter is allowed to express indignation and even outrage about the experience of suffering. The lamenter talks

---

[8]Bessel van der Kolk, *The Body Keeps the Score: Brain, Mind, and Body in the Healing of Trauma* (New York: Penguin, 2014), 2.

back to God and ultimately petitions him for help in the midst of pain. The one who laments can call out to God for help, and in that outcry, there is the hope and even the manifestation of praise."[9] One prayer of lament is found in Psalm 44. David asks God,

> Why do you hide your face?
>> Why do you forget our affliction and oppression?
> For we sink down to the dust;
>> our bodies cling to the ground.
> Rise up, come to our help.
>> Redeem us for the sake of your steadfast love. (Ps 44:24-26)

King David's prayer of lament is an example of how, when faced with injustice, people of color can also cry out to God. It also serves as a model of prayer for White folks to cry out in prayer on behalf of people of color.

Sometimes unsuspecting and surprising events cause lament to surface. In my case, it was an eighty-five-year-old photo. I had not seen a picture of my grandmother until a few weeks ago when her 1935 graduation photo was discovered tucked away in an old shoebox. The photo surfaced just as I finished writing my book about healing racial trauma. In the book I shared my story of oppression, healing, and resilience and those of other African American, Indigenous, Asian, Latino, Bi-racial, and South African friends. But I had not shared the full details of the story of my paternal grandmother Mary. Shortly after her high school graduation, she married her beloved Robert Wise and soon gave birth to three sons, Robert Jr., Edward, and Curtis. They had built a life in Accomack County, Virginia, while a tuberculosis outbreak ran throughout the county, leaving devastation in its wake. My emotional response to my grandmother's photo surprised me in ways that I did

---

[9]Soong-Chan Rah, *Prophetic Lament: A Call for Justice in Troubled Times* (Downers Grove, IL: InterVarsity Press, 2015), 44.

not expect. I wrote an ekphrastic poem as I pondered her image and prayed.

Mary Coston Wise

Finally, I see you.
Weathered black, white
shades of brown.
I weep from longing.

You are eighteen
with furrowed brow
wearing your Sunday best.

It's Accomack County graduation
day 1935. Did you know your arms,
legs crossed, could not shield you
from past, present, future tense?

Did you know your marriage
ends in sweating, coughing,
fever, shaking?

Did you know hospitals are for whites only?
Your uncle, husband, baby boy gone, then you.
Your orphan sons left motherless, aching.

Did you know one day
I'd see you and lament
countless ancestors sacrificed?

Did you know today
I'd seek repair
for countless ancestors sacrificed?

As I looked at the photo, I was awakened to my own grief. I sought out records of the deceased and discovered that on a frigid morning in

December 1939 at 2:20 a.m. Robert had passed away, and baby Curtis soon followed. In November 1940, two days before Thanksgiving and on the day that the new tuberculosis hospital for coloreds had a vacant bed, Mary passed away. She was twenty-two years, four months, and nine days old. I read the death certificates and cried, praying a lamenting prayer.

Support. When we are dealing with grief and trauma, we need hush harbors like those set-apart and secluded places where the enslaved gathered, prayed, worshiped the Lord, and strategized about freedom. These sacred healing spaces can be found everywhere if we look for them, and we can also create them. These spaces can help people and communities process and heal from trauma, affirm life and beauty, and pursue reconciled relationships. We can invite other people of color and White allies to sustain, strengthen, and support us as we heal and transcend our trauma. We need safe people with whom we can openly share when we've been blindsided by racism. They can help us to get as calm as possible, remind us to breathe in and out slowly and deeply. These folks can also offer us a reality check regarding alternative facts and tell us who we really are. Just like the woman with the issue of blood, we can come to Jesus. He will receive us just as he did that woman who was deemed outcast and unclean. He called her daughter and restored her dignity. Jesus bestowed peace, shalom, and freedom from her agony and isolation. He publicly proclaimed that she was healed and cleansed, and he restored her to the community. Jesus does the same for us. When we share our whole story, other people get to know us better, and they may hear elements of their own story.[10] The Lord can use our whole story to help someone else heal.

Forgiveness. Our faith and support can ultimately lead to reconciled relationships. However, we live in an age of outrage, and too often, as

---

[10]See Sheila Wise Rowe, *Healing Racial Trauma* (Downers Grove, IL: InterVarsity Press, 2020), 51.

Psalm 64:3 tells us, we are a people who "sharpen their tongues like swords and aim cruel words like deadly arrows" (NIV). I'm tempted to do this when I experience injustice or am exposed to it online or in the news. I remember Jesus' words to Peter in the Garden of Gethsemane after Peter tried to prevent Jesus' arrest by cutting off the right ear of Malchus, the high priest's servant. "Put your sword back into its place," Jesus said to Peter, "for all who take the sword will perish by the sword. Do you think I cannot appeal to my Father, and he will at once send me more than twelve legions of angels?" (Mt 26:52-53). Jesus reminds us that Abba is fully equipped to deal with his adversaries as well as ours. Racial trauma will not stop just because we have experienced some degree of healing. People of color are continually forgiving others, and in some cases, we have received apologies. Forgiveness is hard when we have to do it seventy times seven times (Mt 18:22 KJV). In Romans 12:17-19, we are reminded,

> Do not repay anyone evil for evil, but take thought for what is noble in the sight of all. If it is possible, so far as it depends on you, live peaceably with all. Beloved, never avenge yourselves, but leave room for the wrath of God; for it is written, "Vengeance is mine, I will repay, says the Lord."

Our forgiveness is not a declaration that what was done was okay. It is a proclamation that judgment belongs to our God, and it is a defiant act of refusing to allow our freedom to be bound by despair, anger, bitterness, and someone's sin. As the Lord stirs hearts toward forgiveness, repentance, and compassion by his grace, we can walk in love and mercy while still striving for justice.

Reconciled relationships. If we want genuinely reconciled relationships, this may involve personal and at times public apology to people of color for past and present harm and also a determination to go a step further. Repentance must include a commitment to stop all actions of injustice and oppression and to repair any damage done. Truly reconciled relationships include repair; without it, the apology and repentance can feel shallow. In Luke 19, we see repair happen as a result of the repentance of Zacchaeus, the chief tax collector, an agent for state-sanctioned systemic oppression. After Jesus invites himself to Zacchaeus's home, Zacchaeus tells Jesus, "Look, half of my possessions, Lord, I will give to the poor; and if I have defrauded anyone of anything, I will pay back four times as much" (Lk 19:8). True reconciliation includes acts of repair, and there is a cost. Truly reconciled relationships involve sisters and brothers in Christ committed to dismantling systemic racism and helping repair the damage done by it. Repair does not always have to involve money. It happens on a micro level when previously disadvantaged individuals are given access and opportunities and on a macro level when there is a systemic overhaul that promotes equity in education, salary, and healthcare.[11]

Action. Activism is often a byproduct of lament. Dr. Susan Delaney says, "We grow around grief, we become bigger. In the end, our feelings of loss become one small part of our enlarged mental and emotional space. Grief may actually be a doorway to something new, like becoming an activist."[12] As people of color pursue healing from racial trauma, justice, and reconciled relationships, we will undoubtedly continue to face racism. But we have the grace of God and other believers to help us to continue to walk. Change can happen as friends, allies, and brothers and sisters of different races and ethnicities genuinely hear each other's hearts and commit to making a difference. Together we can strive for social action that is hopeful, impactful, and life-affirming. Finally, 1 Corinthians 13:12-13 states, "For now we see in a mirror, dimly, but then we

---

[11]See Rowe, "Transcending Racial Trauma."

[12]Maria Cohut, "The Legacy of Grief: Coping with Loss," *Medical News Today*, November 10, 2017. https://www.medicalnewstoday.com/articles/320032#You-wont-get-over-it,-but-thats-O.K.

will see face to face. Now I know only in part; then I will know fully, even as I have been fully known. And now faith, hope, and love abide, these three; and the greatest of these is love." This is what we strive for across the racial divide. Love heals racial trauma, and may it be what motivates our pursuit of justice.

FAITH-ROOTED RECONCILIATION

ORGANIZING FOR SHALOM JUSTICE

Peter Goodwin Heltzel

FROM THE FIRES OF FERGUSON IN 2014 to the nationwide protests sparked by the killing of George Floyd in 2020, we are witnessing the Black revolution erupt today in American cities.[1] Events of the past several years raise the issue of racism that has plagued our nation since its founding. America was built on a slave-based economy, and there has never been a moral reckoning for this injustice. How can Blacks and Whites be reconciled in America until there is an acknowledgment of this injustice, concrete reparations, and a commitment to an ongoing reconstruction of a more just and equitable America?

BLACK THEOLOGY AND BLACK POWER

When Dr. Martin Luther King Jr. was brutally shot dead on April 4, 1968, while leading a living wage movement for sanitation workers in Memphis, James H. Cone's revolutionary fire was ignited. Cone sat down in the basement of his brother Cecil's church and wrote *Black Theology and*

---

[1]This chapter was originally presented as a paper at the 10th Anniversary Celebration of the Center of Reconciliation, Duke Divinity School, Durham, North Carolina, February 11, 2016.

Black Power in six weeks. Cone advocated a Black theology that inspired and equipped Black people to claim their own power as they worked together to dismantle racist institutions and find their true freedom.

"It is time for the church to be relevant by joining Christ in the black revolution," writes Cone.[2] Cone saw the promise of the Black Power movement as a pathway for prophetic Christianity to achieve its destiny in America. On the wrong side of the ocean, being Black in America was to be in a permanent state of exception—eclipsed and oppressed. While Dr. King worked for the integration of African Americans within White society, a younger, radical Stokely Carmichael increasingly called for Black Power. It was on the Meredith March for Freedom in the sweltering summer of 1966 that this internal debate erupted onto the public scene. On June 16, 1966, Carmichael addressed the marchers in Greenwood, Mississippi, announcing that the only way to overcome the oppression of White supremacy was through building Black Power. With the call-and-response structure of Black preaching and praise, Stokely called the question to the Black Mississippian sharecroppers: "What do we want?"

"Black Power. . . . Black Power," they chanted into the darkness, until the tear gas and shots of police pistols shut it down. The spirit of Blackness broke out that long night in Greenwood. This was a turning point in the civil rights movement, which until that moment had focused on integration but increasingly saw a surge of longing for liberation materialize.

During the summer of 1966, Cone was writing his dissertation on Karl Barth at Northwestern University, while in the summer of 1968 he would write a book that would change the face of American theology. As a theology professor at Adrian College in Adrian, Michigan, in 1968,

---

[2]James H. Cone, *Black Theology & Black Power* (New York: Seabury Press, 1969), 126.

Cone was inspired by the racial riots that erupted down in Detroit after King's untimely death. Since "writing is fighting," he sought to write theology with the same focus and passion of the Black activists. While the Black Power movement called for cultural and political change, Cone knew there had to be change in churches and in Christian theology. Given America's racialized faith, a new theology—a Black theology—must be forged to actualize the prophetic energies of Christianity that Jesus of Nazareth had unleashed in Palestine.

Since Howard Thurman's *Jesus and the Disinherited* had been published in 1949, Dr. Martin Luther King Jr. and theologians of the Black social gospel emphasized Jesus as a liberator of the oppressed. Connecting the suffering of the poor Jews in Jesus' day with the suffering of poor Blacks in America, Cone sought a Black theology all the way down: "To say that Christ is black means that Black people are God's poor people whom Christ has come to liberate."[3] While others had viewed Christ as the crucified liberator, Cone explicitly connected Christ to the crucified in American history, especially Blacks who were descended from enslaved Africans. His Black liberation theology upended the White affluent church in America.

Understanding the confrontational character of his theology against the White establishment, Cone anticipated White objections to his Black liberation theology. Cone wrote, "When Black Theology emphasizes the necessity of a theology of revolution (liberation) based on the unity of black people committed to the task of destroying white racism, it is to be expected that many white religious people will ask: 'What about the biblical message of reconciliation?'"[4] Often when Whites hear about Black Power and Black revolution, they get scared. White anxiety drives them to the discourse of reconciliation as a psychological coping

---

[3]James H. Cone, *God of the Oppressed* (Maryknoll, NY: Orbis, 1997), 125.
[4]Cone, *Black Theology*, 143-44.

mechanism and strategy to overlook the glaring racial injustices in America's racial past and present. Understanding White fear, Cone writes, "We must inform them as calmly and clearly as possible that black people cannot talk about the possibilities of reconciliation until full emancipation has become a reality for all black people."[5] For Cone reconciliation cannot take place until the reality of liberation is fulfilled in the lives of all Black people and Black communities in America.

RECONCILIATION OR LIBERATION?

Cone's call for liberation was contested within both White and Black theological ranks. In 1971, Black theologian J. Deotis Roberts wrote *Liberation and Reconciliation*, critiquing Cone's crystal-clear focus on liberation. Because of his commitment to nonviolent peacemaking, Roberts was concerned about an advocacy of violence in Cone's work as well as an assertion of Black identity that left no space for conversation and reconciliation with White people. While Cone emphasized liberation, Roberts argued we need liberation *and* reconciliation: "There can be no liberation without reconciliation and no reconciliation without liberation. The only Christian way in race relations is a liberating experience of reconciliation for the white oppressor as well as for the black oppressed. This is what a black political theology is all about and its message to the whole church of Christ."[6] While Cone emphasized the liberation of Black people, Roberts was resolute in seeing America's racialized faith as oppressing White people too, just in a different way given their distinct subject positions in the racist regime.

As a Baptist theologian trained at the University of Edinburgh and in conversation with Reformed theology, Roberts was more deeply

---

[5] Cone, *Black Theology*, 146.
[6] J. Deotis Roberts, *A Black Political Theology* (Philadelphia: Westminster Press, 1974). While Cone did discuss reconciliation in *Black Theology and Black Power*, he dropped it in *A Black Theology of Liberation*, favoring the language of liberation.

committed to the discourse of reconciliation within Reformed theology, especially in the theology of Karl Barth. The final published volume of Karl Barth's magisterial *Church Dogmatics* is *The Doctrine of Reconciliation*, since he never completed the final volume, *The Doctrine of Redemption*. While Barth's unfinished legacy was to develop a theology of redemption, many Protestant theologians and ethicists like Roberts committed themselves to working out the implications of the doctrine of reconciliation.

Roberts liked reconciliation because of its theocentric framing in two Pauline letters (2 Cor 5:16-6:2; Eph 2:14-16). Paul writes, "In Christ God was reconciling the world to himself . . . and entrusting the message of reconciliation to us" (2 Cor 5:19). In the first instance reconciliation describes the restoration of the relationship "in Christ" between a Holy God and a sinful humanity. While reconciliation as salvation is a gift of grace, justified humans still have work to do. Paul calls us to be ambassadors of reconciliation, proclaiming a "message of reconciliation." Thus, reconciliation works on a transcendent axis (between God and humanity) and on a horizontal axis (between humans and other humans in the context of the community of creation). Roberts finds the work of reconciliation central to the walk of Christian discipleship, describing the deep intra- and interpersonal work that needs to be done among White oppressors and Black victims in White supremacist America.

Roberts's theology of reconciliation was anticipated by the Confession of 1967 of the Presbyterian Church (USA). During the revolutionary sixties, Presbyterians sought to articulate a new confession of faith in light of the civil rights movement, the women's movement, the peace movement, and other movements of social change. Since the Westminster Confession (1646) was considered dated, the Presbyterians called the church to consider what it meant to be disciples in that moment, focusing on issues of racism, poverty, sexuality, and war.

Reconciliation was the orienting theme around which the confession was organized: "God's reconciling work in Jesus Christ and the mission of reconciliation to which he has called his church are the heart of the gospel in any age."[7] Almost every article in the document mentions reconciliation; I found only two references to justice and none to liberation in the document.[8] The section "Reconciliation in Society" is where we see an important confessional attempt to enflesh a theology of reconciliation within a Christian communion. Section 9.44a, which addresses racism, states,

> God has created the peoples of earth to be one universal family. In his reconciling love, God overcomes the barriers between sisters and brothers and breaks down every form of discrimination based on racial or ethnic difference, real or imaginary. . . . Therefore, the church labors for the abolition of all racial discrimination and ministers to those injured by it.[9]

The Presbyterian call to abolish all racial discrimination was brave. It was one of the first mainline Protestant attempts to theologically engage race as a theological and ethical problem.

Is reconciliation adequate as a theological framework for Christian social ethics today? In *Liberation and Reconciliation*, Roberts writes, "Christians are called to be agents of reconciliation. We have been able to love and forgive. . . . The assertion that all are 'one in Christ Jesus' must henceforth mean that all slave-master, servant-boss, inferior-superior frames of reference between blacks and whites have been abolished."[10] While Saint Paul imagines the body of Christ as a new sociality where all differences are relativized, a flat-footed

---

[7]The Confession of 1967, Presbyterian Church (USA), Inclusive Language Version, 2002, www.pcusa.org/site_media/media/uploads/theologyandworship/pdfs/confess67.pdf, 9.06.

[8]Gayraud Wilmore was the only African American on the drafting committee, which was composed primarily of White males who taught theology at Princeton Theological Seminary, and a wife of one of the Princeton professors.

[9]Confession of 1967, 9.44a.

[10]Roberts, *Liberation and Reconciliation*, 34.

appropriation of Paul's vision of unity today does not deal with the problem of power differentials and systemic injustice.

The discourse of reconciliation is ultimately inadequate to deal with the problems of racism and capitalism. When contrasting his view from J. Deotis Roberts, who emphasizes integrating Blacks into a White society in the spirit of Dr. King, Cone pushes for an alternative community of belonging in the spirit of Malcolm, writing, "I believe that Black Theologians need to move beyond 'civil rights' (i.e., *integration* of Black people into a capitalistic, oppressive White society) to a political commitment that seeks to restructure society along the lines of creative socialism."[11] What's at stake in the Cone versus Roberts debate is two very different diagnoses of the problem, as well as a different strategy of how to move ahead.

Roberts saw the problem as the separation between Blacks and Whites and pressed for deep interpersonal relational healing between Blacks and Whites. For Cone the issue was deeper and more urgent—White folks had their heel on Black folks and needed to take it off. Cone understood White supremacy as structural evil. Cone's Black theology took seriously God's reconciling act in Jesus Christ, but he believed reconciliation had to be sought on Black terms and would be accomplished only *after* liberation.

While Roberts advocated a relationship-based reconciliation model, Cone advocated a reparation-based reconciliation model. In his "I Have a Dream" speech, Dr. King said, "We came here today to cash a check. A promise given. We came to collect."[12] Not only had the debt not been paid, but Whites did not acknowledge there was a debt to be paid. Since enslaved Africans had built America on land White colonists of European descent stole from Native people, often in Jesus' name, to

---

[11]Cone, *Black Theology*, 132.
[12]Martin Luther King Jr., "I Have a Dream," in *A Testament of Hope: The Essential Writings and Speeches of Martin Luther King, Jr.*, ed. James M. Washington (New York: HarperCollins, 1986), 217.

acknowledge the debt was to confess the sins of a Christian-sanctioned violent exploitation of people of color and extraction of land. Repentance entailed reparations. For White folks, Cone summarized reconciliation thus: reconciliation to God meant White people were prepared to deny themselves (Whiteness), take up the cross (Blackness), and follow Christ (Black ghetto).[13] But following Christ the Liberator proved a difficult journey for White evangelicals.

CHRIST THE LIBERATOR AND THE STRUGGLE FOR SHALOM JUSTICE

In 1970, Black evangelical theologian Tom Skinner delivered an electrifying speech at the Urbana Missions Conference titled "Christ the Liberator." Skinner challenged evangelical Christians to reimagine the gospel in light of Black suffering, preaching,

> Any gospel that does not talk about delivering to man a personal Savior who will free him from the personal bondage of sin and grant him eternal life and does not at the same time speak to the issue of enslavement, the issue of injustice, the issue of inequality, any gospel that does not want to go where people are hungry and poverty-stricken and set them free in the name of Jesus Christ—is not the gospel.[14]

Skinner's call for Jesus and justice was crystal-clear, but it would take decades for evangelicalism to catch up with him. When Skinner got a divorce, White evangelical leaders looked to another Black evangelical leader to be the spokesperson for the movement.

A Black prophet from Mississippi, John Perkins quickly emerged as the most respected Black evangelical voice. Like J. Deotis Roberts, Perkins opted for the language of reconciliation. He encouraged White

---

[13]Cone, *Black Theology*.
[14]Tom Skinner, "The US Racial Crisis and World Evangelism" (known as "Christ the Liberator") in *Christ the Liberator* (Downers Grove, IL: InterVarsity Press, 1971), 205.

evangelicals to live into an ethic of the three Rs: relocate, reconcile, and redistribute. White evangelicals were encouraged to leave their affluent neighborhoods and relocate in the ghetto, to be reconciled with African Americans through crosscultural friendships, and to redistribute resources from the White community to poor communities of color. This vision of reconciliation took racial difference, including structural segregation, seriously. While it continued a relationship-based model of reconciliation, it was in the context of the community-building efforts in local neighborhoods. Perkins's vision has inspired a nationwide movement of community builders called the Christian Community Development Association. Within Perkins's orbit, reconciliation is understood as cross-racial friendship as embodied in Spencer Perkins and Chris Rice's *More Than Equals*.[15]

Reconciliation understood as communicating and connecting with people of other races does not exhaust the prophetic call of Scripture. Seeking to move beyond the impasse of reconciliation and liberation, I suggest "shalom justice" as way of describing the prophetic imperative in Hebrew Scripture.

Shalom justice is the heart and soul of the vision of Hebrew Scripture. Shalom justice is rooted in a worshipful acknowledgment that God the Creator is present in all creation and is graciously working for the redemption and reconciliation of the world. Shalom—communal and ecological well-being—is the result of the people of God embodying the justice and righteousness of God.[16] While a deeply relational concept, shalom justice is also a call to restore broken systems and work to dismantle structural sites of injustice, pastoring those who are traumatized and hurt in their wake.

---

[15] Spencer Perkins and Chris Rice, *More Than Equals: Racial Healing for the Sake of the Gospel* (Downers Grove, IL: InterVarsity Press, 1993).

[16] Peter Goodwin Heltzel, "Shalom Justice: The Prophetic Imperative," in *Resurrection City: A Theology of Improvisation* (Grand Rapids, MI: Eerdmans, 2012), 22-48.

Injustice is a violation against God. The social dimension of *mishpat* included many different types of social relations and referred to the relationship among Israelites within their tribe, the relationships between the tribes, their relationship with other nations, and their relationship with the community of creation. When nations would deal unjustly with Israel, Israel would cry out through passionate prayers for God's justice to be manifest. It was God and God alone who was the judge of the social dealings among the nations.

The word *mishpat* is used with *tsedaqah*, "righteousness," which is the Bible's most common word pairing (e.g., Jer 22:3-5; Is 28:17-18). *Tsedaqah* calls the people of Israel to do what is right and it becomes *mishpat* when put into practice in the embodied life of God's people. Justice refers to how all people, especially the marginalized, are treated and accepted. The marginalized in the world of the Israelites included foreign women of color, the poor, the disenfranchised, and those who suffered from social structures that privileged the few rich people.

The Hebrew prophets demonstrate that Israel embodies shalom justice in the way it treats its neighbors, especially people who have no one to take care of them. Israel's God is the defender of the poor and the oppressed. Hebrew Scripture is clear in its constant clarion call to care for the widow, orphan, and stranger, and Zechariah adds the poor to this list (Zech 7:10). God of the prophets is concerned about the compassionate care of those with great needs. Whenever Israel lost its focus on caring for those who were victims of injustice and working toward a more equitable society, God would raise up prophets such as Isaiah, who said,

> Is not this the fast that I choose:
> > to loose the bonds of injustice,
> > to undo the thongs of the yoke,

> to let the oppressed go free,
>> and to break every yoke? (Is 58:6).

The prophet Micah calls Israel "to do *mishpat"* in a spirit of humility and tender mercy (Mic 6:8).

FAITH-ROOTED RECONCILIATION

Our work as reconcilers is always fulfilled in the pursuit of shalom justice. Cultivating cross-racial revolutionary friendships can happen in the struggle for justice. While living in intentional community and doing community development work is one important expression of Christian mission, it does not exhaust it. When a man who has been taught to fish can't get to a pond to fish because there is a fence around it, he has to organize.

Faith-rooted organizing is an innovative new model of organizing that gathers people for social change from the deepest wells of our faith.[17] As Christians, we have been great at gathering people for hearing the Word proclaimed and celebrating the sacrament, but it is now time to gather people for faith-rooted social change. It is only through building relational power through the depth of our faith traditions that we can truly trouble the waters and heal the world.

Jesus was an amazing faith-rooted organizer. While his public ministry was only three years, he had a big impact on his society. A poor carpenter for the Northern Galilee, Jesus was called by God to inaugurate the kingdom of God. He shared his vision with the people in his region, calling twelve disciples to follow him as his core team. When he turned his face to Jerusalem like a flint (Lk 9:51), he was hyperfocused on his mission, engaging the powers and principalities of Jerusalem, both

---

[17]For a concise introduction to faith-rooted organizing see Alexia Salvatierra and Peter Goodwin Heltzel, *Faith-Rooted Organizing: Mobilizing the Church in Service to the World* (Downers Grove, IL: InterVarsity Press, 2014).

Roman powers and Jewish powers. As a result of Jesus' interrogation he was crucified on a Roman cross. Jesus' life provides a template of what it means to be a faith-rooted organizer today.

As Walter Wink argues, the "powers and principalities" that Jesus confronted found form in the Roman structures of domination.[18] Sin and the demonic are not abstract but embodied in concrete structures and institutions. These forces shape us and form us. They define who is human and who is not, whose lives are grievable and whose are not. The reigning ideologies today, be they evangelical theology or neoliberal capitalism, press us to see only individuals, the outcomes of the market, and, in different ways, racism as the products of natural processes. The account of nature conflicts with a Christian vision of the world, one where God's provision is natural and our failure to thrive alerts us to the presence of sin.

Social science helps us to name sin, to contest the idea that injustice or racist anthropologies are in any sense natural or inevitable. As theologians and organizers we need the insights of the social sciences to inform our reconciliation studies and ministries of shalom justice. We also need to be aware that social science has been the handmaiden of racism, with pseudoscientific anthropologies (e.g., phrenology) used to justify racism and colonialism. As Christians we can appropriate the social sciences critically, insisting on the dignity of every person even when "science" justifies the sacrifice of a people group. The social sciences help us understand the way society works through systems theory and the structural nature of sin. As Kristen Heyer says, "In its broadest sense social sin encompasses the unjust structures, distorted

---

[18]Walter Wink offers the most comprehensive mapping of the discourse of "powers and principalities" in the New Testament. Walter Wink, *Naming the Powers: The Language of Power in the New Testament* (Philadelphia: Fortress Press, 1984); *Unmasking the Powers: The Invisible Powers That Determine Human Existence* (Philadelphia: Fortress Press, 1986); *Engaging the Powers: Discernment and Resistance in a World of Domination* (Minneapolis: Fortress Press, 1992).

consciousness, and collective actions and inaction that facilitate injustice and dehumanization."[19]

Faith-rooted organizing is a strategy for eradicating social sin. It is for justice and moves toward social change for the good. It is a model that can be used to address poverty, racial injustice, affordable housing, education, immigration, police reform, health reform, environmental justice, sex trafficking, domestic violence, labor trafficking, and other global problems that result from racism, patriarchy, and neoliberal capitalism.

The struggle to embrace the other is not just an interpersonal process. Oppressive social systems keep structures of exclusion and domination intact. Faith-rooted organizing provides us with a set of perspectives and tools that can help us identify the logic and weaknesses of these structures of exclusion. Then we can begin the process of building relational power through face-to-face meetings, monthly group meetings, and campaign development and implementation in order to address the injustices that are oppressing people in our society.

Faith-rooted organizing is a strategy for eradicating social sin. Confessing the social sin of racism, faith-rooted reconciliation calls us to public repentance. Given the legacy of White colonial violence in the United States, prophetic Christians, especially anti-racist White Christians, should engage in reparations and repair among both indigenous people and African Americans. The moral logic of reparations is based on the goodness of the land, the dignity of all people, and the prophetic imperative to "do justice" (Micah 6:8). Acknowledging responsibility for injustice, faith-rooted reparations provide a pathway toward forgiveness, economic justice and racial healing.

---

[19]Kristen E. Heyer, *Kinship Across Borders: A Christian Ethic of Immigration* (Washington, DC: Georgetown University Press, 2012), 37.

CONCLUSION

Improvising for justice is an important way we can reimagine community in our contemporary moment of revolutionary ferment in cities around the world, as we reimagine the Blackness of Christ in an oceanic mode, with an echo of opacity. Jesus as a Jewish jazz improviser for love and justice offers a model of faith-rooted organizing that seeks to transform individuals and social systems. From Black abolitionists to Black civil rights leaders, the Black radical tradition has organized from the deepest wells of faith, long before a Jewish White man named Saul Alinsky showed up in Chicago in the 1930s. As J. Kameron Carter argues, the "in-dignity" that Black folks have suffered, their soulful strength as witnesses of revolutionary intimacy, and the "in-sovereign" revolutionary community they embody, portends a future of fugitive liberation.[20]

From North Carolina to New York, Selma to Syria, Derry to Donbas, a growing group of ordinary citizens is rising up in the name of love to end the violence. We will keep meeting. We will keep marching. We will keep moving until we see "justice roll like a river and righteousness like an ever-flowing stream" (Amos 5:24).

---

[20] J. Kameron Carter, "Paratheological Blackness," *South Atlantic Quarterly* 112/4 (2013): 589-611.

LONGING FORWARD

PEACEMAKING AND VIOLENCE TOWARD WOMEN AND GIRLS

Elizabeth Gerhardt

Blessed are the peacemakers, for they will be called children of God.

MATTHEW 5:9

To work for peace is to work for life.

HENRI NOUWEN

THE PHONE RANG in my newly acquired office.[1] A local pastor introduced himself with a voice that soon became loud and animated. He stated, "I know you have Janet in your shelter. I am counseling this couple, and Jim is very upset that Janet left their home. You are obviously not a Christian or you wouldn't be breaking up families in this community. God wants families to stay together."

---

[1] Portions of this chapter have been adapted from Beth Gerhardt, "Created *Imago Dei*: Trumping Misogyny in All Its Forms": https://imagodeifund.org/created-imago-dei-trumping-misogyny-in-all-its-forms/.

He continued the lecture citing the dangers of the local shelter. I had recently been hired as director of the battered women's program in a local nonprofit agency. I was new to this small New England city and not familiar with its civic and religious leaders. I introduced myself, informed him that the names of shelter residents were confidential, and said I could not therefore disclose whether Janet was a guest. I also informed him that I considered my work Christian and that I understood that our God desired women to be safe and free from violence. Battered women advocates are not interested in breaking up families. Abusers' violence is the cause of the breakdown of these families. I concluded by describing the work I do in tandem with many others as justice building and peacemaking. Finally, I posed this question: "Isn't this God's work?"

This conversation took place over thirty years ago, early in my work to end violence against women. I have asked that same question to countless pastors, church leaders, seminarians, and lay leaders who have attempted to understand how this "fits in" with the mission of the church, the work of peacemaking and justice building. Many understand the work of directly aiding abused women. However, working to end global structural and institutional violence against girls and women has been more difficult for churches to engage as the peacemaking work of Christ.

I understand. On the surface, working to end violence against women appears as an effort to split families. Those working to end violence, sexual assault, gendercide, and domestic violence may appear to be shredding the fabric of social patterns that support male privilege and dominance. This shredding of cultural norms may appear to be more about peace breaking than peacemaking. Justice building is not comfortable. It not only shakes our cultural norms but may threaten many religious ideas about gender roles, church authority, and church mission.

However, the hope created by knowing this shredding of injustice that has embedded itself in our cultural fabric is God's work will enable us to continue this effort. We cannot create a new fabric of peace without tearing at the status quo. Living out the discipleship and the radical life of the gospel is countercultural and threatening to a world where male domination is normative.

A GLOBAL PROBLEM

The recent #MeToo and #TimesUp movements have helped raise universal awareness of the links between individual experiences of sexual violence and the institutional supports of and collusion in this violence. Violent athletic coaches, doctors, Hollywood producers and actors, corporate managers, pastors and religious leaders, teachers, and abusers are found in every corner of our society. They would not be able to perpetrate their crimes unless the organization, institution, or corporation in which the abuse occurred had not colluded in one or more ways. We have many examples. The lack of accountability permits the abuse to continue. As one victim declared, "Denial is easier than devastation." The fear of exposure is often the impetus for churches and other organizations to look the other way, minimize the abuse, or to fail to hold the perpetrator accountable. Families of abusers often fail to disclose, as do institutions, and this also extends to nations that fail to enact laws to protect girls and women or fail to enforce those laws. Violence against women and girls is a devastating individual, family, institutional, and global problem.

If we understand Christian discipleship to mean a call to peacemaking, then it is important to become conscious of the extent of the violence perpetrated against women and girls across the globe and in our own communities due to their gender. There are many resources for gathering the facts regarding the prevalence of global violence against girls and women.² These are a few of the facts: A review of the literature indicates one in three to four women in the United States is battered by an intimate partner. One in four girls in the United States is sexually abused before the age of eighteen, and one in six women has experienced attempted or completed rape. Global violence takes the form of sexual assault, rape as a weapon of war, female genital mutilation, sex trafficking, forced abortions, infanticide of girl babies, honor killings, and the exploitation of women and girls in labor for profit. The World Health Organization defines violence against women and girls as "any act of gender-based violence that results in physical, sexual, or psychological harm or suffering to women, including threats of such acts, coercion, or arbitrary deprivations of liberty, whether occurring in public or private life."³ There are many statistics that support the reality that this violence is pervasive, ongoing, and touches the lives of millions of girls and women and their families. This is gendercide, an attack on persons due their gender alone. Behind every statistic is a story of someone who has had their body and psyche wounded and, in many situations, their lives violently ripped away from them. Gendercide is a crime and a sin, and it needs to be addressed by the whole church, understood as justice building and peacemaking.

All abuse perpetrated against girls and women, both global and local, is rooted in the same underlying belief system that fuels all controlling and violence behavior: getting and maintaining power. By use of coercion; physical, psychological, emotional, and sexual abuse; forced labor; and withholding access to economic and social equality, the

---

²For an extensive list of statistics and resources on the prevalence of violence against women and girls see Elizabeth Gerhardt, *The Cross and Gendercide: A Theological Response to Global Violence Against Women and Girls* (Downers Grove, IL: InterVarsity Press, 2014), 13-58.

³World Health Organization (WHO), VAW Fact Sheet No. 239 (Geneva: WHO, 2009). Statistics have been compiled by the National Coalition Against Domestic Violence, www.ncadv.org/statistics.

perpetrator obtains power. The maintenance of an abuse of power can occur when organizations and institutions fail to hold perpetrators accountable. Domination, patriarchy, and the objectification of women are three supports of power and violence that must be dismantled by a united and concerted effort by all persons and institutions. However, the church has a particular task to unmask evil in all its forms, aid victims, hold known perpetrators accountable, and work to create a just and equitable environment for girls and women to thrive both in society and the church.

THEOLOGICAL ROOTEDNESS

How are we to respond in a faithful manner to the call of Jesus Christ? How do we "long forward" unless we understand our "point of departure"?

> The kind of thinking that starts out from human problems and then looks for solutions from that vantage point, has to be overcome—it is unbiblical. The way of Jesus Christ, and thus the way of all Christian thought, is not the way from the world to God but from God to the world. This means that the essence of the gospel does not consist in solving worldly problems, and also that this cannot be the essential task of the church. However, it does not follow from this that the church would have no task in this regard. *But we will not recognize its legitimate task unless we first find the correct starting point.*[4]

My perspective is rooted in a theology of the cross as a "point of departure," particularly as defined by Dietrich Bonhoeffer and other theologians, activists, and saints of the twentieth century. I am deeply influenced by the theology and ethics of Bonhoeffer and Reinhold

---

[4] Dietrich Bonhoeffer, *Ethics*, trans. Reinhard Krauss, Charles C. West, and Douglas W. Stott; ed. Clifford J. Green, vol. 6 of *Dietrich Bonhoeffer Works* (Minneapolis: Fortress, 2005), 356, emphasis added.

Niebuhr, the activism of Martin Luther King Jr., and the spirituality of Henri Nouwen and Dorothy Day. My understanding of peacemaking and discipleship is reflective of these twentieth-century theological and spiritual masters, and the theological foundation for strategies of peacemaking reflect their spirituality and activism. My approach to peacemaking is integrated within the context of the following themes: a Christian understanding of suffering, the vocation of all Christians to work toward peace and justice, prayer as a means of confession and remembrance of our identity as children and disciples of Christ, and the eschatological dimension of Christian discipleship and hope. These themes provide a context and framework for shaping creative strategies that can alleviate global violence against women and girls. This violence is pervasive in our world and in our own local communities and is one of the most pressing spiritual and justice problem of our time.

Confession. The primary task of the church is to acknowledge the failures of the Christian community, both historically and theologically, in promoting peacemaking among individuals, communities, and nations. Peacemaking begins with confession. It is vital that the church recognize and confess both its failure to promote peace in critical times in history and its promotion of violence in the name of God to promote ideologies based on political, nationalistic, and racial and gender platforms. Unfortunately, we have many examples of this: the collusion of churches in slavery and racist laws and practices, as well as the collusion of the church in National Socialism in Germany in the twentieth century. And we certainly can point to the many examples of church promotion of violence during the past two thousand years, including the countless wars fought in the name of God. It is vital that we acknowledge and confess that we have used God's name to justify various sins of violence and the sin of silence. Within our time and context we often give way to the temptation to collapse political ideologies with the gospel, and therefore we trade our prophetic role of speaking truth to power for political power and recognition. To be peacemakers we need to see ourselves as we truly are and confess our failures to establish peace and justice. Out theologies must be rooted in the realities of others' experiences and social location.

A theology of the cross recognizes the sinfulness and inability of the Christian to establish peace and justice by works, by our own efforts apart from faith. The confession of sin and the failure to live out the Christian call to work for justice and to love the neighbor is a recognition of the limits of the self and human ability. Confession also goes beyond the recognition of our human limitations. It is a humbling of the self at the cross and an awareness that it is God's kingdom, not our own, that we must be about. Being a Christian means to subject oneself in confession to God and take on God's righteousness and call to serve. How can we hear the call of God if we do not begin in humility, in confession, if we do not empty ourselves and our churches of our own agendas, power plays, programs, and assumptions about what it means to move forward?

Peacemaking does not begin with programs or political platforms. Peacemaking begins on our knees, in confession of our own sinfulness and pride. It begins in recognition that the power to change injustice to justice, evil systems to righteous ones, begins with worship of the God who is the source of all power and righteousness. Christian peacemaking begins at the cross of Christ, who bid us to follow and die to self. It is there that we find grace to be so costly. But it also there that we find the power of grace to strengthen us in our tasks.

Dietrich Bonhoeffer was a scholar, author, activist, and ecumenical and church leader during one of the most hellish periods of the twentieth century. However, his role as pastor is the one he most treasured. He devoted himself for a time to leading a seminary in Finkenwalde until the Nazis shut it down. The church in Nazi Germany faced critical questions of identity: Who are we as a church? How do we move forward when faced with such evil? Do we ignore government atrocities and work to preserve ourselves, or do we resist and be proactive against evil by working to establish justice? It appeared from a human perspective that the authentic church of Christ in Germany was dead. What lived and called itself "church" was the political arm of National Socialism and Hitler. The perennial temptation to collapse the gospel and political ideology framed those central identity questions at that time. By resisting that temptation, Bonhoeffer, firmly confident and rooted in the gospel and the historical confessions of the church, was able to lead others forward in resisting an evil that had infiltrated the church. He and the confessing church could move forward because they maintained that the church must always be faithful to the one who calls us not to preserve our churches but be faithful disciples no matter the cost. The prophetic work of the authentic church offers lessons for us in the work of peacemaking and ending violence against girls and women. Who is Jesus Christ today? What is the mission of the church today? These christological and ecclesiological questions echo for the church today. They are important in shaping our application of Christian biblical and theological understanding to the work of ending violence against women and girls.

Discipleship. It is at the end of ourselves at the cross that we also find Christ's call to discipleship. In Luke 14 Jesus challenges the crowds by instructing them, "Whoever does not carry the cross and follow me cannot be my disciple" (Lk 14:27). This is the great paradox of discipleship. A disciple of Christ has to lay down all the plans, programs, and identification with political figures, dreams, and even one's theology. At the foot of the cross there is only death to the self. In death, though, one is then open to the person and work of Christ. Discipleship involves relationship with Christ and taking up the work of Christ.

Therefore, peacemaking is more than a confession of sin of violence and more than offering praise to a mighty God. Peacemaking also means willingness to give up the comfortable secure world we build around ourselves and to come away from our attachments and follow the call of God to heal, work for peace and justice, and serve others. This involves a willingness to enter into the struggles and suffering that inevitably come when speaking and acting against the prevailing culture of violence.

Nevertheless, suffering is not something to be sought after and held as a badge of holiness. In my work with abused women, it is particularly difficult to counsel Christian women because there is such a misunderstanding of the role of suffering in their lives. They were often instructed, sometimes by their abusers, sometimes by well-meaning pastors, that somehow their suffering at the hands of an abuser was redemptive. The advice given to women in many Christian churches has been some form of the following: "Love him more, put up with the abuse, put up with the pain and suffering, and in your suffering God will be with you." Recently, a student informed me that a pastor told a woman who was being battered by her husband to be more cooperative in the bedroom and that would help end the violence. Another pastor reported that he always told abused women that they should suffer in silence and that pain was their cross. He realized he needed to rethink his pastoral advice. True Christian suffering happens in the context in which we live, not something that is imposed on us as a result of violence. We are told by Jesus that if we follow him we will suffer "for my name's sake" (Jn 15:21 KJV). In a violent world, preaching and acting for peace can cause suffering. We need to look no further than Dietrich Bonhoeffer, Oscar Romero, Dorothy Day, and Martin Luther King, among others.

However, it is important to differentiate the suffering of the peacemakers from the suffering imposed on the poor, on the oppressed, on women who are abused and children who are sexually exploited in this world. This is *not* the suffering brought about by the will of God. Evil exists. And there is nothing as heinous as evil, violent acts being passed off as God's will. As peacemaking disciples of Christ, we need to be willing to step out of what is comfortable, discern the evil present in violence, and be willing to act for peace no matter the consequences. How can we stand up for and work for peace and not be overwhelmed by fear? Hope. Hope provides the impetus to resist evil, aid victims, and create paths of reconciliation.

Eschatology. The eschatological dimension of Christian discipleship includes an understanding of the true meaning of Christian hope. Historically, Christian hope has often been used as a means to preserve the status quo rooted in quietism. During the civil rights movement many Christians cautioned Martin Luther King to be patient and not demand equal rights for African Americans. They attempted to assure the resistors that change would occur someday. Why stir up trouble? They maintained that the civil rights leader's actions were "unwise and untimely." King responded to this perversion of Christian hope in his classic "Letter from a Birmingham Jail." In this letter King describes Christian discipleship as the very center of the struggle for freedom, justice, and equality. Indeed he attacks the false notion of Christian hope as passive collusion with evil and violence and promotes a discipleship centered in action:

> In the midst of blatant injustices inflicted upon the Negro, I have watched white churches stand on the sideline and merely mouth pious irrelevancies and sanctimonious trivialities. In the midst of a mighty struggle to rid our nation of racial and economic injustice, I have heard so many ministers say, "Those are social issues with which the gospel has no real concern," and I have watched so many churches commit themselves to a

completely otherworldly religion which made a strange distinction between body and soul, the sacred and the secular. So here we are moving toward the exit of the twentieth century with a religious community largely adjusted to the status quo, standing as a taillight behind other community agencies rather than a headlight leading men to higher levels of justice.[5]

Christian hope rooted in the good news of the gospel proclaims the hope of the not-yet, that the kingdom of God is yet to come in all its fullness *and* that the kingdom of God is here in the now. Biblical Christian discipleship maintains that the work of Christ is for us today. Even in the midst of violence and suffering the Christian confesses Christ by way of service and serves by way of confession. Eberhard Bethge in reflecting on the life and theology of Bonhoeffer wrote that both confession and action are necessary. Confessing Christ without "putting a spoke" in the wheel of evil institutions and violence and without aiding the poor and oppressed is a dead religion. It is a religious practice that has nothing to do with the Jesus of the Scriptures:

> People today that confine themselves to confession and never cross the threshold often ask how a man like Bonhoeffer could theologically justify his identification with the conspirators. The question is frightful, because it is usually raised out of an isolated and isolating situation of detached confessionalism, unconscious of its own complicity with evil. My wife once gave the shortest answer: "How can a confessing Christian theologically justify a lack of action?"[6]

To be called a Christian is not about being a passive receptor of God's grace. It is not a call to adhere to a type of detached confessionalism that

---

[5]Martin Luther King Jr., "Letter from Birmingham Jail," in *A Testament of Hope: The Essential Writings and Speeches of Dr. Martin Luther King, Jr.*, ed. James M. Washington (New York: Harper Collins, 1991), 299.
[6]Eberhard Bethge, *Friendship and Resistance: Essays on Dietrich Bonhoeffer* (Grand Rapids, MI: Eerdmans, 1995), 105.

has no concern for the world. A true Christian follows the Prince of Peace into the world. A Christian who is not a peacemaker and is not about building justice and caring for the neighbor is not a true Christian. Resistance to power that seeks to destroy community is necessary to being a confessing community.

> Bonhoeffer introduced us in 1935 to the problem of what we today call political resistance. The levels of confession and of resistance could no longer be kept neatly apart. The escalating persecution of the Jews generated an increasingly intolerable situation, especially for Bonhoeffer himself. We now realized that mere confession, no matter how courageous, inescapably meant complicity with the murderers, even though there would always be new acts of refusing to be co-opted and even though we would preach "Christ alone" Sunday after Sunday. During the whole time the Nazi state never considered it necessary to prohibit such preaching. Why should it? Thus we were approaching the borderline between confession and resistance; and if we did not cross this border, our confession was going to be no better than cooperation with the criminals. And so it became clear where the problem lay for the Confessing Church: We were resisting by way of confession, but we were not confessing by way of resistance.[7]

Jesus' call to die to self in order to live is the great paradox of discipleship. A disciple of Christ has to lay down all the plans, programs, and identification with political figures, dreams and even one's ideology and theology. At the cross, death to self lies the hope in the person and work of Jesus Christ. But this hope does not only lie in a kingdom yet to come, but in the fulfilling of our call as peacemakers in this world.

The call of discipleship, therefore, requires the radical action of peacemaking. Confession of our faith is realized through the work of ensuring equitable and fair treatment of girls and women. The reality of God's

---

[7]Bethge, *Friendship and Resistance*, 24.

existing kingdom of peace cannot tolerate disruption by way of violence. As Martin Luther King wrote so beautifully, "I cannot sit idly by in Atlanta and not be concerned about what happens in Birmingham. Injustice anywhere is a threat to justice everywhere. We are caught in an inescapable network of mutuality, tied in a single garment of destiny. Whatever affects one directly affects all indirectly."[8]

Discipleship is a call to be an advocate for those who cannot speak for themselves, and discipleship is also a call to resist injustice. Confession and resistance to injustice cannot be separated. Henri Nouwen, another twentieth-century spiritual writer and peacemaker, understood the relationship between spiritual identity and peacemaking. He knew that in prayer we approach a God who calls us out to bring justice and healing to a broken world. Nouwen maintained that the welfare of persons came before national security. He argued that peacemaking was essential to Christian discipleship. The concerns and well-being of the whole of humanity must take priority over all because this is the human family that God has created and loves.[9]

Community. All of these twentieth-century theologians and activists underscored in their writings the importance of community as a necessary element of spirituality and a unifying dimension to peacemaking. Dorothy Day understood that the thousands she fed in the Catholic Worker houses during the Depression were her brother and sisters. Nouwen taught that the poor in Africa and Asia and all over the world were our responsibility and that that responsibility took precedence over national security and economic interests. Martin Luther King argued that the "enemy" of the civil rights workers, the White racists, were children of God and that peaceful, active nonviolence would not only

---

[8]King, "Letter from Birmingham Jail," 290.
[9]For a full discussion on Nouwen's spirituality of peacemaking see Henri Nouwen, *The Road to Peace: Writings on Peace and Justice*, ed. John Dear (Maryknoll, NY: Orbis, 2003).

bring about justice but "win over" these racist White brothers and sisters. Dietrich Bonhoeffer wrote, "We Christians are above all addressed by the command of love to the point that we ourselves must live in peace with every person, just like Christ when he preached peace to the community, exemplified in peace with one's brother and sister, with one's neighbor, with the Samaritan. Unless we have this peace, we cannot preach peace to people."[10] Christian community necessitates a greater connection with the global community.

These theological dimensions of discipleship—confession, the role of suffering in peacemaking, eschatological hope, and the brotherhood and sisterhood of all peoples—provide a point of departure for the work to end violence against women and girls.

STRATEGIES FOR PEACEMAKING

As we struggle to discern the mission of the church today we must find ourselves at the foot of the cross in confession and humility. The death of Jesus leads us to the hope of resurrection and new life. This hope provides the foundation for God's work of peacemaking through the presence of the church in the world. Peacemaking involves the whole of the church ensuring that the gospel is preached and that suffering imposed by violence toward women and girls is denounced. The prophetic word of truth to power involves the denunciation of patriarchy, domination, and the objectification of girls and women. Our churches need to be safe spaces where victims of violence can be heard, recognized, and empowered. The Christian church should be aiding victims, referring to community resources, and supporting those who provide shelter, legal aid, and counseling. Aiding global efforts to provide safe

---

[10]Dietrich Bonhoeffer, "Christ and Peace," in *A Testament to Freedom: The Essential Writings of Dietrich Bonhoeffer*, ed. Geoffrey B. Kelly and F. Burton Nelson (New York: Harper Collins, 1995), 95.

schools for girls, supporting empowerment programs that provide small business loans to poor women, and assisting in many other initiatives provide opportunities for women and girls to live independently and violence-free.

Peacemaking involves resistance to violence in our institutions and all corporate bodies both locally and globally. We must address the culture of violence in our communities that supports violence against girls and women, including violence in media and politics. Androcentric language that shapes attitudes toward women should be challenged both in our churches and communities. Images that objectify women should be continually identified and denounced as part of the fabric of violence. The defensive walls that corporations, institutions, political bodies, and churches keep up to protect abusers must fall. Gender reconciliation involves intentional action to facilitate safe spaces in our communities of faith for deep listening to the pain of those impacted by gender violence. The willingness to be vulnerable and listen to these narratives helps to shape a more just, equitable, and loving community.

Violence against women and girls is a horrific global and local problem that needs to be addressed by all who call themselves disciples of Christ. The church needs to move beyond confession of Christ to acting out our confession by recognizing our past silence and collusion, aiding victims of violence, speaking up against all forms of gender violence, and, wherever possible, work to end the suffering of women and girls throughout the world. The authentic church of Christ is called to create peace for women and girls by working to end forced abortions and sterilizations, female infanticide, domestic violence, female slavery, forced prostitution, mass rape and sexual assault as tools of war, and female genital mutilation as part of a culture of violence for girls and women within the walls of our own church communities. Violence remains a part of the political and cultural fabric of life for women. When systemic violence is perpetrated against women as a consequence of their gender, then the gospel is distorted and undermined.

As we "long forward," let's establish churches that are peacekeepers and peacemakers. As church communities, let's ask ourselves these important questions: Do we humble ourselves before the cross and confess our sins of omission and silence in the face of violence? Do we identify with the poor and oppressed as Jesus did, or do we build walls of comfort around us? Are we really free "for the other"? Where there is evil and passivity to the good, do we speak truth to power? Do we proclaim the gospel knowing it will have political and social implications? Or are we captive to political ideologies that make it difficult for us to be captive to the Word of God? Do we name sin and hold perpetrators of violence accountable? Are we committed to ending denial, minimization of violence, and victim blaming? Peacemaking is countercultural, radical, and risky. However, with Christ as our point of departure, we participate in this work knowing that the grace, hope, and strength of the crucified God are with us and for us.

DISABILITY, IDENTITY, AND THE RESURRECTION OF THE DEAD

CULTURAL COMPETENCY AS NONVIOLENCE

Chibuzo Nimmo Petty

WHETHER OR NOT THERE is an afterlife is a concern held by virtually all humans from the beginning of time. What that afterlife will be like has puzzled philosophers for millennia. It should come as no surprise that the Corinthians were likewise puzzled enough to compel Paul to address the issue. While these ponderings are near-universal, they are uniquely important for believers living with disability and chronic illness. To some, the question of whether there will be disability in the afterlife is a nonsensical one. *Of course not! God forbid!* How can a heavenly (or new earthly) paradise be, well, paradisiacal if it is something of which disability can be a part? That question and its underlying assumptions make a lot of sense at face value but upon further thought begin to look overly simplistic.

Four approaches to disability and the resurrection of the dead have arisen during my research:

1. Resurrection life as solely spiritual (i.e., flat denial of bodily resurrection).
2. Healed disability or chronic illness in the resurrection life.
3. Continued disability or chronic illness in the resurrection life.
4. Transformed disability or chronic illness in the resurrection life.

These approaches differ in a variety of important and nuanced ways.

RESURRECTION AS SOLELY SPIRITUAL

I have encountered many Christians who reject the doctrine of a future bodily resurrection. For those who believe the afterlife is purely spiritual, issues related to the limitations of our earthly bodies become irrelevant. I would like to do more research to more precisely measure the percentage of Christians who hold this view. I was surprised, though, to find that, of those living with a disability or chronic condition whom I surveyed or interviewed for this project, the overwhelming majority held this view. For many, the pain and suffering experienced in this life lead them to yearn for the opportunity to escape this physical body—and, by extension, this physical world. They use a variety of words to describe their future heavenly states, such as "spirit," "ghost," "force," and "energy."[1]

As a minister, I have sat with numerous congregants as they convalesce telling me the road to recovery is just too long and difficult. They tell me they welcome death and the escape from their physical body. I have sat with those receiving palliative care, those nearing death. Sure, many in that position are sad, scared, and lonely. Still, others approach their coming death like a true departure from their current, earthly, and temporal suffering. For many individuals, death and the afterlife are very appealing, not because their bodies will be healed in the next life but

---

[1] "Various Interviews About Resurrection Bodies," interview by author, 2018–2020.

because they will not have a body in the next life to begin with. These individuals are looking forward to their great escape—to their material existence's final voyage, its swan song. Goodbye and good riddance, they say! I have had many interactions with others who have experienced physical or sexual abuse who, likewise, are eager to shed their body which is a constant reminder of some wrong or harm done to them. Similar conversations arise with trans persons contemplating what their bodies might look like in the world to come. Some, though not all, trans persons I spoke with shared an affinity with this view pertaining to their unique situations. I understand that not everyone reading this accepts the idea of trans or otherwise queer-identified persons going to heaven. My point, here, is not to convince you either way but only to express a deep and confused longing that has so often been expressed to me. Surely, this is worth pondering. How might this perspective inform our pastoral care? As someone who struggles deeply with living with chronic illness, being a survivor of abuse, and having a complicated and confused identity, I can certainly empathize with this view. It does not appear to be the biblical view, however. There are times we hate and want out of our bodies. That seems reasonable, even understandable. Yet, God might just have something better in store for us.

HEALED DISABILITY OR CHRONIC ILLNESS

Many believe we will no longer have our disabilities or chronic health issues after the resurrection of the dead. They point to passages saying there will be no more pain and suffering in the kingdom, such as Revelation 21:4, which says Jesus will "wipe every tear from their eyes" and "mourning and crying and pain will be no more." This view was the second most popular among those I questioned who are disabled or chronically ill. It was held by a slight majority of those questioned overall. A complicating concern raised by many in this camp is how there can be no pain in the afterlife if we are aware that many of our loved ones are suffering in hell. One response given was that a lack of suffering and pain means not the absence of seemingly negative emotions but rather a feeling of being fully comforted by God. Another was that we will better understand God's justice in the afterlife, therefore becoming unsad, if you will, for those suffering in hell. I am not sold on either response but can see why addressing this apparent loophole is important to those preferring this approach to the resurrection life.

CONTINUED DISABILITY OR CHRONIC ILLNESS

The third view is one I had not encountered before embarking on this project. It was the minority view by a considerable amount both in my personal interviews and in my broader research. Still, many believe that disability is a central part of identity, just as gender, race, sexual orientation, and so on are, and because it's essential that we will be resurrected as ourselves, we will also be resurrected with multiple sclerosis, autism, and so on. While most modern Americans would not view gender identity variance as a disability, there are some interesting parallels related to identity. Again, while not a universal belief, let us assume trans Christians are resurrected into eternal life. Do they believe their resurrected bodies will match their gender identity? The question, for a trans male, for instance, becomes whether his maleness is a more central part of his identity than his transness. This question was not easily answered by those queer persons I questioned, though most eventually said they believed their sex in the resurrection would match their current gender identity. Proponents of this view also tend to argue that disability is not a thing wrong needed to be made right in the afterlife. Part of it comes down to whether disability is primarily about difference or defect. Scripture says noticeable ethnic differences will remain in the kingdom, for instance (Rev 7:9). That implies, then, that difference is okay—perhaps even celebrated. So disability could be another type of difference instead of something needing to be corrected or healed.

TRANSFORMED DISABILITY OR CHRONIC ILLNESS

Continued Scripture study leads me to believe view four is likely the more biblical view. Proponents would point to Jesus' body after his resurrection because it was clearly spiritual and physical, clearly perfected, and had noticeable holes in it from being crucified—enough that Thomas could put his fingers through them. That example is obviously applied to physical ailments. It is unclear what that transformation would mean for someone who is neurodivergent, for instance. With more time and energy, I look forward to exploring this perspective more fully.

Before diving directly into the concept of disability in Scripture or into different approaches to disability and the afterlife, let us lay out some basic definitions. According to the Americans with Disabilities Act, the legal definition of a person with a disability is a person "who has a physical or mental impairment that substantially limits one or more major life activity."[2] According to the Department of Labor, disabilities include but are not limited to the following:

- autism
- bipolar disorder
- blindness
- deafness
- cancer
- cerebral palsy
- diabetes

---

[2] "What Is the Definition of Disability Under the ADA?" ADA National Network, January 24, 2017, accessed January 18, 2018, https://adata.org/faq/what-definition-disability-under-ada.

- epilepsy
- HIV/AIDS
- impairments requiring the use of a wheelchair
- intellectual disability (previously called mental retardation)
- major depression
- missing limbs
- multiple sclerosis
- muscular dystrophy
- obsessive compulsive disorder
- posttraumatic stress disorder
- schizophrenia.[3]

For our purposes, the term *chronic illness* refers to any condition that is persistent or otherwise long-lasting, including but not limited to those already listed as a disability.

Persons living with disabilities and chronic conditions play an important role in the Gospels. Healings makeup the bulk of Jesus' miracles in the Gospels. Jesus heals blind persons in Matthew 20:29-34; Mark 8:22-26; 10:46-52; Luke 18:35-43; and John 9:1-12. The story of Jesus healing a leper, telling him not to reveal Jesus' identity, the man disobeying, and Jesus subsequently retreating into deserted wilderness appears in all three Synoptic Gospels (Mt 8:1-4; Mk 1:40-45; Lk 5:12-16). Luke 17:11-19 tells an additional story of Jesus sending ten lepers to the high priests for healing. In the story, all are healed on their way with only the Samaritan returning to thank Jesus. The story of Jesus healing a paralytic brought to him on a mat (through a roof in Mark and Luke) also appears in all three Synoptic Gospels (Mt 9:1-8; Mk 2:1-12;

---

[3] "Voluntary Self-Identification of Disability," US Department of Labor, www.dol.gov/ofccp/regs/compliance/sec503/Self_ID_Forms/VoluntarySelf-ID_CC-305_ENG_JRF_QA_508c.pdf, accessed November 11, 2021.

Lk 5:17-26). In the story Jesus tells the man to pick up his mat and walk. Jesus also tells the man his sins are forgiven, which causes serious uproar among the Pharisees and others present. Jesus heals a paralytic in John 5:1-18 as well. The Synoptics also share a story of Jesus healing a woman suffering from continuous vaginal bleeding for twelve years (Mt 9:18-22; Mk 5:21-34; Lk 8:40-48). This listing of Jesus' healing miracles is meant only to be demonstrative; it is not exhaustive. In addition to Jesus healing a number of physical ailments, Jesus performs many exorcisms in the Gospels. While many continue to believe these were spiritual healings, some modern interpreters believe the exorcism recipients were suffering from mental illness rather than demon possession. Beyond these healings and exorcisms, Jesus raises three separate people from the dead in the Synoptic Gospels.

Paul was temporarily blinded during his experience on the road to Damascus. In his second letter to the Corinthians, Paul writes about a thorn in his flesh (2 Cor 12:7). While this could very well refer to a spiritual or emotional torment, one could argue that it was physical—specifically, that Paul suffered from poor eyesight long after vision was returned to him. In Acts, Paul mistakes a stiffened serpent for firewood (Acts 28:1-3). In his letter to the Galatians, Paul makes two remarks that could be interpreted as pointing to a vision issue. Galatians 4:15 says, "What has become of the goodwill you felt? For I testify that, had it been possible, you would have torn out your eyes and given them to me." Then, in Galatians 6:11, he writes, "See what large letters I make when I am writing in my own hand!" Whether Paul was, in fact, disabled remains unclear. Surely he would have interacted with disabled persons and been familiar with the stories of Jesus' healing ministry.

First Corinthians includes the most exhaustive explanation of and support for the resurrection of the dead in the New Testament. After a lengthy discussion of church division, Paul provides the reader with a rousing defense of belief in the resurrection. Paul explains that because Jesus was raised from the dead and is alive, so too *must* we be raised to life since Jesus was the firstfruits of the resurrection life (1 Cor 15:12, 20). After addressing the connection between Christ's resurrection and ours, Paul addresses concerns about resuscitated bodies. The Corinthians, who were Greeks, fully embraced the idea of the spiritual realm. Their dualism, however, separated the spiritual from the physical in a way that made the idea of a literal resurrection of the dead both unbelievable and unappealing. This disconnect likely led some in the church to look down on Paul and his teachings as unrefined.[4] In 1 Corinthians 15:35, they wonder what sort of body they will have. In the succeeding verses, Paul asserts that our new resurrection bodies will be like Christ's. The Corinthians' confusion is reminiscent, at least slightly, of Nicodemus's confusion after Jesus tells him he must be born-again. How can he climb back into his mother's womb (Jn 3:4)?

Paul explains that just as a seed is planted and later transformed by God, so too will humankind be transformed in the resurrection. Paul actually writes that seeds die before flowering, but that was either a basic scientific misunderstanding or intended as a figure of speech. Merrill Tenney, former dean of the Wheaton College Graduate School, explains the analogy well:

> When a grain of wheat is dropped into the ground, its husk quickly decays, and even the live core disintegrates. The life of the seed, rather than its material substance, provides the continuity of existence. As the rootlets begin to grow, they draw nourishment from the earth, and by the chemistry of sun and rain the small seed soon becomes a large plant. The plant bears no external resemblance to the seed, nor is the bulk of its tissue drawn from the seed; nevertheless, the continuity is undeniable.[5]

---

[4]Dan Nighswander, *1 Corinthians* (Harrisonburg, VA: Herald Press, 2017), 330.
[5]Alan F. Johnson, *1 Corinthians* (Downers Grove, IL: Intervarsity Press, 2010), 303.

For Paul, it is important that all individuals be resurrected as themselves truly. This means personality and individuality remain. The seed analogy helps explain this (1 Cor 15:36-38).

Paul moves from seed to skin in 1 Corinthians 15:39. He mentions different types of skin and bodies for humans, animals, birds, and fish. In 1 Corinthians 15:40, he continues by asserting that just as there are different temporal bodies, there are earthly and heavenly bodies. Paul writes that our resurrection bodies will differ from our current ones in splendor—as one star from another (1 Cor 15:41). Paul goes on to contrast the two types of bodies. Our present bodies are sown in corruption, whereas our resurrected bodies will be incorruptible. Our present bodies are dishonorable. Our resurrected bodies will be glorious. Our present bodies are weak. Our resurrected bodies will be strong. Our present bodies are natural in contrast to our future spiritual bodies (1 Cor 15:42-44). If the seed analogy was meant to point to continuity, here Paul focuses on the discontinuity of the two types of bodies. The Greek words used in this last verse, *psychikon* and *pneumatikon*, signal a difference in function rather than in being.[6]

Just as our character has been transformed into Christ's likeness, so too will our bodies be (1 Cor 15:49). He explains this by again referencing last Adam imagery (see also 1 Cor 15:21-22). Paul reminds his readers of the Genesis 2 story where God forms Adam out of the dust then breathes life into him, making him a living being, as well as Genesis 3 where Adam and Eve—and, through them all humankind, generation after generation—fall. It is possible Paul is also referencing Daniel 7 when he writes in 1 Corinthians 15:47 of a second man from heaven. "I saw One like a son of man coming with the clouds of heaven. . . . His dominion is an everlasting dominion that will not pass away" (Dan 7:13-14 HCSB)

---

[6]Johnson, *1 Corinthians*, 305.

surely seems to fit with Paul's broader message here. Regardless, Paul reiterates that Jesus Christ is the quintessential model for our future resurrection bodies (see also Phil 3:20-21).

FURTHER CONSIDERATIONS AND REFLECTIONS

In 1 Corinthians 15, Paul delivers an apologia for a proto-orthodox view of the resurrection against the Hellenistic and pagan understandings of many Corinthians. It's unclear how successful Paul's message was. Christians continue to hold a number of Greek beliefs long after literal veneration of Hades has ceased. Examples include the immortality of the soul and a belief that rituals and initiations (e.g., baptism) play a role in determining the nature of our afterlife.[7] The dualism that Paul derides lives on; in many ways Platonic philosophy has been Christianized with many believing the spiritual or heavenly to be good, solely, and the material to be bad. Additionally, modern American Christians believe a whole host of things about the afterlife that are not biblical. While not directly asking people about soul-body dualism, a recent study by Lifeway shows that many, and in some cases most, Christians hold contradictory and sometimes even heretical beliefs about the character of God, the nature and person of the Holy Spirit, and a variety of issues related to the afterlife, including the centrality of Jesus in salvation, the impact of works, the eternality of hell, and whether all are reunited with loved ones.[8]

Misconceptions about the afterlife are common among my largely Christian social circle. One Methodist I interviewed was so appalled by the idea of a bodily resurrection that she said believing it would "lessen

---

[7]"How the Greeks Changed the Idea of the Afterlife," *National Geographic*, June 08, 2016, www.nationalgeographic.com/magazine/2016/07/greek-gods-ancient-greece-afterlife.

[8]"Americans Love God and the Bible, Are Fuzzy on the Details," LifeWay Research, August 23, 2017, lifewayresearch.com/2017/09/27/americans-love-god-and-the-bible-are-fuzzy-on-the-details.

God's credibility." She went on to question the bodily ascension and remarked that even a perfected body would, as a body, have needs, something she found incomprehensible in the afterlife.[9] It was difficult for this person to conceptualize an afterlife that included their body because their image of an afterlife was not only purely spiritual but one where a person's every need is met. How, they question, can the afterlife be perfect, let alone paradisical, if we are tied down by our body's limitations, even typical or healthy ones? A Lutheran I interviewed said she believed that upon death her spirit would be "set free" from her physical body and that her resurrected body would be her "spiritual self separated from its shell/organic life matter." She continued by saying that resurrection, which can happen during this life, is "the full realization of spiritual life."[10] These responses, while very different from my theology, are not terribly surprising. Through similar conversations I have had over the years, I have come to believe that many if not most of the self-professing Christians I know believe in this sort of spirit-matter dualism. A fellow pastor I interviewed affirmed my findings, stating that in his ministry experience many have implicitly or explicitly believed in this type of dualism—so many that he estimates roughly half of his congregants hold similar views.[11]

Suffice it to say, these examples show that many people struggle to hear Paul's message or, conversely, reinterpret it and give it new meaning. When pressed about 1 Corinthians 15 specifically, one layperson I interviewed asserted that Paul was forced to write so heavily about physical resurrection because he was combating false rejections of Christ's resurrection among troublesome people in Corinth. What is more, this person stated that all of what Paul writes in 1 Corinthians 15 should be

---

[9] "Various Interviews About Resurrection Bodies." Interview by author. 2018–2019. All web and in-person interviewees requested they be kept anonymous.
[10] "Various Interviews About Resurrection Bodies."
[11] "Various Interviews About Resurrection Bodies."

understood as "dealing with ancient peoples who had definite thoughts on life and death, and the supernatural."[12]

In this and other writings, I have explored what I consider to be the leading concern in intercultural ministry, which is oppression-informed pastoral care. As demographics continue to shift in the United States, deacons, pastors, and professional counselors will not get by with pastoral care theories and practices primarily brought forth through the lens of neurotypical, cishet, middle-class Whites. A creative reimagining of pastoral care is needed to support, encourage, honor, and heal those impacted by systemic oppression (e.g., gender, racial, and religious minorities, LGBTQIA+ persons, immigrants, the previously incarcerated). More broadly, I contend that a care-centered approach to intercultural ministry uniquely improves one's cultural competency by requiring them to listen deeply to the experience of others and to respond with compassion and care.

Culture includes much more than race and ethnicity. Culture includes demographics such as gender, age, sexuality, physical or mental ability, class, geographic location, and so on. Those I questioned for the latter portion of this project included members of the millennial, Generation X, and baby boomer generations. Most of the people I questioned were White women contrasting in both race and gender from me as a Black person assigned male at birth. Though I am disabled and chronically ill, I have never attempted to approach hermeneutics specifically from that vantage point. Exploring how that aspect of my identity informs my theology and exegetical style has been invaluable. Seeking out other disabled voices to fill out the tapestry of understanding not only furthered this writing; it undoubtedly started conversations I will be having for weeks and months to come. Reading and interpreting

---

[12]"Various Interviews About Resurrection Bodies."

interculturally improves the way I do ministry in tangible ways. Previous intercultural experiences have done so, and I look forward to seeing how this experience will as well. Might not it do the same for you? How could you be reading more interculturally, beyond the literal and figurative Black and White? Not only do reading and interpreting interculturally honor the biblical text's intercultural reality, perhaps most importantly, reading with an intercultural hermeneutic allows the reader to recognize violence done to those on the margins both in the text and in our pews. Reading interculturally may allow the reader to decolonize their pastoral care. In that way, an intercultural reading of the text is a reading of peace as cultural competency, which is nonviolence in and of itself.

PART FIVE

IMMIGRATION AND ENVIRONMENT

19

OUR FOOD SYSTEM

THE TIE TO IMMIGRATION, MIGRANT WORKERS, EXPLOITATION, AND HUMAN TRAFFICKING

Baldemar Velasquez

I COME TO YOU TODAY SPEAKING AS a farm worker who worked alongside my parents in the fields in Texas, Michigan, Indiana, Ohio, Wisconsin, Florida, and North Carolina.[1] I've learned in organizing poor people for fifty years that our food system is in trouble, that globalization of our food systems is driving inequality around the globe, including in the United States, where we still have a large problem with immigrant workers who are harvesting crops. For the last five years, I've visited our counterpart workers in other countries. Members of the Farm Labor Organizing Committee harvest thirty-two different crops that are under a labor agreement in North Carolina, South Carolina, Virginia, Tennessee, and Ohio.

---

[1] This chapter is adapted from a speech given by the author at the Common Ground Country Fair in Unity, Maine, in September 2018.

GREED, MILITARISM, AND POLICY CREATE POVERTY

We share three things with our counterparts in other parts of the world. One is extreme poverty. It's why a lot of our children work in the fields. I started working in the fields when I was four, not because my parents believed in child labor, but because the alternative was not eating. Poverty is accompanied by greed because food systems in this country and throughout the world are designed by human beings. Somebody's got to put the food on the shelves of our stores, and how it gets there is driven by a corporate design that marginalizes people at the bottom of the production chain. So small farmers and migrant workers are probably some of the biggest victims of our food supply systems.

Connected to poverty and greed is militarism. What's happening throughout the world with any commodity that has a global supply chain is driven by our trade agreements and our foreign policy. I tell people, if you're mad about Mexicans coming across our border, maybe the first thing to think about is not displacing them in their own country by our trade agreements. Human beings have a right to stay home and produce food locally to feed their own families. When Mexican farmers can't compete with American corn farmers, the government will not protect them with tariffs, so they can't sell the excess corn they grow for their own consumption in their own local market to buy the other things a family needs. In the first three years of the North American Free Trade Agreement (NAFTA), a Carnegie Endowment study indicated that we had displaced three million corn farmers. Those farmers and their families had to migrate to find jobs to feed their families. They come to the United States to do agricultural work any way they can. They hire smugglers to bring them over the border. Many pay six thousand to seven thousand dollars to a smuggler to bring them to Ohio. Then they have to work to bring other family members here. Many are members of our union.

The United States enforces these trade agreements in its foreign policies to enable investors to make their money in those foreign countries, especially Mexico and Central America. So our foreign policy is to prop up governments that are conducive to our investments. When we negotiated NAFTA with Mexico, the United States made the Mexican government modify its constitution and its laws, allowing North American investors to have majority ownership of businesses in Mexico—previously illegal. Then American companies, especially our banks, take over. All the Mexican banks are now owned by North American banks, which control the interest they charge to small producers, small farmers, and small shopkeepers in Mexico. So we have a global problem.

What we need is what I'm seeing here. This is my first time in Maine, and I'm stunned by what I see. We need to proliferate all of you all over the country and figure out a way to conform these global corporations to be run by people like you. We can't continue to create the kind of foreign policy and trade agreements we currently have and not encounter the social problems and debates we're experiencing today. The debate on immigration is not addressing the real issues of global economic inequity and the way we push people out of their homes to benefit investors. That has got to stop.

To understand how militarism is tied to our policies, read Philip Agee's *Inside the Company: CIA Diary*.[2] Learn the role the CIA played in overthrowing Salvador Allende and instituting the dictator Pinochet in Chile. Same thing with *Confessions of an Economic Hit Man* by John Perkins.[3] They show how we progress in the dominance of another country to dominate its minerals, resources, land, and labor. We have to stop the proliferation of that inequity. We can do it only by having people become

---
[2] Philip Agee, *Inside the Company: CIA Diary* (New York: Stonehill, 1975).
[3] John Perkins, *Confessions of an Economic Hit Man* (New York: Plume, 2005).

conscious of this inequity and by empowering the people at the bottom to have a voice in those decisions. This is why I'm a labor organizer.

WHY LABOR UNIONS?

If you have a problem with labor unions, I say get over it because everybody's in the union. You are all members of something—of cooperatives, of this organization that puts on this fair. Why? To confront obstacles to make life better for your family, your children, and their future.

I debated a businessman in Ohio who had a hard time with our recruiting high school kids for our immigrant rights marches and our campaigns for Ohio farm workers. I said, "You have a problem with my ministry, I need to talk to you."

He said, "OK. Meet me at my country club." So I had lunch with him at his country club. I asked why he was a member of the country club.

He said, "This is where I meet with people like me to talk about problems we have in common so we can overcome them." He was a member of the Rotary Club and the Chamber of Commerce for the same reason.

I said, "How come all you white guys can have all these unions and we Mexicans can't have one?" I said to him, "Everybody is a member of a union. Just get over it. Because it's easier to deal with people who are in a collective and are organized than people who are individuals."

You can overcome obstacles in your life, maybe—but it will be easier if you do it with other folks. We need to challenge inequities by organizing people on the bottom to find their collective voice. This is what farm workers and immigrant workers need.

SHIFTING BORDERS

I didn't immigrate from Mexico into the United States. A lot of us Mexicans feel the same way. You know the history, right? We were the first victims of the expansion of inequity through US foreign policy and trade policies. It's weird for me to see cities like Los Angeles, San Francisco, Albuquerque, San Antonio. Who do you think named these cities? Not North Americans but Mexicans and indigenous people who were born on this continent. So I say we Mexicans didn't immigrate anywhere; immigrants overrode us and switched the borders. And now that we want to come home to our original homelands, we're illegals. There's a saying in the immigrants' rights movement that we didn't cross any borders; the borders crossed us.

Look at the way the European settlers describe the conquering of that land, how they stole it from the Indians and the Mexicans. They came up with euphemisms like Manifest Destiny, when what was really happening was the theft of those lands, including in the Rio Grande Valley where I was born. They were stolen by land development companies. The McAllen Townsite Company was one of the biggest land thieves in South Texas in the early 1900s. The Texas Rangers were really a vigilante group designed to protect the White investors in those development companies in South Texas, running Mexicans off their own land.

I studied the theft of those lands in the Rio Grande Valley. From 1900 to 1912, titles to those lands changed from Hispanic to Anglo surnames. The 1910 Mexican Revolution was used as an excuse to invade those lands, with leaders saying they were running Mexican bandits off the lands. It's part of the history of this country, how we use the military, economic policies, and economic development as excuses to marginalize the people at the bottom. Many of us descended from those Mexican families in South Texas, and we started migrating all over the country to be able to feed ourselves and our families.

INSPIRED TO ORGANIZE

In fifty years of organizing work I've come across many inspirational people who fed my desire to organize—the only way to defend ourselves.

I spent many days with Cesar Chavez talking about organizing on our long trips. I ran into Dr. Martin Luther King Jr. when he invited me in Atlanta to help plan a poor people's campaign in 1968. The first time I saw Dr. King, in Atlanta, he walked into a room where thirty Latino and Indian leaders gathered to discuss the poor people's campaign. He came in with Andy Young on one side and Ralph Abernathy on the other. When I saw that column of Black pastors come in, I said, "I want to be like those guys." When I saw Cesar Chavez, I said, "I want to be like that guy."

Somewhere sitting out here are the next Dr. Kings, the next Cesar Chavezes, the next revolutionary who's going to organize the people and inspire us to fight inequity in this world, particularly in our food systems. It's got to be you, sitting out there. And don't say it can't be me. Growing up in those fields picking tomatoes, cucumbers, strawberries, cherries, apples, row after row, tree after tree, bush after bush, I thought, "How can life be just this? There's got to be more to life than this." We barely made enough money to buy the food we were picking; we had to buy the cheapest food we could find.

NOTHING BECOMES SOMETHING

No good change comes without sacrifice, because the opposition will use everything it can to stop and undercut you. Cesar Chavez said, "Look, we farm workers have nothing. But nothing becomes something very important, because if you've got nothing, you've got nothing to lose. And the rich have got money to lose." They'll put a lot of money into stopping you, but time is the thing we've got, and there's a lot more time than there is money. So if you don't give up, at some point they've got to talk to you.

CAMPBELL SOUP WIN

Our current campaign is trying to organize 150,000 farm workers in North Carolina. That's the migrant population; most of them are undocumented; some come with guest worker H-2A visas. They're all terribly exploited. A lot are indentured laborers; a lot are smuggled there to benefit agricultural production in North Carolina. The biggest agricultural crop in North Carolina is tobacco, but the workers who harvest tobacco harvest thirty-two different crops—everything from sweet potatoes to cucumbers to strawberries, even Christmas trees in the fall. If we organize those tobacco workers, we automatically organize the farm workers for all these other crops. So Big Tobacco becomes a big target, because the corporations that buy tobacco are the wealthiest. Our job is to get tobacco to put more money into their supply chain, money designated to get to the people on the bottom.

We did that in the eighties by taking on the Campbell Soup Company. Remember their commercial with the two chubby Campbell's kids? We showed them who the real Campbell's kids were. We took pictures of migrant farm worker kids harvesting tomatoes and we put them in ads in *The New York Times*, the *Los Angeles Times*, the *Chicago Tribune*. We did a corporate campaign against Campbell Soup. We took on its banks and its corporate profile, and we boycotted its product for eight years.

We understood that the company set the price. If the company pays only thirty-two dollars per ton for tomatoes, and two-thirds of that is measly wages for your labor, and the profit margin is maybe sixty dollars an acre on a sixty-acre contract, that's not much of a profit margin for the farmer. So we figured that to improve our wages as farm workers and to get some benefits like health care, we had to go to the people who set the prices—the Campbell Soup Company. Everybody said Campbell Soup would not negotiate a contract with a group of workers who were not their employees. Campbell Soup told us, "The farmers are your employers. Go negotiate with the farmers."

We said, "We're going to boycott you until you negotiate a contract directly with us." And in 1986, Campbell Soup did what everybody said it would never do. It signed the first supply chain collective bargaining agreement in labor history. We doubled the price per ton for the farmers, we increased our wages eighty percent, and we made the company buy a Blue Cross Blue Shield health insurance policy for all the tomato pickers.

UNIONIZING TOBACCO AND PRODUCE WORKERS

Now we're asking Big Tobacco to do that for us in North Carolina, because when you organize a tobacco union, you're also organizing the workers who harvest all the other produce. We're telling them to enable farmers to unionize all over the world where people buy tobacco.

Two years ago I had the international union federation assemble all the tobacco-growing sector unions in Africa. Mozambique, Zimbabwe, Uganda, Malawi, and South Africa are the tobacco-producing nations in Africa that compete directly with us, through the same companies. British American Tobacco owns Reynolds American and buys all its tobacco in North Carolina and Africa. They pit us against each other. We said we're not going to allow that to happen anymore.

The supply chain agreements that we pioneered in Ohio with Campbell Soup, Heinz, Dean Foods, Green Bay Foods, and in 2005 with the Mount Olive Pickle Company in North Carolina increased prices to growers and increased wages of workers. Now we want tobacco companies to do that all over the world, because my heart went out to those workers in Africa when I saw them in the plantations in Malawi. It was like walking home. I saw those moms and the tears that rolled down their cheeks because they couldn't feed their children, because their kids were working in those tobacco fields. Do you think those tears of that mom were any saltier than the tears of my mother? Or of any mother who wants to feed her kids and make a life for her family?

I said to my brothers and sisters on that trip, we have to make this demand to British American Tobacco the same here as in the United

States. I asked a brother how much he gets paid in a flue-cured tobacco operation. They get paid about eighty-five cents per day. So we told British American Tobacco in a joint statement with those African unions that we wanted them to implement a practical mechanism on freedom of association outside government participation. They could put it in the purchase agreements for the tobacco they bought all over the world.

Imagine if we duplicated that with every other food commodity. People ask me, "How are you going to solve the child labor problem all over the world?" How did we solve the child labor problem in the United States? We used to have children in the coal mines and textile mills. We solved that problem by unionizing. Workers negotiated their kids out of those sites and into schools. In the eighties, 30 percent of the workforce was children under fourteen years of age in the cucumber fields of Vlasic Pickles, the largest pickle company in America, owned by Campbell Soup. We negotiated to improve their living situation and to get those kids into school in the summer during harvest and to increase the wages of workers to compensate for the lost wages of the children.

TARGETING CONVENIENCE STORES

We can solve the child labor problem now if we have free labor association all over the world. To make this happen, everybody can play a role. We're going after the convenience stores, the retailers that distribute that tobacco. The big convenience stores are Circle K, 7-Eleven, Wawa, and Kangaroo, all part of the McLane Distribution System owned by Warren Buffett. They account for one-third of Big Tobacco's consolidated revenue. So we're asking you to go to your local 7-Eleven, your local Circle K, and tell the manager—you can download a letter from our website (actionnetwork.org/petitions/until-reynolds-signs-an-agreement-with-floc-drop-vuse)—we want you to deliver this letter to the higher-ups in your corporate chain. Tell them you're not going to buy anything in their store until they remove the e-cigarette product Vuse, Reynolds's tobacco product of the future. They're promoting it mostly to young people.

Circle K and 7-Eleven will call Reynolds America and say, "Why are we being harassed by these consumers because you've got this problem with the farm workers?" Reynolds will ask us, "What is it going to take to make this go away?"

SECURITY FROM COMMUNITY

The only thing I own in my name is my car with almost 200,000 miles on it and my guitar. When you've got nothing to lose, that is a big weapon because the opposition can't take anything away from you.

Somebody asked me, what about your future, your security? When you're doing something for somebody else, people are going to help you. I've done this for fifty years. I don't have a pension; I don't have anything to lose. I've never had to worry. Growing up poor helped prepare me for this mission. If I have pinto beans and corn tortillas, I'm happy as a pig in mud. You've got to travel light to be involved in this movement. When you're doing something for somebody else, that draws people to you.

When people talk to me about immigrants and illegal aliens, I say the Bible says do not exploit and oppress the aliens. Do not mistreat them. "You shall govern the aliens with the same laws with which you govern yourself."

To do this fight, you have to have a vision and a commitment, regardless of the cost. I am grateful to do this work, because it brings me into contact with people like Rob Shetterly, who hosted me these last couple of days, and all the great people I met on this trip. You have a heart for others, and you're doing these kinds of things here because you're going to make life better for other people. And if people follow your example, the world will be a whole lot better.

People ask when I'm going to retire. The only time you really retire is when you're twelve feet under. Until then, you've got a lot of experience and life to share. Share it to the fullest ability that you can, impart the humanity you have to others, and do what is commanded of us—to love your neighbor as yourself. The Bible doesn't say love your neighbor if he looks like you or talks like you or is in the same political party. If somehow you're connected to that person, that's your neighbor. Get to know your neighbor. Get to know the person you know the least about. That's the only way we're going to bridge the cultures, the differences and the inequities we have in our lives. Because if you do, you'll have compassion for that person, and you won't be part of a food system that exploits them, that takes advantage of them and promotes inequality throughout their world.

The Scriptures warn that we don't fight against flesh and blood but against powers and principalities. Greed is a principality, and it takes control of people's lives. We need pilgrims like you all to walk it out on this earth, to live it. Don't just talk about it. Together we can make a better world.

IMMIGRATION AND THE CHURCH

WHO IS MY NEIGHBOR?

Marlena Graves

As an undergrad, I was a history major and a secondary education major. My goal was to be a high school history teacher. At one point, I remember sitting in a one p.m. American history class at my Christian college and being completely horrified, reeling from the devastation of what I had learned about the history and culture of White supremacy mixed with Christianity. The professor was lecturing on the Trail of Tears, a result of Andrew Jackson's Indian Removal Act of 1830.

The United States' insatiable lust for Native American lands motivated them to force the Cherokee nation, at gunpoint, to abandon their homes and lands. Soldiers knowingly marched the Cherokee through cholera-infested territory, places like Vicksburg, Mississippi, in order to wipe them out. Soon, I learned that the United States repeatedly reneged on treaties with Native Americans when the treaties no longer served US purposes. The United States violently pushed and shoved them out of their homes, massacred them out of their land. No matter the cost of human lives, they drove the Cherokee and others west of the Mississippi because they wanted the gold discovered on their lands in Georgia and natural resources in Kentucky, Tennessee, and other areas of the South. Many White settlers stole, killed, and destroyed to satisfy their greed. They pestered the government to get rid of the indigenous so they could squat and wickedly claim Native American lands as their own.

The land on which my family and I live in northwest Ohio, in a suburb of Toledo along the Maumee River, is Native land. Of course, all of Ohio was. "Maumee" is an English derivation referring to the Miami tribe.[1] Just a few miles from my house is the Fallen Timbers monument where General Anthony Wayne, dubbed "Mad Anthony Wayne," defeated a confederation of Native American tribes supported and protected by the British. It was the Battle of Fallen Timbers in 1794.[2] I travel up and down the Anthony Wayne Trail, which cuts through Maumee, a suburb of Toledo, and Toledo proper, to drop off my youngest daughter, Isabella, at grandma's house three days a week, and then I proceed north on Anthony Wayne Trail to arrive at my job at the Farm Labor Organizing Committee (FLOC) in historic south Toledo.

In 1795, after the Battle of Fallen Timbers, most of Ohio was handed over to the United States. Not satisfied, the European Americans wanted to expand westward. Yet there was one problem: the indigenous peoples were in their way. It would be one thing if all this land and resource grabbing were done through equitable, good-faith negotiations with the relevant Native American nations. But, alas, most of it was not. Massacres occurred at the hands of those who claimed to follow Christ. The word for these massacres is *genocide*. At least that is what we would call it if we observed it happening in any other place in the world.

I'll give an example: the Sand Creek Massacre. In the course of seven hours, US Army Colonel John Chivington, born in Lebanon, Ohio, in

---

[1] "Maumee River," Britannica, www.britannica.com/place/Maumee-River, accessed February 21, 2019.
[2] "Battle of Fallen Timbers," History.com, updated August 21, 2018, www.history.com/topics/native-american-history/battle-of-fallen-timbers.

1821, ordained in the United Methodist church, led seven hundred men from the Colorado Militia in the genocidal massacre of the peaceful Cheyenne and Arapaho.[3] Estimates of the number murdered range from seventy to five hundred natives.[4] Two-thirds of the dead were women and children. The six-year-old girl who first ran out waving a white flag when the troops arrived was immediately shot and killed.[5] The rest (infants, children, women, men) were scalped and mutilated, including genital mutilation and genitalia cut off. Fetuses were ripped from the womb. Representatives and scouts who went to investigate afterward, such as Robert Ben, testify that almost all were scalped.[6] Colonel Chivington justified his actions:

> Damn any man who sympathizes with Indians. . . . I have come to kill Indians, and believe it is right and honorable to use any means under God's heaven to kill Indians. . . . Kill and scalp all, big and little; nits make lice.[7]

At one point, Teddy Roosevelt had this to say about the Sand Creek Massacre: It was "as righteous and beneficial a deed as ever took place on the frontier."[8] "Righteous" and "beneficial" are not words I'd use. I'd call the Sand Creek Massacre genocidal, warring, rapacious, greedy, inhumane, violent, and evil—to name just a few. In a series about how the United States has treated Native Americans, including those at Sand Creek, those at PBS ask, "Who is the savage?"[9] Indeed, I wonder, just who is the savage?

---

[3] "John Chivington Biography," Sand Creek Massacre: National Historic Site Colorado, National Park Service, updated May 7, 2020, www.nps.gov/sand/learn/historyculture/john-chivington-biography.htm.
[4] "The Sand Creek Massacre Witness Accounts," The Sand Creek Massacre, sandcreekmassacre.net/witness-accounts, accessed: March 5, 2019.
[5] "Sand Creek Massacre Witness Accounts."
[6] "Sand Creek Massacre Witness Accounts."
[7] *The West,* episode 4: "Death Runs Riot," directed by Stephen Ives, written by Dayton Duncan and Geoffrey Ward, executive producer Ken Burns, aired September 15-22, 1996, on PBS, www.pbs.org/kenburns/the-west/documents#episode-four.
[8] "Sand Creek Massacre Witness Accounts."
[9] *The West,* episode 4.

How could this ordained Methodist—who would claim to follow Christ—justify such outrageously immoral behavior? How could Teddy Roosevelt, who would later become our twenty-sixth president, say Sand Creek was one of the most "righteous and beneficial" deeds that ever took place on our frontier? Is it only "righteous" and "beneficial" when such atrocities are committed against the marginalized in our society? People of color? What if the same thing happened to Teddy Roosevelt's own family and his own town? Would he have said the same thing? Surely not. Interestingly enough, as Jesus talks about in his parable, we will go to great lengths to rationalize and justify the planks in our eyes, which allow us to be willfully blind to our own sins, while we claw out the specks, the little faux pas, in other people's or other nations' eyes.

I'll give another example from history.

Need I say anything about the slave trade in the Americas? How Bible-reading, church-attending folk enslaved Africans and used the Bible to justify their crimes against humanity, their brutality, because they had convinced themselves Africans weren't really humans or, at least, were inferior to Europeans? Back when the government was first debating the bill that would eventually become the thirteenth amendment abolishing slavery and involuntary servitude, John Rutledge of South Carolina argued, "Religion and humanity have nothing to do with the questions."[10] In other words, as an article from the University of Missouri-Kansas City School of Law highlights, Rutledge was arguing that slavery was merely about property rights and that religion and humanity should be left out of the discussion.[11] Certain people—in other words, slaves—were less than human. They were property and should be treated as such. In modern parlance, it was, "For goodness

---

[10]"The Thirteenth Amendment: The Abolition of Slavery," Exploring Constitutional Conflicts, UMKC School of Law, law2.umkc.edu/faculty/projects/ftrials/conlaw/thirteenthamendment.html, accessed March 5, 2019.

[11]"The Thirteenth Amendment."

sake, leave the discussion of religion and human rights out of the discussion." Today, do we convince ourselves that people are less than human? In practice, we do. We treat them as less than human. With Native Americans, with African Americans, and, as we will see below, with others, we have a history of "targeting entire groups as suspect," as T.A. Frail says.[12]

FAST-FORWARDING TO THE WORLD WAR II ERA

Anne Franke's father, Otto Franke, desperately tried to get his family to the United States. But Americans worried that those seeking asylum in the United States coming from Europe were Nazis spies. So the United States closed the door on Anne Frank's family. Anne, her sister, and her mother died in Auschwitz—captives of the Nazis. Her father alone survived to publish her diary.

In 1939, the *St. Louis*, a ship with over nine hundred passengers aboard, approached the port of Miami after having been turned away from Cuba. The passengers were seeking asylum as refugees because of poverty and threat to their lives resulting from the World War II conflict and Nazi occupation. President Franklin D. Roosevelt, fifth cousin of Teddy Roosevelt, and our US government also turned away the ocean liner. As a result, 254 of those passengers died in the Holocaust.[13]

Auschwitz.org reports the ways and means of the German Nazis to get rid of those they had exterminated, trying to erase what they had done:

---

[12] T. A. Frail, "The Injustice of Japanese-American Internment Camps Resonates Strongly to This Day," American Incarceration: Special Report, *Smithsonian Magazine*, January 2017, www.smithsonianmag.com/history/injustice-japanese-americans-internment-camps-resonates-strongly-180961422.

[13] Amy B. Wang, "A Ship Full of Refugees Fleeing the Nazis Once Begged the U.S. for Entry. They Were Turned Back," *Washington Post*, January 29, 2017, www.washingtonpost.com/news/post-nation/wp/2017/01/29/a-ship-full-of-refugees-fleeing-the-nazis-once-begged-the-u-s-for-entry-they-were-turned-back.

Bones that did not burn completely were ground to powder with pestles and then dumped, along with the ashes, in the rivers Soła and Vistula and in nearby ponds, or strewn in the fields as fertilizer, or used as landfill on uneven ground and in marshes.[14]

And so those in the surrounding regions and downstream would drink of the dust of human beings and people in the region would breathe in the dust of the bodies—eat it because human dust fertilized their foods, never knowing.

JAPANESE INTERNMENT

Mass hysteria over the "other" during World War II led to the mass incarceration of the Japanese people after Pearl Harbor in 1941. It wasn't just the Germans who put people in concentrations camps; Americans put the Japanese people in concentration camps. White farmers in California were instrumental in getting the Japanese into American concentration camps because they were jealous of the amount of land the Japanese owned and over their agricultural success. Note how racially based hostilities coupled with fear and hysteria during the war and other uncertain times affected innocents—whole people groups—in this case, the Japanese. They were detained and everything they had was stolen from them—land, properties, livelihood—everything was confiscated.[15] The United States apologized in 1976 and there is a monument in Washington, DC, admitting the atrocities. You can see it. I did. But for those seriously harmed? Too little too late.

Of course, this is to say nothing about the lynchings, Jim Crow, and Emmett Till, who was brutally murdered for allegedly whistling at and

---

[14] "The Extermination Procedure in the Gas Chambers," Auschwitz-Birkenau Memorial and Museum, auschwitz.org/en/history/auschwitz-and-shoah/the-extermination-procedure-in-the-gas-chambers, accessed March 5, 2019.

[15] Ryan Reft, "National Security, Racism, Detention: The Relocation of California's Japanese-American Population," KCET, February 6, 2017, www.kcet.org/shows/lost-la/national-security-racism-detention-the-relocation-of-californias-japanese-american.

wrapping his arms around the waist of Carolyn Bryan Donham, who, in 2007, confessed that she had fabricated the story—that she had lied about the whole thing.[16]

NAFTA

In the fight against the expansion of communism, the United States propped up dictators in Central and South America who were corrupt and murdered their own people.[17] The United States passed the North American Free Trade Agreement, displacing an average of half a million Mexican laborers annually because Mexican farmers couldn't compete with American farmers who received government handouts in the form of farm subsidies.[18] In 2018, American farmers received $18 billion in subsidies. Indeed, over the last fifteen years, US farmers have received an annual average of $26.46 billion in subsidies.[19] NAFTA hurled Mexican farmers into poverty. As a result they headed north to cross the border to feed their families. They couldn't let their families starve. Many of them are currently farm workers in the United States They populate the farms, bolstering agriculture here in the United States.

---

[16]Richard Pérez-Peña, "Woman Linked to 1955 Emmett Till Murder Tells Historian Her Claims Were False," *New York Times,* January 27, 2017, www.nytimes.com/2017/01/27/us/emmett-till-lynching-carolyn-bryant-donham.html.

[17]Georgie Anne Geyer, "U.S. Support for Brutal Central American Dictators Led to Today's Border Crisis," *Chicago Sun-Times,* June 20, 2018, chicago.suntimes.com/2018/6/20/18380269/u-s-support-for-brutal-central-american-dictators-led-to-today-s-border-crisis; Robert E. White, "After Chavez, a Chance to Rethink Relations with Cuba," *The New York Times,* March 7, 2013, www.nytimes.com/2013/03/08/opinion/after-chavez-hope-for-good-neighbors-in-latin-america.html; Richard Stockton, "How the U.S. Government Has Supported the Deaths of Hundreds of Thousands," All That's Interesting, October 18, 2016, allthatsinteresting.com/us-dictator-alliances.

[18]Laura Carlsen, "Under NAFTA, Mexico Suffered, and the United States Felt Its Pain," *New York Times,* November 24, 2013, www.nytimes.com/roomfordebate/2013/11/24/what-weve-learned-from-nafta/under-nafta-mexico-suffered-and-the-united-states-felt-its-pain; David Bacon, "How US Policies Fueled Mexico's Great Migration," *The Nation,* January 4, 2012, www.thenation.com/article/how-us-policies-fueled-mexicos-great-migration.

[19]"The United States Farm Subsidy Information," Enviornmental Working Group, farm.ewg.org/region.php?fips=00000&progcode=total, accessed November 11, 2021.

IMMIGRATION AND THE CHURCH

What does all this thus far have to do with immigration and the church and our local and global neighbors? Everything. It shows that left to their own devices and the malformative influences of American culture, those who claim to be Christians, even those who attend church regularly and diligently read their Bibles, have a propensity to hate their local and global neighbors—to bear ill will toward them and promote or support policies that impose serious harms on them. Historically, as I have shown, such ill will—that is, hatred—has borne individual, institutional, and national harm to our local and global neighbors because the church, overall, has become captive to various prevailing ideologies and sociopolitical trends of its period—whatever period the church happens to be in.

LEGALITY, ILLEGALITY, JUST LAWS, AND UNJUST LAWS

Just because a policy is legal doesn't mean it is just or morally right. Examples of unjust and morally abhorrent yet legal policies and practices abound. Here are a few: chattel slavery, Jim Crow and rigid racial segregation in the American South, the Nuremberg Laws, which provided the foundation for the Holocaust,[20] and the Family Planning Services and Population Research Act of 1970, which led to the forced sterilization of many Native American women.[21]

Among religious groups, socially conservative Christians and Muslims would have to agree that some legal policies and practices are unjust and immoral: according to polling data, the clear majority of such Christians and Muslims believe abortion is morally wrong, although many allow for it when the mother's life is in jeopardy (and some would

---

[20] "Nuremburg Race Laws," Holocaust Encyclopedia, United States Holocaust Memorial Museum, last edited September 11, 2019, encyclopedia.ushmm.org/content/en/article/nuremberg-laws.

[21] Brianna Theobald, "A 1970 Law Led to the Mass Sterilization of Native American Women. That History Still Matters," *Time*, November 28, 2019, time.com/5737080/native-american-sterilization-history.

allow it under other extraordinary circumstances).[22] So the clear majority of such Christians and Muslims would insist that simply because abortions are legal in a particular jurisdiction doesn't mean abortion is just and morally right.

Here's another example directed toward socially conservative Christians. Many such Christians and Christian missionaries smuggle Bibles into countries where possessing a Bible and other specific religious literature is illegal. These Christians break other nations' laws to smuggle in Bibles.[23] They also break other nations' laws to proselytize. Often, they go under cover as teachers of English. And yes, they are teaching English, but many are also proselytizing students should the opportunity arise—even though it's against the law in those countries.[24]

In Nazi-occupied Europe, many Christians hid Jewish people and helped them escape even though it was against Nazi law. They broke the law to prevent the death of innocents.[25] And, of course, it wasn't just Christians. In Albania, Muslims hid two thousand Jews even though, let me underscore again, it was against the law.[26] Here's one story from

---

[22] "Politics and Policy," Pew Research Center, August 29, 2018, www.pewforum.org/2018/08/29/politics-and-policy-2/#highly-religious-groups-more-likely-than-others-to-morally-oppose-abortion-homosexual-behavior-and-drinking-alcohol; "The World's Muslims: Religion, Politics and Society," Pew Research Center, April 30, 2013, www.pewforum.org/2013/04/30/the-worlds-muslims-religion-politics-society-morality; "Abortion," BBC, updated September 9, 2007, www.bbc.co.uk/religion/religions/islam/islamethics/abortion_1.shtml.

[23] "A Bible for Every Believer," The Voice of the Martyrs, www.persecution.com/bibles, accessed March 7, 2019; "Brother Andrew's Story," Open Doors, www.opendoorsusa.org/about-us/history/brother-andrews-story, accessed March 7, 2019.

[24] "Why Teaching English Is Such an Important Ministry," Mission to the World, www.mtw.org/stories/details/why-teaching-english-is-such-an-important-ministry, accessed March 7, 2019; "Opportunity: ESL Teachers in Thailand," ABWE International, www.abwe.org/serve/opportunities/esl-teachers-2, accessed March 7, 2019; "How to Teach English Overseas and Be a Missionary Too," TEAM, May 31, 2016, team.org/blog/teach-english-overseas-missions; "English Conversation Partner Opportunity in Southeast Asia," TEAM, team.org/opportunities/english-conversation-partner, accessed March 7, 2019.

[25] "Rescue," Holocaust Encyclopedia, United States Holocaust Memorial Museum, encyclopedia.ushmm.org/content/en/article/rescue, accessed March 8, 2019.

[26] "Albanians Saved Jews from Deportation in WWII," *Deutsche Welle*, December 27, 2012, www.dw.com/en/albanians-saved-jews-from-deportation-in-wwii/a-16481404; Cnaan Liphshiz, "London Mosque to Honor Muslims Who Rescued Jews in the Holocaust," *The Times of Israel*,

The Times of Israel: "To accommodate the Aladjems [a Jewish refugee family], [Rifhat] Hoxha, who died in 1987, shuttered his bakery in the busiest time of the year—police brought the Jews to his shop just ahead of the Eid al-Fitr holiday—and brought them to his home. . . . Then he put them up in a room occupied by his in-laws, who temporarily moved out to make room for the [Jewish] guests." Hoxha's son, Rexhep, commented, "Not only the police knew, but all the neighbors knew as well. There was a circle of silence. It's something connected to our culture. You don't betray your guest, and you certainly don't betray your neighbor."[27] Note the juxtaposition of the words *refugees*, *guests*, and *neighbors* in the story. *The Times of Israel* highlights how invested the Muslim community was in saving the Jews: "As with many other Jews who survived in Albania—most of them refugees from neighboring Greece, Italy, Bulgaria and Serbia—the rescue of the Aladjems was 'an open secret.'"[28]

SO, JUST WHO IS OUR NEIGHBOR?

As the parable of the Good Samaritan opens in Luke chapter 10, we have an expert in the Hebrew law, a biblical scholar, asking Jesus how he can inherit eternal life. Jesus asks him, "What is written in the law?" (Lk 10:26). The lawyer answers, "You shall love the Lord your God with all your heart, and with all your soul, and with all your strength, and with all your mind; and your neighbor as yourself" (Lk 10:27). But, according to the Gospel account, the expert wants to "justify himself" during this public encounter. And so he asks, "Who is my neighbor?" (Lk 10:29). He wants to corner Jesus, to make himself look

---

December 28, 2018, www.timesofisrael.com/london-mosque-to-honor-muslims-who-rescued-jews-in-the-holocaust.

[27]Cnaan Liphshiz, "What Made Muslim Albanians Risk Their Lives to Save Jews from the Holocaust?" *The Times of Israel*, January 19, 2018, www.timesofisrael.com/what-made-muslim-albanians-risk-their-lives-to-save-jews-from-the-holocaust.

[28]Liphshiz, "What Made Muslim Albanians."

wiser than Jesus, and to justify his action (or inaction) toward those around him.[29]

As Jesus continues the parable in Luke 10:30-32, he tells of a man beaten and left for dead on the dangerous road to Jericho, a road full of ambushing bandits. A priest and a Levite see the man beaten up and in terrible condition. Vulnerable, the man desperately needs help. But these religious leaders pass by on the other side. They rationalize their many reasons for avoiding him. Some of their reasons are understandable.[30] Perhaps some of them even make religious sense.[31] But the Samaritan—the one on the bottom of the societal ladder, their enemy, the theological heretic, the unclean one—went out of his way to help the man. The Samaritan even put him up in a hotel and charged the victim's medical bills to his own tab. In this parable, Jesus isn't answering the question of "who is my neighbor?" but telling us what it means to *act as* a neighbor. The expert in the law wanted to find a loophole for his moral obligation to love his neighbor. Jesus wouldn't have it. When Jesus asked who acted as the neighbor, the expert in the law could barely cough up, "The one who helped him." He couldn't even eke out the words "the Samaritan." Isn't it interesting how theological heretics, those despised by society, those considered enemies by many Christians sometimes act as better neighbors than those who claim the name of Christ? How many of us, on the other hand, can act like the lawyer who wanted to find a way out of having to love?

---

[29]Reflecting on this exchange and the lawyer's response in particular, Martin Luther King Jr. writes, "The lawyer was chagrined. 'Why,' the people might ask, 'would an expert in law raise a question that even the novice can answer?' Desiring to justify himself and to show that Jesus' reply was far from conclusive, the lawyer asks, 'And who is my neighbor?' The lawyer was now taking up the cudgels of debate that might have turned the conversation into an abstract theological discussion. But Jesus, determined not to be caught in the 'paralysis of analysis,' pulls the question from mid-air and places it on a dangerous curve between Jerusalem and Jericho" ("On Being a Good Neighbor," in *Strength to Love* [Minneapolis: Fortress, 2010], 22).

[30]King identifies some of these possible reasons in "On Being a Good Neighbor," 25-27.

[31]For example, Numbers 19:11-13 articulates priestly duties to avoid corpse impurity. The religious leaders in Jesus' parable may have mistakenly thought the beaten and battered man was, indeed, dead already. And checking to verify would have put them at risk of violating this religious duty.

Whether Christians consider immigrants and refugees as neighbors or enemies, it doesn't change the way Christians are to treat them—with love. Jesus tells his followers to love their neighbors and their enemies. Love is manifested in concrete actions, not ephemeral feelings. Love works for the good of the other. Love is sacrificial. Pursuing justice requires sacrifice and is seldom convenient, as my boss, FLOC founder and Presidente Baldemar Velasquez, likes to say. Just look to Jesus—his love is manifested in a sacrificial life. He emptied himself on our behalf, Christians confess.

As noted above, I work for the Farm Labor Organizing Committee (FLOC). We are primarily made up of ten to twelve thousand migrant farm workers, mostly in North Carolina on tobacco farms. But our members don't just harvest tobacco; they harvest over thirty-two other crops—mostly fruits and vegetables. People have told us that Mexican agricultural workers are the new slaves, and for good reason.[32] And note that some people use *Mexican* as a catch-all term for everyone south of the US border. In the United States right now, there is a significant antirefugee and anti-immigrant sentiment fueled by fear.[33] The United

---

[32] Oxfam America partnered with FLOC to produce the report "Like Machines in the Fields: Workers Without Rights in American Agriculture," March 2004, www.oxfamamerica.org/static/media/files/like-machines-in-the-fields.pdf. In the epigram to the report, Oxfam America quotes Lucas Benitez: "Behind the shiny, happy images promoted by the fast-food industry with its never-ending commercials, there is another reality. . . . This is the reality of farmworkers who contribute their sweat and blood so that enormous corporations can profit, all the while living in sub-poverty misery, without benefits, without the right to overtime or protection when we organize. Others are working by force, against their will, terrorized by violent employers, under the watch of armed guards, held in modern-day slavery. The right to a just wage, the right to work free of forced labor, the right to organize—three of the rights in the United Nations' Universal Declaration of Human Rights—are routinely violated when it comes to farmworkers in the United States."

[33] In a recent report, the Anti-Defamation League reports, "Anti-immigrant ideology has gained mainstream acceptance, infiltrated policy implementation, been used as a wedge issue to scare constituents and become the fodder of media personalities who regularly demonize immigrants to a wide audience. They frame their messages as reasonable and valid but are promoting xenophobia and preventing a reasonable conversation about real reform to address real challenges in the immigration system." See "Mainstreaming Hate: The Anti-immigrant Movement in the U.S," ADL, November 2018, www.adl.org/the-anti-immigrant-movement-in-the-us#an-overview-of-the-anti-immigrant-movement-in-the-us; Meagan Flynn, "An Invasion of Illegal Aliens': The Oldest Immigration Fear-Mongering Metaphor in America," *Washington Post*,

States' current national stance is strikingly similar to what occurred during World War II and the early civil rights era.[34]

However, our hysteria is now aimed at Latinx people, Haitian people, those from the Middle East and parts of Asia. We are targeting people groups but would never want the same to be done to us. How would we like if it happened to us?

For example, we all know that not all White men are mass murderers, even though the overwhelming majority of those perpetrating mass shootings at schools, places of worship, and commercial locations are White men.[35] What if we incarcerated and took the civil and human rights away from White men because of these mass shooters? Should those around the world consider all White men mass shooters and take mass security precautions because of what they see coming across on their news reels overseas? Hardly.

IMMIGRATION, THE CHURCH, AND MIGRANT FARM WORKERS

Farmers want migrant workers. They'll tell you that migrants know the land and how to farm. Farmers are for immigration reform.[36] If we think our lives have nothing to do with immigration, that there is a distance between us and immigrants, we will soon find out we are terribly wrong.

Whenever you and I eat or drink, we have an immigration problem on our hands. If it weren't for migrants, documented or not, we wouldn't

---

November 2, 2018, www.washingtonpost.com/nation/2018/11/02/an-invasion-illegal-aliens-oldest-immigration-fear-mongering-metaphor-america.

[34] "Mainstreaming Hate," ADL; Isaac Stanley-Becker, "'Our Country Is FULL!' Trump's Declaration Carries Far-Right Echoes That Go Back to the Nazi Era," *Washington Post,* April 8, 2019, www.washingtonpost.com/nation/2019/04/08/our-country-is-full-trumps-declaration-carries-far-right-echoes-that-go-back-nazi-era.

[35] "Mass Shooter Database," The Violence Project, March 2021, www.theviolenceproject.org/mass-shooter-database.

[36] "Agriculture Labor Reform," American Farm Bureau Federation, www.fb.org/issues/immigration-reform/agriculture-labor-reform, accessed March 8, 2019.

have food on our tables. Our food and agricultural system depends on immigrant workers—most from Latin America.[37] When people pray and "give thanks for the hands that prepared our food," it is incumbent upon them to think about and seek justice for those who harvested and processed their food. Our fruits and vegetables, milk, wine, meat, chocolate, and tea—if we didn't grow them, harvest them, or process them ourselves, they came via the hands of immigrants. To put it bluntly, without them we wouldn't eat or drink. They feed us. Farmers know this.

Harvesting crops is backbreaking work that hardly any Americans want to do.[38] If US residents do not want to apply for farm work, workers have to come from somewhere. Most of them come from south of the US-Mexican border. Often they work in slavelike conditions and live in squalid housing.[39] The reality is that they are out of sight and out of mind. This is why FLOC exists. We are fighting alongside migrant farm workers and for them—for their human rights, which include labor rights.

One recent summer, FLOC took a group of African American, Latinx, and White folks on a trip to the fields of North Carolina, to the labor camps where FLOC members work. Theresa, one of the African

---

[37]"As Burton Eller, legislative director for the National Grange, writes, "Those of us living in and working in rural and small town America have a message for our city cousins. We need workers and we need them now. . . . We've become increasingly dependent over the years on migrant labor, legal and illegal, to help run our farms, ranches, processing plants and service industries," "What Agriculture Needs Now Is More Labor," *The Hill,* July 21, 2018, thehill.com/opinion/energy-environment/398162-what-agriculture-needs-now-is-more-labor; see also "U.S. Farms Can't Compete Without Foreign Workers," *Bloomberg Opinion,* June 1, 2018, www.bloomberg.com/opinion/articles/2018-06-01/u-s-farms-need-more-immigrant-workers; Tamar Haspel, "Illegal Immigrants Help Fuel U.S. Farms. Does Affordable Produce Depend on Them?" *Washington Post,* March 17, 2017, www.washingtonpost.com/lifestyle/food/in-an-immigration-crackdown-who-will-pick-our-produce/2017/03/17/cc1c6df4-0a5d-11e7-93dc-00f9bdd74ed1_story.html.

[38]Eller writes, "Why don't we hire local workers from the community? We wish we could. Our neighbors don't want to work under farm conditions for the prevailing pay scale" ("What Agriculture Needs Now").

[39]Oxfam America partnered with FLOC to issue the report "A State of Fear: Human Rights Abuses in North Carolina's Tobacco Industry," 2011, s3.amazonaws.com/oxfam-us/www/static/oa3/files/a-state-of-fear.pdf.

American women on the trip, was aghast. She said, "I grew up poor in the city of Toledo. But I can never again say I was poor, given what I've seen." She was talking about the squalid living and extremely difficult working conditions at the farm labor camps. You'd think these conditions only existed in poorer countries. Not the United States. But FLOC confronts these conditions every day, and we work on the ground with our members, in the state houses, in Washington, DC, with farmers and businesses and human rights organizations, to change these conditions.

Our migrant worker members are taken advantage of. Women and children are sexually harassed and assaulted. Workers' wages are stolen—some employers are creative in finding ways to not pay. Others are physically abused. We help them get workers' compensation, bathroom breaks, and water breaks. These are basic human rights that they are denied. We fight child labor. We also fight human trafficking.

Here I am discussing the agricultural sector, but you cannot go to a hotel, restaurant, or new construction site without running into the need for immigration reform. Many of these workers pay income tax. They have taxpayer identification numbers and the IRS is happy to take their money, even knowing that they are undocumented.[40] They fund our Medicare and social security but get none of the benefits. It is taxation without representation.

What about the fact that many are here undocumented? As noted above, while it is surely a complicated issue, US foreign and economic policy has destabilized Central and South America.[41] We have fueled

---

[40]"The Facts About the Individual Tax Identification Number (ITIN)," American Immigration Council, September 15, 2021, americanimmigrationcouncil.org/research/facts-about-individual-tax-identification-number-itin.

[41]Ciara Nugent, "Why the Threat of U.S. Intervention in Venezuela Revives Historical Tensions in the Region," *Time*, January 25, 2019, time.com/5512005/venezuela-us-intervention-history-latin-america.

the destabilization of these nations' infrastructure. Corrupt people have taken advantage of it and now terrorize their own people. Poverty, hunger, threat of life and limb, and lack of employment are the realities. I don't know about you, but if I had to keep my family from starving or my children from being raped and murdered, I would do whatever it takes to get my family to health and safety. We as a nation are making the lives of many of these people and their families living hells. Many of them are Christians. But whether they are or not doesn't seem to matter.

Telling them to enter the United States legally when there is not a real pathway to do so short of long waits to seek asylum (unless you are Western European, Australian, or rich—you can donate a bunch of money to a business and get into this country much more quickly) when they are hungry or even under the threat of death or under other physical danger won't cut it.

Not having your documents is a misdemeanor.[42] That is the same level of lawbreaking as a speeding ticket. But we as a country are currently treating people seeking asylum, which they can do legally at a port of entry, as criminals. Felons. Recently we instituted the "zero tolerance" immigration policy.[43] Initially we covertly separated children from families. For Christians who herald a pro-life stance, such unjust policy and behavior is certainly violent, and pro-death. We have for-profit detention centers that make money off the number of detainees in their beds, so it is in their best interest to lobby for draconian immigration policies to profit from the suffering of the least of these.[44]

---

[42]Laura Jarrett, "Are Undocumented Immigrants Committing a Crime? Not Necessarily," CNN Politics, February 24, 2017, www.cnn.com/2017/02/24/politics/undocumented-immigrants-not-necessarily-criminal/index.html.

[43]"Attorney General Announces Zero-Tolerance Policy for Criminal Illegal Entry," US Department of Justice, April 6, 2018, www.justice.gov/opa/pr/attorney-general-announces-zero-tolerance-policy-criminal-illegal-entry.

[44]Clyde Haberman, "For Private Prisons, Detaining Immigrants Is Big Business," *The New York Times*, October 1, 2018, www.nytimes.com/2018/10/01/us/prisons-immigration-detention.html.

As the Gospel accounts testify, the Magi, the wise men from the East, broke the law when they didn't report Jesus' whereabouts. Herod told the wise men to come back to him. But as the account goes, God warned them in a dream to return home by another route (Mt 2:7-12). Joseph, Mary, and baby Jesus fled Herod and his gang because they knew Herod sought to harm Jesus, to kill infant Jesus. The Magi acted as neighbors to Jesus, Mary, and Joseph when they disobeyed Herod.

As I have demonstrated, America, including its population of White Christians, has a history of murderous oppression when it comes to indigenous and minority peoples here in the United States. This murderous oppression is contrary to the teachings of Jesus. When it comes to immigration reform and treatment of migrants and asylum seekers, White Christians need to part with their historical and current propensity to oppress people of color and act in similar fashion to the Magi. They need to take their cue from the Albanian Muslims and others during the World War II era who broke unjust laws to do what is right. Even our food system depends on immigrants we are oppressing. Why bite the hands that feed us?

Many migrants and asylum seekers from Central and South America are fleeing poverty and violence. Those who profess to follow the teachings of Jesus and familiarity with their Bibles should be familiar with the parable of the Good Samaritan. If so, they would want to act like the Good Samaritan and not the priest or Levite. If the American church, especially White evangelicals, follow the teachings of Jesus, it is very likely that America will change its draconian immigration policy and other forms of oppression against minorities.

EVERYTHING, NOTHING, SOMETHING

TRADING IN WORLDVIEWING FOR EVERYDAY FAITHFULNESS IN PEACEMAKING AND SUSTAINABILITY

Jacob Alan Cook

THINKING ABOUT MATTERS OF VIOLENCE AND ECOLOGY together is a time-scattered tradition dating at least to the (hi)story gathered in the Hebrew Scriptures. Reverence for the land permeates the text, beginning with the poetic portrayals of God's creative work in setting the cosmos on its foundations and breathing life into it. Formed of earth and bound to it in life and death, the first humans stagger out of the garden into a vast wilderness fit to test their newfound knowledge. By the second generation, genuine "commerce" with the living God and creation has already given way to theories about a god's involvement in human agricultural endeavors.[1] And when poor agronomy gives way to worse theology, one man's jealousy drives him to cut his brother down,

---

[1]Throughout this chapter, I will intentionally bend the term *commerce* in the direction of *communion* as a way of flagging the character of Christian agency in a world that routinely reads all things as mostly about economics.

foreshortening his time on the earth and returning his body to it. To all this, God says,

> What have you done? Listen; your brother's blood is crying out to me from the ground! And now you are cursed from the ground, which has opened its mouth to receive your brother's blood from your hand. When you till the ground, it will no longer yield to you its strength; you will be a fugitive and a wanderer on the earth. (Gen 4:10-12)

Here in the first biblical account of human violence; both God and soil respond to the damage suffered in the commerce of Creator and creation.

Generations later, "when people began to multiply on the face of the ground" (Gen 6:1), God grieves the path human lives are cutting across the land, scarring and corrupting it. Particularly, "the earth was filled with violence" (Gen 6:11), and God's initial concern is not limited to human beings—for by this time, all flesh is caught up in the circle of life and its food web. Unlike the deities featured in the flood stories of other ancient Near Eastern cultures, the biblical God is not merely aggravated by human beings but deeply troubled by their rampant bloodshed and its devastating ecological impact. And by the end of the story, as the stench of burnt offerings rises from the newly washed soil, God's first words land with a thud: "I will never again curse the ground because of humankind, for the inclination of the human heart is evil from youth" (Gen 8:21). Taking notice of the offering, God registers the ongoing wickedness of human hearts. At this point in the biblical story, one could be forgiven for reading God's statement as disapproving of the violence essential to the sacrifices offered. In any case, violence seems to be on the forefront of God's mind, for next God delimits future bloodshed: nonhuman creatures may be killed and eaten, but any creature that kills a human person must reckon with their maker (Gen 9:3-6). Through these stories we may sense the connection between all life in the God-created world and the soil, without which no embodied creature would have a place to stand let alone to make a life. Humankind is the crowning creature, but only within an abundant creation that as a whole gives glory to the living God and laments the violence that breaks the commerce of Creator and creation.

This sensibility is all but lost in the twenty-first century CE—at least on the human beings who take up space in the so-called Western world. Ideological designations like this are but one reminder that all creation has come to be seen primarily in terms of its function within the endeavors of humankind. Scientists studying the earth's systems (starting with atmospheric chemist Paul Crutzen) have suggested that we think of the current geological epoch as not the Holocene but the Anthropocene. And given that the geologic time scale was developed to help scientists correlate significant events in earth's history, it makes sense that the age in which human activity remakes landscapes and changes the atmosphere would bear its autograph as well. As Willis Jenkins muses, "In a sense, humanity has become earth's habitat."[2] Human beings generate the Anthropocene by shaping and ordering both lands and creatures to suit their worldviews—bending all things to their will, with violence when "necessary" or, in some cases, merely "expedient."

One more set of reasons for thinking about matters of violence and ecology together sets the course for this chapter: contemporary Christians tend to approach concerns about each with the same limited methodology. Specifically, given the scale of problems of both violence and sustainability, Christians tend to identify and handle each basic threat at the level of ideology—"the biblical worldview" or "gospel perspective" or some other such signifier. But in this chapter I will argue that

---

[2] Willis Jenkins, *The Future of Ethics: Sustainability, Social Justice, and Religious Creativity* (Washington, DC: Georgetown University Press, 2013), 2.

worldview-level projects easily mask their shortcomings in generating social change by appearing as "very present help in trouble" (Ps 46:1). To begin, I will briefly catalog some such approaches to both sustainability and peacemaking and, with some help from Jenkins, identify categorical problems with perceiving and addressing issues at the worldview level. Then I will explore some pragmatic strategies concerning both issues that highlight the role of creative agency in faithful Christian living, juxtaposing Jenkins's approach to sustainability matters in *The Future of Ethics* with the *Just Peacemaking* paradigm brokered by Glen Harold Stassen. Finally, I will sketch from these two accounts an approach to Christian ethics that foregrounds the commerce of all creation and underscores everyday responsibility.

STRATEGIZING FROM A GOD'S-EYE VIEW

An hour's worth of almost any day's news will contain reports of climate change, violence somewhere, new evidence of pollution and its effects on some local population, and talk and rumors of war. There is enough to make anyone feel sad, angry, hopeless, like we need sweeping changes, and like nothing will ever change. The pervasive nature and overwhelming magnitude of such problems contribute to the question mark over the future of ethics, as Jenkins has argued in his book by that title. What he calls "wicked" problems—those that are "atmospheric" in scale and complex beyond imagination and that spawn from the "accidental" development of human powers beyond intelligible limits and responsibilities—seem to call for solutions at the largest level we can think of. And for many ethicists, that is precisely where we should start: at the level of thought, namely worldviews.[3] As Jenkins explains, "*a cosmological strategy* uses theological discourse to critically interpret cultural worldviews, on the notion that such interpretations can illuminate the

---

[3]Jenkins, *Future of Ethics*, 19.

significance of social problems in an agent's moral imagination."[4] If a person's worldview drives their everyday actions, then working at that level is a primary strategy for generating social change.

Take Christian approaches to matters of violence as an example. Questions typically circle around how to situate the use of violence—especially the practice of war—in view of biblical demands for love and justice. What are Christians permitted to contribute to their nation's war efforts when the time comes? At one end of the spectrum, we can imagine a pacifist response of "nothing" to this question, forbidding Christians from serving in any armed (sometimes any civil) service. The world will not see in the church an alternative society (i.e., God's kingdom) built on forgiveness, after all, if its people continuously prop up earthly kingdoms through corrupt practices like war. At the other end of the spectrum, we can imagine someone who answers "everything" to our question, deferring to civil authorities' judgments regarding the necessity of war—often under the assumption that the United States has a unique role in administering God's justice in the world. For example, as World War II unfolded, Harold Ockenga, the founding president of the National Association of Evangelicals, preached, "In a matter of war, we must admit that the ministers of the State become our conscience before God. What the rulers decree we must obey. We do not have the right to sit in judgment."[5] And during the Vietnam War, Ockenga wrote to President Lyndon Johnson, urging him to use "whatever weapons and firepower necessary to win."[6] Between these poles on the spectrum, we can find a framework for evaluating cases for war and disciplining its practice. The "just war" tradition that materialized in

---

[4]Jenkins, *Future of Ethics*, 74.
[5]Harold Ockenga, "The Christian as a Member of the State" (sermon, October 20, 1940), quoted in Matthew Avery Sutton, *American Apocalypse: A History of Modern Evangelicalism* (Cambridge, MA: Belknap Press, 2014), 277.
[6]Harold Ockenga to the president, May 28, 1966, quoted in Sutton, *American Apocalypse*, 331.

medieval Christian ethics has evolved to address the limits of a state's right to war (*jus ad bellum*), conduct during war (*jus in bello*), and responsibilities after war (*jus post bellum*); foremost among the rules is an assurance that the intent behind warmaking is restoring an order of justice for all.

On matters of ecology, Christian responses fork at this question: For what are humans, as stewards of the earth, responsible in maintaining a sustainable environment for themselves and other creatures? As Jenkins explains, one strategy for relating Christianity to our climate answers "nothing" to this question, taking up avoidance strategies that "use Christian ideas to deny that a problem exists."[7] For example, Cal Beisner's Cornwall Alliance disputes the very possibility that humans could ever harm the earth (e.g., through overuse of fossil fuels) beyond its resilience as God's good creation under God's ongoing, sovereign care. One of the alliance's landmark documents "affirm[s] that by God's design earth and its physical and biological systems are robust, resilient, and self-correcting" and "den[ies] that they are fragile" or "that godly human dominion entails humans' being servants rather than masters of the Earth."[8] Beisner and company embrace and endorse the Anthropocene as humankind realizing God's intention for its role within creation—sustainability is about the earth as sustenance for human life. Another strategy answers "everything" to our question, taking anthropogenic climate change as a given and highlighting its present signs as symbols of judgment and warnings to proceed differently into the future. Here some Christian ethicists take up an apocalyptic strategy,

---

[7]Jenkins, *Future of Ethics*, 46.
[8]E. Calvin Beisner, "The Biblical Perspective of Environmental Stewardship: Subduing and Ruling the Earth to the Glory of God and the Benefit of Our Neighbors," written for the International Church Council Project, June 17, 2014, cornwallalliance.org/landmark-documents/the-biblical-perspective-of-environmental-stewardship-subduing-and-ruling-the-earth-to-the-glory-of-god-and-the-benefit-of-our-neighbors.

"depicting high-carbon culture within the fate of Rome or Babylon," thus "undermin[ing] the normalcy of high-carbon patterns of life" and "mak[ing] climate change a scene in which to seek the irruptive, transforming coming of God."[9] But apocalyptists risk painting a jarring image at the level of poetry and symbol without much hope of practical action. Other ethicists develop an increasingly comprehensive advocacy strategy that looks primarily to inspire societal change, sometimes promoting an ideal reality that would require human societies to respond to God's presence and activity to an extent that even the church has not attained.

Yet the focus on situating larger concepts like violence and sustainability within a full-orbed worldview leaves a sizable gap between theory and the everyday realities of life and practice. Interpreting the degree to which human beings can or should actively form their environs does not necessarily enable everyday Christians to participate in and promote healthy commerce between and among people and nonhuman creation. Resolving the question of war's place in Christian life simply does not inspire a practicable commitment to the best everyday practices for social change, transforming initiatives to promote justice, or conflict resolution through repentance and forgiveness. So even as we reflect on worldview-level principles and ideals, and even as we take into account the ever-changing global realities, Christians need concrete guidance for what everyday faithfulness looks like. Before moving on to some leading examples, I should stake out some space for pragmatic strategies by flagging a few more liabilities in worldviewing.

PROBLEMS OF SCALE IN WORLDVIEWING

Our moral traditions and inherited concepts for understanding nature as well as human possibility and responsibility have been fundamentally

---

[9]Jenkins, *Future of Ethics*, 49.

broken by the scale of problems amassing since the Industrial Revolution. And Jenkins convincingly argues that worldview-level approaches have proven themselves "incompetent" to even understand let alone respond to the wicked problems generated by our technological and societal developments.[10] For example, we now live in a world proliferating advanced nuclear weapons and increasingly autonomous war drones without fully fledged ethics of their use. The future of ethics is in question because our struggle to understand "what is going on"[11] frequently leaves us without any genuine handles by which to grasp responsibility for the world we are already shaping and generate new patterns of everyday faithfulness. In an age when humans are amassing technological powers faster than our moral compass can map them or our ethical drive can regulate them, the earth and all its creatures have become just so many objects in the grand scheme of some human ideology or another. Improving the ideology can go only so far in repairing the genuine commerce of all creation.

Time spent grinding the intellectual wheels too often doubles as time spent deferring tangible action and (if we are being honest) fretting about whether any action could be sufficient to the challenge.[12] The energy we might otherwise give to engaging the conflicts and constructive projects that are near at hand can be sapped away by (1) the cognitive-emotional bandwidth dedicated to big problems and (2) so-called slacktivist engagement with issues. (1) Giving preference to analysis over activity can itself become a practiced response, such that looking for pragmatic solutions in everyday life becomes less ingrained or at least less interesting. But thinking of problems like sustainability or

---

[10] Jenkins, *Future of Ethics*, chaps. 1-2.
[11] Jenkins often refers to this question, which H. Richard Niebuhr saw as the beginning of Christian social ethics; see Niebuhr's *The Responsible Self: An Essay in Christian Moral Philosophy* (New York: Harper and Row, 1963), 60.
[12] Jenkins, *Future of Ethics*, 79.

peacemaking primarily at the scale of national, or even global systems, we can come up with plenty to argue about without much to act on together. (2) The average American spends an almost unbelievable amount of time consuming and engaging online content each day, and the strategy for engaging high-level issues that rests nearest at hand is the public token of support for this or that cause—a tweet here, a post there. Yet empirical studies suggest that, other things being equal, people could be more inclined toward and motivated to provide further, more concrete support for social causes if they did not turn first to social media as an outlet for expressing their position.[13] Once slacktivists have satisfied their "impression-management concerns" by publicly sharing from their worldview on an issue, their inclination and overall motivation to provide further, more concrete support is significantly diminished. In either case, a great deal of energy is radiated through debates about the issues, often at the worldview level, without being channeled into constructive, concrete action.

Jenkins worries that "religious ethicists sometimes overestimate the practical importance of religious beliefs and cultural worldviews while underestimating the moral creativity in religious reform projects."[14] On the one hand, this means that thinkers focused on thinking are overly fond of solutions to problems that start with thinking better and assume those better thoughts will cash out in social change. On the other hand, I might add, being able to give ideal answers from the perspective of a relatively sterile worldview gives us a sense that we are already doing good by thinking well. If our thinking and doing are wrapped up together in our lives, then it is good to spend some time regularly evaluating what we think for errors and sins; however, worldview-level

---

[13]See for instance Kirk Kristofferson, Katherine White, and John Peloza, "The Nature of Slacktivism: How the Social Observability of an Initial Act of Token Support Affects Subsequent Prosocial Action," *Journal of Consumer Research* 40, no. 6 (April 2014): 1149-66.
[14]Jenkins, *Future of Ethics*, 5.

thinking drives us beyond this level to speculating about what is ideally true (i.e., in God's eyes) with the assumption that we should work to refashion the world on its basis. But when we embrace such a story about how things should be, we risk being seduced by the tidiness of a worldview that makes a lot of sense to us in the abstract and, thus, lulled into a false sense of moral security. I can have confidence that I will not participate in the practice of war without considering how I might actively promote justice through nonviolent direct action.

Furthermore, our attempts to generate more ideal worldviews, when they do parlay into advocacy and concrete reform projects, risk participating in the problem at the heart of our broken commerce with God, other persons, and the rest of creation.[15] Driven by an ideal mental picture of the world, human beings are tempted to use their energy to refashion the world and its peoples to more neatly fit their relatively abstract mental picture—and the expedient route to these ends is the way of coercion and objectification. All things can be refigured to suit human ideological desires, further reinforcing a sense of alienation from the natural world; all persons are prospective converts to our worldview and its cause—or should at least be required to play along with our rules when we are in power. Of course, beautiful visions of a transformed world do motivate constructive social action, but the social movements we find so inspiring have not been predicated on comprehensive, worldview-level agreement. Rather, they draw people from their points of deepest concern into a common movement, which they can support (more or less) from within their own more particular views of the world. The ideological other does not reduce to merely another piece of furniture in our mental world; rather, in commerce, other persons may be

---

[15] A deeper, sustained critique of worldviewing, and signposts toward a creaturely alternative, can be found in Jacob Alan Cook, *Worldview Theory, Whiteness, and the Future of Evangelical Faith* (Lanham, MD: Fortress Academic/Lexington Books, 2021).

won as allies in concrete action for change. But to live even partially into the created reality of genuine commerce, we must be freed to get creative with our moral inheritances and faithfully address new problems as they arise.

THEOCENTRIC PRAGMATISM TOWARD CLIMATE CHANGE

At least some of these problems with "moral cosmologies" (in Jenkins's terminology) are among the reasons he argues for shifting energy toward theocentric pragmatism. What Jenkins calls a "pragmatic strategy" operates on the assumption that people are already finding ways to put their religious inheritances (ideas, practices, and otherwise) to use in interpreting and responding faithfully to practical problems of sustainability. Everyday patterns of life carry meaning or content as more than just idea(l)s and can be creatively reinterpreted or reapplied (sometimes on the fly) to address problems arising in a person's embodied context. I cannot do in this short space what Jenkins does in his book by way of building an argument for practicable strategies. Instead, I intend to offer a brief example of the kind of pragmatic response to a local climate issue that Jenkins sees as motivated by religion yet creative with traditional resources—the case of Christian waterman families on Tangier Island. And from this I will draw some preliminary conclusions.

The Chesapeake Bay ecosystem has faced a number of challenges to its sustainability over the last century, from industrial pollution to overfishing to the threat of sea level rise. As such, environmentalists (scientists and activists) have long been active in the restoration and preservation of the bay, as with the founding of the Chesapeake Bay Foundation in 1967. Positioned out in the middle of the bay, Tangier Island, Virginia, has a rich cultural heritage, and its people share a sizable role in the area's fishing industry. Part of its heritage is the Christian faith that much of its current population (roughly 87 percent) confesses.[16] As they perceived the influx of sustainability-oriented messaging from the outside, the Christian watermen of Tangier Island rebuffed proposals to change their practices, even "us[ing] biblical themes of human dominion to support their resistance."[17] And the resistance was in many and varied forms, including illegal fishing and even suspected arson. Among the change agents in this seemingly intractable situation was Susan Drake Emmerich, who came on the scene as a Christian but an outsider—doing doctoral research at the intersection of faith, conceptions of stewardship, and concrete conservation projects. But when "watermen began asking for her help to better understand what they could do to address fisheries declines and ensure a future for the community," Emmerich started talking about stewardship in a biblical idiom that connected with Tangier residents.[18] Emmerich writes of a community church service in which "fifty-eight watermen bowed down in tears and asked God to forgive them."[19] Seeing the ecological challenges present in their embodied context, the waterman started understanding them as theological problems for which God demanded a reconfiguration of their actions. Signing the "Waterman's Stewardship Covenant," these same folks committed to good stewardship practices and to holding one another accountable—flying red ribbons on their boat antennas as a reminder of their pledge.

While this example has clear worldview-level undertones, it highlights how the fishermen "deployed the practice of repentance to

---

[16]Tracy A. Scheffler, "Bridge over Troubled Waters: Faith-Based Stewardship in Chesapeake Bay," *Yale F&ES Bulletin* 105 (2001): 63.

[17]Jenkins, *Future of Ethics*, 173. For more on this story, see the firsthand accounts in Susan Drake Emmerich, "The Declaration in Practice: Missionary Earthkeeping," in *The Care of Creation*, ed. R. J. Berry (Downers Grove, IL: InterVarsity Press, 2000), 147-54, and the documentary film *When Heaven Meets Earth*, directed by Jeffrey Pohorski, coproduced by Susan Drake Emmerich and Jeffrey Pohorski (Skunkfilms Productions, 2007), DVD.

[18]Scheffler, "Bridge," 66.

[19]Emmerich, "The Declaration," 151.

authorize a new pattern of cultural action."[20] The order of operations is significant here as well as the localness of both the problems and the response. The problems had already begun to disrupt the basic patterns of thought and life. Reconfiguring the whole worldview was unnecessary, and really the resources for change were already there to be mobilized once the concrete issues broke through the worldview-level avoidance strategy. This is a practical-wisdom ("we must do *something*") response to a concrete problem, applying religious inheritances in creative new ways to generate novel solutions. It is engaged locally with matters near at hand to do at least something better. The religious conceptuality deployed to do the work may leave something to be desired by the academically trained ethicist, who still cannot deny that real theological, social, and ecological change do take place. As people who inhabit patterns of life that include but are not limited to our (inevitably incompetent) thoughts about the world, when we are freed to see the earth and its people at the local level, we may find that our religious resources are especially motivating in practicable, everyday ways to "seek the welfare of the city" (Jer 29:7) in which we live. And at the end of the day, we might expect those concerned for religious worldviews to revise and expand those views in light of everyday work.

THE JUST PEACEMAKING PARADIGM

As 1990 waned, war raged in Kuwait and the United States was preparing an extensive air campaign. In January 1991—the week before the first US airstrikes—the Society of Christian Ethics debated the justness of this war. Glen Stassen recalled a clear promise to "not only debate whether the war would be just, but also what initiatives should be taken to avoid the war."[21] To his great disappointment, no constructive alternatives

---

[20] Jenkins, *Future of Ethics*, 174.
[21] Glen Harold Stassen, "The Origin of the Just Peacemaking Ethic," essay, 2013 (private collection).

emerged. Stassen was angry but did not sin; instead, he did something. He took an independent initiative in publishing *Just Peacemaking: Transforming Initiatives of Justice and Peace*, which identifies eight biblical steps and seven promising public practices of peacemaking.[22] Importantly, his first draft emerged as he tuned his religious concepts to address the conditions leading to war and sought to understand pragmatic (if partial) practices that had sometimes worked to make peace, resolve conflict, and prevent violence in the world. Soon a conversation coalesced around twenty-three scholars who spent about five years building rapport and consensus, producing a *Just Peacemaking* volume to serve as "the new paradigm for the ethics of peace and war."[23] Rather than focusing solely on the extent to which Christians can justifiably be involved in the practice of war, just peacemaking addresses the question of what Christians can do to promote the peace of their world.

One of Stassen's most cherished examples of the power of just peacemaking practices is what has been called the "Revolution of the Candles." In the opening chapter of his book on just peacemaking, Stassen describes arriving in Berlin for a speaking tour on November 10, 1989, just as the Berlin Wall was opening.[24] His speaking engagements would be centered around peacemaking, which had become a regular theme of East German churches for ten days in November (the *Friedensdekade*). On the ground, tensions came to a head in the spring of 1989 "as a result of two key happenings—the rigged local elections on 7 May and the opening of the border between Hungary and Austria during the summer."[25] From this point on, church leaders took increasingly

---

[22]Glen H. Stassen, *Just Peacemaking: Transforming Initiatives of Justice and Peace* (Louisville, KY: Westminster John Knox, 1992).

[23]Glen H. Stassen, ed., *Just Peacemaking: The New Paradigm for the Ethics of Peace and War*, new ed. (Cleveland: Pilgrim Press, 2008).

[24]Stassen, *Just Peacemaking: Transforming Initiatives*, 22.

[25]Richard V. Pierard, "Religion and the East German Revolution," *Journal of Church and State* 32, no. 3 (Summer 1990): 502. For more on this story, see the firsthand accounts in Jörg Swoboda,

bold, public stands against Erich Honecker's regime and demanded reforms. In advance of his trip, Stassen was told, "The church context influenced the demonstrations to be disciplined and nonviolent. They preached nonviolence, prayed for nonviolence, urged nonviolence on the authorities, and strategized nonviolent action without pause."[26] As Richard V. Pierard tells the story,

> Prayer vigils and memorial services took place in churches across the country.... At the close of the services, particularly on Monday evenings, the assembled crowds would sing "Dona Nobis Pacem" ["Grant Us Peace"] and take to the streets carrying lighted candles. From week to week their numbers grew.[27]

Despite these efforts, police responded with force at some demonstrations. Things began to look different in Leipzig on Monday, October 9, when the evening prayers for peace at seven churches spilled into the streets, and the crowds grew to some sixty thousand people. Though Honecker had issued an order for "a Chinese solution" (in reference to the Tiananmen Square Massacre a few months prior), local leaders—perhaps at the direction of Egon Krenz—did not carry it out. The next week, the number of protestors more than doubled and Honecker was forced out of office, replaced by Krenz. A week later the numbers more than doubled again, and "with amazing rapidity other members of the old guard were ousted and a whirlwind of reforms followed, the most dramatic being the opening border with West Berlin and West Germany on 9 November."[28]

In response to concrete changes that were adversely affecting the situation on the ground, church leaders drew on their inherited resources to generate creative new strategies that drew others into nonviolent

---

The Revolution of the Candles: Christians in the Revolution of the German Democratic Republic, ed. Richard V. Pierard, trans. Edwin P. Arnold (Macon, GA: Mercer University Press, 1996).
[26]Stassen, *Just Peacemaking: Transforming Initiatives*, 23.
[27]Pierard, "Religion," 503.
[28]Pierard, "Religion," 504.

direct action for reform. They could not have possibly foreseen the positive outcome; in fact, it stands to reason that many were bracing for increasing bloodshed in response to even nonviolent demonstration. However, their faith resources gave them confidence that God was working to transform their situation, hearing their prayers for peace, and working toward that end. In the face of challenges that strain our idealist pictures of the world at the point of how we might faithfully exercise our responsibility to God and for others, just peacemaking (especially as Stassen originally developed it) sheds light on some creative pathways for making a positive impact.

Just peacemaking is offered as a "research program" to be tested in its interpretation of specific conflicts, focusing on responsiveness to unfolding concrete realities rather than idealist generalizations.[29] In its most recent iteration, the just peacemaking paradigm mobilizes the resources of faith to respond without grand, worldview-level rethinking. Stassen continuously spread the good news about the ten effective practices of just peacemaking and cultivated a coalition of Christian scholars to support that ethic from within their own theological and ethical frameworks. Perhaps more significantly, Stassen and key allies worked with an interfaith group of scholars to deploy their own religious traditions to support this new paradigm. As a multiworldview vision bloomed through an ongoing conversation among about thirty scholars representing the Abrahamic faiths (Judaism, Christianity, and Islam), project leaders further clarified the research program aspect of just peacemaking: "Certainly, in the future the Just Peacemaking paradigm may shift to address additional topics and grapple more completely with the richness and complexity of our scriptures and religious practices."[30] This

---

[29]On this use of "research program," see Stassen's discussion of Nancey C. Murphy, Imre Lakatos, and Alasdair MacIntyre in *A Thicker Jesus* (Louisville, KY: Westminster John Knox, 2012), chap. 4.

[30]Susan Brooks Thistlethwaite, ed., *Interfaith Just Peacemaking: Jewish, Christian, and Muslim Perspectives on the New Paradigm of Peace and War* (New York: Palgrave Macmillan, 2011), 6.

set of best practices offers sites for reconsidering how one's own faith commitments might respond while promoting goodwill and commerce among all.

RENEWING AGENCY AND COMMERCE FOR THE FUTURE

Many Christians think of God as primarily concerned about the big picture, possessed by an ideal vision and whether or not humans remain blameless in light of it. In a world framed by both idealism and concreteness, the threat of giving ground to one side in order to benefit the other is ever-present and generates a great deal of heartburn. Will my sense of everyday responsibility require me to part with my ideals at some point? Will my idealist vision of the world prevent me from being as engaged as I might otherwise be? I submit that our increasingly comprehensive pictures of how everything in the world should work are only as good as the life they enable us to live, the sense of responsibility they generate within us as we engage the unpredictable and accidental circumstances that make up life. Faithfulness in the unfolding (hi)story of God's communion with creation means avoiding the Charybdis of blinding ourselves to the global realities of our time without foundering on the Scylla of allowing our attention to big-picture ideals and realities to sap energy away from actually acting on what is nearest at hand.

I do not mean to reinforce the sense that Christians are primarily living within the "Western world" rather than the kingdom of God, as sometimes argued by voices on the pacifist end of the spectrum.[31] Rather, I am advocating an ethic of everyday faithfulness that frees Christians to be agents of the kingdom of God who nurture its mustard seeds wherever they find them growing. Christian ethics is about

---

[31]See for example Myles Werntz's argument against the just peacemaking paradigm in "War in Christ's World: Bonhoeffer and Just Peacemaking on War and Christology," *Dialog* 50, no. 1 (Spring 2011): 90-96.

creatively working with what the world throws at us with a living faith and a sometimes incompetent inherited tradition that functions more like a set of precedents than a detailed prescription. And concrete action, even if undertheorized, provides the basis for solidarity and commerce with others across time and space. If we struggle for justice here, we will more easily see how others are engaged in analogous struggles elsewhere (and more committed to joining in their responses).[32] Our social change efforts are best served by our practical efforts at a local level, which may become analogs in interactions with others who are seeking change for their locales as well. We simply do not need to be on the same page in terms of worldview first, and if that is where we direct our first efforts, the apocalyptists may be on target.

Jesus calls each disciple to follow after him in a genuine relationship of growth and in the grace that makes relationships possible in the first place. So a Christian view of social change hinges not on transforming the world on the basis of a full-orbed, ideal Christian worldview. Rather, social change understood as the fruit of everyday faithfulness is about a community relearning its place in the overall economy of things in the God-created world and drawing others into full-orbed commerce—if not full communion. Even in Christian iterations of just war theory, after a conflict subsides, most human beings at risk on the "other" side will (hopefully) be rehabilitated and restored to community. So, if human beings are designed to live in commerce with God, each other, and all of creation—before ever being tasked with transforming the world into the form of a principled biblical worldview—then how can we reconceive the material we have inherited so that it enables us to live creatively and faithfully in the tension with other creatures? From Jenkins and Stassen, we learn that each person becomes responsible at each point of

---

[32]In this way of thinking, I have learned from Michael Walzer's little book *Thick and Thin: Moral Argument at Home and Abroad* (Notre Dame, IN: University of Notre Dame Press, 1994).

contact with the world they live in—creatures, places, and things. In this dynamic, we grow and learn over time; even our view of the world changes over time as we encounter others and see things from their vantage. And because we risk living faithfully in a world of ambiguity, we remain open to God's Spirit so that we might continuously seek repentance and forgiveness when we discover that we have made mistakes in our thinking and our living—like the Christian watermen of Tangier Island.

ENVIRONMENTAL VIOLENCE

Kathy Khang

My immigrant parents are the environmental activists I didn't know mattered. They were my first teachers and mentors in many aspects of my spiritual life and development. They taught me and continue to model a kindness to the earth and an understanding of stewardship and creation care I still wrestle with. They reused and recycled before there were special bins and labels because it was a manner and matter of survival. When you are poor and a stranger in a strange land everything is a luxury and necessity truly is the mother of invention.

The ugly broken lamp currently in my bedroom was picked up out of the trash sometime in the early 1970s by the building super, fixed, and then given to my parents, who could not afford to buy a new lamp. That lamp came with me to my first apartment because even though I could afford a new lamp my parents had instilled a strong value for reusing items that still had function. I've seen the same lamp at vintage shops selling for more than $30, and I have kept it in hopes of rewiring it. What once was garbage is now considered a vintage find with a price tag.

Uncooked food left over at the end of the day at the restaurant where my father worked as a busboy would be brought home to eat as a special late-night meal, an indulgence for them, and that habit remains as they bring home all the leftovers, whether from a restaurant or dinner at my house. I have packets of ketchup, a collection of mismatched plastic utensils, and glass jars (that once held strawberry jam) holding the abundance of soy sauce poured out of the plastic packets—all from carryout meals. Bacon fat is saved for fried rice made of the leftover rice. No glue? Use a grain or two of cooked rice. Anything and everything can be saved and used and maybe reused, and they are not ashamed or worried at any possible stigma their behavior may impart. You do not waste what God has given.

The first two chapters of Genesis paint an image of the Creator delighting in the beauty of creation of the earth and sky, land and earth, creatures to inhabit and multiply on and in land, sky, and water. God creates the land and separates the sky and water, and "God saw how good it was" (Gen 1:10 CEB). Creation repeatedly is described as "good," a reminder that creation is and should be good. But is the creation of garbage, waste that will sit on or in the land and water, good? No. Is the creation of pollution that lingers in the air and can lead to disease good? No. That kind of creation, that which perpetuates a system of disease and death and a cycle of consumerism, is violence that actually destroys what God sees as good.

The creation of garbage isn't something I have considered as violent until recently. Violence instead has involved weapons and war, most often between people, whether individuals engaging in gun violence or entire countries going to war. I thought of violence as not only the act but also the intent to harm or destroy. My purchasing several pounds of chicken breast on a slab of Styrofoam is not based on an intent to harm. I just need to feed my family. But the industrial farms producing this relatively affordable chicken for the masses destroy and harm much. Chickens are raised in inhumane conditions and are bred and raised to be ready for slaughter at the fastest rate possible, risking disease.[1] This produces the convenient skinless chicken breast at $1.89 per pound wrapped completely in unrecyclable materials, transported across the country in refrigerated trucks. The cycle is overwhelming, and assuming it's void of intent to destroy, it is doing exactly that.

The other night we were enjoying a night with friends and ordered from a local restaurant to feed more than a dozen of us. It wasn't just the convenience of having the food of our choice made to our liking and delivered to where we were that made me consider the impact on the earth. It was as we were cleaning up, throwing away containers that could not be recycled or reused, that I stopped and took notice. Even as the conversation filled my soul I could not stop thinking about the bags of garbage our group had produced in the name of fellowship. We did not intend to destroy anything. Our intent was to enjoy an evening of adult conversation and good company among friends, not to inflict violence on one another or the earth. But we did.

Violence against creation is something I don't have to think about, much like violence against Black and Brown siblings, Black and Brown bodies. Violence against creation is a step removed from my daily existence as a Korean American woman living in a four-bedroom home in the suburbs. I can opt in and out because of my social location. I have options that most of the world does not. We in the Western world all have options most of the world does not—multiple modes of transportation varying in convenience, cost, and so on. If we are thirsty, we have the options of looking for a water fountain, drinking tap or well water, going to our refrigerator where a dispenser provides filtered water, pouring from a filtered pitcher, or even grabbing a recyclable but single-use plastic bottle. Often the level of convenience is what drives the

---

[1] Annie Lowrey, "The Human Cost of Chicken Farming," *The Atlantic,* November 11, 2019, www.theatlantic.com/ideas/archive/2019/11/human-cost-chicken-farming/601687.

violence and impact further and further away from the daily lives of those of us who most benefit. I often think about my friend and former colleague Sandra Van Opstal taking college students to live near the garbage slums of Cairo. There they lived with the consequences as part of their lives, but here my garbage wrapped in a plastic bag gets put out into a plastic garbage can completely out of sight and out of mind until there is another bag of trash to take out. Bottled water, fast fashion, single-serving convenience food, disposable diapers for infants and adults, and out-of-season produce all improve a facet of life, but there is little to remind us daily what those conveniences are costing us in the longer run even as we are reminded that clean water is not a given for everyone. For many of us it again is a matter of convenience.

Recently we went from having four to two people living full-time in our home. We recycle everything we can and compost produce scraps in the back yard. We have two rain barrels and a small vegetable and herb garden. I am conscious of what I buy and what it's packaged in. Back-to-college shopping included trips to resale and rummage shops. We have managed to reduce our garbage production so much that we do not have enough garbage to justify a weekly garbage pickup—even when five of us were living here. Our recycling bin often overflows, but even that is a sign that our consumption might be too high if we are still producing that much packaging waste that may or may not actually be recycled.

Even as the truck picks up our weekly recyclables, they are taken out of sight and therefore out of mind. I don't see a mound of garbage or even a facility sorting what can and cannot be returned to the consumer cycle. Many of us reading this book will never live near one of the more than three thousand active landfills in the United States, nor do we consider the global impact of countries like the United States and the UK exporting their trash.² ³ Garbage—more specifically, the elimination of waste—has become a global industry, with developing and underdeveloped countries and their residents most impacted by the pollution produced. The residents of the garbage slums of Cairo and other locations are our siblings in Christ. The creatures affected by our garbage are God's creation. Just the other day I saw a story about a dead whale washing ashore with a stomach full of plastic, and a Google search will show that this is not a rare event. My convenience is costing the lives of animals.⁴

As Christians we talk about being created in God's image, invited into the work of caring for and stewarding the earth too often without concrete suggestions, even in the context of our Sunday worship services. How does the convenience of disposable plastic communion cups impact the environment even as we reflect on how the bread and wine or juice compels us to consider how Christ's body was broken and his blood was shed for us? How are we, in the very act of remembrance, hurting the earth? Our fellowship meals often are full of plastic utensils, plastic cups, and Styrofoam plates; our church cafés use coffee cups covered in plastic lids to protect the sanctuary floor. VBS curricula packages sell craft kits, plastic banners to make sure the surrounding neighborhood knows the details.

A church we attended for years held an annual food fight as a youth group activity. Yes, kids would bring food to throw at each other. I sent my kids one year and then had a conversation with a youth leader about the tradition. The same church held a weekly midweek meal,

---

²"Summary," Zero Waste, www.zerowasteamerica.org/landfills.htm, accessed November 13, 2021.
³Robert Frerck, "Where Does All That Garbage Go?" Blue Ocean Network, blueocean.net/where-does-all-that-garbage-go, accessed November 13, 2021.
⁴Gianluca Mezzofiore, "Young Sperm Whale Found Dead in Sicily with Stomach Full of Plastic," CNN, May 20, 2019, www.cnn.com/2019/05/20/europe/sperm-whale-sicily-plastic-stomach-intl-scli/index.html.

which was a lifeline that provided a communal meal. Another church family noticed how many paper plates and napkins and plastic cups and utensils were being used in a single evening, estimated the cost benefit of purchasing bulk plates, cups, and utensils, and eventually the switch was made, setting off conversations about our own family practices.

The global Covid-19 pandemic posed an interesting opportunity and challenge to churches to reconsider not only how to preach the gospel virtually, but also what resources were necessary in doing church when being together in a physical building was out of the equation. We questioned the very definition of "church" if we couldn't be together in a building that required water and electricity (again, social location plays into this, because these are not assumed requirements elsewhere in the global church, but they most certainly are in most Western churches). What would it look like for local churches to take an audit of how and when their buildings are in use and how those uses are a way to live out the gospel? How many fewer copies of bulletins need to be printed, and could those that are printed be made accessible for those with visual impairments? Or is there another way to communicate the flow of service and the announcements? Musical worship presents its own challenges, depending on the technical and production resources—will worship leaders use this upending as an opportunity to also evaluate energy usage or discern whether new equipment is a true need or a desire?

Some churches are open campuses, multiuse rooms that double as preschools, youth centers, soup kitchens, evening housing for those experiencing homelessness, meeting space for various community groups. While my family was on vacation, we walked past a church on our way to a hike. The church parking lot was gated, and the signage made it clear that trespassers were unwelcome. As society returns to a new normal, how will churches better steward their physical spaces in partnership with the community or even other churches to be more welcoming? What are new ways to steward a building or even a parking lot so that other local needs might be met instead of building another building or covering another lot with asphalt?

How do our worship and physical church space inflict violence against the very earth we were meant to steward?

I never heard Sunday school teachers or pastors teach about stewarding the earth in the same way we were taught to steward our money or our talents and abilities. In fact, when we look at the way many local churches operate, it is not with the mindset of stewarding the earth but rather approaching the earth as a vending machine by which God provides for our personal needs. More and more I am unnerved and bothered by what my convenience costs others.

The violence is a cycle. The violence we inflict on the earth comes back to harm us. Whales dying with bellies full of plastic may not feel that close to home, but consider the convenience (and luxury) of drinking a cold bottle of water that breaks down into microplastics—microscopic pieces of plastic that never naturally degrade—which have in turn shown up in drinking water.[5] Pesticides and antibiotics used in factory farming seep into water supplies and into the very food that is produced, impacting public health. Dependence on fossil fuels continues to contribute to global climate change. Wildfires around the world are being triggered by historic heatwaves, causing untold damage even in uninhabited places.

Recently, scientists tracked a wildfire in Siberia: "According to CAMS data, wildfires in Siberia emitted since June more than 188 megatonnes of carbon, which is equivalent to about 505 megatonnes of carbon

---

[5]"The Dangers of Microplastics in Drinking Water," Multipure, March 2020, www.multipure.com/purely-social/science/dangers-microplastics-drinking-water.

dioxide. In comparison, Europe's biggest polluter Germany emitted 750 megatonnes carbon dioxide in the entire year 2018."[6]

Violence begets violence.

Too often, Western Christianity and specifically US evangelicalism want to feign nonpolitical stances on everything except abortion and prayer in schools. The reality is that the Western church benefits from politics, specific public policy and tax laws that allow religious exemptions. Here in the United States our tithes are tax-deductible. Religious institutions are actively involved in shaping public policy for their interests. What would be the impact if efforts to stop legal abortion were matched in money, energy, and theological framework for the care and restoration of creation? What would it look like if Christians were the loudest and most ardent supporters of breaking dependence on oil, fast fashion, and overall immediate gratification and convenience? What would it look like for local churches and entire denominations to examine how their own systems—including budgets and annual meetings—could be reoriented to care for the whole of creation instead of centering individual convenience?

Through the years I've slowly, very slowly, been urged, nudged, and sometimes forced to consider how my many choices make an impact in the world, the community, my family, my soul.

Lights off. Buying less. Set the thermostat. Some of it is habit. Dad always, always reminded us to turn the lights off and the water off and the AC off and the heat off when possible.

If you're not in the room it doesn't need a light.

If you're brushing your teeth you aren't cleaning the sink. Turn off the water.

---

[6]Tereza Pultarova, "The Devastating Wildfires of 2021 Are Breaking Records and Satellites Are Tracking It All," Space.com, August 11, 2021, www.space.com/2021-record-wildfire-season-from-space.

If you can put on an extra sweater or a pair of slippers you don't need to turn on the heat quite yet.

Can the hole in your shirt/sweater/socks be mended or patched up?

It has made me consider how I am connected to the earth in a physical and spiritual way. I am not a formless soul floating and flitting about. I am embodied, living and breathing in contact and relationship with the earth and others. I do not believe the earth has a soul in the way you and I have a soul, but I believe that the earth and I are formed and created by the same God. We are connected to one another and to this earth through our Creator, and the whole of creation does cry out. Out my window I can see some of the earth's cries in shades of green, brown, white, yellow, pink, red, blue, and purple ,while some of it is in pollution, animals and fauna threatened by the same.[7]

It matters because every week as the church we pray,

> Our Father in heaven,
> > hallowed be your name.
> > Your kingdom come.
> > Your will be done,
> > > on earth as it is in heaven. (Mt 6:8-10)

May our actions be not in response to cultural and social trends but to my God, doing no undue harm to the earth. May God's kingdom have a chance to be here on earth because God's people cared for the earth as much as we care about a ticket to heaven. Amen.

---

[7]Kathy Khang, "Earth Day 2010: Does Going Green Matter?" Kathy Khang, April 21, 2010, www.kathykhang.com/2010/04/21/earth-day-2010-does-going-green-matter.

CONCLUSION

PRACTICAL STEPS TOWARD COMMUNAL FLOURISHING

Shawn Graves and Marlena Graves

IN THIS VOLUME we have the perspectives of those who have worked to cultivate the beloved community where one may find true communal flourishing, even in this beautiful world plagued with violence.

Perhaps as a result of our engagement with the ideas found in this collection we have a newfound, renewed, or invigorated commitment to working out the gospel of peace in this violent world. We'll conclude by identifying some strategies we might implement in our individual and collective lives to realize shalom, that gospel-shaped positive peace. No doubt there are more strategies; some are sprinkled throughout the essays in this volume. Whichever nonviolent peacemaking strategy we seek to implement, intellectual and moral sensitivity to the details of the relevant context—conjoined with courage and humility—is crucial in determining our particular way forward.

Conclusion

1. ADDRESS THE UNDERLYING FACTORS PERPETUATING VIOLENCE

It does no good to perpetually treat the symptoms while ignoring the disease itself. It's reasonable to think that violence is a tragic symptom of a network of deeper, underlying conditions. As the World Health Organization (WHO) notes, "No single factor explains why some individuals behave violently toward others or why violence is more prevalent in some communities than in others. Violence is the result of the complex interplay of individual, relationship, social, cultural and environmental factors."[1] Consequently, any strategy directed toward reducing and preventing violence will include attempts to address these factors. WHO identifies some of the larger societal factors contributing to violence:

- Cultural norms that support violence as an acceptable way to resolve conflicts
- Attitudes that regard suicide as a matter of individual choice instead of a preventable act of violence
- Norms that give priority to parental rights over child welfare
- Norms that entrench male dominance over women and children
- Norms that support the use of excessive force by police against citizens
- Norms that support political conflict

Other factors include health, educational, economic, and social policies that maintain high levels of economic or social inequality between groups in society.[2]

Elsewhere, WHO claims, "Violence of all types is strongly associated with social determinants such as weak governance; poor rule of law; cultural, social and gender norms; unemployment; income and gender inequality;

---

[1] Etienne G. Krug et al., eds., *World Report on Violence and Health* (Geneva: World Health Organization, 2002), 12.
[2] Krug, *World Report on Violence*, 13.

rapid social change; and limited educational opportunities."³ Christians seeking to cultivate positive peace locally, nationally, and internationally may intelligently and sensitively direct their energies, resources, and talents toward projects aimed at addressing such underlying factors. In addition, Christians should seek to identify where in their communities, particularly their Christian communities, these factors may be found. For example, Christians might consider how their churches further entrench male dominance over women and children through patriarchal teachings and practices and how their emphasis on, and celebration of, the military may reinforce cultural norms that support violence as a way to resolve conflict.

2. INVEST RESOURCES IN NONVIOLENT CAMPAIGNS

Nonviolent campaigns and organizations need funders for operating costs and the support of volunteers to organize and sustain initiatives. We ought to financially support these organizations and campaigns and consider how we might dedicate our time to a worthy cause.

3. RESIST CHRISTIAN NATIONALISM

According to Paul Miller, "Christian nationalism is the belief that the American nation is defined by Christianity, and that the government should take active steps to keep it that way."⁴ Or, as Samuel Perry and Andrew Whitehead put it, Christian nationalism is *"an ideology that idealizes and advocates a fusion of Christianity* with American civic belonging and participation."*⁵ As indicated by the asterisk, they note that "Christianity" here refers to:

---

³"Global Status Report on Violence Prevention 2014: Executive Summary," World Health Organization, December 9, 2014, www.who.int/publications/i/item/WHO-NMH-NVI-14.2.
⁴Paul D. Miller, "What Is Christian Nationalism?" *Christianity Today,* February 3, 2021, www.christianitytoday.com/ct/2021/february-web-only/what-is-christian-nationalism.html.
⁵Samuel L. Perry and Andrew L. Whitehead, "Christian Nationalism Talks Religion, but Walks Fascism," *Religion in Public* (blog), February 5, 2020, religioninpublic.blog/2020/02/05/christian-nationalism-talks-religion-but-walks-fascism.

something far beyond (and we believe altogether different from) mere orthodoxy. "Christian" in this sense represents more of an ethno-cultural and political identity that denotes a specific constellation of religious affiliation (evangelical Protestant), cultural values (conservative), race (White), and nationality (America-born citizen).[6]

Of course, this phenomenon is not unique to our contemporary circumstances. There's good reason Malcolm X observed,

> The whole church structure in this country is white nationalism, you go inside a white church—that's what they preaching, white nationalism. They got Jesus white, Mary white, God white, everybody white—that's white nationalism.[7]

As such, Christian nationalism marks clear boundaries of who's properly regarded as an American and licenses a particular political agenda authorizing doctrines and policies of exclusion.

In addition, Christian nationalists, viewing the United States as a Christian nation, see the United States as God's special vessel for accomplishing God's purposes in the world. This has the effect of baptizing American foreign policy, including its extensive military operations, occupations, and campaigns, as the execution of God's will in the world.

Christian nationalism is an idolatrous conflation of one's nation with the kingdom of God, of members sharing their own ethnocultural and political identity with the true citizens of the kingdom of God and one's beloved political agenda with the way of the kingdom of God. Miller states,

> Christian nationalism takes the name of Christ for a worldly political agenda, proclaiming that its program is *the* political program for every true believer.... It is taking the name of Christ as a fig leaf to cover its

---

[6]Perry and Whitehead, "Christian Nationalism."
[7]Malcolm X, "The Ballot or the Bullet," American RadioWorks, American Public Media, April 12, 1964, americanradioworks.publicradio.org/features/blackspeech/mx.html.

political program, treating the message of Jesus as a tool of political propaganda and the church as the handmaiden and cheerleader of the state.[8]

This ought to be worrisome for anyone seeking to set aside violence, exclusion, and conflict in an effort to cultivate positive peace in this world.

4. PRACTICE SKEPTICAL PACIFISM AND TRANSFORMATIONAL PACIFISM

Skeptical pacifism presses the following questions: How will we ever know that violence is truly necessary? How will we ever know that we have exhausted all nonviolent ways of addressing the conflict? In addition, skeptical pacifism involves adopting a skeptical posture toward governments' attempts to justify war and violence to their own citizens and the broader international community. According to Andrew Fiala,

> In this approach, skepticism . . . is based upon the fact that citizens have no good reason to trust that their governments are telling them the truth about war and its justification. This skepticism is derived from historical judgments about the tendency of governments to manipulate information in order to provoke the citizenry toward war.[9]

As one might anticipate, transformational pacifism is directed toward reforming and rehabilitating culture in such a way that resorting to violence, particularly as a first or early strategy, becomes unthinkable. Fiala describes it as follows:

> Transformational pacifism is understood as aiming at a transformation of psychological, cultural, social, and moral sensibility away from acceptance of violence and war. Transformational pacifism articulates a broad framework of cultural criticism and includes an effort to reform educational and cultural practices that tend to support violence and war. The

---

[8]Miller, "What Is Christian Nationalism?"
[9]Andrew Fiala, "Pacifism," Stanford Encyclopedia of Philosophy, September 15, 2018, plato.stanford.edu/entries/pacifism.

goal of transformational pacifism is a world in which war and violence appear to be archaic remnants of less civilized past.[10]

Just as we might hope that we have put gladiatorial violence behind us culturally, regarding it as barbaric, so a transformational pacifist hopes that all forms of violence go the way of gladiatorial combat.

5. CELEBRATE AND REMEMBER ICONS OF PEACE

Many communities, including many Christian communities, have made a habit of celebrating and remembering veterans of various wars throughout history. Christians should consider celebrating and remembering icons of peace—those who have worked tirelessly, creatively, and nonviolently to bring about shalom in their particular context.[11] By doing so we normalize and valorize the way of nonviolence in our communities. We expand the cultural imagination, prompting people to go beyond the usual, and dominant, violent methods to resolve conflict.[12]

6. LEARN FROM, ELEVATE THE PLATFORMS OF, AND SUPPORT—IN WHATEVER WAY SOLICITED— HISTORICALLY MARGINALIZED AND SILENCED PEOPLE

Who is in our orbit? Does it consist mostly of White men? White male authors? White male speakers? White male scholars? White businessmen? In America, the ruling class consisting of White men has extracted labor and wealth from people of color and the poor for their advantage. This reality goes unnoticed by the majority of people. Thus we must intentionally elevate the platforms of people of color, women,

---

[10] Fiala, "Pacifism."
[11] One can find some examples throughout Jim Forest's *Loving Our Enemies: Reflections on the Hardest Commandment* (Maryknoll, NY: Orbis, 2014). Of course, many other examples can be found elsewhere.
[12] Fiala writes, "Indeed, it may be argued that to resort to violence is to admit to a failure of imagination and to give up hope that more humane forms of problem solving and conflict resolution can be effective." "Pacifism."

and other historically marginalized and silenced groups who have deep wisdom, knowledge, and understanding that White men do not have. We ought to financially support their endeavors. It will not happen on its own. As Martin Luther King Jr. observed, "We know through painful experience that freedom is never voluntarily given by the oppressor; it must be demanded by the oppressed."[13]

Put differently, those in power and possessing privilege rarely give up the two. Christians, however, are to be different. We should lead the way in uplifting, celebrating, and supporting—this is the commandment of Scripture though not the way of the world. So we ought to intentionally bring in conference and retreat speakers of color, let the marginalized and oppressed speak for themselves—and not speak for them. We ought to support their businesses and books and ministries. One might see it as doing a favor for others, but the reality is that it is a joyful work of justice, a way of practicing the beloved community. And in so doing, we are doing a favor for our impoverished selves while we pursue justice and cultivate shalom.

7. INSIST ON TELLING THE TRUTH

Rejecting the Christian nationalist's mythmaking about the United States and its history and trajectory, Christians committed to a nonviolent movement toward positive peace will insist on telling the truth, confronting squarely and soberly both history and the current moment. Bryan Stevenson notes,

> We have committed ourselves in this country to silence about our history, to ignorance about our history, to denying our history. And that's the first part of this relationship that has to be repaired. We've got to be willing

---

[13]Martin Luther King Jr., "Letter from a Birmingham Jail," International Education and Global Engagement, California State University Chico, August 1963, www.csuchico.edu/iege/_assets/documents/susi-letter-from-birmingham-jail.pdf.

> now to talk honestly about who we are and how we got here.... So I believe it's important for anyone who identifies as an American, as a citizen of this country, to not simply embrace all the things about American history that we think are glorious and wonderful, but to also acknowledge and accept the things about our history that are tragic and devastating.[14]

Without truth, there is no reconciliation. Without truth, there is no reasonable hope for cultivating shalom. Stevenson adds,

> I think every entity, every institution has to commit to this process of truth-telling. I think it's really important that people understand that if you're genuinely engaged and recovering from human rights abuses, you have to commit to truth-telling first. You can't jump to reconciliation. You can't jump to reparation or restoration until you tell the truth. Until you know the nature of the injuries, you can't actually speak to the kind of remedies that are going to be necessary.[15]

Individual Christians and Christian communities ought to insist on—and practice—telling the truth in seeking reconciliation and redemption. As Ida B. Wells claimed, "The way to right wrongs is to turn the light of truth upon them."[16] Truth telling is essential to the pursuit of positive peace.

8. RECOGNIZE THAT THE NONVIOLENT PURSUIT OF POSITIVE PEACE IS DISRUPTIVE TO SYSTEMS AND STRUCTURES WITH THE POTENTIAL TO UPEND ENORMOUSLY PROFITABLE INDUSTRIES

One can anticipate that there will be resistance. Government leaders, titans of industry, corporate executives, local employers, colleagues, and

---

[14]Bryan Stevenson as interviewed by Ezra Klein, "Bryan Stevenson on How America Can Heal," Vox, July 20, 2020, www.vox.com/21327742/bryan-stevenson-the-ezra-klein-show-america-slavery-healing-racism-george-floyd-protests.

[15]Stevenson and Klein, "Bryan Stevenson."

[16]Ida B. Wells, "Southern Mob Rule" (lecture delivered at Metropolitan AME Church October 31, 1892, in Washington, DC); see chroniclingamerica.loc.gov/lccn/sn84025891/1892-10-22/ed-1/seq-3.

neighbors will push back. They will try to take down resisters. There may be job loss or smears to one's reputation. They will say it can't be done, that it's not practical to upend these violent and unjust institutions and industries, systems, and structures—the same way oppressors claimed that ending enslavement and the slave trade would prove to be devastatingly impractical because it would tank the economy. Plan and resist, and do so with the support of the beloved community.

9. ACKNOWLEDGE THAT NONVIOLENT RESISTANCE MAY APPEAR TO BE A POSITION RESERVED FOR THE PRIVILEGED OR A PLOY USED BY THE POWERFUL TO PRESERVE THE STATUS QUO

Threats to one's job, family, health, or reputation aren't as easily confronted when one is especially vulnerable, when one is economically insecure, exposed, without reasonable access to protection and health care, and without stable social grounding or rootedness. This needs to be acknowledged and taken very seriously indeed.

In addition, it ought to be acknowledged that urging nonviolent resistance can be—and has been—regarded as a sinister way for the powerful and violent oppressor to pacify the oppressed and preserve the status quo. It's worth considering Malcolm X's response in 1963 to Louis Lomax's question: "Reverend Martin Luther King teaches a doctrine of nonviolence. What is your attitude toward this philosophy?" Here's how Malcolm X replied:

> The white man supports Reverend Martin Luther King, subsidizes Reverend Martin Luther King, so that Reverend Martin Luther King can continue to teach the Negroes to be defenseless—that's what you mean by nonviolent—be defenseless in the face of one of the most cruel beasts that has ever taken people into captivity—that's this American white man, and they have proved it throughout the country by the police dogs and the police clubs. A hundred years ago they used to put on a white sheet

and use a bloodhound against Negroes. Today they have taken off the white sheet and put on police uniforms and traded in the bloodhounds for police dogs, and they're still doing the same thing. Just as Uncle Tom, back during slavery used to keep the Negroes from resisting the bloodhound or resisting the Ku Klux Klan by teaching them to love their enemies or pray for those who use them despitefully, today Martin Luther King is just a twentieth-century or modern Uncle Tom or religious Uncle Tom, who is doing the same thing today to keep Negroes defenseless in the face of attack that Uncle Tom did on the plantation to keep *those* Negroes defenseless in the face of the attack of the Klan in that day.[17]

Malcom X continues:

Now the goal of Dr. Martin Luther King is to give Negroes a chance to sit in a segregated restaurant beside the same white man who has brutalized them for four hundred years. The goal of Martin Luther King is to get the Negroes to forgive the people the people who have brutalized them for four hundred years, by lulling them to sleep and making them forget what those whites have done to them, but the masses of black people today don't go for what Martin Luther King is putting down.[18]

These are powerful and weighty words that ought to be reckoned with by anyone, White Christians in particular, who insists on nonviolence.

10. BE AWARE OF THE TENDENCY TO CONFUSE OUR CULTURALLY INFORMED INTERPRETATION OF SCRIPTURE WITH SCRIPTURE ITSELF

Christopher Hall notes,

North American evangelicals read the Bible—and the world—through Western eyes. Indeed, all human beings come to the Bible with cultural

---

[17] Malcolm X, "A Summing Up: Louis Lomax Interviews Malcolm X," Teaching American History, 1963, teachingamericanhistory.org/library/document/a-summing-up-louis-lomax-interviews-malcolm-x.
[18] Malcolm X, "A Summing Up."

habits, deeply ingrained patterns of interpreting the world that inevitably shape—and sometimes warp—our interpretation and understanding of Scripture.[19]

He rightly adds, "This insight is now commonplace in discussions about biblical interpretation in popular and academic circles."[20] Christian resistance to nonviolent pursuits of positive peace may stem from interpretations of Scripture that are born and raised in a culture that is captive to violence and militarism.

We are personally aware of an administrator at a conservative evangelical Christian university who insisted that affirming nonviolence amounted to a straight denial of the authority of Scripture. Apparently, he couldn't entertain the idea that it was his interpretation of Scripture, not Scripture itself, that was being challenged. He's not alone; many American Christians in particular confidently assume their interpretation of Scripture is completely consonant with its original intended meaning. As Hall notes, no one is immune to this. But learning history, including global church history, and engaging in sustained conversations with Christians in different streams of Christianity, particularly historically marginalized and oppressed Christians—those "with their backs constantly against the wall. . . . the poor, the disinherited, the dispossessed"[21]—will help with myopic interpretations of Christianity.

As noted above, there are more strategies one might employ to promote and cultivate nonviolently the beloved community; some can be found or developed by engaging in slow conversation with the essays in this volume, and others can be found elsewhere. Of course, it's

---

[19]Christopher Hall, "How Does Culture Affect the Way We Understand Scripture?" *Christianity Today*, April 21, 2015, www.christianitytoday.com/biblestudies/bible-answers/theology/how-does-culture-affect-way-we-understand-scripture.html.
[20]Hall, "How Does Culture."
[21]See Howard Thurman's *Jesus and the Disinherited* (Boston: Beacon, 1976), 13.

Conclusion

unreasonable to think that a single approach or strategy is fitting for all sets of circumstances. This is why it's important to recall that as we proceed, we need a virtuous attitude and approach along with careful, intelligent attention to the details of our specific contexts.

"Do not be overcome by evil, but overcome evil with good" (Rom 12:21). In that same vein, we conclude this volume with these words from South African Nobel Peace Prize laureate and chair of South Africa's Truth and Reconciliation Project, Archbishop Desmond Tutu:

> Do your little bit of good where you are; it's those little bits of good that overwhelm the world.[22]

And:

> Evil, injustice, oppression, all of those awful things, they are not going to have the last word. Goodness, laughter, joy, caring, compassion, the things that you do and you help others do, those are going to prevail.[23]

---

[22]Desmond Tutu, "Ten Pieces of Wisdom from Desmond Tutu to Inspire Change Makers in 2016," Desmond Tutu Peace Foundation, January 3, 2016, www.tutufoundationusa.org/2016/01/03/ten-quotes-from-desmond-tutu-to-inspire-change-makers-in-2016.

[23]"Desmond Tutu: 'Caring and Compassion Will Prevail over Evil and Injustice,'" World Council of Churches, May 20, 2008, www.oikoumene.org/news/desmond-tutu-caring-and-compassion-will-prevail-over-evil-and-injustice.

LIST OF CONTRIBUTORS

Sarah Azaransky earned her PhD from the University of Virginia and is associate professor of social ethics at Union Theological Seminary in New York City. She is author of *The Dream Is Freedom: Pauli Murray and American Democratic Faith* and *This Worldwide Struggle: Religion and the International Roots of the Civil Rights Movement* and editor of *Religion and Politics in America's Borderlands*. Azaransky was the coauthor of the successful application for Pauli Murray's childhood home in Durham, North Carolina, to be named a National Historic Landmark.

Gregory A. Boyd earned his PhD from Princeton Theological Seminary and his MDiv from Yale Divinity School. He is senior pastor at Woodland Hills Church in Maplewood, Minnesota, serves as president of Reknew Ministries (reknew.org), and is an adjunct professor at Northern Seminary.

Mae Elise Cannon earned her PhD in history from the University of California, Davis, and a DMin in spiritual formation from Northern Theological Seminary. She is an ordained pastor in the Evangelical Covenant Church and the executive director of Churches for Middle East Peace. She is the author of several books, including the award-winning *Social Justice Handbook: Small Steps for a Better World* and the recent *Beyond Hashtag Activism: Comprehensive Justice in a Complicated Age*. Among other things, she has served as the senior director of advocacy and outreach for World Vision-US and as a consultant to Compassion International for child advocacy issues in the Middle East.

Jacob Alan Cook earned his PhD from Fuller Theological Seminary and is a postdoctoral fellow at Wake Forest University School of Divinity. He is the author of *Worldview Theory, Whiteness, and the Future of Evangelical Faith*. During his doctoral studies, Jake served as the associate director of Fuller's Just Peacemaking Initiative, and he has published chapters on Christian identity, peacemaking, and ecological theology.

List of Contributors

Elizabeth Gerhardt earned her ThD from Boston University and is professor of theology and social ethics at Northeastern Seminary in Rochester, New York. Gerhardt teaches in the areas of historical theology and social ethics. Academic writing and research interests include gender reconciliation, Bonhoeffer studies, and the intersection of spirituality, a theology of the cross, and social justice. Gerhardt is the author of *The Cross and Gendercide: A Theological Response to Global Violence against Women and Girls*.

Marlena Graves earned her MDiv from Northeastern Seminary in New York and is currently a PhD student in American culture studies at Bowling Green State University in Ohio. In addition to several other books, she is the author of *The Way Up Is Down: Finding Yourself by Forgetting Yourself*, which received *Christianity Today*'s Award of Merit in Spiritual Formation, and the award-winning *A Beautiful Disaster: Finding Hope in the Midst of Brokenness*. She is an adjunct professor at Winebrenner Seminary and is also a member of Ink: A Creative Collective.

Shawn Graves earned his PhD in philosophy from the University of Rochester in New York and currently serves as associate professor of philosophy at the University of Findlay in Ohio. He has published research articles in journals such as *Oxford Studies in Philosophy of Religion*, *Faith and Philosophy*, and *Sport, Ethics, and Philosophy*. He has also contributed chapters on Christianity and ethics to volumes published by Oxford University Press, Eerdmans, and Mercer University Press.

Ted Grimsrud earned his PhD in Christian ethics from the Graduate Theological Union in Berkeley, California, and is currently senior professor of peace theology at Eastern Mennonite University in Harrisonburg, Virginia. He began teaching there in 1996. Before that he pastored for ten years in various Mennonite congregations.

T. C. Ham earned his PhD from Dallas Theological Seminary and is professor of biblical studies at Malone University. His concentration in biblical studies is in the Hebrew Bible with a special interest in the Wisdom literature, particularly the book of Job. Born in South Korea and raised in a multicultural home, Ham finds matters related to culture and language fascinating. His research interests in biblical and theological studies focus on cultural and linguistic features of the Bible.

Lisa Sharon Harper earned her master's degree in human rights from Columbia University and is the founder and president of Freedom Road, a groundbreaking consulting group that crafts experiences that bring common understanding and common commitments that lead to common action toward a more just world. Harper is a public theologian whose writing, speaking, activism, and training have sparked and fed the fires of re-formation in the church from Ferguson and Charlottesville to South Africa, Brazil, Australia, and Ireland. Her book *The Very Good Gospel* was named 2016 Book of the Year, and the Huffington Post identified Harper as one of fifty Women Religious Leaders to Celebrate on International Women's Day.

List of Contributors

Drew G. I. Hart earned his PhD from Lutheran Theological Seminary in Philadelphia and is an assistant professor of theology at Messiah University. He has ten years of pastoral experience. He is director of Messiah University's Thriving Together: Congregations for Racial Justice program and cohost of Inverse Podcast. Hart is the author of *Trouble I've Seen: Changing the Way the Church Views Racism* and *Who Will Be a Witness? Igniting Activism for God's Justice, Love, and Deliverance*. He was the recipient of bcmPEACE's 2017 Peacemaker Award and the 2019 W. E. B. Du Bois Award in Harrisburg, Pennsylvania, and was Elizabethtown College's 2019 Peace Fellow.

Peter Goodwin Heltzel earned his PhD from Boston University and is visiting researcher at Boston University School of Theology. Author of *Jesus and Justice: Evangelicals, Race and American Politics*, Heltzel focuses his theological scholarship on equipping the church to dismantle institutional racism.

Aaron James earned his PhD in theology from the University of Dayton. He is an associate professor of philosophy at Illinois Central College in East Peoria, Illinois.

Michael Jimenez earned his PhD from Fuller Theological Seminary and teaches history at Vanguard University. He is the author of *Remembering Lived Lives: A Historiography from the Underside of Modernity* and *Karl Barth and the Study of the Religious Enlightenment: Encountering the Task of History*.

Kathy Khang is a writer, speaker, and yoga teacher based in the north suburbs of Chicago. She is the author of *Raise Your Voice: Why We Stay Silent and How to Speak Up* and *Psalms, with Guided Meditations*, volumes 1 and 2, and has written for *Sojourners*, Christians for Social Action, and *Faith and Leadership*.

Willi Hugo Perez Lemus earned his PhD in sociology and political science from the University of Santa Monica, Spain, with a dissertation focused on Central American Mennonite responses to violence in their communities. He is the rector of Semilla, the Latin American Anabaptist Seminary in Guatemala City, a position he has held for fifteen years. He previously worked as the director of Redpaz, a Central American interfaith peace network.

Thomas R. Yoder Neufeld earned his ThD from Harvard University Divinity School and is professor emeritus at Conrad Grebel University College at the University of Waterloo (New Testament and Peace Studies [1983–2012]). He has served as hospital and prison chaplain as well as in several pastorates. He is presently chair of the Faith and Life Commission of the Mennonite World Conference. He is author of *Ephesians* (Believers Church Bible Commentary), *Recovering Jesus: the Witness of the New Testament*, and *Killing Enmity: Violence and the New Testament*.

Chibuzo Nimmo Petty earned his MDiv in intercultural leadership from Bethany Theological Seminary and is a creative, organizer, and minister, living with family in Cleveland, Ohio, whose passion is the intersection of cultural competency and pastoral care. Petty's writing and editing can also be found in the Church of the

Brethren's biannual academic journal *Brethren Life & Thought* and more regularly on its affiliate blog *DEVOTION*.

Sheila Wise Rowe is a graduate of Tufts University and Cambridge College and holds a master's degree in counseling psychology. For twenty-five years she's offered counseling and spiritual direction and taught counseling internationally. She is the director of The Rehoboth House and cofounder of the Cyrene Movement. She is a member of the Community Ethics Committee of Harvard Medical School. Her essays can be found in numerous blogs, newspapers, and journals, and she speaks at colleges, churches, organizations, and seminaries across the country. Her latest book, *Healing Racial Trauma: The Road to Resilience* won the 2021 book award in Christian Living/Discipleship from *Christianity Today*.

Eric A. Seibert earned his PhD from Drew University and is professor of Old Testament at Messiah University. He is the author of a number of books and articles, including *Disarming the Church: Why Christians Must Forsake Violence to Follow Jesus and Change the World*. His most recent book is *Enjoying the Old Testament: A Creative Guide to Encountering Scripture*. Seibert served as president of the Eastern Great Lakes Biblical Society from 2010 to 2011 and enjoys speaking about topics related to problematic portrayals of God in the Old Testament and the need to use the Bible responsibly, in ways that promote peace.

Baldemar Velasquez is the founder and president of the Farm Labor Organizing Committee (FLOC). Velasquez is an internationally recognized leader in the farm worker and immigrants' rights movements. His commitment to justice and human dignity have led to recognition by many labor, government, academic, and progressive organizations, including a John D. and Catherine T. MacArthur Fellowship (Genius Grant), the National Hispanic Heritage Award bestowed by the National Council of La Raza, a Development of People Award by the Campaign for Human Development of the US Catholic Conference, and the Bannerman Fellowship. In addition, he received the Aguila Azteca Award by the government of Mexico, the highest award presented by the Mexican government to a noncitizen. In 2009 Baldemar was elected to the AFL-CIO executive council.

Adrienne Wiebe earned her PhD from the University of Alberta based on participatory action research in a Mayan community in Guatemala and is an applied anthropologist. For thirty years she has lived and worked in Latin America and Canada with indigenous communities, migrants and refugees, and other marginalized populations. She has worked with Pueblo Partisans in Guatemala, Mennonite Central Committee in Mexico, Oxfam in global programs, and the Aboriginal Health Program in Alberta. She is currently the manager for international projects in Latin America for Change for Children, a Canadian-based NGO.

Randy S. Woodley earned his PhD from Asbury Theological Seminary and currently serves as distinguished professor of faith and culture at George Fox University and Portland Seminary. His work can be found in venues such as *Time* magazine, the Huffington Post and *Christianity Today*. Woodley is a legal descendent of the United Keetoowah Band of Cherokee Indians in Oklahoma. He cohosts the *Peacing It All Together* podcast with Bo Sanders. He and his wife are cosustainers of Eloheh Indigenous Center for Earth Justice/Eloheh Farm, a regenerative teaching center and farm in Yamhill, Oregon. His books include *Decolonizing Evangelicalism: An 11:59 p.m. Conversation, The Harmony Tree: A Story of Healing and Community, Shalom and the Community of Creation: An Indigenous Vision,* and *Living in Color: Embracing God's Passion for Ethnic Diversity*.

GENERAL INDEX

Alexander, Michelle, 184-85, 264
Anderson, Elizabeth, 174
anger, 54, 73, 236, 282, 286
Anzaldúa, Gloria, 126
Aquinas, Thomas, 227
atonement, 39, 59, 71-73
Augustine, 202, 226-27
baptist vision, 106-8, 113-18
Bainton, Roland, 199
Baker, Ella, 182
Baker-Fletcher, Karen, 273
Barth, Karl, 138-39, 142
Bauckham, Richard, 40-42, 50, 52
beloved community, 161-64, 173, 184-85, 391, 397-98, 401
Bethge, Eberhard, 313-14
Black Lives Matter, 183-84, 265
Bonhoeffer, Dietrich, 223, 307, 309-10, 316
Boring, Eugene, 44
Brimlow, Robert, 198
Brueggemann, Walter, 166, 258, 272
Caird, G. B., 45
Carr, Craig, 112-13
Carretto, Carlo, 164-65
Charles, J. Daryl, 218, 220
Chavez, Cesar, 145-46, 340
chronic illness, 319-24
civil rights, 119, 148, 175, 179-80, 183, 295, 302, 312, 315, 358
 Civil Rights Movement, 27, 163, 183, 264-66, 290, 293, 312
Clay, Henry, 89

Collins, John, 11
Cone, James, 268-69, 289-92, 295-96
conscientious objector, 12, 123, 198-99
Cowles, C. S., 18
Cullors, Patrisse, 183-84
Davies, Norman, 204
Day, Dorothy, 315
 De Las Casas, Bartolome, 87
Delaney, Susan, 287
Derrida, Jacques, 138-39, 142
Didion, Joan, 141-42
dignity, 35, 102, 112, 134, 153, 162, 171-72, 174-78, 184, 273, 285, 300-301
 human dignity, 102, 172-73, 176-78
disability, 319-24
discipleship, 236, 293, 305, 308, 310-16
enemies, 8, 13, 38, 44, 47, 51, 54-55, 58, 60-61, 65, 69, 72-74, 83, 88, 91-92, 106, 108, 114-15, 149, 153, 155-56, 159-60, 164, 191, 194-95, 200, 204, 220, 226, 234, 245-46, 251, 256, 269, 356-57
exploitation, 73, 126, 134, 159, 170, 179, 185, 230, 243, 296, 306
faith-rooted organizer, 299, 301-2
Feagin, Joe, 263-65
fear, 128, 140, 162, 210, 242, 247, 251-53, 279-80, 292, 305, 312, 351, 357
Fiala, Andrew, 395
flourishing, 154-55, 158, 164, 168, 173, 176, 391
Forest, Jim, 151, 165-66
forgiveness, 59, 61, 64-66, 72, 99, 115-17, 234, 236, 245, 248, 252, 281, 285-86, 301, 367, 369, 381

409

General Index

Frankena, William, 150, 179
Frankfurt, Harry, 151
Franklin, Benjamin, 90
Fretheim, Terence, 16
Friesen, Steven, 56
gangs, 143, 240-41, 248-49
genocide, 11, 82, 88-89, 219, 347
Glaude Jr., Eddie, 163-64
Gordon, Jane Anna, 133-34
Graves, Marlena, 153
Griffith, Lee, 191, 193-94
Gushee, David, 219-20, 237
Gutiérrez, Gustavo, 153-54, 170-71
Hall, Christopher, 400
harmony, 92-93, 96-98, 102, 166, 244, 258, 260-61
Harper, Lisa Sharon, 219-20
Hays, Richard, 12, 75
Heyer, Kristen, 300
Hill, Thomas, 172
Holmes, Arthur, 172
Holmes, Robert, 165
hooks, bell, 151-52, 179-80
Howard-Snyder, Frances, 151
human rights, 117, 148, 168-71, 175, 179-80, 183, 185, 190, 194, 196, 230, 233-34, 250, 350, 358-60, 397
immigrant, 31, 34, 138, 335, 338-39, 344, 357-59, 362
Jefferson, Thomas, 88-89
Jenkins, Willis, 365-67, 369-71
Jim Crow, 262, 351, 353
  The New Jim Crow, 264
Johansen, Bruce, 90-91
Johnson, James Turner, 226-28
Jones, L. Gregory, 159-60
justice, 10, 23, 27-30, 33, 36, 162, 165-70, 182-84, 214-17, 226, 231-32, 234-37, 244-46, 260, 269, 287-88, 296-302, 304, 308-16, 357, 359, 367-69, 397
  restorative justice, 248
  gender justice, 249
just war, 199-201, 214-15, 218, 220, 224-36, 367, 380
Kennedy, John F., 83, 144-45
King, Martin Luther, Jr., 2, 105-10, 113-17, 149, 155-56, 160-63, 168, 176-77, 273, 312-13, 315-16, 396
Kinsella, David, 112-13
Konyndyk DeYoung, Rebecca, 154

Kreeft, Peter, 225-26, 236
Lawson Jr., James, 180-82
Lewis, C. S., 150, 156-57
Lewis, John, 181
Long, Stephen, 198
love, 8, 13, 20, 29, 33, 45, 47, 55, 57-61, 63, 68-74, 106, 114, 116, 128, 148-66, 168-71, 173, 176-85, 191, 193, 200, 223, 225, 227, 231-32, 234, 236-37, 244-46, 250, 252, 273, 279, 281-83, 286, 288, 294, 301-2, 309, 311, 315-16, 345, 355-57, 367, 399
  love ethic, 148-50, 171, 179, 185
Luiselli, Valeria, 143-44
Maier, Harry, 47
Malcolm X, 394, 399-400
Martens, Elmer, 13
martyrdom, 41, 46
McClendon Jr., James Wm., 106-9, 113
Medicine, Sweet, 97-98
Merton, Thomas, 150
Miller, Paul, 393-94
Mills, Charles, 135
Mohawk, John, 83-84
Monroe, James, 89
Mooney, James, 100-101
Native Americans, 82, 87-88, 91-92, 94, 98, 133, 346-50
  Indigenous People, 83, 86-87, 92-94, 98, 100, 102, 104, 274, 347, 362
Nelson-Pallmeyer, Jack, 8
neoliberalism, 163
New Testament, 27-28, 52, 58-59, 66, 72, 215, 217, 224, 258, 325
Niebuhr, Reinhold, 221-22
Nine/Eleven, 122, 190, 195, 276-77, 280
nonresistance, 60
nonretaliation, 59
nonviolence, 10, 22, 58, 60, 97, 108-10, 116-17, 119-20, 122-27, 129, 135-36, 145, 162-63, 180-82, 198, 224, 244-46, 252, 271, 273, 315, 377
Nouwen, Henri, 315
Nozick, Robert, 152
Nussbaum, Martha, 152, 173-74
Ockenga, Harold, 367
Old Testament, 7-12, 14, 16-21, 53-54, 245
Oord, Thomas, 150
oppression, 43, 159, 179, 185, 190, 224, 233, 235, 245-46, 254, 267, 272, 283, 287, 290, 330, 362

General Index

pacifism, 12-13, 23, 109, 112, 127-28, 131, 171, 197-200, 202, 212-15, 217-22, 230, 233, 269, 394-95
    Christian pacifism, 9-10, 12-13, 18, 108, 197-200, 217, 221, 268
Pahl, Jon, 269-70
Patterson, Eric, 227, 229
peace, 10-11, 13-14, 20-23, 27-28, 33, 35-36, 58-61, 64-75, 79-81, 88, 92, 96-98, 102-4, 123-25, 155, 162, 165-66, 169-71, 193, 199, 206, 215-17, 224-26, 228, 232, 235-39, 243-54, 258-63, 268-74, 276, 285, 293, 204-5, 308-9, 311-12, 314-17, 331, 376-78, 391-92, 394-98
    peacemakers, 8, 80, 97-98, 101-3, 258, 263, 309, 314-15, 318
    peacemaking, 20, 72, 81, 91-92, 97, 99, 103, 170, 228, 233-37, 247, 257, 263, 268-70, 272, 292, 304, 306, 308-9, 311-12, 315-18, 366, 371, 376, 378, 391
Pentagon for Peace, 79-81, 102
Perkins, John, 296-97
Perry, Samuel, 393
power, 26, 30-31, 41-42, 44-48, 50, 52 56-57, 61, 64-65, 72-73, 98, 118, 125, 130, 135, 138, 162, 176, 181, 185, 192-93, 196, 205-6, 209, 212, 218, 220, 222, 237, 240-41, 245-46, 251-53, 259-60, 263, 266-67, 270-71, 273, 279, 295, 299, 300-301, 306-7, 309, 314, 316, 318, 345, 372, 376, 396
    Black Power, 290-91
Quiros, Ansley, 182
racial trauma, 276-83, 286-88
rage, 62, 64-65, 183, 273
Rah, Soong-Chan, 282-83
Ramsey, Paul, 231-32
Rawls, John, 152
reconciliation, 23, 65, 71, 106, 108, 116, 180, 245, 248, 252-54, 272, 274, 276, 287, 291-97, 300-301, 312
Reddish, Mitchell, 45
resurrection, 60, 72, 246, 316, 319-22, 325-29
righteousness, 28-30, 36, 166, 169, 191, 217, 245, 259, 297-98, 309
Roberts, J. Deotis, 292-95
Romero, Oscar, 161, 171, 178
Rule of Christ, 62, 64, 66
Rumscheidt, H. Martin, 223-24
Schlabach, Gerald W., 224
Schüssler Fiorenza, Elisabeth, 41
Schwartz, David, 164

Sermon on the Mount, 58, 60-61, 72, 191, 245, 258, 273
shalom, 10, 22-24, 26-28, 33, 35-36, 92, 96-97, 102, 165-66, 168-70, 176, 215-17, 236, 244-45, 250-52, 254, 257-61, 272, 297-300, 391, 396-97
Shenandoah, Leon, 98
Sider, Ron, 219-20, 224-25, 235-37
Singer, Peter, 110-12
Skinner, Tom, 296
slavery, 25, 67, 70, 262, 308, 317, 349, 353, 399
Smedes, Lewis, 169
Smith, Efrem, 180
Soble, Alan, 152
social responsibility, 163, 231
Sprinkle, Preston, 11-12
Staberock, Gerald, 194
Stafford, William, 120-36
Stassen, Glen, 233-35, 375-78
Stevenson, Bryan, 154, 168, 185, 397-98
Stump, Eleonore, 150-51, 158-59
subordination, 59, 66-67, 69-70, 271
sustainability, 365-66, 368, 370, 373-74
Tenney, Merrill, 326
terrorism, 89, 262
Thurman, Howard, 128, 148, 153
Tometi, Opal, 183
Tonstad, Sigve, 45
Truman Doctrine, 211
truth, 48, 50-52, 55, 59, 82-83, 101-2, 161, 166, 181, 190, 193, 244, 251, 275, 279, 309, 316, 318, 395, 397-98
Tutu, Desmond, 401
United Nations, 85, 175, 208, 234
Velleman, J. David, 152-53, 157-58, 171-72
Vietnam, 12, 95, 122, 146, 200, 210, 231, 367
violence, 7-8, 10-14, 36-37, 43, 50-51, 58-74, 102-3, 122-25, 135, 140-47, 160-62, 191, 195, 198, 201, 205, 212, 214, 217-20, 222-25, 227-31, 238-48, 250-54, 261-62, 264, 268-72, 301, 304-8, 310-13, 316-18, 362-67, 383-85, 388-89, 391-95
    urban violence, 240-42
    violence against women, 242, 262, 265, 304-6, 308, 310-11, 316-18, 392
    violent imagery, 39-40, 42, 47, 50-51, 53, 55-56
    violent symbols, 39, 56
war, 1, 7-21, 23, 37, 47-53, 55-56, 67, 82-83, 89, 92, 94-99, 103, 141-43, 165, 194-214, 222, 229, 239-40, 367-68, 375-76

General Index

war on drugs, 264
war on terror, 122, 191, 230
war strategies, 79-80, 102
Weaver, J. Denny, 268
well-being, 24, 26-27, 33, 151-52, 155, 157, 166, 170, 180, 244, 254, 258-59, 297, 315
White supremacy, 87, 121, 135, 257, 261-63, 265, 267-68, 271-73, 276, 290, 295, 346
Whitehead, Andrew, 393
Willard, Dallas, 154
Wink, Walter, 237, 300
Wolterstorff, Nicholas, 150, 168-69, 173
Woodley, Randy S., 166, 170
World War II, 95, 123, 198-99, 200, 203-13, 221, 350-51, 358, 362, 367
Yoder, John Howard, 270-71

SCRIPTURE INDEX

OLD TESTAMENT

Genesis
1–2, *193*
1:1, *383*
1:27, *173*
2, *327*
3, *46, 193, 327*
3:1-5, *46*
4:1, *364*
5, *20*
6:1, *364*
6:11, *364*
8:21, *364*
9:3-6, *364*
9:6, *173*
15:7, *24*
16:13, *153*
18:19, *28*
28:13, *25*
32, *73*
45:1-15, *20*
49:9, *43*
50:2, *26*

Exodus
6, *25*
6:6-8, *25*
14:26-30, *8*
15, *49*
15:26, *24, 26*
19–20, *24*
22:21-24, *31*
22:24, *32*
22:25, *30*
23:1, *33*
23:3, *33*
23:6, *33*
23:8, *33*
23:9, *33*
29:38, *50*

Leviticus
1:3, *50*
3:1, *50*
19, *34*
19:10, *30, 34*
19:9-10, *34*
19:17-18, *63*
25, *216*
25:13, *216*
25:16-17, *216*
25:23-24, *216*
25:25-28, *216*
25:39-43, *216*

Numbers
19:11-13, *356*
25:12, *259*
31:1-3, *8*

Deuteronomy
1, *29*
2, *8, 11*
7:1-2, *8, 11*
10:18, *31*
14:29, *31*
15:12, *31*
15:12-15, *31*
15:12-18, *35*
16:11, *31*
16:14, *31*
23:9-14, *49*
24, *34*
24:17, *29, 31*
24:19, *31, 34*
24:19-22, *34*
24:20-21, *31*
26:12-13, *31*
27:19, *29, 31*
32:4, *33*
32:35, *13*
33:21, *28*

Joshua
1, *8*
6–11, *11, 12*

Ruth
2:7, *35*

1 Samuel
15:1-3, *8*
21:5, *49*
25, *20*

2 Samuel
8:15, *28*
11:9-13, *49*

Scripture Index

1 Kings
10:9, *28*

2 Kings
17:1-23, *9*
20:5, *26*
24:1-4, *9*

1 Chronicles
18:14, *28*

2 Chronicles
9:8, *28*
16:12, *26*

Job
13:4, *26*
37:23, *28*

Psalms
1, *30*
5:11, *252*
14, *30*
33:5, *28*
34:14, *258*
36:7, *28*
42:1-2, *157*
44:24-26, *283*
46:1, *366*
55:22, *252*
72:1, *28*
72:2, *259*
72:12-14, *265*
82:3, *30*
85:1, *244*
85:9, *259*
94:6, *31*
98:1-3, *49*
99:4, *28*
103:3, *26*
103:6, *28*
106:3, *28*
144:9-10, *49*
146:9, *31*
147:3, *26*

Proverbs
8:20, *28*
16:8, *28*
21:3, *28*

Isaiah
1:17, *29*
1:27, *28*
2:3-4, *217*
2:4, *244*
5:7, *28*
5:16, *28*
9:6, *28, 225*
9:6-7, *245*
11:1-4, *260*
11:1-9, *260*
11:5-9, *260*
28:17, *28*
28:17-18, *298*
32:16, *28, 235*
32:17, *244, 259*
33:5, *28*
34:1, *51*
42:1, *49*
49:26, *54*
53:5, *26*
53:9, *50*
54:17, *28*
56:1, *28*
58:2, *28*
58:6, *299*
59:8-9, *28*
59:9, *28*
59:14, *28*
63:1-6, *53*
63:4, *51*

Jeremiah
4:2, *28*
6:14, *96, 274*
7:5-7, *30*
7:6, *31*
8:22, *26*
9:23, *28*
22:3, *28, 30, 31*
22:3-5, *298*
22:15, *28*
23:5, *28*
29:4-7, *259*
29:7, *375*
33:15, *28*

Lamentations
1:15, *53*

Ezekiel
18:5, *28*
18:19, *28*
18:21, *28*
18:27, *28*
22:7, *31*
33:14, *28*
33:16, *28*
33:19, *28*
34:25, *259*
37:26, *259*
39:17-19, *54*
45:9, *28*

Daniel
7, *327*
7:13-14, *327*

Hosea
2:18, *259*

Joel
3:13, *53*

Amos
5:7, *28*
5:24, *28, 302*
6:12, *28*

Micah
6:8, *244, 299, 301*
7:9, *28*

Zephaniah
3:13, *50*

Zechariah
4:6, *245*
7:1, *298*
7:9-10, *30*
7:10, *31*

Malachi
2:5, *259*
3:5, *31*

APOCRYPHA

Wisdom of Solomon
6:1-11, *69*

NEW TESTAMENT

Matthew
1, *225*
2, *260, 324*
2:7-12, *362*
5–7, *60, 245*
5:3-12, *191*

Scripture Index

5:9, *247, 258*
5:38-42, *60*
5:38-48, *58, 246*
5:39-45, *56*
5:43-48, *61, 65*
5:45, *13*
5:48, *61*
6:8-10, *390*
6:9-13, *61*
6:12, *65*
6:19-33, *234*
8:1-4, *324*
9:1-8, *324*
9:18-22, *325*
18, *61, 65, 66*
18:1, *62*
18:1-5, *61, 70, 246*
18:6, *62*
18:6-9, *62*
18:15-20, *62*
18:22, *286*
18:23-35, *64*
18:35, *65*
22:34-40, *148*
23:24, *246*
25:31-46, *62, 173*
26:5, *246*
26:52, *192, 218, 236*
26:52-53, *286*
26:53, *218*
27:11-14, *192*
27:46, *55*

Mark
1, *246, 324*
1:4, *324*
1:14-15, *245*
2:1-12, *324*
5:3, *279*
5:21-34, *325*
5:24-28, *274*
5:32-33, *279*
8:22-26, *324*
9:37, *246*
12:13-17, *68*
12:28-31, *148*

Luke
1, *355, 356*
1:46-55, *245*
4, *217*

4:17-21, *246*
4:18-19, *216*
5:12-16, *324*
5:17-26, *325*
6:17-19, *246*
6:27, *61*
6:27-36, *56, 60*
6:35, *13, 17, 61*
6:36, *61*
8:4, *325*
9:51, *299*
10:25-28, *148*
11:2-4, *61*
11:4, *65*
14, *310*
14:27, *310*
16:19-22, *155*
17:11-19, *324*
18:35-43, *324*
19, *287*
19:1-1, *260*
19:8, *287*
19:42, *258*
22:51, *192*
23:34, *114, 237, 246*

John
1, *245*
3:4, *326*
3:16, *173*
3:19, *52*
4, *246*
5:1-18, *325*
5:22-24, *52*
9:1-12, *324*
9:39-41, *52*
12:48, *52*
13:1-2, *70*
13:1-17, *66*
14:9, *17*
14:17, *253*
14:27, *259*
15:21, *311*
17:14-15, *253*
18:1-11, *192*

Acts
1, *245*
17:29, *173*
28:1-3, *325*

Romans
4:25, *55*
5:6-11, *73*
8:32, *55*
12:1-2, *69*
12:1-21, *67*
12:13-14, *69*
12:14, *69*
12:14-21, *56*
12:17-19, *286*
12:17-21, *68, 69*
12:19, *13*
12:19-20, *60, 69*
12:21, *401*
13, *67, 68*
13:1-7, *67, 69*
13:7, *68*
13:8, *69*
13:8-10, *148*
13:8-14, *67, 68*
13:12, *69*
13:14, *69*

1 Corinthians
1:18, *45, 72*
15, *328, 329*
15:2, *326*
15:4, *327*
15:12, *326*
15:21-22, *327*
15:35, *326*
15:36-38, *327*
15:39, *327*
15:41, *327*
15:42-44, *327*
15:47, *327*
15:49, *327*

2 Corinthians
5:16–6:2, *293*
5:19, *293*
12:7, *325*

Galatians
4:15, *325*
5:13-14, *148*
6:2, *281*
6:11, *325*

Ephesians
2, *58, 71*
2:11-22, *72, 259*

415

Scripture Index

2:14, *58, 96*
2:14-16, *293*
2:16, *61*
2:17, *58*
4:25-27, *63*
5:21, *70*
5:21–6:9, *67*
5:25-33, *70*
6:1, *251*
6:13-20, *252*

Philippians
2:1-11, *66*
2:6-11, *70*
3:2, *328*

Colossians
1:15, *17*
1:19-20, *254*
3:18–4:1, *67*

2 Timothy
3:17, *252*

Hebrews
1, *282*
1:3, *17*
13:2, *259*

James
2:1-9, *155*
2:8, *148*
2:15-16, *27*
2:15-17, *155*
3:18, *258, 259*

1 Peter
2:13–3:7, *67*
5:6-7, *252*

1 John
3:16, *45*
4:2, *173*
4:7-12, *148*
4:8, *45*

Revelation
1:1, *39*
1:3, *39, 40*

1:5, *48*
1:9, *46*
1:16, *48*
2, *42, 47, 53*
2:1, *46, 54*
2:7, *47*
2:11, *47*
2:12, *48*
2:13, *46*
2:16, *48*
2:17, *47*
2:28, *47*
3:5, *47*
3:12, *47*
3:14, *48*
3:21, *44, 47*
4–5, *39, 42*
5:2, *42*
5:4, *42*
5:5, *43, 47*
5:6, *43, 45*
5:9, *44, 48*
6:1, *54*
6:9, *46*
6:9-10, *41*
6:16, *37*
7, *48*
7:4-8, *48*
7:4-9, *43*
7:9, *48, 322*
7:9-14, *46*
7:14, *49, 52*
11:7, *46, 47*
11:9, *48*
11:18, *54*
12:7-8, *47*
12:9, *42, 46, 47, 53*
12:11, *41, 46, 47, 48*
12:15-16, *46*
12:17, *46, 47*
13:1, *48, 54*
13:4, *46*
13:7, *47, 48*
13:7-8, *46*
13:14, *42, 47*

14, *49, 53*
14:1, *49, 54, 55*
14:3, *49*
14:4, *46, 49, 50*
14:5, *48, 50*
14:6, *48*
14:8, *55*
14:8-9, *54*
14:15, *53*
14:18, *53*
14:19-20, *53*
15:2, *47*
15:2-3, *46*
15:3-4, *49*
16:6, *54*
16:14, *47*
17:6, *46, 54, 55*
17:14, *47, 48*
18, *55*
18:3, *55*
18:23, *42*
19, *39, 52*
19:1, *46*
19:1-4, *50*
19:3, *51*
19:8, *52*
19:11, *37, 47, 48, 52*
19:13, *37, 51*
19:14, *46, 52*
19:15, *38, 48, 52, 53, 55*
19:17, *54*
19:17-18, *54*
19:18-19, *53*
19:19, *38, 47*
19:21, *38, 48, 53, 54*
20:2, *46*
21:1-5, *261*
21:7, *47*
21:24, *53*
21:24-26, *53*
21:25, *53*
21:27, *53*
22:2, *53*
22:6, *39*